CAMBRIDGE TEXTS IN THE
HISTORY OF PHILOSOPHY

═══

J. G. FICHTE
Foundations of Natural Right

CAMBRIDGE TEXTS IN THE
HISTORY OF PHILOSOPHY

Series editors

KARL AMERIKS
Professor of Philosophy at the University of Notre Dame

DESMOND M. CLARKE
Professor of Philosophy at University College Cork

The main objective of Cambridge Texts in the History of Philosophy is to expand the range, variety and quality of texts in the history of philosophy which are available in English. The series includes texts by familiar names (such as Descartes and Kant) and also by less well-known authors. Wherever possible, texts are published in complete and unabridged form, and translations are specially commissioned for the series. Each volume contains a critical introduction together with a guide to further reading and any necessary glossaries and textual apparatus. The volumes are designed for student use at undergraduate and postgraduate level and will be of interest not only to students of philosophy, but also to a wider audience of readers in the history of science, the history of theology and the history of ideas.

For a list of titles published in the series, please see end of book.

J. G. FICHTE

Foundations of
Natural Right

According to the Principles of the Wissenschaftslehre

EDITED BY
FREDERICK NEUHOUSER
Cornell University

TRANSLATED BY
MICHAEL BAUR
Fordham University

CAMBRIDGE
UNIVERSITY PRESS

PUBLISHED BY THE PRESS SYNDICATE OF THE UNIVERSITY OF CAMBRIDGE
The Pitt Building, Trumpington Street, Cambridge, United Kingdom

CAMBRIDGE UNIVERSITY PRESS
The Edinburgh Building, Cambridge CB2 2RU, UK   www.cup.cam.ac.uk
40 West 20th Street, New York, NY 10011–4211, USA   www.cup.org
10 Stamford Road, Oakleigh, Melbourne 3166, Australia
Ruiz de Alarcón 13, 28014 Madrid, Spain

First published 2000

Printed in the United Kingdom at the University Press, Cambridge

Typeset in Ehrhardt 11/13pt   System 3b2   [CE]

A catalogue record for this book is available from the British Library

Library of Congress cataloguing in publication data
Fichte, Johann Gottlieb, 1762–1814.
[Grundlage des Naturrechts nach Principien der Wissenschaftslehre. English]
Foundations of natural right / J. G. Fichte; edited by Frederick Neuhouser;
translated by Michael Baur.
p.   cm. – (Cambridge texts in the history of philosophy)
Includes bibliographical references and index.
ISBN 0 521 57591 5 (hardback) – ISBN 0 521 57301 7 (paperback)
1. Natural law.   2. Political science.   3. State, The.
I. Neuhouser, Frederick.   II. Title.   III. Series.
JC181.F6213   2000
320′.01–dc21   99–056852

ISBN 0 521 57301 7 hardback
ISBN 0 521 57591 5 paperback

Contents

Introduction	*page* vii
Chronology	xxix
Further reading	xxxi
Translator's note	xxxiv

Foundations of Natural Right, according to the Principles of the Wissenschaftslehre	I
Introduction	3
First main division: deduction of the concept of right	18
Second main division: deduction of the applicability of the concept of right	53
Third main division: systematic application of the concept of right; or the doctrine of right	85
First chapter of the doctrine of right: deduction of original right	101
Second chapter of the doctrine of right; on the right of coercion	123
Third chapter of the doctrine of right: on political right, or right within a commonwealth	133
Part II, or applied natural right	165
First section of the doctrine of political right: concerning the civil contract	165
Second section of the doctrine of political right: on civil legislation	183

Contents

Third section of the doctrine of political right: 249
  on the constitution
Outline of family right   264
  (first appendix to the doctrine of natural right)
Outline of the right of nations and cosmopolitan right   320
  (second appendix to the doctrine of natural right)

Index   335

Introduction

J. G. Fichte wrote *Foundations of Natural Right* in 1795–6, shortly after he had stunned the German philosophical world with his ambitious attempt to reconceive the foundations of Kant's Critical Philosophy in his *Wissenschaftslehre* (*Doctrine of Knowledge*), first published in 1794. Fichte was only thirty-four years old when he finished the *Foundations*, but by this time he already occupied a prestigious Chair at the University of Jena and was widely regarded (though not by Kant himself) as the brilliant young philosopher who would carry on the philosophical revolution that Kant had begun. Although politics played a prominent role in Fichte's thought from the beginning to the end of his career, this relatively early book remains his most comprehensive and sophisticated work in political philosophy.

Published in 1796–7, just before Kant addressed many of the same issues in his *Metaphysics of Morals* (1797),[1] the *Foundations* represents Fichte's attempt to establish the basic principles of a liberal political order by bringing a Kantian perspective to bear on the problems of legitimacy and right (*Recht*) that had been raised, but imperfectly resolved, by Hobbes, Locke, and Rousseau. (The German term *Recht* has no single English equivalent; it encompasses all of what English-speakers mean by "right," "law," and "justice.") Most importantly, Fichte's treatise is a defense of the claims that all individuals – all adult rational beings, regardless of social class – possess a set of natural rights

---

[1] The situation is more complicated than this. Part I of the *Foundations* was published before the whole of *The Metaphysics of Morals*, but the first part of the latter work, the "Doctrine of Right," appeared in January 1797 and hence before the publication of Part II of the *Foundations* in autumn of the same year. This enabled Fichte to make reference in Part II (§20.V) to certain of Kant's claims in the first part of *The Metaphysics of Morals*. (See editor's notes to §20.V.)

(including inviolability of the body, private property, and the right to subsistence) and that the central purpose of a legitimate political order is to protect those rights from infringement by other individuals and by the state itself. The fundamental thesis of Fichte's theory – the "principle of all right" – is that "each is to limit his freedom, the sphere of his free actions, through the concept of the freedom of the other" in such a way that the other, too, "can exist as free" (§10). But Fichte recognizes that a principle of such generality is too indeterminate to be practical, since it fails to specify where, precisely, the limits of freedom are to be drawn. In order for the principle of right to be realized, then, individuals must agree among themselves to constitute a state that will both delimit and enforce the boundaries of their freedom. In other words, the rights that all individuals have by nature can be realized only in a state founded on a social contract among free and rational individuals. It follows from this that the rights Fichte defends in the *Foundations* are not natural in the sense that they existed, or could exist, in some community of human beings prior to the establishment of a political order. Rather (as we shall see below), these rights are natural in the normative sense that they are necessary if human beings are to realize their true "nature" as free and rational individuals.

At the same time, the *Foundations* is more than just a work in political philosophy; it also plays a crucial role in Fichte's larger project of discovering the answers to *all* of philosophy's fundamental questions within a single, uninterrupted system. Fichte's aim in this text, then, is not simply to solve the traditional problems of political philosophy but also to find the method and resources for doing so in the very approach he used in the *Wissenschaftslehre* to address the basic questions of epistemology and metaphysics. (This ambition is explicitly announced in the full title Fichte gave to his work: *Foundations of Natural Right According to the Principles of the Wissenschaftslehre*.[2]) Thus, together with the *Wissenschaftslehre* and his later *System of the Doctrine of Morals*, or *Sittenlehre* (1798), the *Foundations* constitutes an integral part of Fichte's first completed system of philosophy.

It is this feature of Fichte's project that accounts for the obscure and

[2] Readers who are interested in pursuing the relation between the *Foundations* and the *Wissenschaftslehre* should note that beginning in 1796 Fichte's lectures on the latter were based on a new, thoroughly revised version of that work, the *Wissenschaftslehre nova methodo*. This work appears in English translation as *Fichte: Foundations of Transcendental Philosophy*, ed. Daniel Breazeale (Ithaca, NY: Cornell University Press, 1992).

difficult discussions of rationality, self-positing, and "the I" with which the text begins. Fichte's aim, briefly, is to demonstrate political philosophy's systematic connectedness to the other subfields of philosophy – and thereby to establish its "scientific" status – by deducing the basic concepts of political philosophy from the same first principle that grounded the *Wissenschaftslehre* and (later) the *Doctrine of Morals*. It is Fichte's conviction here and during most of the 1790s that the only principle that can ground a complete system of philosophy is "the I," the defining quality of which is said to be "self-positing" activity, or "activity that reverts into itself" (§1). Since the latter are simply technical terms for self-consciousness – in being conscious of itself the I directs its conscious activity back on itself and thereby "posits," or "intends," itself – Fichte's systematic aspirations in the *Foundations* will be satisfied if he can show that the self-consciousness of individuals in some way *requires* the principles of right (*Recht*). The strategy he relies on to show this is adapted from Kant's transcendental method in the *Critique of Pure Reason*: Fichte aims to "deduce" the basic concepts of political philosophy by showing them to be conditions of the possibility of self-consciousness (just as, for Kant, applying the a priori categories of the understanding to objects of experience is a condition of the I's consciousness of itself as a unitary subject). The *Foundations*, then, inquires into the conditions under which individual subjects can achieve self-consciousness, and it argues that right, or political justice, constitutes one of those conditions.

Bringing together these two aspects of the work, we can summarize Fichte's main aims in the *Foundations* as follows: to give an account of what right (or justice) consists in, to show that it is not an arbitrary human invention but a necessary idea that has its source in reason itself, and to provide a sketch of what a human society would look like in which right were fully realized.

Historical and political context

Fichte was born in 1762 in a small village in rural Saxony. His father, the first of his family to be liberated from serfdom, worked as a linen weaver and earned an income that was barely sufficient to support himself, his wife, and their eight children. Except for the cities of Dresden and Leipzig, feudalism still dominated the region. Production in Saxony, as in most of Germany, was overwhelmingly agricultural. Capitalist relations had only recently begun to develop, and most parts of Germany were still untouched by them. The indigence of Fichte's family was a common condition in eighteenth-century rural Saxony. It stood in marked contrast to the more comfortable circumstances of the still tiny middle class and, even more noticeably, to the vast holdings of the landed nobility. The young Fichte responded to this conspicuous disparity in wealth with an intense moral disgust that never left him, even when academic success enabled him to escape his own poverty and enter the middle class.

Although little is known about Fichte's earliest political views, including his first reactions to the French Revolution, it is clear that by the early 1790s he was following events in France with great interest. Political affairs in Germany captured his attention as well, as is evidenced by a letter from 1790 in which he sympathetically describes a local peasant revolt that he takes to have been inspired by the example of the French. Yet, as Fichte himself sensed, such uprisings were bound to remain ineffectual in Germany as long as there was no substantial middle class to give support and direction to the peasants' struggle. Three years later, in 1793, Fichte caused a minor stir with the publication of two radical political treatises, one criticizing the ruling nobility for its suppression of the freedom of thought, the other defending the French Revolution and arguing for the legitimacy of violent revolt in general.[3] Written during the Jacobin ascendancy in France, and so at a time when most German intellectuals had distanced themselves from the Revolution, the latter work offered a scathing moral critique of the feudal order and a bold defense of a people's right to abolish an illegitimate regime by whatever means necessary. From the publication of these early texts Fichte acquired a reputation as a political radical that remained with him for as long as he lived.

Although the *Foundations* lacks the enthusiastic tone that charac- terizes his first texts, many of its central doctrines are continuous with the political views that originally inspired Fichte to defend the Revolu-

---

[3] The first of these is *Reclamation of the Freedom of Thought from the Princes of Europe, Who Have Oppressed It Until Now*, trans. Thomas E. Wartenberg, in James Schmidt (ed.), *What is Enlightenment?: Eighteenth-Century Answers and Twentieth-Century Questions* (Berkeley, CA: University of California Press, 1996). The second is *Contributions toward Correcting the Public's Judgment of the French Revolution* (*Beiträge zur Berichtigung der Urteile des Publikums über die französische Revolution*). The latter work has not been translated into English.

tion with such vehemence. Indeed, his later theory can be seen, in large part, as Fichte's attempt to find a rigorous philosophical justification of the most important of his earlier views. Most significantly, the center-piece of the *Foundations* – its defense of equal rights for all persons – is clearly continuous with Fichte's youthful opposition to the inherited class privileges of feudalism and, more specifically, to the idea that some individuals can possess a right to the body and labor of others. As Fichte must have conceived it, the doctrine of original rights is an elaboration of the principles that underlie the Declaration of the Rights of Man. At a more general level, the *Foundations*'s attempt to establish the validity of the principles of right via an argument from the conditions of self-consciousness can be understood as Fichte's version of the idea, implicit in Revolution ideology, that human reason is the source of eternal principles of right in accordance with which existing political institu-tions are to be judged and, if necessary, reformed or replaced. The *Foundations* also gives expression to the republicanism of the Revolution – the idea that sovereignty resides ultimately in the popular will and that in a just state the governed must have some role in governing. This idea is at the core of Fichte's account of the state, insofar as its principal theoretical device, the social contract, makes consent of the governed an essential condition of legitimate authority. Finally, the central role that Fichte's later theory accords to personal freedom is a continuation of his earlier rejection of the paternalism implicit in the idea of princely rule. Grounding the principles of right in freedom rather than happiness is Fichte's response to paternalism's chief claim – the principle that apologies for tyranny tacitly assume – that happiness is the aim of political society and that only through direction from above can citizens achieve it.

Outline of the argument

Despite Fichte's various attempts to summarize the basic plan of his text, the *Foundations* is not an easy work to grasp as a whole. Indeed, it could be argued that its principal value resides in a few scattered strokes of brilliance rather than in its project as a whole. Even if this is true, however, there is some merit in attempting to understand how Fichte intended those parts to constitute a single undertaking. Not surpris-ingly, the organization of the text itself offers the best starting point for grasping the structure of its argument. First, however, it is necessary to decide which of its organizational features are truly relevant to this task. In this regard it is important to note that the *Foundations* was originally published in two parts, the first in March 1796 and the second just one year later. Although Fichte distinguishes the two parts by calling the second "Applied Natural Right," there is in fact more continuity in their contents than this attempt to distinguish them suggests. Part II begins with a long and important discussion of the state, but, as Fichte admits (both in II(6) of the Introduction and in the opening paragraph of Part II), this is more a continuation of a discussion begun in Part I than the first step into a new, fundamentally distinct realm of "applied" right. In the end, this division of the text reflects more of Fichte's publication schedule and writing speed than a genuine shift in content.

A more reliable guide to the work's philosophical structure is its division into three *Hauptstücke*, or Main Divisions (which are followed by two appendices and preceded by a general introduction). As their titles indicate, each Main Division has a distinct philosophical task: the first "deduces" the concept of right, the second demonstrates its "applicability," and the third "applies" the concept to the empirical world. In order to grasp the overall project of the *Foundations* we must understand what these distinct tasks are and how, roughly, Fichte plans to accomplish them.

1 Deduction of the concept of right

We have already indicated very generally how Fichte conceives of the first of these tasks: to deduce the concept of right is to demonstrate that it is a necessary condition for the possibility of self-consciousness. But what, more specifically, does this entail? Perhaps it is best to begin by defining the starting and end points of the argument more precisely. If the concept of right is to be shown to be necessary for self-conscious-ness, we need to know what that concept consists in and what kind (or aspect) of self-consciousness it is supposed to be a condition of. According to the Introduction, the concept of right is "the concept of the necessary relation of free beings to one another" (Introduction, II.2) or, more informatively, the "principles in accordance with which a community among free beings as such could be established" (Introduc-tion, II.4). These principles, as we see at the end of the first Main

Division, can be summarized in the injunction that "each is to limit his freedom through the concept of the possibility of the freedom of the other" (§4.III). In the same part of the Introduction Fichte also provides a helpful description of the phenomenon that the concept of right is supposed to make possible. According to this passage, the concept of right is to be deduced by showing that "the rational being cannot posit itself as a rational being with self-consciousness without positing itself as an *individual*, as one among several rational beings that it assumes to exist outside itself" (Introduction, II.2). In other words, the claim at the heart of Fichte's deduction is that an awareness of oneself as a rational subject requires as its condition a consciousness of one's *individuality* (in a sense yet to be determined) and that this consciousness depends on taking oneself to stand in certain law-governed relations – relations specified by the concept of right – to other individuals of the same type.[4]

Before proceeding to outline the steps of Fichte's argument, let us pause to note what is contained in the idea of self-consciousness on which the deduction rests. It is extremely important to recognize that the self-consciousness at issue here includes consciousness of oneself as a *rational* subject, where "rational" implies "self-positing," or – especially in the context of practical philosophy – "self-determining." In other words, the self-consciousness from which the principles of natural right are to be deduced is not simply the awareness of oneself as the numerically identical subject of diverse representational states; it includes, beyond mere self-identity, the consciousness of oneself as rational, or free. (If it did not include this element, it would not be genuine *self*-consciousness, according to Fichte, since if what I am aware of is not self-determining, it cannot be an I.) Moreover, Fichte's formulation of his task in the Introduction signals that the argument of the *Foundations* is to focus on a particular aspect of self-consciousness: one's awareness of oneself as a free *individual* – a being distinct from, but also the same as, the other members of one's species. The connection that Fichte means to establish between individuality and the principles of right rests on the provocative claim that consciousness of

---

[4] Fichte's thesis that humans can realize their individuality only through relations to others is a provocative claim that greatly influenced succeeding philosophers and continues to be of interest today. Friedrich Schleiermacher and Wilhelm von Humboldt are just two examples of thinkers who incorporated versions of Fichte's thesis into their own thought.

oneself as an individual requires that one's free agency have a socially recognized domain in the external world, a domain within which the subject is able to give objective reality to the idea of its own freedom. (Fichte's starting point could be further qualified by noting that he is concerned only with how self-consciousness is possible for a "finite" being; this aspect of his undertaking is elaborated below, in conjunction with the argument of §1.) With these qualifications in mind, Fichte's aim in the first Main Division can be reformulated more precisely: it is to show that taking oneself to be bound by the principles of right – principles that impose equal and reciprocal limits on the freedom of all – is a necessary condition of taking oneself to be an *individualized locus of free agency* and, further, that this awareness of one's individuality is required in order to be conscious of oneself as free and rational.

The main steps of Fichte's deduction are easy to trace – they are set out as three separate "theorems" – but reconstructing the arguments they rely on is considerably more difficult. In the first step (§1) he argues that a subject could not be self-conscious without ascribing to itself "a free efficacy," or "an activity whose ultimate ground lies purely . . . within itself." Fichte's claim, in other words, is that self-consciousness is possible only if the subject thinks of itself as having the capacity for a certain kind of free activity. This claim is easily recognized as a version of the thesis that practical reason has primacy over theoretical, and Fichte explicitly formulates his view in these terms in the first Corollary to §1: "the practical I is the I of original self-consciousness; . . . a rational being perceives itself immediately only in willing and would not perceive itself, and thus would also not perceive the world . . . , if it were not a practical being. Willing is the genuine and essential character of reason."

It is important to look more closely at how Fichte characterizes the activity that the practical subject is supposed to ascribe to itself in order to be self-conscious, namely, as "the act of *forming* the concept of an intended efficacy outside us, or the concept of an *end*." (It is worth noting here that Fichte focuses on the same capacity of the subject that Kant will single out in the *Metaphysics of Morals* as the defining feature of moral personhood: the ability to set practical ends for oneself.) Although this free activity is originally characterized as one that is wholly internal to consciousness – the mere forming of an end – it is an activity of consciousness that also makes implicit reference to a world outside itself: forming an end includes a determination to act in the world. This reference to an external world is crucial to Fichte's argument. Its importance is reflected in the fact that the *Foundations* expressly sets out to investigate the conditions of self-consciousness for *finite* subjects (that is, for subjects who are always necessarily related to an objective world and hence "limited" – that is, *not* fully self-determined – in the sense that they are bound, both theoretically and practically, by a world that is neither themselves nor entirely of their own making). The text's founding idea – that political rights are among the necessary conditions of self-consciousness – is predicated on the view that finite subjects can become conscious of themselves as self-determining only when the objective world to which they are necessarily related mirrors that picture of themselves. Thus, it is only by seeing the results of its free agency in an independently existing world (or, more precisely, in what ordinary consciousness takes to be an independent world) that a finite subject can intuit its own self-determining character; it is only in acting on objects that a finite subject can be aware of itself as self-determining. From here it is only a short step to the inference drawn in §2 – that for a finite being self-consciousness requires positing an independent, sensible world as the sphere within which its free agency can be realized.

The deduction's second theorem (§3) makes one of the *Foundations*'s most original and exciting claims, and it is essential to Fichte's project of showing that rights are necessary conditions of self-consciousness. Its claim is that ascribing to oneself free efficacy (or agency) in the sensible world requires ascribing the same capacity to other rational beings. Fichte argues here that in order for a subject to be conscious of its own agency, it must first find that agency, as an object for its consciousness, in the external world. The thought here appears to be that the subject cannot come to an awareness of itself as practically free simply by seeing the results of its agency in the world, for in order to act freely, it would first have to know itself as free. The subject, then, must learn about its freedom in some other manner; it must somehow experience itself as free prior to any actual instances of its agency. Fichte's claim in §3 is that the only possible solution to this problem is to suppose that external evidence of one subject's agency is provided by another free subject. This occurs through a "summons" that one already formed subject makes to another. The summons is a call to act, a call to realize one's free efficacy, which takes the form of an imperative: You *ought* to "resolve to exercise [your] agency" (§3, III). Fichte concludes from this that the freedom of one subject (which includes consciousness of its freedom) requires the existence of others; free individuality is possible only in relation to other subjects, and so *intersubjectivity* is a necessary condition of self-consciousness. As Fichte sums up his result in the first Corollary to §3: "The human being . . . becomes a human being only among human beings; . . . it follows that *if there are to be human beings at all, there must be more than one.*"

From here Fichte moves to the final step of the deduction of the concept of right (§4). Its claim is that positing the existence of other rational beings requires thinking of oneself as standing in a particular relation to them, a relation that turns out to be the "relation of right." The argument behind this claim is that in order to be conscious of myself as a free *individual*, I must be able to distinguish my own free agency from that of the other subjects whose existence I necessarily posit (as established in §3). According to Fichte, this requires "ascribing exclusively to myself a sphere for my free choice" (§4, II), a sphere to which other free beings have no access. But, given that I share the external world with other free beings, this is possible only if my individuality is *recognized* by those beings as setting limits to their own free agency. (And the same, of course, is required of me in relation to them if they are to attain consciousness of themselves as free individuals.) This recognition is more than just a theoretical acknowledgment of my status as a free being; it also requires that I be treated as such by other subjects or, in other words, that my free agency acquire a real and protected existence in the external world. But this is nothing more than the requirement that I possess a set of rights that are respected by others, which is what Fichte means by "standing in a relation of right" to other rational beings.

This argument concludes the first Main Division of the *Foundations* and its deduction of the concept of right. Although Fichte has made a plausible case for the claim that rights play an important role in the formation of individuals' conceptions of themselves as free, it must be wondered whether he has shown all that he intended. One principal worry is whether the concept of individuality invoked at the beginning of the deduction is precisely the same concept at work in its conclusion. The former is simply the idea of the individual as a discrete unit of free causal efficacy – the sole ground of its own actions – but it is unclear that this concept is sufficient to ground the necessity of the relation of right. Fichte's claim is that recognition by others of the inviolability of one's external sphere of action is necessary if one is to be able to distinguish one's own agency from that of others. But this would appear to entail the highly implausible conclusion that individuals can be conscious of themselves as discrete units of causal efficacy only by inhabiting a political order that protects individual rights. (As we shall see below, Fichte comes to realize the implausibility of this claim and attempts to weaken it later in the text.) It may well be that standing in a relation of right to others serves to form one's conception of oneself as an individual, but, if so, what that relation fosters is a consciousness of oneself not as a discrete unit of causal efficacy but as a being whose capacity for agency gives it a special *dignity* or *value* that makes it *deserving of* an exclusive sphere of activity that is respected by others. This is not to suggest that rights are completely irrelevant to the concept of individuality with which the deduction begins, but only that they cannot be understood as transcendental conditions of it. It is more plausible to understand rights, not as conditions that make it possible for individuals to become conscious of themselves as discrete units of agency, but as principles that guarantee that the external world will allow adequate space for the *expression* of their conceptions of themselves as such – in other words, principles that ensure that the free agency of individuals can be *realized*.[5]

2 *Demonstrating the applicability of the concept of right*

After having deduced the concept of right, Fichte turns his attention to establishing its applicability. Although it is initially difficult to figure out just what this means, the last section of §7 nicely sums up the four tasks Fichte takes himself to have carried out in the text's second Main Division: (1) He has provided a "sure criterion" for applying the concept of right, which is to say that he has given us a way of distinguishing those beings in the sensible world who are potential

---

[5] Indeed, this is precisely how Hegel, in his doctrine of Abstract Right, transforms Fichte's account of the relation between rights and the consciousness of freedom: rights are viewed by Hegel as necessary conditions for the *expression* of a certain conception of oneself as free, not as transcendental conditions for having that self-conception. See G. W. F. Hegel, *Elements of the Philosophy of Right*, ed. and trans. Allen W. Wood (Cambridge: Cambridge University Press, 1991), §§34–40.

bearers of rights from those that are not. (Fichte's solution is that any being with a human form, or body, is to be regarded as a rational being and hence as a possible bearer of rights.) (2) He has shown that what the concept of right purports to govern – "the mutual influence of free and rational beings upon one another" – is a real possibility. (Interaction among rational beings is possible because their free agency is mediated by bodies that inhabit the same sensible world. An important step in this proof is the argument of §5, that having a body is a necessary condition of self-consciousness, since the ability to carry out one's ends requires an immediate link between one's will and the sensible world in which the will's ends are to be achieved. Thus, human consciousness is necessarily embodied, and our bodies play an essential role in consti-tuting us as rational beings.) (3) He has specified the kind of laws that principles of right give rise to by showing that they apply to free actions of rational beings, not to behavior that is the result of mere natural forces. (In other words, laws based on right are *normative* principles – that is, laws whose efficacy depends on conscious beings recognizing them as such, in contrast to laws of nature, which govern events independently of any knowledge of them.[6]) (4) He has determined under what conditions the principles of right are valid, namely, wher-ever "a community, a reciprocal influence among free beings as such, is to exist." (In this context Fichte introduces a point that has important consequences for his later account of political obligation. The point is that the validity of laws of right, unlike that of moral laws, is merely conditional. It is conditional on the agreement of other individuals to submit themselves to laws of right and, more importantly, on one's own arbitrary decision to live in a community of free beings. Thus, from the perspective of political philosophy alone there is no absolute obligation to respect the rights of others. A community of free beings cannot exist unless the principles of right are followed, but individuals are obligated by those principles only if they choose to make the existence of such a community one of their ends. This view is obviously in tension with Fichte's earlier claim in §4 that thinking of oneself as standing in a relation of right to other subjects is a necessary condition of self-consciousness, since such a relation cannot be both a condition of self-consciousness and a matter left up to arbitrary choice. It is not

---

[6] Kant makes this distinction in his *Groundwork of the Metaphysics of Morals*, trans. H. J. Paton (New York: Harper & Row, 1964), p. 80.

surprising, then, that in §7, and again in his opening remark in the First Appendix, Fichte modifies his earlier position, maintaining only that an original summons from another rational being is necessary for self-consciousness, not enduring relations of right. This move, however, appears to invalidate the crucial transition from §3 to §4 and raises the question of how, then, the concept of right can be claimed to be an a priori concept of reason rather than an arbitrary human invention.)

3 Applying the concept of right

In the third Main Division Fichte proceeds to apply the concept he has just deduced and shown to be empirically applicable. His task here is to show how the sensible world must be ordered if the concept of right is to be realized within it. This is accomplished in three chapters, each of which treats one of the central doctrines that together complete the main project of the *Foundations*: original right, the right of coercion, and political right (or right within the state). Original rights are rights that individuals have independently of any actual political order and that must be safeguarded and respected within a just state. (The thesis that there are such rights is what makes Fichte's theory part of the "natural right" tradition, though he is careful to point out that original rights are not natural in the sense that they could be realized in a pre-political "state of nature." Original rights would have normative validity in the absence of a state, but they can be "actual" – explicitly acknowledged and enforced – only in a political order.) Original rights are introduced as "the conditions of personality" (§9) (or of free agency), and as such they belong to individuals simply by virtue of the quality that makes them persons, the capacity to set ends for themselves. Original rights secure the conditions of personality not by enabling individuals to set ends but by guaranteeing their ability to translate their ends into effective action. Thus, original rights secure the freedom of individuals to *act* as they will by restricting the actions of others (including those of the state) so as to create for all individuals an exclusive, external sphere of freedom within which their free agency can be realized. The principle that underlies all original rights is expressed by the formula: "No one has a right to an action that makes the freedom and personality of another impossible" (§8, I). The rights that Fichte derives from the conditions of free individual agency fall into two broad classes: those that concern the inviolability of the body and those that guarantee the individual a sphere of "free influence within the entire sensible world" (§11, V), including the rights to self-preservation and private property.

In the following chapter Fichte establishes a further right individuals have independently of the state, the right of coercion. He deduces this right by observing that outside a state there is no rational basis for believing that one's original rights will be respected by others and hence no guarantee that the conditions of one's free agency will be secured. Thus, if the free agency of individuals is to be realized – or, more precisely, if the right to its realization is to be enforceable – individuals must have the right (permission) to "violate . . . the freedom and personality" of any person who violates their original rights (§8, II). The right to coerce others to respect one's original rights, though "natural" in the sense indicated above, is not itself an original right, because it ceases to be a right of individuals once the state is formed. In fact, it is precisely because according this right to individuals is incompatible with the realization of original rights – it makes their enforcement highly irregular – that the state is necessary.

As Fichte's treatment of the right of coercion makes clear, the necessity of the state is grounded in the need to establish a reliable "law of coercion" that will deter individuals from violating the original rights of others and punish actual offenders. Thus, the third and final chapter in Fichte's account of how right can be realized in the sensible world is concerned with *Staatsrecht*, or political right, and it constitutes by far the longest part of that account. (Part Two of the *Foundations*, "Applied Natural Right," is to a large extent just a continuation of this topic.) In explaining the nature and purpose of the state Fichte relies on the familiar idea of a social contract in which individuals give up a part of their rights (here, the right of coercion) to a more powerful third party, the state, which guarantees the enforcement of their more basic, original rights. Yet Fichte's version of the social contract has several distinctive features. The most obvious of these is that founding the state requires not just one contract but (at least) three.[7] Although these contracts are usually treated as though they were three separate agreements, it is best to regard them, as Fichte himself sometimes does (§17, B.I), as three parts of a single contract, all of which are necessary for the state to be

---

[7] In addition to the three most important contracts I discuss here, Fichte also refers to a subjection contract (§17.B.V) and an expiation contract (§20).

complete. The first of these agreements is the property contract, in which each citizen promises all other citizens to respect their property on the condition that they exercise the same restraint with respect to his. ('Property' here is understood in a broad sense that includes all rights to the exercise of freedom (§17, B.I).) Because promises alone are not sufficient to guarantee that this agreement will be respected, a second pact, the protection contract, is required. Here each citizen agrees to make a positive contribution (of services, goods, or money) towards establishing a coercive power capable of enforcing the first contract.

The need for the third pact, the unification contract, is more difficult to grasp. It is supposed to follow from the fact that in the protection contract individuals make a commitment (to contribute towards the protection of the rights of all) that extends not to each member of the state individually but to a corporate entity that, strictly speaking, does not yet exist. As Fichte formulates the point, "*Who* requires that [one] contribute in this way? With whom does [one] actually negotiate it, and who is the second party in this contract?" (§17, B.IV). Fichte's thought here seems to be that in the protection contract citizens obligate themselves to pursuing an end that is more than just a composite of the ends held by private individuals (the desire, in each case, that one's own rights be respected). In this contract citizens agree not only to help protect the rights of each individual but also to support the collective body that guarantees the rights of all. In doing so citizens tacitly consent to be guided by a "common" (or general) will that is not reducible to the private wills of individuals but is instead the collective will of a new corporate entity. In Fichte's view, the unification contract is required in order to bring this new entity into existence and so is presupposed by (and hence deducible from) the first two contracts. This third contract is an agreement of every individual with every other that results in the formation of an organized whole with its own will, or ends, namely: the protection of the rights of all individuals and the maintenance of the corporate body that alone is able to achieve that end.

Fichte's unification contract is highly reminiscent of Rousseau's version of the social contract, which is described as having the following result: "Instantly, in place of the private person of each contracting party, [the] act of association produces a moral and collective body, . . . which receives from this same act its unity, its common *self*, its life, and its will."[8] Fichte is clearly thinking of Rousseau when he writes that "as a consequence of the unification contract, the individual becomes a part of an organized whole, and thus melts into one with it" (§17, B.V). It is not completely clear what Fichte's talk of melting into an organized whole ultimately comes to, but surely one point he means to be making is that the parts that make up the state – human individuals – cannot realize their true nature on their own, outside the state, since it is only in a just political order that proper accord is given to their status as free, rational agents. A second implication of the metaphor appears to be that – as Rousseau, too, asserted – becoming a citizen entails more than merely signing on to a particular sort of contract; it also requires thinking of oneself in a new way – not as a separate being with only private ends but as a member of a community who cares about the general ends prescribed by the principles of right. Fichte's reasons for holding this view are somewhat less clear than Rousseau's, but he seems to think that if the state is not to be directed wholly from above, and hence be tyrannical, the individuals who are its parts must themselves both know and will the universal ends it seeks to achieve.[9] Thus, Fichte's theory shares with Rousseau's the curious feature that although the original purpose of the contract is defined individualistically (as the protection of each individual's original rights), its actual implementation requires a high degree of social-spiritedness among its participants – specifically, the ability to subordinate one's private ends to the universal aims of the just state. In distinction to Rousseau, however, Fichte insists that a citizen does not give himself completely to the state; rather, as a citizen he retains the freedoms defined by his original rights and to this extent "remains an individual, a free person, dependent only on himself" (§17, B.V). The implication of Fichte's view is that a state in which right is fully realized requires its members to have (at least) dual identities, both as citizens who are parts of a collective self and as private individuals with substantial interests separate from those of the whole.

---

[8] Jean-Jacques Rousseau, *On the Social Contract*, ed. Roger D. Masters, trans. Judith R. Masters (New York: St. Martin's Press, 1978), p. 53.

[9] This point is hinted at in §17, B.IV, where Fichte emphasizes that, in contrast to a natural organic entity such as a tree, every part of the state – each individual – must be related to the state's ends via "consciousness and . . . will." In this passage Fichte anticipates Hegel's view of the state as an organic entity within which every individual "knows and wills" its laws ("the universal") and so enjoys the freedom appropriate to citizenship (*Elements of the Philosophy of Right*, §260).

The remaining two sections of Fichte's account of political right are devoted to civil law and the state's constitution. The first of these discusses in detail the various classes of positive law and the principles underlying them. The second rejects the separation of powers, argues that both monarchy and aristocracy are legitimate forms of government, and determines the nature and tasks of the police.[10] (It is here that Fichte articulates in great detail his notorious provisions for requiring that citizens always carry with them a government-issued identity card with likeness and that they register their whereabouts at all times with the police.) These sections are followed by appendices on family right and international right that, although historically interesting, fall outside the main philosophical tasks of Fichte's theory of natural right.

The enduring significance of Fichte's theory

Even if it is true, as has been suggested here, that the central argument of the *Foundations* fails at several crucial junctures, Fichte's theory contains a number of innovative ideas that make it an achievement of enduring philosophical importance. The most prominent of these is expressed in his claim, made throughout the text, to have established the principles of political philosophy independently of moral theory. The theory of right, as one formulation would have it, is "a separate science standing on its own" (Introduction, II.5). Fichte's central claim here is that, contrary to the views of most of his Kantian contemporaries, the theory of right cannot be deduced from the moral law (understood here as the law that underlies Kant's categorical imperative). In his earlier work in defense of the French Revolution[11] Fichte himself had attempted to ground political philosophy in Kant's moral theory by deriving the inalienable rights of individuals from their duty to follow the categorical imperative. According to this view, political rights were understood as restrictions placed on the actions of others for the purpose of providing individuals with the freedom necessary to fulfill

---

[10] Nineteenth-century German speakers gave a much broader meaning to the term "police" (*Polizei*) than it has in contemporary usage, and Fichte uses the term here in its extended sense. The Prussian General Legal Code of 1794 ascribed to the police a variety of functions beyond law enforcement, including building regulation, fire protection, maintaining public health, and providing assistance to the poor. This usage is closer to the sense of the Greek word from which it derives (*politeia*), which means simply "constitution."

[11] See note 3 above.

their moral duties. (If, for example, I have a moral duty to perfect my natural talents, then I have an inalienable right to whatever freedom of action their perfection requires.) Fichte's earlier view accorded to the state a further role in helping individuals to achieve moral virtue: it was charged with the *moral education* of its citizens – with taming and reforming their natural inclinations so as to make them more disposed to do what duty requires. This view of the relation between moral and political philosophy can be summed up by saying that the latter's task is to determine how the social world must be organized if the external conditions of moral action are to be realized. On this view, the morality of its citizens is the state's highest, and only, final end.

The transformation that Fichte means to effect in the *Foundations* is best understood as a change in the conception of the subject that grounds political philosophy. His earlier theory could be said to be grounded in the idea of a morally autonomous subject, in that its principles are derived by articulating the social conditions necessary for individuals to achieve moral autonomy. The *Foundations*, in contrast, derives the principles of right from a different conception of the subject, the "person" (or, equivalently, the free individual who is conscious of himself as a discrete unit of agency). According to this view, a system of rights is rationally necessary not because it helps to make us moral. (It can, Fichte thinks, but this is not the perspective a theory of right properly takes on the matter.) Rather, a system of rights is rationally necessary because it fosters and gives expression to the *individuality* of citizens as defined in the opening sections of the text. One reason why Fichte is led to his later view is that it alone (he believes) is able to explain why, for example, private property is a necessary part of a just political order. His thought here is that the need for private property cannot be established if the only conception of subjectivity one recognizes is that of a self-legislating being in Kant's sense (one that legislates universal principles of action, valid for all subjects). Subjects could be autonomous in this sense even if private property did not exist. Fichte's innovation is to claim that the need for private property, and for rights more generally, can be understood only in relation to individuality (as he conceives it), the value of which is not simply derivative of the value of moral autonomy. In other words, the rational necessity of private property (and of all other original rights as well) lies in the fact that in order to realize themselves as persons, human subjects require an

exclusive sphere of activity within which they are free to carry out ends
that are entirely their own – ends that, once translated into actions,
mark them in the external world as individuals, distinct from all others.

A second important innovation of the *Foundations* is closely related to
the first. It is the distinction Fichte draws between two conceptions of
freedom – personal freedom and moral autonomy – that correspond to
the two conceptions of subjectivity just discussed. In other words, one
important implication of Fichte's separation of right from morality is
that the former comes to be grounded in a new, distinctively political
conception of freedom. This means that the freedom the rational state
strives to realize for its citizens is different in kind from the freedom
that characterizes the (Kantian) moral subject: political philosophy aims
to promote personal, or "formal," freedom – the ability to act according
to one's freely chosen ends, unhindered by the interference of others –
whereas moral theory finds its ideal in a more substantive form of self-
determination, determining one's actions in accordance with universal
moral principles that come from oneself. According to the political
conception of freedom, the ends an individual sets for himself are his
own – determined by himself – simply because they are chosen by him,
and actions based on those ends are worthy of a kind of respect from
others, regardless of whether they are self-determined in the weightier
sense that is of concern to moral philosophy. It could be argued that
Fichte's distinction between moral and political freedom is already
implicit in Kant's appeal to a concept of external freedom in the
Metaphysics of Morals.[12] Even if this is true, however, Fichte must be
credited with articulating the distinction more clearly than his prede-
cessor, and with inspiring Hegel's fully explicit distinction in the
Philosophy of Right between personal and moral freedom, the two
conceptions of self-determination that ground his "Abstract Right" and
"Morality," respectively.[13]

Thirdly, and perhaps most importantly, the *Foundations* provides the
first extended discussion of the concept of recognition (*Anerkennung*)

---

[12] Immanuel Kant, *The Metaphysics of Morals*, trans. Mary Gregor (Cambridge: Cambridge
University Press, 1996), pp. 146–7, 157–8. In contrast to Kant, however, Fichte seems not to
regard the capacity to set ends as parasitic on the subject's status as a moral being. Whereas Kant
insisted that the ability to set ends for oneself was possible only for a being that was also morally
autonomous (bound by the laws of one's own reason), Fichte appears to believe that the former
is possible independently of the latter.
[13] *Elements of the Philosophy of Right*, §§36–9, 105–12.

and the role it plays in the constitution of free, rational subjects. (Fichte was no doubt influenced here by Rousseau's treatment of *amour-propre* in *Emile* and the *Discourse on Inequality*.[14] Hegel, of course, makes recognition a centerpiece of his social and political thought, but few readers today realize that Fichte was the first to develop the central ideas of this doctrine.) This aspect of Fichte's political theory has major implications for his understanding of the nature of subjectivity in general and the conditions under which it is fully realized. Fichte's innovation is to have highlighted the significance of intersubjectivity by arguing that recognition of and by another human subject is a condition for the possibility of self-consciousness. Given that the *Foundations* is a work in political philosophy, it is most natural to take its doctrine of recognition as primarily a claim about the importance of having one's free agency recognized by others within a state that safeguards individual rights. This, however, is not the kind of recognition Fichte refers to when he originally argues for its status as a condition of self-consciousness (§3). As we have seen, the recognition he appeals to there is a summons, made by one subject to another, to engage in free activity, and the real-world phenomenon he has in mind is education (*Erziehung*) rather than political rights. According to either way of understanding Fichte's doctrine, however, the underlying thought is the same: relations to other free subjects are essential to one's own subjectivity, since one can acquire a conception of oneself as free only by being treated as such by another being whom one in turn takes to be free. One of the provocative implications of this thought is that the conditions of realizing oneself as an individual, distinct from other subjects, include a form of what the tradition of German idealism calls "universal" self-consciousness. For, according to Fichte's doctrine of recognition, the consciousness of one's own individuality entails having relations to other beings that one takes to be of the same general type as oneself: free, rational, and self-aware. One reason, then, that Fichte's argument has had such an enduring influence on Continental philosophy after him is that it promises to provide a rational justification – grounded in the conditions of something as basic as self-consciousness itself – for the relations of reciprocity and equality among subjects that modern

[14] Jean-Jacques Rousseau, *Emile*, trans. Allan Bloom (New York: Basic Books, 1979) and *The First and Second Discourses*, trans. Roger D. Masters and Judith R. Masters (New York: St. Martin's Press, 1964).

political thought, and modern philosophy more generally, take as one of their guiding ideals.

Finally, we must not neglect the more specifically political innovations of Fichte's theory.[15] The most conspicuous of these is his much-criticized doctrine of the state's undivided sovereign power, which is held in check only by the "ephorate," a group of wise and trusted men, elected by the people (or their representatives), who have the authority to dissolve the government when it violates the principles of right or the manifest will of the citizenry (§16, VI, IX–XII). A more positive legacy of the *Foundations* is its defense of strict privacy rights for individuals (§19, II.G–I) and of an unrestricted right to emigrate (Second Appendix, §22). Fichte can also be credited with encouraging a new and historically influential way of thinking about the function and significance of political membership. By putting the relation between right and self-consciousness at the center of his theory, he suggests that the political realm is not best understood as a social arena that already constituted individuals enter in order to satisfy ends that they have prior to existing in the state. The natural implication of his view, rather, is that politics plays a deeper, *formative* role in constituting individuals' self-conceptions – that is, in bringing them to think of themselves as free persons who, simply by virtue of their ability to determine their own practical ends, are deserving of a set of rights identical to those of every other person.

But perhaps the *Foundations*'s most important political innovation is its inclusion of issues of economic justice among the central concerns of political philosophy. Fichte's account of natural rights goes beyond those of earlier writers (such as Locke and Rousseau) by widening the scope of natural rights to include, for example, the rights to subsistence and gainful employment (§11, IV–V; §19, II.D). Beyond this, Fichte argues that the state must play an active role in regulating economic activity in order to insure that everyone who works – as every citizen must – is also able to live from his income (§18, III–IV). Finally, Fichte's state is charged with the task of redistributing wealth in order to eliminate poverty and, as Rousseau emphasized, all forms of economic dependence that are incompatible with personal freedom (§18, III–V).

---

[15] Many of the ideas in this paragraph and the next come from Allen W. Wood's discussion of Fichte's political views in "Fichte's Philosophical Revolution," *Philosophical Topics*, 19 (Fall 1991), 21–2.

(It should be noted that Fichte ignores this principle when he discusses, in the First Appendix, the relation between husbands and wives: women's complete financial dependence on their husbands is said to be in accordance with both "nature and reason.") The philosophical underpinnings of these political doctrines can be found in the fact that Fichte conceives of personal freedom not primarily as a freedom from the interference of others (though noninterference is an important part of the content of original rights) but as a freedom, or ability, to act in the external world – an ability to be *effective* in translating one's ends into real action (§11, IV). Thus, the rights that Fichte defends are not, at base, rights to be left alone – which in contemporary liberal societies often include the "freedoms" to starve, to be homeless, and to have no access to health care – but entitlements to the basic social conditions of human agency. (Applying this principle to the right to work, Fichte writes: "In a nation where everyone goes naked the right to work as a tailor would be no right" (§18.III).) Original rights, then, can be understood as directed at securing the social conditions of agency for all (male) persons.[16] It is not difficult to see how Fichte's concern with economic justice follows from this way of conceiving of personal freedom. He defends the right to subsistence, for example, on the grounds that "self-preservation is the condition of all other actions and of every expression of freedom" (§11.IV). Thus, even though Fichte's theory remains squarely within the liberal tradition, it at the same time provides a framework for defending many of the ideas espoused by socialist thinkers in the following century. If for no other reason than this Fichte's *Foundations of Natural Right* continues to deserve our attention now, when uniting the best of liberalism with economic justice remains the most urgent political challenge of the day.

---

[16] Because they have not surrendered their personhood through marriage, single women who are no longer subject to their fathers' authority count as fully fledged persons for Fichte, except that they are not allowed to hold political office (First Appendix, §§35–7).

Chronology

1762   Born Rammenau, Saxony, 19 May.

1780   Enters the Jena theology seminary.

1784   Breaks off studies without completing a degree.

1788   Accepts position as private tutor to a family in Zurich.

1790   Engagement to Johanna Rahn, niece of the poet F. G. Klop-
        stock. Leaves Zurich for Leipzig, where he begins study of
        Kant's works.

1791   Travels to Warsaw to seek employment, then to Königsberg to
        ask Kant for financial support, and finally to Gdansk to work
        again as a private tutor.

1792   Fichte's first publication, *Attempt at a Critique of all Revela-
        tion*, is published with Kant's help.

1793   Marries Johanna Rahn in Zurich and begins work on his new
        philosophical system. Publishes two popular writings on
        political philosophy: *Reclamation of the Freedom of Thought
        from the Princes of Europe* and *Contributions toward Correcting
        the Public's Judgment of the French Revolution*.

1794   Takes up prestigious position at University of Jena as the
        successor of Karl L. Reinhold. Publication of first version of
        the *Wissenschaftslehre*.

1796   Birth of only child, I. H. Fichte, who later edited his father's
        works. *Foundations of Natural Right*, Part I.

1797   *Foundations of Natural Right*, Part II.

1798   *System of Ethical Theory*.

1799   Atheism controversy. Loses his academic position at Jena over
        charges of atheism.

1800   Moves to Berlin. *The Vocation of Man* and *The Closed Commercial State.*

1806   Napoleon's troops defeat Prussia at Jena and occupy Berlin.

1807   Appointed as Professor in Königsberg but leaves for Copenhagen when French troops threaten to reach East Prussia. Returns to Berlin after Peace of Tilsit.

1807–8 Delivers lectures in Berlin that become *Addresses to the German Nation.*

1810   Appointed as Professor and Dean of the Philosophical Faculty at the newly founded Humboldt University in Berlin.

1811   Named Rector of Humboldt University.

1812   Dismissed as University Rector and begins work on a final version of *Wissenschaftslehre.*

1813   War against Napoleon resumes.

1814   Dies of fever caught from his wife, who herself contracted it while nursing Prussian soldiers.

Further reading

Although there is a growing body of secondary literature on Fichte in English, surprisingly little of it is devoted specifically to the *Foundations of Natural Right*. Yet because the *Foundations* is an integral part of Fichte's larger philosophical system, the wider literature is relevant to understanding this text, and some familiarity with it is advisable. A general introduction to the aims of Fichte's first philosophical system is Frederick Neuhouser's *Fichte's Theory of Subjectivity* (Cambridge: Cambridge University Press, 1990). Allen W. Wood's "Fichte's Philosophical Revolution," *Philosophical Topics*, 19 (1991), 1–28, provides a short but excellent introduction to Fichte's thought as a whole, including a discussion of the *Foundations* in §§10–11. The account of Fichte's theory of self-consciousness given by Dieter Henrich in "Fichte's Original Insight," *Contemporary German Philosophy*, 1 (1982), 15–52 played a key role in generating interest in Fichte among contemporary Anglo-American philosophers.

Readers interested in Fichte's practical philosophy in general might want to consult F. W. J. Schelling's *System of Transcendental Idealism* (1800), the "Third Proposition" of which is a response to Fichte's attempt to ground both ethics and political philosophy in a principle of self-consciousness. Allen W. Wood's "Fichte's Philosophy of Right and Ethics" (in *The Cambridge Companion to Fichte*, ed. Günter Zöller (Cambridge: Cambridge University Press, forthcoming)) discusses Fichte's practical philosophy as a whole. For related topics, see Daniel Breazeale's "The Theory of Practice and the Practice of Theory," *International Philosophical Quarterly*, 36 (1996), 47–64, which offers an insightful discussion of Fichte's claim that practical reason has primacy over theoretical. (Breazeale's introductions to the early works he edits and translates in *Fichte: Early Philosophical Writings* (Ithaca, NY: Cornell University Press, 1988) also provide an excellent overview of Fichte's early thought.) A recent book by Günter Zöller, *Fichte's Transcendental Philosophy: The Original Duplicity of Intelligence and Will* (Cambridge: Cambridge University Press, 1998), discusses related themes from Fichte's *System of Ethics*, including freedom, the will, and the primacy of practical reason. A more critical assessment of Fichte's practical philosophy is provided by Karl Ameriks in chapter 4 of his *Kant and the Fate of Autonomy: Problems in the Appropriation of the Critical Philosophy* (Cambridge: Cambridge University Press, 2000).

Readers interested specifically in Fichte's political philosophy of the 1790s would do well to begin with two wide-ranging books that situate Fichte's thought in relation to other strands of German political thought: Frederick C. Beiser, *Enlightenment, Revolution, and Romanticism: The Genesis of Modern German Political Thought 1790–1800* (Cambridge, MA: Harvard University Press, 1992) and Reinhold Aris, *History of Political Thought in Germany from 1789 to 1815*, 2nd ed. (London: Frank Cass, 1965). Two articles that treat the historical and philosophical context of the *Foundations* in particular are Daniel Breazeale, " 'More than a Pious Wish': Fichte on Kant on Perpetual Peace," in *Proceedings of the Eighth International Kant Congress*, ed. Hoke Robinson, I (Milwaukee: Marquette University Press, 1995), 943–59; and Anthony J. La Vopa's "Fichte and the French Revolution," *Central European History*, 22 (1989), 130–59.

Although a comprehensive treatment of the *Foundations* in English has yet to be written, there are several books and articles that helpfully discuss some of its most important ideas. Susan Shell, " 'A Determined Stand': Freedom and Security in Fichte's *Science of Right*," *Polity*, 25 (1992), 95–122, offers a survey of the *Foundations*'s main themes, including some that are barely addressed elsewhere: the right of coercion, the constitution, the police, and issues relating to sex and marriage. In chapter 8 of her *Sexuality, State, and Civil Society in Germany, 1700–1815* (Ithaca, NY: Cornell University Press, 1996), Isabel V. Hull provides an interesting discussion of Fichte's treatment of sexual difference in the *Foundations* and assesses its importance for his political theory as a whole.

The separation of political from moral philosophy is discussed by

Frederick Neuhouser in "Fichte and the Relationship between Right and Morality," in *Fichte: Historical Context/Contemporary Controversies*, ed. D. Breazeale, T. Rockmore (Atlantic Highlands, NJ: Humanities Press, 1994) and by Luc Ferry, "The Distinction between Law and Ethics in the Early Philosophy of Fichte," (*Philosophical Forum*, 19 (1987–8), 182–96).

Fichte's theory of rights is the topic of several recent papers: Luc Ferry and Alain Renaut, "How to Think about Rights," (in *New French Thought: Political Philosophy*, ed. Mark Lilla (Princeton, NJ: Princeton University Press, 1994)); Susan Shell, "What Kant and Fichte Can Teach Us about Human Rights," (in *The Philosophy of Immanuel Kant*, ed. Richard Kennington (Washington, DC: Catholic University of America, 1985)); and Gary B. Herbert, "Fichte's Deduction of Rights from Self-Consciousness," (*Interpretation*, 25 (1997), 201–2). The specific right to private property is discussed in Jay Lampert, "Locke, Fichte, and Hegel on the Right to Property," (in *Hegel and the Tradition*, ed. Michael Baur and John Russon (Toronto: University of Toronto Press, 1997)).

The *Foundations*'s most widely discussed claims are those associated with its deduction of intersubjectivity as a necessary condition of self-consciousness. Fichte's concepts of the summons, recognition, and "the other" are the topic of a number of secondary works, which include Allen W. Wood, *Hegel's Ethical Thought* (Cambridge: Cambridge University Press, 1990), chapter 4; Robert R. Williams, *Recognition: Fichte and Hegel on the Other* (New York: State University of New York, 1992), Part II; and Paul Franks, "The Discovery of the Other: Cavell, Fichte, and Skepticism," *Common Knowledge*, 5 (1996), 72–105. Ludwig Siep, *Anerkennung als Prinzip der praktischen Philosophie* (Freiburg: Karl Alber, 1979; untranslated), is a classic treatment of recognition that begins with a brief but influential account of its role in Fichte's political theory.

Finally, the editors of the German series *Klassiker Auslegen* are in the process of publishing a volume devoted to the *Foundations of Natural Right*, edited by Jean-Christoph Merle. It will contain commentaries on the individual sections of the text, some of which will be in English. More information on this project and on future publications can be found by accessing the continually updated Fichte bibliography on a website maintained by Curtis Bowman, located at: http://www.phil.upenn.edu/~cubowman/fichte.

Translator's note

This translation is based on the critical edition of Johann Gottlieb Fichte's *Grundlage des Naturrechts nach Principien der Wissenschaftslehre*, published under the auspices of the Bavarian Academy of Sciences, in *J. G. Fichte - Gesamtausgabe*, vol. I, 3, ed. Reinhard Lauth and Hans Jacob (Stuttgart–Bad Cannstatt: Friedrich Frommann Verlag (Günther Holzboog), 1966) and vol. I, 4, ed. Reinhard Lauth and Hans Gliwitsky (Stuttgart-Bad Cannstatt: Friedrich Frommann Verlag (Günther Holzboog), 1970). The numbers inserted throughout the translation (in square brackets and in bold type) refer to the pagination of the "I. H. Fichte edition" of the *Grundlage des Naturrechts*, published in *Johann Gottlieb Fichtes sämmtliche Werke*, vol. 3, ed. I. H. Fichte (Berlin: Veit & Comp., 1845/46), and reprinted in *Fichtes Werke*, vol. 3, ed. I. H. Fichte (Berlin: Walter de Gruyter & Co., 1971). Since many libraries and individuals have the I. H. Fichte edition, and since page numbers from the I.H. Fichte edition are referenced in the *Gesamtausgabe* as well as in the Felix Meiner *Werkausgabe* of Fichte's works (but not vice versa), the editor and I agreed that it would make most sense to include page numbers from the I. H. Fichte edition rather than from the *Gesamtausgabe* edition on which this translation is based. The textual differences between the two editions are not substantial enough to merit additional references to the pagination of the *Gesamtausgabe* edition.

My work on this translation benefited immensely from Frederick Neuhouser's very helpful suggestions and corrections along the way, for which I am extremely grateful. Of course, I remain solely responsible for any remaining shortcomings.

I would also like to thank Karl Ameriks, General Editor of Cambridge

Texts in the History of Philosophy, and Hilary Gaskin, Commissioning Editor at Cambridge University Press, for the patience and understanding they showed me when I requested, on more than one occasion, extra time to work on this translation. I am also grateful to Margot Gill, Chair of Harvard University's Committee on General Scholarships, for funding that spared me from having to work in a law office (like most of my fellow law students) during the summers of 1996 and 1997, and thus allowed me to concentrate on Fichte. I would also like to thank Robert Himmelberg, Dean of Fordham University's Graduate School of Arts and Sciences, for financial support under the "Ames Fund" that enabled me to hire assistants, in the spring of 1999, for the onerous task of typing and saving hundreds of manual editorial changes in electronic form. Finally, and most importantly, I would like to thank my wife Christine: for helping with various aspects of this translation in particular (e.g. proofreading, editing, and re-typing), and for her bountiful *Liebe* and *Großmut* in general.

Notes

The editorial footnotes are numbered, while Fichte's own notes are lettered. When both appear on the same page Fichte's notes are given above the editorial notes.

Foundations of Natural Right, according to the
Principles of the *Wissenschaftslehre*

[1] Introduction

I How a real [*reelle*] philosophical science is distinguished from a merely formulaic philosophy

(1) The character of rationality consists in the fact that that which acts and that which is acted upon are one and the same; and with this description, the sphere of reason as such is exhausted. – For those who are capable of grasping it (i.e. for those who are capable of abstracting from *their own I*), linguistic usage has come to denote this exalted concept by the word: *I*; thus reason in general has been characterized as "I-hood" [*Ichheit*]. What exists *for* a rational being exists *in* the rational being; but there is nothing in the rational being except the result of its acting upon itself: what the rational being intuits, it intuits within itself; but there is nothing in the rational being to be intuited except its own acting: and the I itself is nothing other than an acting upon itself.[a]1 – [2]

---

[a] In order not to suggest the idea of a substratum that contains within itself this power of acting, I do not even want to call the I an *acting something* [*ein Handelndes*]. – Some have raised the objection (among others) that the *Wissenschaftslehre* grounds philosophy in an I, conceived of as a substratum that exists independently of the I's activity (an I as a thing-in-itself).2 But how could one argue in this way, since the derivation of any substratum from the I's necessary mode of acting is distinctive of that mode of acting and especially suited to it? I can say perfectly well how certain people could and had to argue in this way. These people cannot begin anything at all without a substratum, because they are unable to raise themselves from the point of view of common experience to the point of view of philosophy. Accordingly, they supplied the *Wissenschaftslehre* with the idea of a substratum, which they themselves brought out of their own reserves, and then they chastised the *Wissenschaftslehre* for their own incompetence; moreover, they chastised it, not because they themselves had seen the error of conceiving of the I as a substratum, but because Kant rejects such a substratum of the I.3 Their substratum has its source elsewhere – in the old thing-in-itself, outside the I. They find a justification for this in the letter of Kant's writing about a manifold for possible experience. They have never understood

3

It is not worth the trouble to involve oneself in further explications of this. This insight is the exclusive condition of all philosophizing, and until one has elevated oneself to it, one is not yet ripe for philosophy. Also, all true philosophers have always philosophized from this point of view, only without knowing it clearly.

(2) That inner acting of the rational being occurs either *necessarily* or *with freedom*.

(3) The rational being *is*, only insofar as it *posits* itself *as being*, i.e. insofar as it is conscious of itself. All *being*, that of the I as well as of the not-I, is a determinate modification of consciousness; and without some consciousness, there is no being. Whoever claims the opposite assumes a substratum of the I (something that is supposed to be an I without being one), and therefore contradicts himself. Thus necessary actions, those that follow from the concept of the rational being, are simply those that condition the possibility of self-consciousness; but all of these actions are necessary and certain to follow, just as certainly as there exists a rational being. – The rational being necessarily posits itself; thus the rational being necessarily does everything that belongs to the positing of itself, and everything that lies within the scope of the action expressed by this positing.

(4) In acting, the rational being does not become [3] conscious of its acting; for *it itself* is *its acting* and nothing else: but what the rational being is conscious of is supposed to lie outside what becomes conscious,

what this manifold is for Kant, and where it comes from. When will these people stop trying to have their say about things for which their own nature fails them?

1 The characterization of the "I" (or subject) in this and following paragraphs derives from Fichte's conception of the subject as essentially "self-positing," which he first articulates in §1 of the 1794 *Wissenschaftslehre*. (See *The Science of Knowledge*, trans. Peter Heath and John Lachs (Cambridge: Cambridge University Press, 1982).) According to this view, the subject is not a thing, or substance, but rather something that constitutes itself through its own self-reflexive, conscious acts. Sometimes Fichte expresses this claim – that, in the case of the I, "that which acts and that which is acted upon are one and the same" – by calling the I a *Tathandlung* (see n. 1, p. 25).

2 To conceive of the I as a thing in itself is to think of it as existing like a thing – that is, as having an existence independent of its conscious apprehension of itself. Fichte first mentions and criticizes this view of the subject in his review (1794) of G. E. Schulze's anonymously published book *Aenesidemus*. (See *Fichte: Early Philosophical Writings*, ed. Daniel Breazeale (Ithaca, NY: Cornell University Press, 1988), pp. 64–74.) Excerpts from Schulze's book appear in English in *Between Kant and Hegel: Texts in the Development of Post-Kantian Idealism*, ed. George di Giovanni and H. S. Harris (Indianapolis: Hackett Publishing Co., 2000), pp. 104–35.

3 Kant criticizes the idea of the subject as a substance (an independently existing substratum of thought) in his "Paralogisms of Pure Reason." See Immanuel Kant, *Critique of Pure Reason*, ed. Paul Guyer and Allen W. Wood (Cambridge, UK: Cambridge University Press, 1998), B 399–432.

and therefore outside the acting; it is supposed to be the *object*, i.e. the opposite of the acting. The I becomes conscious only of what emerges for it in this acting and through this acting (*simply and solely through this acting*); and this is the object of consciousness, or the thing. There is no other thing that exists for a rational being, and since one can talk of a being and of a thing only in relation to a rational being, it follows that there is no other thing at all. Whoever talks about some other thing does not understand himself.

(5) What emerges in the I's *necessary*[b] acting (although, for the reason indicated, the I does not become conscious of its acting) itself appears as necessary, i.e. the I feels constrained in its presentation [*Darstellung*] of what emerges. Then one says that the object has *reality*. The criterion of all reality is the feeling of having to present something *just as* it is presented. We have seen the ground of this necessity; the rational being must act in this way if it is to exist as a rational being at all. Hence, we express our conviction concerning the reality of a thing as: "this or that exists, as sure as I live," or "as sure as I am."

(6) If the object has its ground solely in the I's acting, and is completely determined through this acting alone, then, if there is to be a diversity among objects, this diversity can [4] emerge solely through the I's diverse ways of acting. Every object has become determinate for the I in just the manner that it is for the I, because the I acted determinately in just the manner that it acted; but that the I acted in such a manner was necessary, for just such an action belonged among the conditions of self-consciousness. – When one reflects on the object and distinguishes it from the way of acting through which it emerges, then the acting itself becomes a mere *conceiving*, comprehending, and grasping of a given. It becomes this, since (for the reason offered above) the object appears to be present, not as a result of this acting, but rather without any contribution of the (free) I. Accordingly, one is right to call this way of acting, when it occurs with the abstraction described above, a *concept*.[c]

---

[b] The *Wissenschaftslehre*'s claim, "what exists, exists through the I's acting (through productive imagination, in particular)," has been interpreted as if it were a claim about a *free* acting; but once again, this is due to an inability to elevate oneself to the concept of activity in general, a concept that was adequately articulated in the *Wissenschaftslehre*. This inability made it easy for some to decry this system as the most outrageous fanaticism. But the charge of fanaticism would be much too weak. Confusing what exists through free acting with what exists through necessary acting, and *vice versa*, is really madness. But then who has proposed such a system?

[c] A reader who, in the joy that he has now finally found a word that is familiar to him, rushes to transfer to this word everything that he has previously understood by the word *concept*, will soon

(7) Only through a certain determinate way of acting does there emerge a certain determinate object; but if the acting occurs with necessity in this determinate way, then this object also emerges with certainty. Thus the concept and its object are never separated, nor can they be. The object does not exist without the concept, for it exists through the concept; the concept does not exist without the object, for it is that through which the object necessarily emerges. Both are one and the same, viewed from different sides. If one looks to the I's action as such, with respect to its form, then it is a concept; if one looks to the content of the action, to its matter, to *what* happens in abstraction from the fact *that* it happens, then it is an object. – When one hears some Kantians talking about *a priori* concepts, one is led to believe that these concepts just stand there in the human mind prior to [5] experience, somewhat like empty compartments, and wait until experience puts something into them. What kind of thing could a concept be for these people, and how could they have come to accept the Kantian doctrine, understood *in this way*, as true?

(8) As has been said, *prior to what emerges from an instance of acting*, the *acting* itself and the determinate way of acting cannot be perceived. For ordinary people and from the point of view of common consciousness, there are only objects and no concepts: the concept disappears in the object and coincides with it. The discovery of the concept in [*bei*] the object was a product of philosophical genius; that is, it required the talent of finding, in and during the acting itself, not only that which emerges in the acting, but also the acting as such, as well as the talent of uniting these completely opposed directions within one act of comprehension and thus grasping one's own mind in its action. In this way, the sphere of consciousness gained a new territory.

(9) Those men of philosophical spirit made their discoveries known. – Nothing is easier than to bring forth, *with freedom* and where no necessity of thought prevails, every possible determination in one's mind and to let one's mind act arbitrarily, in any manner that might be suggested by someone else; but nothing is more difficult than to observe

be utterly confused and will understand nothing further; and that would be through his own fault. This word should denote nothing more and nothing less than what has been described here, whether or not the reader might have previously thought the same thing by such a concept. I am not referring to a concept that is already present for the reader; rather, I intend first to develop and determine such a concept in the reader's mind.

one's mind as it acts in its *real* [*wirklichen*] – i.e. its necessary – acting as described above, or, if one is in a position to do so, to observe that the mind must act in this determinate way. The first way of proceeding yields concepts without an object, an empty thinking; only in the second does the philosopher become the observer of a real [*reellen*] thinking by his own mind.[d]

[6] The former is an arbitrary mimicking of reason's original ways of acting as learned from someone else, after the necessity that alone gives meaning and reality to these ways of acting has disappeared; the latter alone is the true observation of reason in its way of proceeding. From the former there emerges *an empty, formulaic philosophy* that believes it has done enough if it has proved that one can think of something at all, without being concerned about the object (about the conditions of the necessity of this thinking). A real [*reelle*] philosophy presents concepts and the object at the same time, and never treats one without the other. The aim of Kant's writings was to introduce such a philosophy and to do away with all merely formal philosophizing. I cannot say whether this aim has been noticed by even one philosophical writer so far. But I can say that the misunderstanding of this system has shown itself in two ways: the first is exemplified by the so-called Kantians insofar as they took this system, too, to be a formulaic philosophy. They took it to be an inverted version of the previous formulaic philosophy, and thus they philosophized in as empty a manner as had ever been done, only from the opposite side. The second way of misunderstanding Kant's system is exemplified by the astute skeptics, who saw quite well what was actually missing in philosophy, but did not notice that the deficiency was remedied in the main by Kant. Merely formal thinking has done an

---

[d] The philosopher who thinks in a merely formulaic way thinks of this or that, observes himself in this thinking, and then presents as truth the entire series of what he was able to think, simply *because* he was able to think it. *The object* of his observation is himself as he proceeds *freely*, either without all direction, trusting everything to luck, or according to a goal given to him from without. The true philosopher observes reason in its *original and necessary* way of proceeding, through which the philosopher's I and everything that is for it exists. But since the true philosopher no longer finds this originally acting I present in empirical consciousness, he presents the I at its starting point through the only act of choice that is allowed to him (the free resolve to want to philosophize), and he lets the I (under his observation) go on acting, beginning from this starting point and according to its own laws, which are well known to the philosopher. Thus, the object of the true philosopher's observation is reason in general as it proceeds necessarily, according to its inner laws, without any external goal. The philosopher who thinks in a formulaic way observes an individual (himself) in his lawless thinking; the true philosopher observes reason in general, in its necessary acting.

indescribable amount of damage in philosophy, in mathematics,[e] in [7] the doctrine of nature, and in all pure sciences.

II What the doctrine of natural right, as a real philosophical science, has to achieve in particular

(1) According to what has been said above, that a certain determinate concept is originally contained in reason and given through it, can [8] mean nothing other than that the rational being, just as certainly as it is

---

[e] In mathematics this shows itself especially in the misuse of algebra by merely formal minds. Thus – to give a striking example – some have not yet been able to see clearly that [7] squaring the circle is impossible and contradictory in its concept. In the *Hallischen Annalen*, the reviewer of my essay, *Concerning the Concept of the Wissenschaftslehre*[4] (or rather the reviewer of a few notes in that essay) asks me whether squaring the circle is impossible because *straight* and *curved* have nothing in common.[5] He thinks he has been very clever in asking this question; he has a look around, laughs, and leaves me standing there in my shame. I look at him and laugh at the question. In all seriousness, that is my opinion. *Ansam philosophiae non habes,*[6] he says with pity; and I answer him: great wisdom has robbed you of healthy common sense. – With regard to this point, dear sir, I am not at all lacking in knowledge, but in understanding. When I was still in school, I saw perfectly well that a circle's circumference should be equal to a polygon of infinitely many sides, and that one could get the area of the former if one knew the area of the latter: but I was never able to understand the possibility of this way of measuring, and I hope to God that He will not let me understand this possibility as long as I live. What then is the concept of something that is infinite? Is it the concept *of a task* of dividing the side of the polygon to infinity, and therefore the task of an *infinite determining*? But then what is the measurement for which you want to use the infinite here? Could it really be something *determinate*? If you keep dividing to infinity, as you should in accordance with the task, then you do not arrive at any measuring. But if you start to measure, then you must have previously stopped dividing; and thus your polygon is finite and not infinite, as you profess. But because you can comprehend the procedure for describing something that is infinite (i.e. because you can comprehend the empty concept of the infinite) and can label it, for example, with an A, you are no longer concerned about whether you have really acted and can act in this way, and you vigorously get down to work with your A. You do the same thing in several other cases as well. Healthy common sense marvels respectfully at your deeds, and modestly takes the blame for not understanding you; but when someone less modest gives even the smallest indication of his opinion, you cannot explain his inability to understand a matter that is so extraordinarily clear to you and by which you are not bedeviled in the least, except to suggest that the poor man must not have learned the foundations of the sciences.

[4] This text was published just before the 1794 *Wissenschaftslehre* as a prospectus for Fichte's first academic lectures on his system. It provides an introductory account of the *Wissenschaftslehre's* basic structure and method. It is translated in English in Breazeale, *Fichte: Early Philosophical Writings*, pp. 94–135.

[5] The review in question was written by Jakob Sigismund Beck and published in *Annalen der Philosophie und des philosophischen Geistes* in February 1795.

[6] You have no handle on philosophy. This is Fichte's response to Beck's criticism of some remarks Fichte makes in *Concerning the Concept of the Wissenschaftslehre* (1794) about space and the foundations of geometry (Breazeale, *Fichte: Early Philosophical Writings*, pp. 120–1n). After ridiculing Fichte's discussion, Beck exclaims: "*Ansas philosophiae non habes!*" (You have no handles on philosophy!). Fichte omitted the ridiculed passage in the text's second edition.

a rational being, acts necessarily in a certain determinate way. The philosopher's task is to show that this determinate action is a condition of self-consciousness, and showing this constitutes the deduction of that concept. The philosopher has to describe this determinate action itself with respect to its form, as well as to describe what emerges for reflection in this acting. By doing this, the philosopher simultaneously provides proof of the concept's necessity, determines the concept itself, and shows its application. None of these elements can be separated from the others, otherwise even the individually treated pieces will be treated incorrectly, and then one will be philosophizing in a merely formal manner. The concept of right should be an original concept of pure reason; therefore, this concept is to be treated in the manner indicated.

(2) This concept acquires necessity through the fact that the rational being cannot posit itself as a rational being with self-consciousness without positing itself as an *individual*, as one among several rational beings that it assumes to exist outside itself, just as it takes itself to exist.

It is even possible to present in a sensory manner what one's mode of acting in this positing of the concept of right is like. I posit myself as rational, i.e. as free. In doing so, the representation of freedom is in me. In the same undivided action, I simultaneously posit other free beings. Thus, through my imagination I describe a sphere for freedom that several beings share. I do not ascribe to myself all the freedom I have posited, because I posit other free beings as well, and must ascribe to them a part of this freedom. In appropriating freedom for myself, I limit myself by leaving some freedom for others as well. Thus the concept of right is the concept of the necessary relation of free beings to one another.

(3) What is contained first and foremost in the concept of freedom is nothing but the capacity to construct [*entwerfen*], through absolute spontaneity, concepts of our [9] possible efficacy [*Wirksamkeit*]; and the only thing that rational beings ascribe to one another with necessity is this bare capacity. But if a rational individual, or a person, is to find himself as free, then something more is required, namely, that the object in experience that is thought of through the concept of the person's efficacy actually correspond to that concept; what is required, therefore, is that something in the world outside the rational individual follow from the thought of his activity. Now if, as is certainly the case, the effects of rational beings are to belong within the same world, and thus

be capable of influencing, mutually disturbing, and impeding one another, then freedom in this sense would be possible for persons who stand with one another in this state of mutual influence only on the condition that all their efficacy be contained within certain limits, and the world, as the sphere of their freedom, be, as it were, divided among them. But since these beings are posited as free, such a limit could not lie outside freedom, for freedom would thereby be nullified rather than limited *as freedom*; rather, all would have to posit this limit for themselves through freedom itself, i.e. all would have to have made it a law for themselves not to disturb the freedom of those with whom they stand in mutual interaction. –

(4) And so we would then have the *complete object* of the concept of right; namely, *a community among free beings as such*. It is necessary that every free being assume the existence of others of its kind outside itself; but it is not necessary that they all continue to exist alongside one another *as free beings*; thus the thought of such a community and its realization is something arbitrary or optional [*willkürliches*]. But *if* it is to be thought, how – through what concept, through what determinate mode of acting – is it thought? It turns out that, in thought, each member of the community lets his own external freedom be limited through inner freedom, so that all others beside him can also be externally free. This is the concept of right. Because the thought and task of such a community is arbitrary, this concept, [10] if thought as a practical concept, is merely technical–practical: i.e. if one asks, in accordance with what principles could a community among free beings as such be established if someone wanted to establish one, the answer would have to be: in accordance with the concept of right. But this answer by no means asserts *that* such a community ought to be established.

(5) This entire presentation of the concept of right has refrained from refuting in detail those who attempt to derive the doctrine of right from the moral law; this is because, as soon as the correct deduction is given, every unbiased mind will accept it of its own accord, even if the incorrectness of the other deductions has not been shown; but as for biased minds and those who have their own axes to grind, every word uttered for the purpose of refuting them is wasted.

The rule of right, "limit your freedom through the concept of the freedom of all other persons with whom you come in contact," does indeed receive a new sanction for conscience through the law of absolute agreement with oneself (the moral law); and then the philosophical treatment of conscience constitutes a chapter of morality; but this is not part of the philosophical doctrine of right, which ought to be a separate science standing on its own. One might say that several learned men who have put forth systems of natural right would have dealt with that chapter of morality without knowing it, had they not forgotten to state why compliance with the moral law (which they must always have had in mind regardless of the formula they used to express it) conditions the agreement of the rational being with itself. Similarly – I mention this in passing – the teachers of morality have generally not considered that the moral law is merely formal and therefore empty, and that a content cannot be obtained for it through sleight of hand, but must be rigorously deduced. It is possible to indicate briefly how the matter stands in our case. I must think of myself as necessarily in community with other human beings with whom [11] nature has united me, but I cannot do this without thinking of my freedom as limited through their freedom; now I must also act in accordance with this necessary thought, otherwise my acting stands in contradiction with my thinking,^{f} – and thus I stand in contradiction with myself; I am bound in conscience, by my knowledge of how things ought to be, to limit my freedom. Now in the doctrine of right there is no talk of moral obligation; each is bound only by the free, arbitrary [*willkürlichen*] decision to live in community with

---

^{f} I have read somewhere that the principle of moral theory is: "The manifold actions of the free will ought to agree with themselves."[7] This is a very unfortunate application of the postulate of the absolute agreement of the rational being with itself, a postulate that I proposed in the *Lectures concerning the Scholar's Vocation*.[8] In response, one only has to think of becoming a thoroughly consistent villain, as J. B. Erhard (Niethammer's *Philosophisches Journal*, 1795) portrays the devil in his "Devil's Apology";[9] then the actions of the free will agree perfectly with themselves, for they all contradict a conviction concerning what ought to be, and [the criterion of] such a moral doctrine has been satisfied.

[7] Fichte probably had in mind Carl Christian Erhard Schmid's *Outline of Natural Right* (1795), §§94–7. Schmid attempts to characterize rational (moral) agency by invoking Kant's idea of a unified manifold in the first *Critique*: rational actions are those that are "related by a unity;" moral agency consists in a manifold of actions that "thoroughly agrees with itself."

[8] *Some Lectures concerning the Scholar's Vocation*, published in 1794, contains public lectures that Fichte delivered in the same year to the university community in Jena. Their aim was to communicate the most important ideas of Fichte's new system to nonphilosophers, especially its moral implications. See Breazeale, *Fichte: Early Philosophical Writings*, pp. 144–84, especially p. 149.

[9] Johann Benjamin Erhard, a medical doctor and philosopher, was the author of "Devil's Apology," which appeared in 1795 in the second issue of volume 1 of *Philosophisches Journal einer Gesellschaft Teutscher Gelehrten*.

others, and if someone does not at all want to limit his free choice [*Willkür*], then within the field of the doctrine of right, one can say nothing further against him, other than that he must then remove himself from all human community.

(6) In the present text, the concept of right has been deduced as a condition of self-consciousness, along with the object of right; this concept has been derived and determined, and its application guaranteed, as is required of a real science. This has been done in the first and second sections of this investigation. The concept of right is further determined, and the way it must be realized in the sensible world is demonstrated, in the doctrine of civil rights [*Staatsbürgerrechte*]. The investigations into original right [*Urrecht*] and the right of coercion [*Zwangsrecht*] serve as preparation for the doctrine of civil right. The three chapters necessary for the complete determination of civil right (those listed in the book as covering the civil contract, civil legislation, and the constitution) have already been worked out [12] and presented in lectures to my listeners;[g] they will appear at the next book fair, along with the doctrines of the right of nations, cosmopolitan right, and family right, under the title, *Applied Natural Right*.[10]

III Concerning the relation of the present theory of right to the Kantian theory

Apart from some excellent hints by Dr. *Erhard* in several of his most recent writings,[11] and by *Maimon* in an essay on natural right in Prof. Niethammer's *Philosophical Journal*,[12] the author of the present work

[g] It was not possible to print these chapters along with the present text; therefore, they remained behind, and this gave me the opportunity to add to them the other parts of the general doctrine of right. – As a result, there arises just one difficulty for the present book. Based on previous experience I am justified in assuming that not all critics who read my principles will simultaneously acquire a competence to apply them. Thus I ask anyone who does not have a sure self-consciousness of this competence already confirmed by experience not to rush into applying them further, but to await my text.

[10] These chapters were published in 1797 as Part II of the *Foundations of Natural Right*, "Applied Natural Right." They are included in the present volume under the same name.

[11] See n. 9. In addition to "Devil's Apology," Erhard wrote *On the People's Right to a Revolution* (1795) and a review (1795) of Fichte's *Contributions toward Correcting the Public's Judgment of the French Revolution*, published in *Philosophisches Journal einer Gesellschaft Teutscher Gelehrten*, 2, 47–84.

[12] The essay in question is "On the First Grounds of Natural Right" (1795) by Salomon Maimon (1753–1800), a self-taught Polish-Russian Jew whose criticisms of Kant heavily influenced Fichte's attempt to reconstruct Kant's philosophical system. This essay appeared in *Philosophisches Journal einer Gesellschaft Teutscher Gelehrten*, 1, 141–74.

had found no trace of any philosopher having questioned the usual way of dealing with natural right, until, after completing the foundations of his theory of right according to the principles of the *Wissenschaftslehre*, he was most pleasantly surprised by Kant's extremely important[h] work, *Perpetual Peace*.[14]

A comparison of the Kantian principles concerning right (insofar as these principles emerge from the work just cited) [13] and the system presented here, may perhaps be useful to some readers.

On the basis of the work just cited, it is not possible to see clearly whether Kant derives the law of right from the moral law (in accordance with the usual way of doing things) or whether he adopts another deduction of the law of right. But Kant's remark concerning the concept of a permissive law [*Erlaubnisgesetz*][15] makes it at least highly probable that his deduction agrees with the deduction given here.

A right is clearly something that one can avail oneself of or not. Thus a right follows from a merely permissive law, and it is a permissive law because it is limited only to a certain sphere, from which it can be

---

[h] What is one to think of the acumen of part of the public, when one hears this work placed in the same class with the ideas of the Abbé St.-Pierre, or with Rousseau's ideas on the same topic?[13] These two said only that the realization of this idea [of perpetual peace] would be desirable, to which every sensible person no doubt responds that the idea would not be impossible, if human beings were different from how they still presently are. *Kant* shows that this idea is a *necessary* task of reason and that the presentation of this idea is an end of nature that nature will achieve sooner or later, since she works endlessly towards it and has actually already reached so much that lies on the way to the goal: thus Kant's position is undoubtedly a very different view of the same topic.

[13] Charles Irénée Castel de Saint-Pierre (1658–1743), commonly known as the Abbé de Saint-Pierre, was an eighteenth-century publicist and reformer who wrote extensively on politics, morality, and social issues. In his "Traité pour rendre la Paix perpétuelle en Europe" (1713) he advocated a confederated Europe ruled by a central assembly as a means to world peace and stability. In response, Jean-Jacques Rousseau (1712–1778) wrote his "Extrait du projet de paix perpétuelle de Monsieur l'Abbé de Saint-Pierre" (1761), in which he criticized the Abbé for being overly optimistic and neglecting the important role that glory and prestige inevitably play in human affairs. Translated excerpts from Rousseau's treatise can be found in *The Indispensable Rousseau*, ed. John Hope Mason (London, Quartet Books, 1979).

[14] Immanuel Kant's *Perpetual Peace* was published in 1795, just one year before the publication of Part I of Fichte's *Foundations of Natural Right*. It provided the philosophical public, including Fichte, with a glimpse of some of the elements of the more complete political theory that Kant would go on to develop in *The Metaphysics of Morals* (1797), trans. Mary Gregor (Cambridge: Cambridge University Press, 1996). In addition to establishing basic principles of international law and arguing that a federation of republics is the surest means to world peace, Kant invokes the idea of a social contract to explain political authority, defends the division of powers, and denies that a people has the right to revolt against an established authority. See "Perpetual Peace: A Philosophical Sketch," in *Kant: Political Writings*, ed. Hans Reiss (Cambridge: Cambridge University Press, 1970), pp. 93–130.

[15] See "Perpetual Peace," pp. 97–8n.

inferred that outside the sphere of the law one is free from it, and if there is no other law concerning this object, one is generally left solely to one's own arbitrary choice [*Willkür*]. This permission is not explicitly contained in the law; it is merely inferred from an interpretation of the law, from its limited character. The limited character of a law manifests itself in the fact that it is conditioned. It is absolutely impossible to see how a permissive law should be derivable from the moral law, which commands unconditionally and thereby extends its reach to everything.

Our theory fully agrees with Kant's claims that the state of peace or lawfulness among human beings is not a natural state, but must be instituted; that one has the right to coerce even someone who has not yet attacked us, so that, by submitting to the authority of the government, the coerced person might afford us the requisite security; and in our theory these propositions have been proved in the same way in which they are proved by Kant.

Our theory is just as much in agreement with the Kantian argument for the propositions that the association of the state can be constructed only on the basis of a contract that is original, but necessarily entered into; [14] further, that the people itself does not exercise executive power, but rather must transfer it, and that therefore democracy, in the proper sense of the word, is a constitution fully contrary to right.[16]

But I have been led to different thoughts regarding the claim that, for the purpose of maintaining the security of right in the state, it is sufficient to separate the legislative and executive powers, as Kant seems to assume (merely *seems*, for in this work it was evidently not Kant's intention to given an exhaustive treatment of the subject). Here I shall briefly summarize the main points of the present treatise.

The law of right includes the idea that, when human beings are to live alongside one another, each must limit his freedom, so that the freedom of others can also exist alongside that freedom. But the law of right says nothing to the effect that a particular person should limit his freedom

---

[16] By "democracy" both Fichte and Kant usually mean a state in which supreme executive authority (as opposed to the authority to make law) resides in the people as a whole. For Kant, democracy in this sense is necessarily despotic, because in such a state laws would be both made and executed by the same body (see "Perpetual Peace," pp. 100–1). This is what Fichte calls democracy "in the proper sense of the word," although he also uses "democracy" in a narrower sense to refer to a state in which those who hold executive power are directly elected by the people (§16, VI).

specifically through the freedom of a particular second, third, or fourth person. That I must restrict myself specifically in relation to these particular human beings derives from the fact that I live in community specifically with them; but I live in community specifically with them as a result of my free decision, not through any obligation. Applied to the civil contract, this means it is originally up to the free and arbitrary choice of every individual to determine whether he wants to live in this particular state or not, although if he wants to live among other human beings at all, then it is not up to his arbitrary choice to determine whether he enters into a state, or whether he wants to remain his own judge; but, just as he expresses his will to enter into a particular state and just as he is accepted into such a state, so he is, by virtue of this simple, reciprocal declaration, subjected without further ado to all the limitations that the law of right requires for this group of human beings; by virtue of the words, "I want to live in this state," he has accepted all the laws of that state. The law of the state, with regard to its *form*, becomes his law by virtue of his consent, but the law of the state, with regard to its *content*, is determined without any consent by him by the law of right and the circumstances of this state.

[15] Furthermore, the law, "limit your freedom through the freedom of all others," is merely formal and, as set forth thus far, is not capable of being applied; for just how far should the sphere of each individual extend within which no one may disturb him and beyond which he, for his part, may not go without being regarded as someone who disturbs the freedom of others? On this, the parties must reach some agreement in good faith. Applied to the state, this means: on entering the state, each must come to an understanding with it concerning a certain range for his free actions (property, civil rights, etc.). What then limits him to precisely this sphere? Evidently, his own free decision; for without this decision, he would have just as much right as others to everything that remains left over and available to them. But then what determines how much can be granted to each individual for himself? Evidently the common will, in accordance with the rule: this particular number of human beings should be free alongside one another in this particular sphere for [the sake of] freedom in general; thus, so much belongs to each individual.

Now the citizens must be kept within these limits by coercion, and a certain, impending harm (in case they overstep them) must deter their will from deciding to overstep them. It is clear that this punishment, which is determined by criminal law, must be known to them if it is to have an effect on their will; furthermore, it is clear that, by entering into the state, they have made themselves subject to this harm, in case they overstep the law.

But then who is to *proclaim* the common will (which is, of course, completely *determined* by *the nature of the matter*) concerning both the rights of individuals and the punishment of those who overstep their rights? Who, then, is to *clarify and interpret* that necessary decree of nature and of the law of right? No one would be more ill-suited than the masses, and by aggregating individual votes one is likely to obtain a very impure version of the true common [16] will. This task can belong to no one other than he who constantly oversees the whole and all of its needs, and who is responsible for the uninterrupted rule of the strictest right; in other words, it can belong to no one other than the administrator of the executive power. He provides the content of the law, which is given to him by reason and by the circumstances of the state; but the law gets its form, its binding power for the individual, only through the individual's consent, not specifically to this determinate law, but to be united with this state. For these reasons and in this sense, our theory claims that the legislative power in civil legislation and the executive power are not to be separated, but must remain necessarily united. Civil legislation is itself a branch of the executive power, insofar as it is only right in general that is being executed. The administrator of the executive power is the natural interpreter of the common will concerning the relationship of individuals to one another within the state; he is the interpreter, not exactly of the will that the individuals actually have, but rather of the will that they must have if they are to exist alongside one another; and this is so, even if not a single person should, in fact, have such a will (as one might well assume to be the case from time to time).

The law concerning how the law is to be executed, or the *constitution*, is of a completely different kind. Every citizen of the state must vote in favor of the constitution, which can be established only through absolute unanimity; for the constitution is the guarantee that each receives from all the others, for the sake of securing all his rights within the society. The most essential component of every constitution is the ephorate as it is established in the present theory. I leave it to the judgment of unbiased experts to determine whether the ephorate is sufficient to secure the rights of all without the separation of the legislative and executive powers, a suggestion that has been made by others but seems impracticable to me. (*The extent to which Kant* approves of this separation, which is quite correct *in part*, is not apparent from his essay.)

[17] First main division
Deduction of the concept of right

§1 First theorem

A finite rational being cannot posit itself without ascribing a free efficacy to itself

(I) *If a rational being is to posit itself as such, then it must ascribe to itself an activity whose ultimate ground lies purely and simply within itself.* (The antecedent and the consequent are reciprocal propositions: one denotes what the other denotes.)

Activity that reverts into itself in general (I-hood, subjectivity) *is the mark of a rational being.* Positing oneself (reflection upon oneself) is an act of this activity. Let this reflection be called A. *Through the act of such activity, the rational being posits itself.* All reflection is directed at something as its object, B. What kind of something, then, must the object of the requisite reflection, A, be? – The rational being is supposed to posit itself in this reflection, to have itself as an object. But the mark of the rational being is activity that reverts into itself. Therefore, the final and highest substratum, B, of the rational being's reflection upon itself must also be an activity that *reverts into itself and determines itself.* Otherwise, the rational being would not posit itself as a rational being and would not posit itself at all, which contradicts our presupposition.

The rational being presented here is a *finite* rational being. *But a finite rational being is one that can reflect only upon something limited.* These two concepts are reciprocal concepts; one denotes what the other denotes. Therefore, the activity B that reverts into itself would have to be

18

limited; i.e. outside B, there would also have to be a C posited by the reflecting activity that is not this activity but opposed to it.

[18] (II) *Its activity in intuiting the world cannot be posited by the rational being as such,*

for this world-intuiting activity, by its very concept, is not supposed to revert into the intuiter; it is not supposed to have the intuiter as its object, but rather something outside and opposed to the intuiter; namely, a world.

(Afterwards, however, the rational being can ascribe this *acting*, i.e. the intuiting, to itself and can raise it to consciousness; the rational being can posit itself as intuiting. In fact, from the point of view of a transcendental philosophy, one even realizes that the intuiting is itself nothing more than an I that reverts into itself and that the world is nothing more than the I intuited in its original limits. But, in order to be capable of ascribing something to itself, the I must already exist for itself; this is simply the question of how the I can exist originally for itself, and this cannot be explained out of the intuiting of the world; rather, intuiting the world becomes possible only by virtue of the I's existing for itself, which is what we are seeking.)

(III) *But the activity we are seeking can be posited by the rational being in opposition to the world, which would then limit the activity; and the rational being can produce this activity in order to be able to posit it in opposition to the world; and if such an activity is the sole condition of the possibility of self-consciousness (and self-consciousness must necessarily be ascribed to the rational being, in accordance with its very concept), then what is required for such self-consciousness must occur.*

(a) If we are to advance in our speculation towards a presentation of a doctrine of natural right, then we who are philosophizing, though not yet the rational being about which we are philosophizing, must be aware of the rational being's activity in intuiting the world. This activity is *constrained* and *bound*, if not with respect to its form (i.e. that the activity occurs) then with respect to its content (i.e. that the activity, once it occurs in a particular case, proceeds in a certain way). We must represent the objects as we take them to be apart from any [19] contribution from us; our representing must conform to their being. Therefore, an activity opposed to such representational activity would have to be *free* with respect to its content; one would have to be able to act in a variety of ways.

Furthermore, the free activity is supposed to be limited by the world-intuiting activity, i.e. the world-intuiting activity is itself that free activity in the state of being bound; and conversely, the free activity is the activity involved in intuiting the world when the character of being bound falls away: the objects are objects solely because, and insofar as, they are not supposed to exist by virtue of the I's free activity; and this free activity must be curbed or held in check [*aufgehalten*] and limited, if the objects are to exist. But free activity aims at nullifying the objects, insofar as they bind it. Therefore, it is an *efficacy* directed at objects, and intuition is an efficacy that has been nullified, one that has been freely surrendered by the rational being itself.

This is the activity to be posited, B, in its relation to the intuiting of the world and the world itself. But now this activity, B, necessarily is supposed to be the rational being's reversion into itself, and insofar as it is directed at objects, it is not such a reversion. Thus, considered in relation to the rational being itself, this activity must be a free self-determination to exercise efficacy. Insofar as this activity is directed at the object, it is determined with respect to its content. But this is not how the activity, originally and in accordance with its essence, is supposed to be; thus it is determined by itself; it is determined and determining at the same time. Thus it is genuinely an activity that reverts into itself.

What has just been said can be presented systematically in the following way: The activity to be demonstrated is *to be posited in opposition* to the intuiting and is to that extent absolutely free, because the intuiting is bound; the activity is directed at the rational being, or, what amounts to *the same thing*, the activity reverts into itself (for the rational being and its activity are one and the same) because the intuiting is directed at something outside the rational being; to this extent, the activity is the *act of forming* the concept of an intended efficacy outside us, or the concept of an *end* [*Zweck*]. At the same time, the activity is to be [20] *related* to – i.e. posited as identical to – the intuiting; then the activity is an efficacy directed at objects, but (and this is a point not to be overlooked) it is an efficacy that follows immediately from the concept of an end, and is the same as the intuiting, only viewed from a different perspective.

(b) By means of such an activity, the self-consciousness we are seeking becomes possible. The activity is something that has its ultimate ground in the rational being itself, and it is to be posited as such by means of its possible opposition to something that does not have its ground in the rational being. The I (the rational being itself, as such) would now be limited and determinate, and therefore capable of being grasped by reflection: that is, the practical I would be the I for reflection, the I that is both posited by itself and to be posited by itself in reflection; and something could be ascribed to this I (as logical subject) by a possible predicate, just as the intuition of the world is ascribed to the I here.

(c) Self-consciousness becomes possible *only* by means of such an activity. For what has been presented here contains nothing other than the characteristics that were shown above to be conditions of self-consciousness; namely, that there is an activity that reverts into itself or an activity that has its ultimate ground in the rational being itself, that this activity is finite and limited, that it is posited as limited (i.e. in opposition and relation to something that limits it) and as occurring simply through the fact that the activity is reflected upon.

Therefore, such an activity and the positing of it are necessarily presupposed, just as self-consciousness is presupposed, and both concepts are identical.

Corollaries

(1) What is being claimed is that the practical I is the I of original self-consciousness; that a rational being perceives itself immediately only in willing, and would not perceive itself and thus would also not perceive the world (and therefore would not even be an intelligence), if it were not a practical being. Willing is the [21] genuine and essential character of reason; according to philosophical insight, representing does of course stand in reciprocal interaction with willing, but nevertheless it is posited as the contingent element. The practical faculty is the innermost root of the I; everything else is placed upon and attached to this faculty.

All other attempts to deduce the I in self-consciousness have been unsuccessful, because they must always presuppose what they want to deduce; and the reason they were bound to fail is evident here. – After all, how could one assume that an I would emerge through the connection of several representations – none of which contained the I itself – if they were simply combined together? Things can be connected within the I only after the I exists; thus prior to all connection, the I must exist, and this obviously means – as it always does here – that it exists *for the I*.[a]

(2) Thus willing and representing stand in constant, necessary reciprocal interaction, and neither is possible if the other is not present at the same time. One will readily acknowledge – as it has been for a long time – that all willing is conditioned by representing: I must represent whatever I will. In contrast, the claim that all representing is conditioned by willing is likely to encounter resistance. But there can be no representing, unless there is something that represents, and no representing can be posited with consciousness, unless something that represents is posited. But that which represents is – not [**22**] *accidentaliter*, insofar as it now represents, but rather *substantialiter*, insofar as it exists at all and is something – either something that actually wills or something that is posited and characterized by its capacity to will. – Mere [theoretical] intelligence does not constitute a rational being, for it cannot exist on its own, nor does the practical faculty alone constitute one, because it, likewise, cannot exist on its own; rather, only the two, together in unity, complete the rational being and make it a whole.

(3) Only through this reciprocal interaction between the I's intuiting and willing does the I itself – and everything that exists for the I (for reason), i.e. everything that exists at all – become possible.

First of all, the I itself. – The possibility of the I itself, one might say, is supposedly preceded by a reciprocal interaction between the I's intuiting and willing; there is supposed to be something that stands in reciprocal interaction within the I, even before the I itself exists; and this is contradictory. But this is precisely the illusion that is to be avoided. Intuiting and willing neither precede nor follow the I, but rather are themselves the I; both occur only insofar as the I posits itself, they occur only in this positing and only by positing *that* they occur; it

---

[a] The I *that* is said to reflect (so too the I *that* is said to determine itself to exercise efficacy, the I *that* is said to intuit the world, etc.) *precedes* [all else]. It does so, obviously, for the I that is engaged in philosophical reflection, which, to be sure, is also an I and thus bound by the laws of its being; and it does so *in consequence of these laws alone*. This is the I that is discussed in the first principle of the *Wissenschaftslehre*.

Now *for* this reflecting I, another I is supposed to be an object, i.e. this reflecting I is supposed to be an object for itself. How is this possible? That is the issue here. – Attentive readers, forgive me for this note. It is not intended for you, but for superficial and distracted readers, who need it here. These readers are asked to refer to this note whenever they happen to need it again.

is absurd to think of something occurring outside and independent of this positing; conversely, the I posits itself insofar as both the intuiting and the willing occur and insofar as it posits *that* both occur. It is equally absurd to think of any positing of the I that does not involve these two. At the very least, it is unphilosophical to believe that the I is anything other than its *own deed and product simultaneously*. As soon as we hear of the I as active, we do not hesitate to imagine a substratum that is supposed to contain this activity as a bare capacity. This is not the I, but rather a product of our own imagination, which we construct in response to the demand to think the I. The I is not something *that has capacities*, it is not a capacity at all, but rather is *active*; it is what it does, and when it does nothing, it is nothing.

[23] It has been asked: how does the representing subject come to believe that, outside its representation, there exists an object of that representation, and that this object is constituted as it is represented? If one had only thought correctly about what this question meant to express, one would have already proceeded beyond it and arrived at the correct concepts. – The I itself makes the object through its acting; the form of its acting is itself the object, and there is no other object to think of. A being whose mode of acting necessarily becomes an object is an I, and the I itself is nothing more than a being whose mere mode of acting becomes an object. If the I acts with its full capacity – one has to express it this way in order to express it at all – then it is an object for itself; if it acts with only a part of its capacity, then it has as an object something that supposedly exists outside itself.

To grasp oneself in this identity of acting and being acted upon (not just in the acting, not just in the being acted upon, but in the *identity* of both), and to catch oneself in the act, so to speak, is to comprehend the pure I and to achieve the viewpoint of all transcendental philosophy. This talent seems to be completely lacking in some people. If a person – even when he takes pains to grasp this identity – can view these two sides of the I only as separate and isolated, and if he always only happens to grasp either what is active or the object of the activity, then, because of this separation, he will obtain completely contradictory results, which can be united in appearance only, since they were not united from the very beginning.

§2 Inference

*By thus positing its capacity to exercise free efficacy, the rational
being posits and determines a sensible world outside of itself*

(I) It *posits* the sensible world. Only what is absolutely self-active or
practical is posited as subjective, as belonging to the I, and [24] through
the limitation of it, the I itself is limited. Whatever lies outside this
sphere is, for precisely this reason, posited as something that is neither
produced nor producible through the I's activity; thus it is excluded
from the I's sphere, and the I is excluded from its sphere. There
emerges a system of objects, i.e. a world that *exists independently of the I*
(that is, of the practical I, which here is taken to be the I in general), and
independently of which *the I likewise exists* (once again, the practical I,
which determines its own ends); therefore, these two exist outside each
other, and each has its separate existence.

Corollaries

(1) The transcendental philosopher must assume that everything that
exists, exists only *for* an I, and that what is supposed to exist for an I,
can exist only *through* the I. By contrast, common sense accords an
independent existence to both and claims that the world would always
exist, even if understanding did not. Common sense need not take
account of the philosopher's claim, and it cannot do so, since it occupies
a lower standpoint; but the philosopher certainly must pay attention to
common sense. His claim is indeterminate and therefore partly incorrect
as long as he has not shown how precisely *common sense follows
necessarily* only from his claim *and can be explained only if one presupposes
that claim*. Philosophy must deduce our belief in the existence of an
external world.

Now this has been accomplished here on the basis of the possibility of
self-consciousness, and our belief in the existence of an external world
has been shown to be a condition of this self-consciousness. Since the I
can posit itself in self-consciousness only practically, but in general can
posit only what is finite, and hence must also posit a limit to its practical
activity, it follows that the I must posit a world outside itself. Every
rational being proceeds originally in this way, and so, too, undoubtedly
the philosopher.

[25] Now although the philosopher later arrives at the insight that the rational being must first posit its suppressed practical activity in order to be able to posit and determine the object (and that therefore the object itself is by no means immediately given, but is originally produced only in consequence of something else), this insight does not create any obstacles for common sense. For common sense cannot become conscious of these operations as they have just been postulated (since they condition the possibility of all consciousness and thus lie outside its sphere), and it does not engage in the speculations that guide the philosopher's beliefs. This insight does not create any obstacles for the philosopher either, once he comes to occupy the standpoint of common sense.

One might ask: if reality belongs only to *that which* is necessarily posited by the I, then what reality is supposed to belong to those actions that lie outside the sphere of all consciousness and are not posited within consciousness? – Obviously, no reality except insofar as it is posited, and thus merely a reality for philosophical understanding. If one wanted to unite the operations of the human mind systematically in an ultimate ground, one would have to assume that this and that were actions [*Handlungen*] of the human mind; every rational being who attempts such a systematization will find himself in this necessity; this and nothing more is what the philosopher asserts. These original actions [*Tathandlungen*][1] of the human mind have the same reality that is possessed by the causality of things in the sensible world on one another and by their universal reciprocal interaction. For those primitive peoples (whose monuments we still have) who barely unified their experiences, but instead allowed individual perceptions to lie scattered about within their consciousness, there was no – at least no very advanced – causality or reciprocal interaction among things. They

---

[1] *Tathandlung* is best known as the term Fichte invents in the 1794 *Wissenschaftslehre* to denote the subject's self-positing character (*The Science of Knowledge*, §1). Literally, it means "fact-act" (or "deed-act") and is supposed to capture the idea that the existence (or "fact") of the I is identical with its activity – that the I has no existence (as a substance) beyond its conscious activities. In his "Second Introduction to the *Wissenschaftslehre*" Fichte defines *Tathandlung* as an "activity that presupposes no object but instead produces its object itself . . . an *acting* that immediately becomes a *deed*" (see J. G. Fichte, *Introductions to the Wissenschaftslehre*, trans. Daniel Breazeale (Indianapolis: Hackett Publishing Co., 1994), p. 51). In the present context Fichte calls the actions of the human mind *Tathandlungen* because he wants to emphasize the mind's active role in positing, or constituting, objective reality: reality is a fact, or deed, that results from the actions of the conscious subject.

regarded almost all objects in the sensible world as living things and made them into free, first causes, such as they themselves were. It is not just that a universal connection among things had *no reality* for them, but rather that it *did not at all exist* for them. However, anyone who connects his experiences into a unity – and the [26] task of doing so lies on the path of synthetically progressive human reason and had to be undertaken and carried out sooner or later – must necessarily connect them in that way; for him the entire ensemble of connections given in this way has reality. As soon as the human mind reverts back into itself after completing this task (as it did for the first time completely and with clear awareness in the work of one of its most eminent representatives, Kant), and finds that everything it believes it perceives outside itself was actually produced by and from itself, then the task that arises for reason in its constant synthetic progression is similarly to unite all these operations of the human mind in one ultimate ground; and this unification has the same reality possessed by the universal connection among things, and for the same reason. This final task for the synthetic faculty, after the completion of which humankind returns once again to analysis (which from then on acquires a completely different meaning) also had to be resolved sooner or later; only one might wish that those who lack the ability to participate in this business would pay no attention to the reality that is being highlighted here – just as they have never paid attention to it before – and would not insist on reducing it to the kind of reality they are familiar with. – To claim that a pure I and its preconscious operations have no reality because they are not present in common consciousness is the same as saying what an uneducated savage would say if he were to speak: "Your causality and your reciprocal interaction have no reality because they cannot be eaten."

(2) The deduction of our belief in the existence of a sensible world outside us immediately entails something about the extent of this belief, and about the state of mind within which it occurs: for nothing that is grounded extends further than its ground, and as soon as one knows the ground of a particular mode [27] of thinking, one also knows its scope. Our belief in the existence of a sensible world outside us extends to the point where our practical capacity is distinguished from and opposed to our theoretical capacity; it extends to the point where our representation of the influence of things upon us, and our counter-influence upon them, extends, for it is only by virtue of such influence and counter-

influence that our practical capacity is posited as limited. This is also why philosophers have always derived their proof of the reality of an external world from the influence that that world has upon us; of course, this proof presupposes what is supposed to be proved, but it is pleasing to common sense, since it is the same proof that common sense employs.

But how does the speculative philosopher bracket this belief for a moment, so that he can go beyond it in his investigations? Evidently, by rejecting the very distinction that conditions it. If we consider just the activity of representing and want to explain it alone, then a necessary doubt will arise about the existence of things outside us. The transcendental idealist comprehends practical and theoretical activity at the same time as activity in general, and thus necessarily concludes – because there is no passivity in the I, as indeed there cannot be – that the entire system of objects for the I must be produced by the I itself. But precisely because he has comprehended both, he can also, at the proper time, separate the two and exhibit the standpoint that ordinary common sense necessarily occupies. The dogmatic idealist completely excludes practical activity from his investigations; he considers only theoretical activity and wants to ground it through itself, and so it is only natural that he must make theoretical activity into something unconditioned. – This mode of speculation is possible for both kinds of philosophers only so long as they remain within the seclusion of thought, but as soon as their practical activity is aroused, they immediately forget their speculative beliefs and return to the commonsense view of things, because they must. There has never been an idealist who extended his doubt or his supposed certainty [28] to his actions, nor can there ever be one; for such an idealist would then be unable to act at all, in which case he would also be unable to live.

(II) Through that positing of free activity, the sensible world is simultaneously determined, i.e. it is posited as having certain unchanging and general characteristics.

First of all – the concept of the rational being's efficacy is constructed by means of absolute freedom; thus, the object in the sensible world, as the opposite of such efficacy, is established, fixed, and unalterably determined. The I is infinitely determinable; the object, because it is an object, is determined all at once and forever. The I is what it is in *acting*, the object in *being*. The I exists in a state of endless becoming, there is nothing permanent in it at all: the object is as it is forever; it is what it was and what it will be. Within the I lies the ultimate ground of its acting; within the object, the ultimate ground of its being: for the object contains nothing but being.

Next – the concept of efficacy, which is constructed with absolute freedom and could be varied under the same circumstances *ad infinitum*, extends out to an efficacy in the object. Thus the object must be infinitely alterable, in consequence of an infinitely variable concept; one must be able to make of the object whatever one can will to make of it. The object is fixed, and thus by virtue of its constancy it could indeed *resist* the I's influence, but the object is not capable of any alteration by itself (it cannot *instigate* any effect); thus it cannot *act* contrary to the I's influence.

Finally – the rational being cannot posit itself as having efficacy without also positing itself as representing; it cannot posit itself as having an effect on a particular object without all the while representing that particular object; it cannot posit any particular effect as completed without positing the object at which the particular effect was directed. That is, since the object is posited as nullifying the I's efficacy, yet the efficacy is supposed to persist along with the object, there is [**29**] a conflict here that can be mediated only through an oscillation of the imagination [*ein Schweben der Einbildungskraft*], between both of these moments, an oscillation through which *time* comes to be.[b] This is why efficacy directed at an object occurs successively in time. Now if the efficacy is exercised on one and the same object, and is therefore regarded at each present moment as conditioned by the preceding moment and, mediately, by the efficacy exercised in all preceding moments, then the state of the object at each moment is likewise regarded as conditioned by its state in all preceding moments, from the first cognition of the object onwards. Thus the object remains the same object, even though it is endlessly altered; that is, the substratum

---

[b] In connection with this, one can read Jacobi's *Dialogue on Idealism and Realism*,[2] where he convincingly shows that representations of time, which in themselves contradict the pure concept of causality, are applied to that concept only from the representation of our own efficacy upon things.

[2] In his *David Hume on Belief, or Idealism and Realism* (1787), Friedrich Heinrich Jacobi (1743–1819) argued that our representation of time, as well as our concepts of cause and effect, depended on our practical engagement with the world and could not be explained, as Kant had attempted to do in the first *Critique*, from the perspective of theoretical reason alone. For more on Fichte's concept of oscillation, or *schweben*, see n. 1, p. 175.

brought forth by the imagination in order to connect the manifold in the same object (that which underlies the accidents that ceaselessly exclude one another and is called "bare matter") remains the same. This is why we can posit ourselves only as altering the form of things, but never the matter, and why we are conscious of our capacity to alter the forms of things *ad infinitum* but of our incapacity to create or annihilate those things. It is also why, for us, matter can be neither increased nor diminished and why from the standpoint of ordinary consciousness (but certainly not from the standpoint of transcendental philosophy), matter is originally given to us.[c]

[30] §3 Second theorem

The finite rational being cannot ascribe to itself a free efficacy in the sensible world without also ascribing such efficacy to others, and thus without also presupposing the existence of other finite rational beings outside of itself

Proof

(I) (a) According to the proof conducted above (§1), the rational being cannot posit (perceive and comprehend) an object without simultaneously – in the same, undivided synthesis – ascribing an efficacy to itself.

(b) But it cannot ascribe an efficacy to itself without having posited an object upon which such efficacy is supposed to be exercised. The positing of the object as something that is determined through itself, and thus as something that constrains the rational being's free activity, must be posited in a prior moment in time; it is only through this prior moment that the moment in which one grasps the concept of efficacy becomes the present moment.

(c) Any act of comprehension is conditioned by a positing of the rational being's own efficacy; and all efficacy is conditioned by some prior act of comprehension by the rational being. Therefore, every possible moment of consciousness is conditioned by a prior moment of consciousness, and so the explanation of the possibility of consciousness

---

[c] A philosophy that starts from the facts of our consciousness of what is *found* when one regards the I simply as something acted upon cannot advance beyond the point where matter is given; thus such a philosophy proceeds with complete consistency when it claims that matter is originally given to us.

already presupposes consciousness as real. Consciousness can be explained only circularly; thus it cannot be explained at all, and so it appears to be impossible.

Our task was to show how self-consciousness is possible. In response to that task, we answered: self-consciousness is possible if the rational being can – in one and the same undivided moment – ascribe an efficacy to itself and posit something in opposition to that efficacy. Let us suppose that this occurs at some moment, Z.

[31] Now the further question is: under what condition is this required occurrence possible? And then it immediately becomes clear that the efficacy to be posited can be posited only in relation to some particular object, A, towards which the efficacy is directed. It would be wrong to say that perhaps an efficacy *in general*, a merely *possible* efficacy, could be posited here; for that would amount to an indeterminate thought, and the practice of arguing from general presuppositions may well have already done enough damage to philosophy for the time being. A merely possible efficacy, or an efficacy in general, is posited only by abstracting from some particular, or from all *actual*, efficacy; but before one can abstract from something, the thing must be posited, and here – as always – the indeterminate concept of something *in general* is preceded by a determinate concept of a determinate something *as actual*, and the former is conditioned by the latter. – It would be equally wrong to say that the efficacy can be posited as an efficacy directed at some object, B (which is also to be posited at moment Z), for B is posited as an object only insofar as there is no efficacy being exercised upon it.

Accordingly, the moment Z must be explained on the basis of another moment in which the object, A, is posited and comprehended. But A, too, can be comprehended only under the condition that made it possible for B to be comprehended; that is to say, the moment in which A is comprehended is also possible only under the condition of a preceding moment, and so on *ad infinitum*. We have not found any possible moment in which we might attach the thread of self-consciousness (through which alone all consciousness becomes possible), and thus our task is not solved.

For the sake of understanding the entire science to be established here, it is important that one achieve a clear insight into the reasoning just presented.

(II) The reason the possibility of self-consciousness cannot be explained without always presupposing it as already actual lies in the fact that, in order to be able to posit its own efficacy, the subject of self-consciousness [32] must have already posited an object, simply as an object. This is why we were always driven beyond the moment within which we wanted to attach the thread of self-consciousness to a prior moment, where the thread already had to be attached. The reason for the impossibility of explaining self-consciousness must be canceled. But it can be canceled only if it is assumed that *the subject's efficacy* is synthetically unified with the *object* in one and the same moment, that the subject's efficacy is itself the object that is perceived and comprehended, and that the object is nothing other than the subject's efficacy (and thus that the two are the same). Only with such a synthesis can we avoid being driven to a preceding one; this synthesis alone contains within itself everything that conditions self-consciousness and provides a point at which the thread of self-consciousness can be attached. It is only under this condition that self-consciousness is possible. Therefore, as surely as self-consciousness occurs, so must we accept the synthesis that has just been hypothesized. Thus the strict synthetic proof is complete; for the synthesis that we have described has been substantiated as the absolute condition of self-consciousness.

The only remaining questions concern what, then, the hypothesized synthesis might mean, what is to be understood by it, and how what it requires is possible. Thus from now on our task is simply to analyze further what has been demonstrated.

(III) It seems that the synthesis suggested here presents us with a complete contradiction in place of the mere incomprehensibility that it was supposed to eliminate. The synthesis is supposed to yield an object; but the nature of an object is such that, when it is comprehended by a subject, the subject's free activity is posited as constrained. But this object is supposed to be the subject's own efficacy; however, the nature of the subject's efficacy is to be absolutely free and self-determining. Both are supposed to be unified here; the natures of both object and subject are supposed to be preserved without either being lost. How might this be possible?

Both are completely unified if we think [33] of the subject's being-determined as *its being-determined to be self-determining*, i.e. as a summons [*eine Aufforderung*] to the subject, calling upon it to resolve to exercise its efficacy.

Since what is required here is an object, it must be given in sensation, and in *outer*, not inner, sensation: for all inner sensation arises only through the reproduction of outer sensation; the former therefore presupposes the latter; thus if one were to assume that the object is given in inner sensation, then, once again, one would be presupposing self-consciousness as actual; but it is the possibility of self-consciousness that is supposed to be explained. – But the object is not comprehended, and cannot be other than as a bare summons calling upon the subject to act. Thus as surely as the subject comprehends the object, so too does it possess the concept of its own freedom and self-activity, and indeed as a concept given to it from the outside. It acquires the concept of its own free efficacy, not as something that *exists* in the present moment (for that would be a genuine contradiction), but rather as something that *ought* to exist in the future.

(The question before us was: how can the subject find itself as an object? In order to find *itself*, it would have to find itself as only self-active; otherwise, it would not find *itself*; and, since it does not find anything at all unless it *exists*, and does not exist unless it finds itself, it follows that it would not find anything at all. In order to find itself as an *object* (of its reflection), it would have to find itself, not as *determining* itself to be self-active – the question here is not how the issue might be in itself from the transcendental point of view, but only how it must appear to the subject under investigation – , but rather as determined to be self-active by means of an external check [*Anstoß*],[3] which must nevertheless leave the subject in full possession of its freedom to be self-determining: for otherwise, the first point would be lost, and the subject would not find itself as an I.

In order to make this last point clearer, I shall anticipate a few points that will come up again later. The subject cannot find itself necessitated to do anything, not even to act in general; for then it would not be free,

---

[3] *Anstoß*, usually translated as "check," is the term Fichte uses in the *Wissenschaftslehre*'s account of how an absolute, entirely active subject can represent an objective, external world. According to this view, the content of sensation is not the result of a thing's affection of a passive subject. Rather, the content of sensation is produced when an infinite activity of the subject is checked, or blocked, by an inert, wholly passive *Anstoß* and then reflected back to the subject. The *Anstoß* is invoked in order to explain why the intuiting subject normally takes what is really its own activity to be affection by an external, independent thing (Fichte, *Science of Knowledge*, pp. 189–93, 203–6, 220–2). In the present context *Anstoß* might be better rendered as "impetus," since it refers to an activity that impinges on the I from without (from another subject) and hence is not merely an inert "check" on the first subject's own activity.

nor an I. Even less can it, if it is to resolve to act, find itself necessitated to act in this or that particular way; for then, once again, it would not be free nor an I. [34] How and in what sense, then, must the subject be determined to exercise its efficacy, if it is to find itself as an object? Only insofar as it finds itself as something that *could* exercise its efficacy, as something that is summoned to exercise its efficacy but that can just as well refrain from doing so.)

(IV) The rational being is to realize its free efficacy; this demand [*Anforderung*] upon it belongs to the very concept of a rational being, and just as certainly as the rational being grasps this concept, so too does it realize its free efficacy, and in one of two ways:

either by *actually acting*: What is demanded is only activity in general; but it is explicitly contained in the concept of such activity that, within the sphere of possible actions, the subject is to choose *one* action through free self-determination. The subject can act only in *one* way; it can determine its faculty of sensation (which in this case is its faculty of exercising efficacy in the sensible realm) in only *one* way. Just as certainly as it acts, so too does it choose this one way by means of absolute self-determination, and to that extent it is absolutely free; it is a rational being and also posits itself as such:

or by *not acting*: Even then it is free; for, in accordance with our presupposition, it is supposed to have grasped the concept of its efficacy as something demanded of it and apparent to it. By now proceeding contrary to the demand it is aware of and refraining from acting, it likewise chooses freely between acting and not acting.

The concept that has been established is that of *free reciprocal efficacy* in its most precise sense; and nothing other than this. To any free effect I can attach the thought of a free, *contingent* counter-effect; but that is not the required concept in its proper precision. If the concept is to be determined with precision, then *effect* cannot at all be distinguished in thought *from counter-effect*. Both must constitute the *partes integrantes* of an undivided event. Such a thing is now being postulated as a necessary condition of a [35] rational being's self-consciousness. Such a thing must occur, as our proof has shown.

The thread of consciousness can be attached only to something like this, and then this thread might well extend without difficulty to other objects as well.

Our presentation has succeeded in attaching this thread. Our proof has shown that under this condition the subject can and must posit itself as a freely efficacious being. If the subject posits itself as such a being, then it can and must posit a sensible world; and it can and must posit itself in opposition to this sensible world. – And now that the main task is resolved, all the activities of the human mind can proceed without further ado, in accordance with the mind's own laws.

(V) Up until now, our analysis of the synthesis that we established has been merely *expository*; our task was only to clarify what we comprehended in the mere concept of the synthesis. The analysis will proceed even further: but from now on, it will be one that *draws inferences*; that is, the subject – in consequence of the posited influence upon itself – may have to posit several other things as well: how does this happen, or what does it posit – in accordance with the laws of its own being – in consequence of its first positing?

The influence upon the subject, as we have described it, was a necessary condition of all self-consciousness; it occurs just as certainly as self-consciousness occurs, and so it is a necessary fact. If, in accordance with the necessary laws of rational beings, several other things must simultaneously be posited together with such laws, then the positing of them is also a necessary fact, like the first.

Insofar as the influence upon the subject, as we have described it, is *something that is sensed*, it is a limitation of the I, and the subject must have posited it as such; but there is no limitation without something that does the limiting. Thus the subject, insofar as it has posited this influence upon itself, must have simultaneously posited something *outside itself* as the determining ground of this influence; this external something is the something that is sensed, and this much is understood without difficulty.

But this influence is a *determinate* influence, and by positing it as determinate, [36] one posits not merely a ground for it in general, but rather a *determinate* ground. What kind of ground must this be, what characteristics must belong to it, if it is to be the ground of this determinate influence? This question will occupy us a bit longer.

The influence upon the subject was understood as a summons to the subject to exercise its free efficacy, and – everything depends on this – it could not be understood any other way; indeed it would not be understood at all, if it were not understood *in just this way*.

The content of this influence upon the subject is the summons, and

34

its ultimate end is [to bring about] the free efficacy of the rational being to whom the summons is addressed. The rational being's activity is by no means to be determined and necessitated by the summons in the way that – under the concept of causality – an effect is determined and necessitated by its cause; rather, the rational being is to determine itself in consequence of the summons. But if the rational being is to do this, it must first understand and comprehend the summons, and so it is dependent on some prior cognition of the summons. Thus the external being that is posited as the cause of the summons must at the very least presuppose the possibility that the subject is capable of understanding and comprehending; otherwise its summons to the subject would have no purpose at all. The purposiveness of the summons is conditional on the understanding and freedom of the being to whom it is addressed. Therefore, the cause of the summons must itself necessarily possess the concept of reason and freedom; thus it must itself be a being capable of having concepts; it must be an intelligence, and – since this is not possible without freedom, as has just been shown – it must also be a free, and thus a rational, being, and must be posited as such.

This inference is established here as necessary, as originally grounded in the nature of reason, and as one that takes place with certainty independently of any scientific help from us; beyond this, we might add a few further words for the sake of clarification.

The following question has been raised, and with good reason: which effects can be explained only by reference to a rational cause? The [37] answer, "those that must necessarily be preceded by some concept of them," is true but not sufficient, for there always remains the higher, somewhat more difficult question: which, then, are those effects about which one must judge that they were possible only in accordance with a previously constructed concept? Every effect, once it exists, can very well be comprehended, and the manifold within it fits itself into a conceptual unity more gracefully and felicitously, the more intelligence the observer himself has. Now this is a unity that the observer himself has brought into the manifold, by means of what *Kant* calls reflective judgment;[4] and reflective judgment must necessarily bring such a unity

---

[4] Fichte's discussion of how effects in the empirical world can be recognized as having a rational cause (through a concept) relies heavily on Kant's treatment of reflective judgment in the *Critique of Judgment* (1790). Determinative judgment starts from a given rule or principle and subsumes particulars under it (recognizes them as things to which the general rule applies). Reflective judgment, in contrast, starts with particulars and discovers the rule (or concept) that unifies

into the manifold, if there is to be *an* effect for the observer at all. But who can guarantee to the observer that, just as he now orders the *actual* manifold under his concept, so too, prior to the effect, the *concepts* of the manifold he perceives were themselves ordered, by another intelligence, under the concept of the unity that the observer now conceives; and what could justify the observer in drawing such an inference? Thus it must be possible to point to a higher ground of justification; otherwise, the inference to a rational cause is entirely groundless, and – by the way – if this inference were not correctly drawn in at least some sphere of cognition, then (in accordance with the compulsory laws of reason) it would even be physically impossible to make incorrect use of such an inference, for then the inference could not even be present [as an idea] within the rational being.

There is no doubt that a rational cause, just as certainly as it is one, constructs for itself the concept of a product that is to be realized through its activity. In acting, it directs itself in accordance with this concept and always, as it were, keeps it in view. This is called the concept of an end.

But now a rational being cannot grasp the concept of its efficacy *without having a cognition of the object of this efficacy*. For it cannot determine itself to act – and this obviously means with consciousness of this self-determination, for only through such consciousnesss does it become a free [38] activity – , without positing its activity as constrained. But what it posits when it posits a particular activity as constrained, is an object outside of itself. This is why – by the way – even if one wanted to ascribe intelligence and freedom to nature, it is impossible to ascribe to it the capacity to grasp the concept of an end (and this is precisely why intelligence and freedom must be denied to nature), because there is nothing outside nature upon which it could exercise its efficacy. Everything that can be the effect of such efficacy is itself nature.

Thus a sure criterion for determining that something is the effect of a rational being would be this: the effect can be thought as possible only under the condition that there is some cognition of the object of the

them. Recognizing empirical states of affairs as the effects of reason would involve reflective judgment because the observer must supply a rule that unifies (makes sense of) the manifold to be explained. See Immanuel Kant, *Critique of Judgment*, trans. Werner S. Pluhar (Indianapolis, Hackett Publishing Co., 1987), Introduction: IV.

effect. But there is only one thing whose possibility can be thought only through cognition – rather than through some merely natural force – and that is cognition itself. Thus if the only possible object of an effect – and here that also means its end – were the production of cognition, then one would necessarily have to assume that the effect had a rational cause.

But in this case, the assumption that the production of cognition was intended would have to be necessary. That is, it would have to be impossible to think that the action had any other end, and the action itself would have to be incomprehensible and not actually comprehended at all, unless it were comprehended as one that intended to produce cognition. – It is sometimes said that nature teaches us this or that lesson; but in saying this, one certainly does not mean that the natural event has no purpose other than to teach us; rather, one means that a person can (among other things) learn from nature through observation, if he should want to do so and if he should direct his free observation towards that end.

Now the situation that has just been described is present here [in the case of the summons]. The cause of the influence upon us has no end at all, if it does not have as its end that we should cognize it as such; thus it must be assumed that a rational being is this cause.

What was supposed to be demonstrated has now been demonstrated. [39] In accordance with I–IV above, the rational being cannot posit itself as such, except in response to a summons calling upon it to act freely. But if there is such a summons, then the rational being must necessarily posit a rational being outside itself as the cause of the summons, and thus it must posit a rational being outside itself in general (according to section V).

Corollaries

(1) The human being (like all finite beings in general) becomes a human being only among human beings; and since the human being can be nothing other than a human being and would not exist at all if it were not this – it follows that, *if there are to be human beings at all, there must be more than one.* This is not an opinion that has been adopted arbitrarily, or based on previous experience or on other probable grounds; rather, it is a truth that can be rigorously demonstrated from the concept of the human being. As soon as one fully determines this

concept, one is driven from the thought of an individual human being to the assumption of a second one, in order to be able to explain the first. Thus the concept of the human being is not the concept of an individual – for an individual human being is unthinkable – but rather the concept of a species.

The summons to engage in free self-activity is what we call up-bringing [*Erziehung*].[5] All individuals must be brought up to be human beings, otherwise they would not be human beings. In connection with this, the question inevitably arises: if it is supposedly necessary to assume that there was an origin of the entire human race and therefore a first human couple – and this is surely a necessary assumption at a certain point in one's reflection – then who brought up the first human couple? They must have been brought up; for the proof given here is a general one. A human being could not have brought them up, for they are supposed to be the first human beings. Therefore, another rational being (one that was not human) must have brought them up – obviously, only to the point where humans could start bringing up each other. A spirit took them into its care, exactly [**40**] as is portrayed in an old, venerable document that generally contains the deepest and most sublime wisdom and presents results to which all philosophy must return in the end.[6]

(2) Only free, reciprocal interaction by means of concepts and in accordance with concepts, only the giving and receiving of knowledge, is the distinctive character of humanity, by virtue of which alone each person undeniably confirms himself as a human being.

If there is any human being at all, then there is necessarily a world as well, and certainly a world such as ours, one that contains both non-rational objects and rational beings within it. (This is not the proper place to proceed further and establish the necessity of all the particular objects in nature and their necessary classification, even though this can be established, just like the necessity of a world in general.[d]) Thus the question concerning the ground of the reality of objects is answered.

---

[d] Whoever cannot understand this should simply have patience and should conclude from his lack of understanding only what it actually implies, namely, that he cannot understand it.

[5] *Erziehung* could also be translated as "rearing" or "education." It normally refers to the process of educating children to become, among other things, autonomous and morally responsible beings.

[6] Gen. 1–2.

The reality of the world – and this obviously means the world for us, i.e. for all finite reason – is a condition of self-consciousness; for we cannot posit ourselves without positing something outside us, to which we must ascribe the same reality we attribute to ourselves. It is contradictory to ask about a reality that supposedly remains after one has abstracted from all reason; for the questioner himself (we may presume) has reason, is driven by reason to question, and wants a rational answer; he, therefore, has not abstracted from reason. We cannot go outside the sphere of our reason; the case against the thing in itself [*die Sache selbst*] has already been made, and philosophy aims only to inform us of it and keep us from believing that we have gone beyond the sphere of our reason, when in fact we are obviously still caught within it.

[41] §4 Third theorem

The finite rational being cannot assume the existence of other finite rational beings outside it without positing itself as standing with those beings in a particular relation, called a relation of right [Rechtsverhältniß]

Proof

(I) *The subject must distinguish itself, through opposition, from the rational being that (as a consequence of the preceding proof) it has assumed to exist outside itself.* The subject has now posited itself as containing within itself the ultimate ground of something that exists *within it* (this was the condition of I-hood, of rationality in general); but it has likewise posited a being outside itself as the ultimate ground of this something that exists within it.

The subject is supposed to be able to distinguish itself from this being. In accordance with our presupposition, this is possible only under the condition that the subject can distinguish between how much the ground of the given something lies *within it,* and how much that ground lies *outside it.* With regard to form, i.e. with regard to the fact that there is activity at all, the ground of the subject's efficacy lies simultaneously *within itself* and in the being *outside itself.* If the external being had not exercised its efficacy and thus had not summoned the subject to exercise its efficacy, then the subject itself would not have exercised its efficacy. The subject's activity as such is conditioned by the activity of the being outside it. It is also conditioned with regard to its content; a particular sphere is allotted to the subject as the sphere of its possible activity.

But within the sphere allotted to it, the subject has freely chosen; it has absolutely given to itself the nearest limiting determination of its own activity; and the ground of this latter determination of the subject's efficacy lies entirely *within the subject alone*. Only in this way can the subject posit itself as an absolutely free being, as the sole [42] ground of something; only in this way can it separate itself completely from the free being outside it and ascribe its efficacy to itself alone.

Within this sphere, that is, from the outer limit of the product of the being outside it, X, to the outer limit of its own product, Y, the subject has chosen from among the possibilities contained in the sphere: the subject constitutes its own freedom and independence out of these possibilities and by comprehending them as the sum of the possibilities that it could have chosen.

Within the sphere just described, a choice had to be made if the product, Y, was to become possible as something individuated among all the possible effects given by this sphere.

But within this sphere, only the subject could have chosen, and *not the other*; for, according to our presupposition, the other being has left this sphere undetermined.

That which alone made a choice within this sphere is *the subject's* I, the individual, the rational being that becomes determinate through opposition to another rational being; and this individual is characterized by a determinate expression of freedom belonging exclusively to it.

(II) *In this process of distinguishing through opposition, the subject acts in such a way that the concept of itself as a free being and the concept of the rational being outside it (as a free being like itself) are mutually determined and conditioned.*

There can be no opposition, unless in the same undivided moment of reflection the sides that are opposed are also posited as equal, related to each other, and compared with one another. This is a formal theoretical proposition, which has been rigorously proved in the appropriate place,[7] but which, I hope, might be plausible to healthy common sense, even without proof. We shall apply this proposition here.

---

[7] Presumably Fichte is referring to §§2–3 of his 1794 *Wissenschaftslehre* (*The Science of Knowledge*).

40

The subject determines itself as an individual, and as a free individual, by means of the sphere within which it has chosen one from among all the possible actions given within that sphere; and it posits, in opposition to itself, another individual outside of itself that is determined by means of another sphere within which it has chosen. [43] Thus the subject posits both spheres at the same time, and only through such positing is the required opposition possible.

The being outside the subject is posited as free, and thus as a being that could also have overstepped the sphere that presently determines it, and could have overstepped it such that the subject would be deprived of its ability to act freely. But the being outside the subject did not freely overstep this sphere; therefore, it materially limited its freedom through itself; that is, it limited the sphere of those actions that were possible for it by virtue of its formal freedom. All this is necessarily posited in the subject's act of opposing itself to another rational being – as is everything else we shall yet establish (without, for the sake of brevity, repeating the present reminder).

Furthermore, through its action, the being outside the subject has – in accordance with our presupposition – summoned the latter to act freely; thus it has limited its freedom through a concept of an end in which the subject's freedom is presupposed (even if only problematically); thus it has limited its freedom through the concept of the subject's (formal) freedom.

Now the subject's cognition of the other being as rational and free is conditioned first by the other being's self-limitation. For – in accordance with our proof – the subject has posited a free being outside itself only in consequence of the other being's summons to the subject to engage in free activity, and thus only in consequence of the other being's self-limitation. But this being's self-limitation was conditioned by its own (at least problematic) cognition of the subject as a possibly free being. Thus the subject's concept of the other being as free is conditioned by the same concept this being has of the subject and by this being's action, which is determined by its concept of the subject.

Conversely, the actualization of the other being's categorical knowledge of the subject as free is conditioned by the subject's own knowledge and by its acting in accordance with such knowledge. If the subject had no knowledge of a free being outside itself, then something [44] that ought to have occurred, in accordance with the laws of reason, would not have occurred, and the subject would not be rational. Or if such knowledge did indeed arise in the subject, but the subject did not limit its freedom as a result of this knowledge so as to allow the other the possibility of acting freely as well, then the other could not infer that the subject was a rational being, since such an inference becomes necessary only by virtue of the subject's self-limitation.

Thus the relation of free beings to one another is necessarily determined in the following way, and is posited as thus determined: one individual's knowledge of the other is conditioned by the fact that the other treats the first as a free being (i.e. limits its freedom through the concept of the freedom of the first). But this manner of treatment is conditioned by the first's treatment of the other; and the first's treatment of the other is conditioned by the other's treatment and knowledge of the first, and so on *ad infinitum*. Thus the relation of free beings to one another is a relation of reciprocal interaction through intelligence and freedom. One cannot recognize the other if both do not mutually recognize each other; and one cannot treat the other as a free being, if both do not mutually treat each other as free.

The concept established here is extremely important for our project, for our entire theory of right rests upon it. Thus we shall attempt to make it clearer and more accessible by means of the following syllogism.

(I) *I can expect a particular rational being to recognize me as a rational being, only if I myself treat him as one.*

(1) The conditioned in the proposition established here is:

(a) *not* that the rational being in itself, apart from me and my consciousness, recognizes me within his own conscience (such belongs to the sphere of morality) or in the presence of others (such is a matter for the state); but *rather* that he recognizes me as a rational being in conformity with *his and my* consciousness, synthetically united in one (i.e. in conformity with a consciousness common to both of us) such that – just as surely as he wants to be regarded as a rational being [45] – I can compel him to acknowledge that he knows that I am one as well.

(b) *not* that I can actually prove that I have been recognized by rational beings in general as their equal; but *rather* that this particular individual, C, has recognized me as such.

(2) The *condition* is:

(a) *not* that I merely grasp the concept of C as a rational being, but *rather* that I actually *act* in the sensible world. A concept in the innermost regions of my consciousness remains accessible only *to me*, and not to anyone outside me. Something is given to the individual C only by experience, and I give rise to such experience only by acting. The other cannot know what I think.

(b) *not* that I merely refrain from acting contrary to the concept of C as a rational being, but *rather* that I actually act in conformity with it, that I actually enter into reciprocal interaction with C. Otherwise, we remain separate and are absolutely nothing for each other.

(3) *The ground of the connection.*

(a) Unless I exercise some influence upon him, I cannot know or demonstrate to him that he possesses any representation of me at all, of my mere existence. Even assuming that I appear as an object in the sensible world and lie within the sphere of those experiences possible for him, there always remains the question, "has he reflected upon me?", and only he himself can answer that question.

(b) Unless I act upon him in conformity with the concept of him as a rational being, I cannot demonstrate to him that he – just as surely as he himself possesses reason – must necessarily have regarded me as a rational being. For every expression of force can originate from a natural power operating in accordance with mechanical laws; only the moderation of force by means of concepts is the unmistakable and exclusive criterion of reason and freedom.

(II) *But in every possible case, I must expect that all rational beings outside me recognize me as a rational being.*

[46] The necessity of this universal, ongoing expectation must be shown to be the condition of the possibility of self-consciousness. But there is no self-consciousness without consciousness of individuality, as has been proved. Now all that remains to be proved is that no consciousness of individuality is possible without this expectation, that the latter follows necessarily from the former. What is supposed to be proved would then be proved.

(A) (1) I posit myself as an individual in opposition to C only by ascribing exclusively to myself a sphere for my free choice that I deny to him, in accordance with the concept of individuality in general.

(2) I posit myself as a rational and free being in opposition to C only by ascribing reason and freedom also to him; and thus only by assuming that he has likewise chosen freely in a sphere distinct from my own.

(3) But I assume all of this only as a consequence of the fact that – in

accordance with my own assumption – he has, in *his* choice, in the sphere of his freedom, taken my free choice into consideration, has purposively and intentionally left a sphere open for me; this is in accordance with the preceding proof. (It is only as a consequence of my having posited him as treating me as a rational being that I posit him as a rational being at all. My entire judgment concerning him proceeds from me and from my treatment of him, as must be the case in a system that has the I as its foundation. I infer his rationality in general only on the basis of this *particular* expression of his reason and on it alone.)

(4) But the individual C cannot have acted upon me in the described manner without, at least problematically, having recognized me; and I cannot posit him as acting upon me in this way without positing that he recognizes me, at least problematically.

(5) Everything that is problematic becomes categorical when the condition is supplied. What is problematic, is in part categorical *qua* [47] proposition. This observation is important, but still frequently overlooked; the connection between the two propositions is asserted categorically; if the condition is given, then it is necessary to assume the conditioned. The condition was that I recognize the other as a rational being (and do so in a manner that is valid for both *him* and *me*), i.e. that I should *treat* him as a rational being – *for only in action does there exist such a recognition valid for both*. Now *I must* necessarily treat him thus, just as *certainly* as *I* posit *myself* as a rational individual in opposition to him – this is true, of course, only to the extent that I proceed rationally, i.e. with theoretical consistency.

Now just as certainly as I recognize him, i.e. treat him in the way described, so too is he with equal certainty *bound* or *obliged* by virtue of his initially problematic expression – he is required by virtue of theoretical consistency – to recognize me *categorically*, and indeed to do so *in a way that is valid for both of us*, i.e. he is required to treat me as a free being.

What takes place here is a unifying of opposites into one. Under the present presupposition, the point of union lies in *me*, in *my consciousness*: and the unity is conditioned by my capacity for consciousness. – For his part, he fulfills the condition under which I recognize him; and he in turn prescribes this condition to me. From my side, I fulfill the condition – I actually recognize him and thereby oblige *him*, as a consequence of the condition that he himself has set up, to recognize me categorically: and I oblige *myself*, as a consequence of my recognition of him, to treat him likewise.

Corollary

As has been demonstrated, the concept of individuality is a *reciprocal concept*, i.e. a concept that can be thought only in relation to another thought, and one that (with respect to its form) is conditioned by another – indeed by an *identical* – thought. This concept can exist in a rational being only if it is posited as *completed* by another rational being. Thus this concept is never *mine*; rather, it is – in accordance with my own admission and the admission of the other – *mine and his*, [48] *his and mine*; it is a shared concept within which two consciousnesses are unified into one.

Each of my concepts determines the one that follows it in my consciousness. The concept of individuality determines a *community*, and whatever follows further from this depends not on me alone, but also on the one who has – by virtue of this concept – entered into community with me. Now this concept is necessary, and this necessity compels both of us to abide by the concept and its necessary implications: we are both *bound* and *obligated* to each other by our very existence. There must be a law that is common to us both and commonly recognized as necessary, a law by virtue of which we mutually abide by the ensuing implications; and this law must exhibit the same character by virtue of which we entered into that very community. But this is the character of rationality; and the law of reason that governs all further implications is called agreement with oneself, or *consistency*, and is scientifically presented in general *logic*.

This whole unification of concepts described here was possible only in and through actions. Thus any ongoing consistency exists only in actions as well: this consistency can be required and is only required for actions. It is actions that matter here, rather than concepts; we are not concerned with concepts in themselves, apart from actions, because it is impossible to talk about them as such.

(B) In each relation into which I enter with the individual C, I must refer to the recognition that has occurred and must judge him in accordance with it.

(1) It is presupposed that I enter into several relations, points of contact, instances of reciprocal treatment, with *him*, with one and the

same individual C. I must therefore be able to attribute the given effects *to him*, i.e. to connect the given effects with those that I have already judged to be his.

(2) But insofar as he is posited, he is posited both as a particular sensible being and as a rational being at the same time; both [49] characteristics are synthetically united in him. The former is posited in consequence of the sensible properties of his influence upon me; the latter, solely in consequence of his having recognized me. Only in the union of both properties is he posited by me at all, only thus does he become an object of knowledge *for me*. Thus I can attribute an action to *him* only insofar as it is connected, in part with the sensible properties of his previous actions, and, in part, with his recognition of me; I can attribute an action to him only insofar as the action is *determined* by both.

(3) Assuming that his action is indeed determined by the sensible predicates of his prior actions – and this is necessary in consequence of nature's own natural mechanism – but not determined by his having recognized me as a free being, i.e. assuming that, by means of his action, he robs me of the freedom that belongs to me and thus treats me as an object; in that case, I am still forced to attribute the action *to him*, to the same sensible being C. (For example, the voice is the same, the gait is the same, and so forth.) Now by virtue of the act of recognition (and perhaps by virtue of a series of actions determined by such recognition), the concept of this sensible being C has been united in my consciousness with the concept of rationality, and I cannot separate what I have once united. But those concepts are posited as necessarily and essentially united; I have posited sensibility and reason in unity as the essence of C. Now, in his action X, I must necessarily separate these concepts, and thus I can continue to ascribe rationality to him only as something *contingent*. My treatment of him as a rational being now also becomes *contingent* and conditioned, and occurs only if he himself treats me as such. Thus in *this case*, I am able, with perfect consistency (which is my only law here), to treat him as a merely sensible being, until both *sensibility and rationality* are once again united in the concept of his action.

My claim in such a case would be this: his action, X, contradicts his own presupposition, namely, that I am a rational being: he [50] has acted inconsistently. By contrast, I have, prior to his action, X, abided by the rules; and I likewise abide by the rules if, in consequence of his inconsistency, I treat him as a merely sensible being. With this, I place myself at a standpoint that is higher than that of either one of us; I transcend my individuality, appeal to a *law* that is valid for us both, and apply that law to the present case. I thus posit myself as *judge*, i.e. as his superior. Hence the superiority that everyone ascribes to himself when claiming to be in the right vis-à-vis the one against whom he has the right. – But, insofar as I appeal to that common law in my opposition to him, I invite him to be a judge along with me; and I demand that in this case he must find my action against him consistent and must approve of it, compelled by the laws of thought. The community of consciousness continues to exist. I judge him by reference to a concept that he himself – according to my claim – must possess. (Hence the *positive element* in the concept of right, whereby we believe that we impose on the other an obligation not to resist our way of treating him, but even to approve of it. The source of this obligation is certainly not the moral law: rather, it is the law of thought; and what emerges here is the syllogism's practical validity.)

(C) *What holds between me and C also holds between me and every rational individual with whom I enter into reciprocal interaction.*

(1) Any other rational being can be present to me only in the very same manner and under the same conditions that C was present to me; for only under these conditions is the positing of a rational being outside me possible.

(2) The new individual, D, is other than C insofar as his free action – so far as its sensible predicates are concerned (for with respect to the consequences that follow from their necessary recognition of me, all actions of free beings are necessarily identical to one another) – cannot be connected with the [51] sensible predicates of the actions of other individuals posited by me. In order to know the identity of an acting individual, I had to be able to connect the distinguishing characteristics of his present actions with his previous actions. Where this does not occur, I cannot attribute the present action to any rational being already known to me; but since I still must posit some rational being, I posit a new one.

(Perhaps it will not be redundant to summarize under a single perspective the point of the proof just undertaken, a point that has been dissipated in a multitude of different parts. – The proposition to be proved was: just as certainly as I posit myself as an individual, so too must I with equal certainty expect all rational beings known to me, in all cases of mutual interaction, to recognize me as a rational being. Thus a certain act of self-positing is supposed to contain a postulate addressed to others, indeed a postulate extending to every case where it can be applied; this postulate can be discovered by mere analysis of this certain act of self-positing.

I posit myself as an individual in opposition to another particular individual, insofar as *I* ascribe *to myself* a sphere for my freedom from which I exclude the other, and ascribe a sphere *to the other* from which I exclude myself – obviously, this occurs merely in the thinking of a fact and in consequence of this fact. Thus I have posited myself as *free* alongside him and without harming the possibility of his freedom. Through this positing of my freedom, I have *determined* myself; being free constitutes my essential character. But what does *being free* mean? Evidently, it means being able to carry out the concepts of one's actions. But this carrying out always *follows* the concept, and the perception of what one takes to be the product of one's efficacy is always – relative to the formation of the concept of such a product – *in the future*. Thus freedom is always posited into the future; and if freedom is supposed to constitute a being's character, then it is posited for *all* of the individual's future; freedom is [52] posited in the future to the extent that the *individual himself* is posited in the future.

But now my freedom is possible only through the fact that the other remains within his sphere; therefore, just as I demand my freedom for all the future, so too I also demand that the other be limited, and – since he is to be free – limited by himself for all the future: and I demand all this immediately, insofar as I posit myself as an individual.

This demand upon the other is contained in the act of positing myself as an individual.

But the other can limit himself only in consequence of a concept of me as a free being. Nevertheless, I demand this limitation absolutely; thus, I demand *consistency* from him, i.e. I demand that all of his future concepts be determined by a certain prior concept, by the knowledge of me as a rational being.

Now he can recognize me as a rational being only under the condition that I treat him as one, in accordance with my concept of him as a rational being. Thus, I impose the same consistency upon myself, and his action is conditioned by mine. We stand in reciprocal interaction with regard to the consistency of our thinking and our acting: our thinking is consistent with our acting, and my thinking and acting are consistent with his.)

(III) The conclusion to all of this has already emerged. – *I must in all cases recognize the free being outside me as a free being, i.e. I must limit my freedom through the concept of the possibility of his freedom.*

The relation between free beings that we have deduced (i.e. that each is to limit his freedom through the concept of the possibility of the other's freedom, under the condition that the latter likewise limit his freedom through the freedom of the former) is called the *relation of right*; and the formula that has now been established is the *principle of right*.

This relation is deduced from the concept of the individual. Thus what was to be proved has now been proved.

Furthermore, the concept of the individual was previously proved to be a condition of self-consciousness; thus the concept of right is itself a condition of self-consciousness. Therefore, the [53] concept of right has been properly deduced *a priori*, i.e. from the pure form of reason, from the I.

Corollaries

(1) Therefore, in consequence of the deduction just carried out, it can be claimed that the concept of right is contained within the essence of reason, and that no finite rational being is possible if this concept is not present within it – and present not through experience, instruction, arbitrary human conventions, etc., but rather in consequence of the being's rational nature. It is, of course, self-evident that the *expression* of this concept in actual consciousness is conditioned by the givenness of some particular instance where the concept applies; it is equally self-evident that this concept does not originally lie in the soul, like some empty form, and wait for experience to put content into it (as some philosophers seem to conceive of *a priori* concepts). But it has also been proved that there must necessarily be some instance where the concept actually applies, because no human being can exist in isolation.

Therefore, it has been shown that a certain concept (i.e. a certain modification of thought, a certain way of judging things) is necessary for the rational being as such. Let us provisionally call this concept X. This

X must be operative wherever human beings live together, and it must be expressed and have some designation in their language. It is operative on its own, without any help from the philosopher, who deduces this X only with difficulty. Now whether this X is exactly the same as what ordinary usage refers to as *right* is a question that common sense must decide (that is, common sense as it is left to itself, not common sense that has been numbed and confused by the arbitrary explanations and interpretations of philosophers). Provisionally, let us declare – as we have every right to do – that the deduced concept, X, whose reality has just been proved by this deduction, is to be called in this investigation *the concept of right*, and not any other possible concept: [**54**] in calling it thus, we assume responsibility for whether or not we can rely on this concept to answer all the questions common sense can raise concerning right.

(2) The deduced concept has nothing to do with the moral law; it is deduced without it, and this fact is enough to prove that it cannot be deduced from the moral law, for there cannot be more than one deduction of the same concept. Furthermore, all attempts at such a deduction have failed completely. The concept of *duty*, which arises from the moral law, is directly opposed to the concept of right in most of its characteristics. The moral law commands duty categorically: the law of right only permits, but never commands, that one exercise one's right. Indeed, the moral law very often forbids a person to exercise his right, and yet – as all the world acknowledges – that right does not thereby cease to be a right. In such a case one judges that the person may well have had a right to something but that he ought not to have exercised it in this situation. In that case, then, is the moral law (which is one and the same principle) at odds with itself, simultaneously granting and denying the same right in the same situation? I know of no reasoning that might offer anything plausible in response to this objection.

The question of whether the moral law might provide a new sanction for the concept of right is not part of the doctrine of natural right, but belongs instead to an account of real morality and will be answered within such an account at the appropriate time. In the domain of natural right, the good will has no role to play. Right must be enforceable, even if there is not a single human being with a good will; the very aim of the science of right is to sketch out just such an order of things. In this domain, physical force – and it alone – gives right its sanction.

Thus, separating natural right from morality does not require any artificial measures, which always fail to achieve their goal anyway. For if one has begun with nothing but morality – actually, not even morality, but only the metaphysics of morals – then, in the wake of any artificial separation, one will never [55] find anything in one's investigations besides morality. Both sciences are already – originally and without any help from us – separated by reason itself, and they are completely opposed to one another.

(3) The concept of right is the concept of a relation between rational beings. Thus, it arises only under the condition that rational beings are thought in relation to one another. It is nonsense to talk about a right to nature, to land, to animals, etc., considered only on their own or in direct relation to a human being. Reason only has power – and by no means a right over – these things, for in this relation the question of right does not arise at all. The fact that one can have scruples about enjoying this or that thing is quite another matter; but this is an issue for the tribunal of morality, and it does not arise out of concern that the things – but rather that our own spiritual condition – might be harmed by such enjoyment; we debate with ourselves, not with the things, and we take ourselves, not the things, to task. Only if another person is related to the same thing at the same time that I am does there arise the question of *a right to the thing*, which is an abbreviated way of talking about – and this is what it should really be called – *a right in relation to the other person*, i.e. a right to exclude him from using the thing.

(4) Rational beings enter into reciprocal interaction with one another only through actions, expressions of their freedom, in the sensible world: thus the concept of right concerns only what is expressed in the sensible world: whatever has no causality in the sensible world – but remains inside the mind instead – belongs before another tribunal, the tribunal of morality. Thus it is nonsense to speak of a right to the freedom of thought, freedom of conscience, and so forth. There is a faculty that performs these inner actions, and there are duties, but no rights, with respect to them.

(5) The question of right between rational beings is possible only if the rational beings actually have some relation to one another, and can thus act such that the action of one has consequences for the other; [56] this follows from the preceding deduction, which always presupposes a real reciprocal interaction. There is no relation of right between those

who do not know each other or those whose spheres of efficacy are completely separate from one another. One completely misunderstands the concept of right if, for example, one talks about the rights of the dead vis-à-vis the living. One can very well have duties of conscience concerning the memory of the dead, but not obligations that exist as a matter of right.

Second main division
Deduction of the applicability of the concept of right

§5 Fourth theorem

The rational being cannot posit itself as an individual that has efficacy without ascribing to itself, and thereby determining, a material body

Proof

According to the proof carried out above, the rational being posits itself as a rational individual – from now on we shall refer to this as *the person* – by *exclusively ascribing* to itself a *sphere for its freedom. He* is the person who exclusively makes choices within this sphere (and not any other possible person, who might make choices in some other sphere); thus, no other person is *this person*, i.e. no other person can make choices within the sphere allotted only to him. This is what constitutes the person's individual character: through this determination, the person is *the one* that he is, this or that person, called by this or that name.

[57] Our only task here is to analyze the action indicated above, to see what actually occurs when this action takes place.

(I) The subject ascribes this sphere to itself, and determines itself by means of it. Thus the subject posits this sphere in opposition to itself. (The subject itself is the logical subject in any possible proposition one might think of; and the sphere we have mentioned is the predicate; but subject and predicate are always posited in opposition to one another.) Now what is the subject first and foremost? Obviously, it is that which is active solely in itself and upon itself; that which determines itself to think of an object or to will an end; that which is spiritual; pure I-hood.

Now, *in opposition* to this subject *there is posited* a limited sphere for the subject's possible free actions, but a sphere that nevertheless belongs exclusively to this subject. (By ascribing this sphere to itself, the subject limits itself, distinguishing itself from the absolute, formal I and thereby becoming a determinate, material I, or a person. One would hope that these two quite distinct concepts, which are contrasted here with sufficient clarity, will no longer be confused with one another.)

To say that this sphere is posited in opposition to the subject means: this sphere is excluded from the subject, posited outside it, separated from the subject, and completely divorced from it. Considered more determinately, this means first and foremost: the sphere is posited as *not present* wherever the self-reverting activity is present, and the self-reverting activity is posited as *not present* wherever this sphere is present; both are mutually independent and contingent in relation to one another. But whatever relates to the I in this manner belongs – in accordance with what has been said above – to *the world*. Thus the sphere identified here is posited first and foremost as *a part of the world*.

(II) This sphere is posited by an original and necessary activity of the I, i.e. it is *intuited*, and it thereby becomes something real. – Since it would not be reasonable to assume that the reader is already familiar with certain results of the *Wissenschaftslehre*, I shall briefly describe those that are needed in the present context. – One doesn't have the slightest idea what transcendental philosophy – and Kant especially – is speaking of if one thinks that, when an act of intuition occurs, there exists outside the intuiter and the intuition some further thing, perhaps some matter, [58] at which the intuition is directed (somewhat like the way common sense tends to conceive of bodily vision).[1] What is intuited

---

[1] In claiming that the act of intuiting gives rise to what is intuited, Fichte is espousing a view that is quite different from Kant's account of empirical intuition as it is usually understood. In the "Transcendental Aesthetic" of the *Critique of Pure Reason* Kant claims that for human subjects intuition "takes place only insofar as the object is given to us," and that "this, in turn, is possible only if [the object] affects the mind in a certain way" (B 33). He later distinguishes the matter, or content, of an appearance from its form, and claims that the former must be given to (finite) subjects through sensation, while the latter is supplied by the human mind (B 34). Fichte's claim that "what is intuited comes to be through the intuiting itself" certainly applies to the I as he conceives it – this is part of what it means to call the subject "self-positing" – but here Fichte extends this principle to all forms of intuition, including empirical. The view that, even in empirical intuition, the act of intuiting gives rise to what is intuited is implicit in Fichte's doctrine of the check (*Anstoß*) in the 1794 *Wissenschaftslehre* and is explicitly asserted in *Wissenschaftslehre nova methodo* (1796/99). See n. 3, p. 32 and *Fichte: Foundations of Transcendental Philosophy*, ed. Daniel Breazeale (Ithaca, NY: Cornell University Press, 1992), pp. 192–5.

comes to be through the intuiting itself, and only through it; the I reverts into itself, and this activity yields both the intuition and the intuited at once. Reason (the I) is by no means passive in intuition, but absolutely active; in intuition, reason is the *productive imagination*.[2] Intuition, in "seeing," projects something outward, somewhat like – if one wants an analogy – the way in which the painter projects the completed shape out of his eye onto the surface and *"looks towards,"* so to speak, before the hand (which is slower) can copy the outline of the shape. The sphere that we have identified is posited here in the same way.

Furthermore – the I that intuits itself as active intuits its activity as an *act of drawing a line*. This is the original schema for activity in general, as will be discovered by anyone who wants to awaken that highest intuition within himself. This original line is *pure extension*, that which is common to time and space and from which they first emerge through differentiation and further determination. This original line does not presuppose space, but rather space presupposes it; lines in space (i.e. the boundaries of things extended in space) are something entirely different from it. In just this manner the sphere we are discussing here is produced in lines and thereby becomes *something extended*.

(III) This sphere is *something determinate*; therefore, the act of producing it has its limits somewhere, and the product is interpreted by the understanding (the faculty of grasping things in a fixed manner) as a completed whole, and only thus is it actually *posited* (i.e. fixed and held fast).

The person becomes determinate by virtue of this product; he is the same person only insofar as this product remains the same, and he ceases to be the same person when the product ceases to be the same. But now, according to what has been said above, just as certainly as the person posits himself as free, so too must he posit himself as enduring. Thus he also posits the product as continually the same, as at rest, fixed,

---

[2] Fichte's claim that the intuiting subject is not passive but "absolutely active" is consistent with his account of the I's role in empirical intuition, but it is manifestly not Kant's view; (see previous note). Fichte's use of the Kantian term "productive imagination" may be his attempt to suggest that his own view is, at least implicitly, held by Kant, too, but if so, it is a highly implausible suggestion. Kant's doctrine of the productive imagination is notoriously obscure, but it is very unlikely that in positing an *a priori* synthesis of the imagination he meant to retract his position in the "Transcendental Aesthetic" and claim that the intuiting subject is active, producing the content of what it intuits (*Critique of Pure Reason*, A 118–25). For more on Fichte's concept of the productive imagination see n. 1, p. 175.

and unchanging, as a whole that is completed all at once. But extension that is at rest and made determinate once and for all is [**59**] *extension in space*. Thus that sphere is necessarily *posited* as a limited body that is spatially extended and that fills up its space. Moreover, in analysis, this sphere is necessarily *found* as just described. It is only analysis of this sphere that we can become conscious of, since the synthesis now being described (or the production of the sphere) is presupposed in order to make the analysis possible, which in turn is presupposed in order to explain the possibility of consciousness.

(IV) The material body we have derived is posited as the *sphere of all the person's possible free actions*, and nothing more. Its essence consists in this alone.

According to what has been said above, to say that a person is free means: the person, merely by constructing a concept of an end immediately becomes the cause of an object corresponding perfectly to that concept; the person becomes a cause simply and solely through his will as such: for to will means to construct a concept of an end. But the body just described is supposed to contain the person's free actions; thus it is in the body that the person would have to be a cause in the manner just described. Immediately by means of his will, and without any other means, the person would have to bring forth in this body whatever he wills; something would have to take place within this body, exactly as the person willed it.

Furthermore – since the body thus described is nothing other than the sphere of the person's free actions, the concept of such a sphere is exhausted by the concept of the body, and *vice versa*. The person cannot be an absolutely free cause (i.e. a cause that has efficacy immediately through the will) except in the body; if a determinate act of willing is given, then one can infer with certainty that a particular change in the body corresponds to it. Conversely, no determination can occur in the body, except as a result of the person's efficacy; and from a given change in the body, one can infer with equal certainty that the person possesses a particular concept corresponding to such change. – This last proposition will acquire its proper determinacy and full meaning only later.

(V) Now how and in what manner are concepts supposed to be expressed in a material body by means of change within it? [**60**] Matter, by its very essence, is imperishable; it cannot be annihilated, nor can new matter be created. For this reason, the concept of change in the posited body could not apply to matter. Furthermore, the posited body is supposed to endure without interruption; thus the same pieces of matter are supposed to remain together and continuously constitute the body; and yet, this body is also supposed to be changed by each of the person's acts of will. How, then, can it endure without interruption and still be (as we are to expect) continually changed?

The body is matter. Matter is infinitely divisible. The body, i.e. the material parts in it, would remain and yet the body would be changed, if the parts changed their relation to one another – i.e. their relative position. The relation of the manifold parts to one another is called *form*. Thus the parts, *insofar as they constitute the form*, are supposed to remain; but the form itself is supposed to be changed. – (I say, "*insofar as they constitute the form*": for particular parts could continually separate themselves from the body without thereby harming the permanence required of such a body, provided only that those parts are replaced by others in the same, undivided moment.) – Thus: *motion of the parts*, and thereby change in the body's form, comes about immediately by means of the person's concept.

(VI) In the body we have been describing, the person's concepts of causality are expressed by means of change in the position of the body's *parts* in relation to one another. These concepts, i.e. the person's acts of willing, can be infinitely varied; and the body, which comprises the sphere of the person's freedom, may not restrict them. Thus each part would have to be able to change its position in relation to the others, i.e. each would have to be able to move while all the others remain at rest; each part, *ad infinitum*, would have to have its *own* movement, attributed only to it. The body would have to be configured such that it would always be up to freedom to think a part as larger or smaller, as more complex or simpler; furthermore, it would always be up to freedom to think any set of parts as a single whole, and thus as itself one part in [**61**] relation to a larger whole; and conversely, to divide up again everything that is thought as a unity in this way. Determining what is to be a part at any given moment would have to depend on a concept. Furthermore, if something is thought as a part, it would have to have its own characteristic movement, which would, once again, depend on a concept. – Something that is thought as an individual part in this relation is called a *member*; it must, in turn, contain *members*; and within each of these there must, once again, be *members*, and so on *ad infinitum*. The question of what is to be regarded as a member at any given moment must depend on the concept of causality. The *member* is in motion, to the extent that it is regarded as a member; what is then the whole in relation to such a member is at rest: what is a part in relation to that member is likewise at rest, i.e. it has no movement of its own, though it does indeed have movement in common with the whole to which it currently belongs (i.e. the member). This kind of bodily composition is called *articulation*. The body we have deduced is necessarily articulated, and must be posited as such.

A material body [*Körper*] such as the one described, whose permanence and identity we tie to the permanence and identity of our own personality – a body we posit as a closed, articulated whole, and within which we posit ourselves as a cause that acts immediately through our will – is what we call *our human body* [*Leib*]; and thus what was supposed to be proved has now been proved.

§6 Fifth theorem

The person cannot ascribe a body to himself without positing it as standing under the influence of a person outside him, and without thereby further determining it

Proof

(I) According to our second theorem, the person cannot posit himself with consciousness, unless he posits that there has been an influence upon him. The positing of such an influence was the exclusive condition of all consciousness, [62] and the first point to which the whole of consciousness was attached. This influence is posited as having been exercised upon the *particular person, the individual, as such*; for, as we have demonstrated, the rational being cannot posit itself as a rational being in general, but only as an individual; thus an influence that the rational being posits as having been exercised upon itself is necessarily an influence upon the individual, since for itself the rational being is and can be nothing other than an individual.

According to the proofs carried out above, to say that a rational being has been affected is to say that its free activity has been canceled in part and in a certain respect. Only through this cancellation of its free activity does an object come to be for an intelligence, and only thereby does such an intelligence infer that something exists that is not due to itself (or to its activity).

Thus to say that a rational being as an individual has been affected is to say that an activity that belongs to it as an individual has been canceled. Now the complete sphere of the rational being's activity, as an individual, is its body; thus, the efficacy in this body, the capacity in it to be a cause merely by means of the will, would have to be restricted, or – more concisely – an influence would have to have been exercised upon the person's body.

If, in consequence of this, one were to assume that an action belonging to the sphere of the person's possible actions were canceled or rendered impossible for the moment, then the required influence would be explained.

But the person is supposed to attribute this influence *to himself*; he is supposed to posit the momentarily canceled activity as one of his own possible activities in general – as contained within the sphere of the expressions of his freedom. Thus the person must posit this activity, in order to be able to posit it as canceled; accordingly, the activity must really be present, and by no means can it be canceled. (It would be wrong to say, for instance, that the person could have *previously* posited this activity as his own, and could now – by running through the sphere of his present freedom – recall that, if his freedom were whole and complete, he would have to possess a further determinate capacity that he in fact does not. For, apart from all the other reasons why this presupposition is [63] untenable, we are dealing with the moment to which all consciousness is attached and prior to which no previous consciousness may be presupposed.)

Thus, if consciousness is to be possible, the same determinate activity of the person must simultaneously, in the same undivided moment, *be both canceled and not canceled*. Our task is to investigate how this can happen.

(II) Any activity of the person is a certain way of determining his articulated body; thus, to say that an activity of the person is restricted means that a certain determination of his articulated body has been rendered impossible.

Now the person cannot posit that *his* activity is restricted, that a certain determination in *his* articulated body is impossible, without simultaneously positing that the same determination is possible; for the person posits something as his body, only under the condition that it is possible for him to determine it by his mere will. Thus the very determination that is supposed to be impossible (and precisely insofar as it is supposed to be impossible) would have to be posited by the person as possible; and, since the person cannot posit anything unless it *is* (for him), the person would actually have to produce this determination. But this activity, even though it is actually produced, must remain continually restricted and canceled, for the person produces it precisely in order to be able to posit it as canceled. Thus we can grasp this much for the time being: this determination of the body's articulation is, in a certain way, actually produced by the will's efficacy, and at the same time – in another way – it is canceled by an influence from outside.

Furthermore – in the moment to be described now, the person is supposed to find himself as free within his sphere, ascribing his body entirely and thoroughly to himself. If the person did not posit that it is at least possible for him to reproduce, through his mere will, the given determination of his body's articulation (even in the sense in which the determination is and remains canceled), then to that extent he could not at all ascribe his body to himself or posit that there has been an influence upon himself – [64] and this contradicts our presupposition. The fact that the person does not cancel the given restriction must depend – in accordance with the assumption of such a restriction – on the person's own free will; and the person must posit that it is possible to cancel the restriction.

How, then, is the person to posit this possibility? Certainly not as a consequence of previous experience, for what is at issue here is the beginning of all experience. Thus the cancellation of the restriction on the body's articulation, insofar as it occurs, would occur only through the person's positing, out of the production of that determination, in the manner in which the determination is actually produced, provided that the person did not restrain his will from canceling it.

Now what, then, is actually posited in the situation just described? Evidently, a double manner of determining the body's articulation, which for now might even be called a double articulation, or a double *organ*, the two sides of which relate to each other in the following way: the first organ (within which the person produces the canceled movement and which we shall call the *higher organ*) can be modified by the will without thereby becoming the other (which we shall call the *lower organ*). To this extent, the higher and lower organs are distinguished from one another. But furthermore: if the modification in the higher organ is not to lead automatically to a modification in the lower, then the person must also restrain his will from thereby modifying the lower organ: thus the higher and lower organs can also be unified through the will; they are one and the same organ.

Thus the person's perception of the required influence upon him involves the following: The person must tacitly accept the influence, must give himself over to it; he must not cancel the modification that has been produced in his organ. The person could cancel this modification through his mere will, and – if this is not supposed to happen – he must limit the freedom of his will. Furthermore, he must freely and internally reproduce the modification produced in his organ. We have said that a possible expression of the person's freedom is canceled. This certainly does not mean that the person can no longer act in some particular [65] direction or towards a certain goal; it means only that something has been produced in the person that he himself is able to produce, but that is now produced in such a way that he must ascribe it not to his own efficacy, but to the efficacy of a being outside of himself. In general, nothing is found in the perception of a rational being that it does not believe itself capable of producing, or the production of which it cannot ascribe to itself; the rational being has no sense of anything else, and so everything else lies absolutely outside the rational being's sphere. What has been produced in the person's organ is freely reproduced by him through his higher organ, but in such a way that he does not influence the lower organ; for if he did, the same determination would certainly exist in the articulated body, only not as a perceived determination, but as one produced by the person himself; not as a determination arising from an external efficacy, but rather as one arising from the subject's own efficacy. For example, a person cannot see if he does not first accept an influence upon himself and then internally reproduce the form of the object, that is, actively construct the object's outline; [similarly,] there can be no hearing if the sounds are not internally imitated by the same organ that produces those sounds in speech. However, if this inner causality should extend as far as the external organ, then the result would not be hearing, but speaking.

If the situation is as we have described it, then the human being's articulated body is *sense*. But as everyone can see, the body is sense only in relation to something present in the body that is the product of an efficacy that could have been the subject's own, but that in the present case is instead the product of the efficacy of a cause outside the subject.

With this kind of influence upon him, the person remains entirely and perfectly free. The person can immediately cancel what the external cause has produced in him; and he expressly posits his ability to do so, and thus posits that the existence of such an influence depends solely on the person himself. Furthermore, if there is to be any influence upon the person, then the person must freely imitate it: thus the person expressly realizes his [66] freedom, simply in order to be able to perceive. (With this, by the way, the *absolute freedom of reflection* has been described and fully determined.)

Now in this way, the articulated body of the person has been further determined, as was required. It has been posited as sense; and in order for it to be posited as such, a higher and lower organ have been ascribed to it; of these two, the lower organ (through which the body first enters into relation with objects and rational beings outside it) can stand under an external influence, but the higher organ never can.

(III) This influence on the subject is supposed to be such that only a rational being outside the subject can be posited as its cause. This rational being's end would have been to exercise some influence on the subject. But, as we have shown, there can be no influence on the subject at all, unless the subject, through his own freedom, accepts the impression that has been made upon him and internally imitates it. The subject himself must act purposively, i.e. he must limit the sum of his freedom (freedom that could just as well cancel the impression made upon him) to the attainment of the intended end of cognition. It is precisely such self-limitation that is the exclusive criterion of reason. Therefore, the subject himself must bring to completion the attainment of the external being's end; and thus this external being – if it is to have possessed any end at all – would have to have counted on such completion by the subject. Thus the being outside the subject must be regarded as a rational being to the extent that – in presupposing the subject's freedom – it has *limited* its own freedom to this particular manner of influencing the subject.

But it is always possible that the external being may have exercised this kind of influence on the subject only by chance, or because it could not have acted otherwise. There is still no reason to assume that the external being limited itself, if it cannot be shown that it also could have acted otherwise, that the fullness of its power would have led it to act in a completely different way, and that it necessarily limited the fullness of its power and had to do so through the concept of the subject's rationality, [**67**] so that an influence like the one described could occur.

Thus in order to be able to conclude that the external being limited itself, I would have to posit that an influence could have been exercised upon me in an opposite manner, and that the being assumed to exist outside me could have exercised its influence in this opposite manner.

What is the opposite manner? The nature of the described influence was such that the question of whether there was to be any influence upon me at all depended entirely on the freedom of my will, since I first had to accept the influence upon me, and posit it as having occurred; otherwise, there would have been no influence upon *me*. Thus an opposite kind of influence would have to be one where the question of whether or not I was aware of the influence did not depend on my freedom; rather, I would have to be aware of it as surely as I was aware of anything at all. How is such an influence possible?

The first kind of influence that we have been describing depended on my freedom primarily because I was able – through the mere freedom of my will – to annul the form that was brought about in my articulated body. With the opposite kind of influence, such annulment must not depend solely on the freedom of my will; the form brought about in my body would have to be fixed, indestructible (at least not capable of being immediately annulled by my higher organ); my body would have to be bound to this form and completely restricted in its movements. As a result of such complete restriction, I would necessarily have to reflect on the restriction. Such necessity would not pertain to the form (i.e. to the fact that I am a reflective being at all, a fact that is grounded solely in the essence of reason), but rather to the matter (i.e. to the fact that, if I reflect at all, I would necessarily have to reflect on the influence that has occurred). For the free being must find itself only as free. Therefore, as surely as it reflects on itself, it internally imitates a determination that has been brought about in it, under the condition that its own free will could annul that determination. The person limits [**68**] his own freedom. But if – in accordance with our presupposition here – the given determination cannot be annulled by the mere causality of the will, then such self-limitation is not required; something that belongs in the reflection of the free being, as free, is missing, and the free being therefore feels compelled in its reflection. As surely as the free being reflects upon something, it feels compulsion; for everything in the articulated body is necessarily connected, and every part influences every other part, in consequence of the concept of articulation.

In view of the opposite kind of influence postulated above, I must necessarily posit that my body's free movement can be restricted in the way described; and thus, once again, my body is further determined. As a condition of this restriction, I must posit resistant, solid matter existing outside me that is capable of resisting the free movement of my body; thus – by virtue of this further determination of my body – the sensible world is also further determined.

This resistant, solid matter can restrict only a part of my free movement, not all of it; for in the latter case, the person's freedom would be completely annihilated; in that case, I would be dead, dead in relation to the sensible world. Thus, by means of the free movement of the rest of my body, I must be able to release the restricted part of my body from being compelled; thus I must also exercise some causality on resistant matter. The body must have physical power to resist the impression of such matter, if not immediately by willing, then mediately by skill, i.e. by applying the will to the part of the body's articulation that is still free. But then the organ of this causality must itself be composed of such resistant, solid matter; and the free being's superior power over this external matter arises solely from its freedom to act in accordance with concepts. Matter, in contrast, operates only in accordance with mechanical laws and thus has only *one* mode of exercising efficacy, while the free being has several.

If my body is composed of resistant, solid matter and has the power to modify all matter in the sensible world [69] and to shape it in accordance with my concepts, then the body of the person outside me is composed of the same matter and has the same power. Now my body is itself matter, and thus a possible object that the other person can affect through mere physical force; it is a possible object whose movement he can directly restrict. If he had regarded me as mere matter and wanted to exercise an influence on me, he would have exercised an influence on me *in the same way* that I influence anything I regard as mere matter. He did not influence me in this way, thus his concept of me was not that of mere matter, but that of a rational being, and through this concept he limited his capacity to act; and only now is the conclusion fully justified and necessary: the cause of the influence upon me as described above is nothing other than a rational being.

With this, the criterion of the reciprocal interaction between rational beings as such has been established. They influence each other necessarily under the condition *that the object of their influence possesses sense*; one does not influence the other as if it were a mere thing to be modified by physical force for one's own purposes.

(IV) With the kind of influence we have been describing, the subject's organ has actually been modified by a person outside him. Now this has happened neither through immediate bodily contact with this person nor by means of solid matter; for if it had happened in one of these ways, one could not infer that the influence was caused by a person, and the subject would not perceive himself as free. – In each case, the subject's organ is something material, since his entire body is material: thus the organ is necessarily modified by matter outside it, the organ is given a particular form and maintained in that form. The mere will of the subject could cancel this form, and thus the subject must restrain his will so that the form is not annulled. Thus the matter that produces this form in the subject's organ is not resistant, solid matter; it is not matter whose parts cannot be separated by the mere will; rather, it is a finer, subtler matter. A [70] subtler matter of this kind must necessarily be posited as a condition of the required influence among rational beings in the sensible world.

The modification of the organ affected by freedom is not supposed to influence the organ affected by compulsion, but is supposed to leave it perfectly and completely free. Thus the finer matter must be able to influence only the former organ, but not the latter. The finer matter must not be able to restrict or bind the latter organ; there must therefore be a kind of matter whose component parts have absolutely no discernible connection to lower sense, i.e. the sense affected by compulsion.

In the situation just described, I acquire the capacity to affect this subtle matter in turn through my mere will, by affecting the higher organ through the lower; for we have expressly stated that I would have to refrain from producing such a movement of the lower organ, in order not to annul the determination produced in the higher one and, thus, also in order not to give another determination to the subtler matter, which stands in immediate relation to the higher organ. *Therefore, the subtler matter is capable of being modified by me, through my mere will.*

In anticipation of possible confusions, I shall add a few more remarks here. – A double – i.e. a higher and lower – organ has been posited. The higher organ is the one that is modified by the subtler matter; the lower organ is the one that can be restricted by the resistant matter, the matter whose parts can be separated only with difficulty.

Either: an influence is exercised upon the person as a free being, as has been described. In that case, the higher organ is modified by a particular form of the subtler matter and maintained as thus modified. In order to perceive, the person must restrain the movement of his lower organ insofar as it is in relation to the modified part of the higher organ;[3] however, the person must at the same time also – though only internally – imitate the particular movement he would have to make if he himself were to produce the given, determinate modification in the higher organ. For example, if a shape in space is to be perceived by sight, then the feel of the object (i.e. the pressure that would have to be exerted in order to produce the shape by sculpting it) would have to be internally imitated (but with lightning speed, unnoticed by the [71] ordinary observer); but the impression in the eye, as the schema of such imitation, would be retained. This, then, is why uncultivated people – i.e. those who have not yet been adequately taught (people whose basic human functions have not yet been refined into skills) – touch physical objects that have raised or embossed surfaces (or even the surfaces of paintings, engravings, or the books they read) when they want to get a good look at them. It is impossible for someone to speak and to hear at the same time, for he must imitate the external sounds by constructing them with the organ of speech. And this is also why some people occasionally ask what has just been said to them; for they have heard it all right, but have not taken it in; and indeed sometimes when it is not repeated for them, they actually know what was said, because then they

---

[3] In a letter to Johann Smidt (1798) Fichte makes the following clarifications of his difficult remarks on the higher and lower organs of sense: "(1) I distinguish the higher, or *inner*, organ from the lower, or *outer*, organ. (2) Both are *sense*; the first is inner sense, the second outer. (3) Outer sense is lower sense that [also] becomes higher sense; (there lies the error in my presentation [in the *Foundations*])." He then proposes that the text be amended to read: "In that case the higher *sense* is modified by a particular form of the subtler matter and maintained as thus modified. In order to perceive, the person must restrain the movement of his *higher organ, and through that, the* lower organ insofar as the latter is in relation to the modified part of the higher organ" (changes are emphasized).

have to imitate the sounds they had previously failed to reproduce. Others are even accustomed to repeating out loud what has been said to them, and only then do they take in what was said. – In this case, the body serves as sense, indeed as the higher sense.

Or: a modification is produced in the higher organ[4] by the person's mere will, and the person simultaneously wills that his lower organ should be moved thereby in accordance with an end. If the person's lower organ is not restricted, then the intended movement of it would ensue – and from that, the intended modification of either the subtler or the coarser matter, depending on the end the person has set for himself. Thus, for example, shapes to be painted or characters to be written down are first formed in the eye, as an active organ, and projected upon the surface, before they are actually affixed to the surface by the hand, which is slower than the eye and operates under its guidance and command. – In this case, the body serves as an instrument.

If the intended movement of the lower organ does not ensue (the movement of the higher organ always ensues, as long as the human being is alive), then the lower organ is restricted, it [72] feels resistance, and the body then serves as sense, but as lower sense.

If a rational being exercises an influence upon another as upon mere matter, then the latter being's lower sense is certainly – indeed, necessarily – affected as well. And, as is always the case with this sense, it is affected quite independently of the fact that the latter being is free. One should not assume, however, that this affection was intended by the rational being that caused it. This rational being wanted only to bring about his own end in the affected matter, to express his concept in it. In the concept of his end, he took no account of whether or not such matter would actually feel his influence upon it. Thus, the reciprocal interaction of free beings *as such* always occurs by means of the higher sense; for only this sense is such that it is impossible to have an effect upon it without presupposing that it is the higher sense; and thus the aforementioned criterion for the reciprocal interaction among rational beings remains correct: in this kind of interaction, one must presuppose that the object being affected possesses sense.

(V) As a condition of self-consciousness, it has been posited that there must be an external influence upon the person; and in conse-

---

[4] In a letter to Smidt (see previous note) Fichte advocates replacing 'organ' with 'sense' in this sentence.

quence of this, that the person's body must have a certain composition; and in consequence of this, that the sensible world must be constituted in a certain way. Hence, first of all: if consciousness is to be possible, then the sensible world must be constituted in *this way* and must stand in *this* relation to our body; and furthermore, there is, of course, nothing in the sensible world except what stands in relation to our body; nothing exists for us except as a result of this relation. – One should not forget that these inferences are to be understood transcendentally. To say that something *is* a certain way means that we must posit it as such: and because we must posit it in that way, it is so. The presence of a body was inferred from the concepts of independence and freedom. But freedom exists only insofar as it is posited: and therefore, since what is grounded cannot extend beyond its ground, the body can exist only for one who posits it.

The further determination of the body and, through it, of the sensible world, is inferred from the necessary community of free beings, which in turn is the condition of the possibility of self-consciousness, and thus depends on our [73] first point. Since free beings, as such, are to exist in community in the world, the world must be constituted in *just this way*. But now a community of free beings exists only insofar as it is posited by such beings; therefore, the world also exists in a certain way, only insofar as they posit it as such. – This they do, not *freely*, but with absolute necessity; and what is posited in this way has reality for us.

(VI) I ascribe to myself a lower and a higher organ, which relate to each other in the manner described; in consequence of this, I assume that there exists in the sensible world external to me a coarser and a subtler matter that relate to my organs in the manner described. Such positing is a necessary condition of self-consciousness and belongs therefore to the very concept of the person. Thus, if I posit a being outside me as a person, I must necessarily assume that he also posits other persons outside himself, or – what amounts to the same thing – I must ascribe to him the real possession and use of two organs that are distinguished in the same manner; I must assume the real existence *for him* of a sensible world that is determined in the manner described.

This transference of my necessary mode of thinking to a person outside me also belongs to the concept of the person. Thus I must suppose that the person outside me – in the event that he posits me as a person – assumes the very same things about me that I assume about myself and about him; and I must suppose that he simultaneously assumes that I am also assuming the very same things about him. The concepts of the determinate articulation of rational beings, and of a sensible world outside such beings, necessarily go together; they are concepts about which rational beings necessarily and without any prior arrangement agree, because *the same way of intuiting* is found in every rational being, in *each one's own personality*, and all rational beings must be thought of in this way. Each rational being, just as surely as he is one, can justifiably presuppose of others – can expect of them and can appeal to this fact – that they have the same concepts of these objects.

(VII) A new objection arises here, and only after it is answered will the body of a rational [74] being be fully determined. The objection is this: it has been claimed that I would not become self-conscious at all, and could not, unless a rational being outside me exercised some influence upon me. Now if it is entirely up to me whether or not I want to give myself over to this influence – and, further, if it is up to me whether and *how* I want to exercise an influence in return – then the possibility of such an expression of my freedom still depends on the other rational being's influence on me.

I become a rational being – *actually*, not merely *potentially* – only by being *made* into one; if the other rational being's action did not occur, I would never have become rational. Thus my rationality depends on the free choice, on the good will, of another; it depends on chance, as does all rationality.

But the situation cannot be thus; for if it were, I as a person would not be independent first and foremost; rather, I would only be the accidental result of another person, who in turn would be the accidental result of a third person, and so on *ad infinitum*.

This contradiction can be resolved only by presupposing that the other was *compelled* already, in his original influence upon me, compelled as a rational being (i.e. *bound* by consistency) to treat me as a rational being; and indeed, that he was compelled to do so by *me*; therefore, that – already in his first, original influence upon me, in which I depend on him – he at the same time depends on me; and accordingly, that that *original* relation is already a reciprocal interaction. But prior to his influence upon me, *I am not an I at all*; I have not posited myself, for the positing of myself is, after all, conditioned by his influence and is possible only through it. But I am supposed to exercise my efficacy.

Thus I am supposed to exercise my efficacy without exercising it; I am supposed to exercise my efficacy without activity. We will see how this can be thought.

(α) *To exercise efficacy without exercising it* can only signify a mere capacity. This mere capacity is supposed to exercise efficacy. But a capacity is nothing but an ideal concept, and it would be an empty thought to ascribe to such a capacity the exclusive predicate of reality – efficacy – without assuming that the capacity [75] was realized. – Now the entire capacity of the person in the sensible world is realized in the concept of his body, which exists as surely as the person exists and endures as surely as the person endures. This body is a completed totality of material parts and therefore has a determinate, original shape (as discussed above). My body therefore would have to exercise some efficacy, be active, without *me* exercising my efficacy through it.

(β) But my body is *my* body only insofar as it is put into motion by my will; otherwise, it is only a mass of matter. It is active as my body only insofar as *I* am active through it. Now in the present case I am said not yet to be an *I* at all and thus also not active; my body is therefore also not active. Thus my body would have to exercise an efficacy by virtue of its shape and its mere existence in space; and indeed, it would have to exercise an efficacy such that every rational being would be obliged to recognize me as a being capable of reason and to treat me in accordance with that presupposition.

(γ) First of all, the most difficult point: how can something exercise any efficacy by means of its mere existence in space, without any motion?

The influence is supposed to be exercised upon a rational being *as rational*; thus it must not be exercised through immediate contact with, or restriction of, the rational being's lower organ; rather, it must be exercised upon its higher organ, and thus via the *subtler matter*. Now it was assumed above that this matter is a medium for the reciprocal influence of rational beings upon one another, since such matter could be modified by the movement of the higher organ itself. But that is not supposed to be the case here. Here, the human body is supposed to exercise an influence in a state of rest, without any activity: thus in this case, the subtler matter must be posited as capable of being modified by a *mere shape at rest*, and – in consequence of this modification – of modifying the higher sense of another possible rational being. – Thus far the human body has been regarded merely as a spatial shape, and thus what has been proved concerning it must be valid – and must be posited as valid – for all shapes.

[76] (It has not been proved that the subtle matter just discussed – i.e. the subtle matter through which a mere spatial shape is said to exercise its efficacy – is specifically distinct from the subtle matter derived above; rather, it has only been proved that the subtle matter must have both of these properties. The first claim would be proved if it could be shown that the matter that can be modified by a mere shape cannot be directly moved by the movement of the organ, but rather is imperturbable and immovable with respect to it. A proof of this is not really relevant to our present argument, but I want to provide it here, so that the various issues do not get scattered too far apart.[)] – The shape of the person outside me must continue to be the same shape for him, if he is to appear to himself as the same person; and his shape must continue to be the same for me if he is to appear to me as the same person. Now suppose that we stand in reciprocal interaction with one another via the moveable subtle matter (e.g. we speak with one another). Then this matter, A, would continually change, and if it were the matter in which our shapes were imprinted, they would also continually change for us both; but this contradicts our presupposition, namely, that – in conformity with both of our representations – the same persons must stand in reciprocal interaction with each other. Therefore, the matter in which our shapes are imprinted must be immovable and imperturbable amidst the constant motion of matter A; thus the matter in which our shapes are imprinted must be incapable of being modified for our organ; it must therefore be a matter, B, distinct from A: *air* or *light*. (Appearances in light can be modified by us only mediately, i.e. only to the extent that the shape itself can be modified.)

(δ) My body must be visible to the person outside me; it must appear to him through the medium of light, and it must have appeared to him, *as surely as he exercises an efficacy on me*. With this, the first and smallest part of our question has been answered. Now according to our necessary presupposition, this appearance of my body must be such that it cannot be understood or comprehended at all except under the presupposition that I am a rational being; i.e. its appearance must be such that I could say to the other: just as you behold this shape, so must you [77] necessarily take it to be the representation of a rational being in the sensible world, if you yourself are a rational being. – How is this possible?

First of all – what does it mean to *understand*, or *comprehend*? It means to *posit as fixed*, to *determine*, to *delimit*. I have comprehended an appearance if, through it, I have attained a complete cognitive whole that, with respect to all of its parts, is grounded in itself; i.e. if each part is grounded or explained through all the others, and *vice versa*. Only in this way is it completed or delimited. – I have not comprehended something if I am still in the midst of explaining it, if my interpretation of it is still in a *state of oscillation* and therefore not yet fixed; i.e. if I am still being led from one part of my cognition to the others. (I have not yet comprehended some contingent A, if I have not thought of a cause for A, and this means – since a particular kind of contingency must belong to A – if I have not thought of a particular cause for it.) Hence, to say that I cannot understand an appearance except in a certain way, means this: I am always driven from the individual parts of the appearance to a certain point; and only when I have arrived at this point can I order the parts that I have gathered together and comprehend them all together in a cognitive whole. Hence, to say that I cannot understand the appearance of a human body except by assuming it to be the body of a rational being, means this: in gathering together the parts of the appearance of the human body, I cannot stop until I have arrived at the point where I must think of it as the body of a rational being. I shall carry out this genetic proof in strict terms, i.e. I will present its main moments. The proof cannot be presented in complete detail here. On its own, this proof constitutes a separate science, anthropology.

(ε) First of all, it would have to be necessary to think of the human body as a *whole* and impossible to separate its parts conceptually, as can be done in the case of objects that are merely raw matter, e.g. rubble, piles of sand, and so forth. But anything constituted such that it must necessarily [78] be thought as a whole, is called an *organized product of nature*. First of all, the human body must be an organized product of nature. What an organized product of nature is, and why and to what extent it is to be thought only as a whole, can best be understood by comparing it with a *product of artifice*; the latter is similar to the product of nature insofar as it, too, can be thought only as a whole. In both kinds of product, each part exists for the sake of the others, and thus for the sake of the whole; and therefore, in observing either kind of product, the faculty of judgment is driven from the positing of one part to all the others, until it has completed its comprehension. But in the product of nature, the whole also exists for the sake of the parts; it has no purpose other than to produce these parts in a specific way. In a product of artifice, by contrast, the whole does not point back to the parts, but rather to an end outside itself; it is an instrument for something else. Furthermore, in the product of nature each individual part produces itself by its own inner force, and so all the individual parts produce the whole; but with the product of artifice, this inner formative drive had to be killed off before it could even become a product of artifice; the product of artifice does not depend on this inner formative drive, but rather on being composed in accordance with mechanical laws. For this reason, the product of artifice points to a creator outside itself, while the product of nature, by contrast, continually produces itself, and maintains itself precisely insofar as it produces itself.

(ζ) An appearance is fully understood through the assumption that it is a product of nature, if everything found in it refers back to its organization, and can be fully explained by reference to the purpose of its determinate organization. For example, the highest and final – the most developed – stage of the organizational force in the individual plant is the seed. Now the seed can be fully explained by reference to the plant's being organized as purpose: by means of the seed, the species is reproduced; by means of it, the plant's organization returns back into itself, and recommences its course from the beginning. The act of organization is not ended, but rather drives itself onward in an eternal cycle. [79] Thus to say that an appearance is not fully comprehended through the assumption that it is a product of nature, means this: the final and highest product of the formative drive cannot be referred back to this drive as its means, but rather points to another purpose. In such a case, explanation may well proceed for some time in conformity with the laws of organization (and so it is not as if these laws cannot be applied at all, as is the case with the product of artifice); but one reaches a point at which one can no longer explain things in terms of these laws; i.e. the final product of the formative drive cannot be referred back to them. In such a case, the circuit is not closed and the concept is not completed, i.e. nothing is *comprehended*: the appearance is not understood. (Of course, by reproducing the species, the human being also completes the circuit of organization. The human being is a consummate plant; but he is also more.)

Now such a being would be an instance of *articulation*, which must necessarily be visible and which is a product of the process of organization. But articulation does not in turn produce organization, but points instead to another purpose, i.e. articulation is fully comprehended and reduced to a unity only through another concept. This could be the concept of determinate *free movement*, and then the human being would be an *animal*.

(η) But the human body cannot be understood even through this assumption. Thus the articulation of the human body would have to be such that it could not be comprehended through any *determinate* concept at all. Its articulation would have to point not to some *determinate sphere* of arbitrary movement, as in the case of animals, but rather to all conceivable movements *ad infinitum*. The articulation would not have any determinacy but only an infinite determinability; it would not be formed in any particular way but would be only formable. – In short, all animals are complete and finished; the human being is only intimated and projected. The rational observer is completely unable to unite the parts of the human body except in the concept of *his equal*, in the concept of freedom given to him by his own self-consciousness. In order to be able to think something here, the rational observer must supply the concept of himself, [80] because none is given to him; but with that concept he can now explain everything. Every animal *is* what it is: only the human being is originally nothing at all. He must become what he is to be: and, since he is to be a being for himself, he must become this through himself.[5] Nature completed all of her works; only from the human being did she withdraw her hand, and precisely by doing so, she gave him over to himself. Formability, as such, is the character of humanity. Because it is impossible to superimpose upon a human shape any concept other than that of oneself, every human being is inwardly compelled to regard every other human being as his equal.

---

[5] This passage is a striking illustration of the extent to which Fichte's conception of subjectivity anticipates some of the foundational principles of existentialism. It is worthy of note that, contrary to most existentialists, Fichte takes the lack of a given human nature to imply a certain political ideal, namely, universal equality of rights.

Corollaries

(1) A vexing question for philosophy, which, as far as I know, it has not yet anywhere resolved, is this: how do we come to transfer the concept of rationality on to some objects in the sensible world but not on to others; what is the characteristic difference between these two classes of objects?

Kant says: act so that the maxim of your will can be the principle of a universal legislation.[6] But then who is to be included in the kingdom governed by such legislation and thus share in the protection it affords? I am supposed to treat certain beings such that I can will that they, in turn, treat me in accordance with the same maxim. Yet every day I act upon animals and inanimate objects without ever seriously posing the question raised above. Now someone will say to me: it is obvious that we are speaking only of beings that are capable of representing laws, and therefore only of rational beings. With this, I admit, I have replaced the first indeterminate concept with another, but I certainly do not have an answer to my question. For then how do I know which particular object is a rational being? How do I know whether the protection afforded by that universal legislation befits only the white European, or perhaps also the black Negro; only the adult human being, or perhaps also the child? And how do I know whether it might not [81] even befit the loyal house-pet? As long as this question is not answered, that principle – in spite of all its splendor – has no applicability or reality.

Nature decided this question long ago. Surely there is no human being who, upon first seeing another human being, would immediately take flight (as one would in the presence of a rapacious animal) or prepare to kill and eat him (as one might do to a beast), rather than immediately expecting reciprocal communication. This is the case, not through habituation and learning, but through nature and reason, and we have just derived the law that makes it the case.

However, one should not think – and only a few need to be reminded of this – that the human being must first go through the long and difficult reasoning process we have just carried out, in order to understand that a certain body outside him belongs to a being that is his

---

[6] This is Fichte's paraphrase of Kant's categorical imperative, the supreme principle of the latter's moral theory. Kant gives several formulations of the categorical imperative, but the one closest to Fichte's statement of it here is: "So act that the maxim of your will could always hold at the same time as a principle in a giving of universal law." See Kant's *Critique of Practical Reason* (1788), trans. Mary Gregor (Cambridge, UK: Cambridge University Press, 1997), §7.

equal. Such recognition either does not occur at all, or it is achieved instantaneously, without one being aware of the reasons for it. Only the philosopher is required to give an account of such reasons.

(2) We shall dwell a few more moments on the outlook that has been opened to us.

(a) Every animal, a few hours after its birth, moves and seeks nourishment at the breast of its mother. It is guided by *animal instinct*, the law of certain free movements, a law that also grounds what has been called the animal's *mechanical drive*. To be sure, the human being has a plant-like instinct, but he has no animal instinct at all in the meaning given here. He needs the freely given assistance of other human beings, and without it would die shortly after birth. When the human offspring has left its mother's body, nature withdraws her hand from it and cuts it loose, so to speak. Because of this, *Pliny*[7] and others have inveighed forcefully against nature and her creator. This may have its rhetorical point, but it is not philosophical. For it is precisely nature's abandonment of him that proves that the human being, as such, neither is nor should be nature's pupil. [82] If the human being is an animal, then he is an utterly incomplete animal, and for that very reason he is not an animal. It has often been thought that the free spirit existed for the sake of caring for animal nature. Such is not the case. Animal nature exists for the sake of bearing the free spirit in the sensible world and of binding it with the sensible world.

Because of this utter helplessness, humanity is made to depend on itself. This means first and foremost that the species is made to depend on the species. Just as the tree maintains its species by shedding its fruit, so too does the human being maintain itself, as a species, by caring for and raising its helpless offspring. In this way, reason produces itself, and only in this way is reason's progress towards perfection possible. In this way, the generations are linked to one another, and every future generation preserves the spiritual achievements of all preceding ones.

(b) The human being is born naked, the animal clothed. In her creation of animals, nature has completed her work and has imprinted the seal of that completion upon it; by means of a rougher cover, nature has protected the finer organization of the animal against the influence of the coarser matter. In human beings the first and most important

[7] Pliny the Elder (23–79) was a Roman official and the author of a 37-volume work, *Natural History*. The view alluded to here is found in Book VII.

organ, that of touch, is spread throughout the entire skin and exposed directly to the influence of the coarser matter: not because of nature's neglect, but because of her respect for us. That organ was designed to touch matter immediately, so that matter could be made to conform to our ends in the most precise of ways. But nature left us free to determine in which part of our body we want to locate our capacity to shape matter, and which parts we want to regard as mere mass. We have located this capacity in our finger tips, for a reason that will soon become apparent. It is located there, because we have so willed it. We could have given the same refined feeling to every part of our body, if we had so willed it; this is demonstrated by people who sew and write with their toes, who talk without moving their lips, and so forth.

(c) As we already noted above, every animal has innate skills pertaining to bodily movement. Consider, for example, the beaver, the bee, and so forth. The human being has nothing of this kind, and even [83] the newborn's position in lying on its back is [not innate but] given to it, in order to prepare it to walk upright in the future. – It has been asked whether the human being was designed to walk upright or on four feet. I believe he is designed to do neither; it has been left up to him, as a species, to choose his manner of motion for himself. A human body can run on four feet, and humans who were raised among animals have been discovered who could do this with incredible swiftness. In my view, the human species has freely lifted itself up from the earth and has thereby earned for itself the capacity to cast its gaze in every direction, in order to survey half of the universe in the skies. By contrast, the eyes of the animal, because of their position, are riveted to the earth, which brings forth its nourishment. By lifting himself up from the earth, the human being has wrested from nature two instruments of freedom: two arms that, relieved of all animal functions, hang from the body only to await the will's command and be made suitable for its ends. Through its daring, upright gait – an everlasting expression of its audacity and skill – the species, in maintaining its balance, also maintains its freedom and reason in constant practice; it remains perpetually in a state of becoming, and gives expression to this. By its upright position, the species transports its life into the kingdom of light, and constantly flees from the earth, which it touches with the smallest possible part of itself. For the animal, the earth serves as both bed and table; the human being raises his bed and table above the earth.

(d) The cultivated human being is characterized most distinctly by a spiritual eye and a mouth that reflects the heart's innermost stirrings. I am not talking about the fact that the eye can move around freely by the muscles that secure it and that its gaze can be cast in this or that direction; this mobility is also increased by the human's upright position, but it is still mechanical in itself. Rather, I am calling attention to the fact that for the human, the eye, in and of itself, is not simply a dead, passive mirror, like the surface of still water, [84] or an artificially produced mirror, or the eye of an animal. It is a powerful organ that self-actively circumscribes, outlines, and reproduces spatial shapes. It self-actively sketches out the figure that is to emerge from raw marble or that is to be projected upon a canvas before the chisel or paint brush is set in motion; it self-actively creates an image for a freely constructed mental concept. Through this live, continual weaving together of parts, the eye, so to speak, tears off and throws away the earthly matter of those parts; the eye is transfigured into light and becomes a visible soul. – This is why the more spiritual a person's self-activity is, the more spiritual is his eye; the less spiritual his self-activity, the more his eye remains a dull, fog-covered mirror.

The mouth, which nature designed for the lowest and most selfish of functions – that of nourishment – becomes, through the human's self-cultivation, the expression of all social sentiments, just as it is the organ of communication. As the individual, or – since we are talking here about fixed parts of the species – as the race becomes more animal-like and more self-seeking, the mouth protrudes more; as the race becomes more noble, the mouth recedes beneath the arch of the thinking forehead.

All of this, the whole expressive face, is nothing as we emerge from the hands of nature; it is a soft mass of confluent tissues within which one can detect, at most, only what is yet to become of it once one imposes on it an idea of one's own development; – and it is precisely because of this incompleteness that the human being is capable of such formability.

All of these things – not considered in isolation, the way philosophers split them up, but rather in their amazing, instantaneously grasped connection, as given to the senses – these are what compels everyone with a human countenance to recognize and respect the human shape everywhere – regardless of whether that shape is merely intimated and must still be transferred (albeit with necessity) to the body that intimates it, or whether that shape already exists at a certain level of completion. [85] The human shape is necessarily sacred to the human being.

§7
Proof that the concept of right can be applied through the propositions established

(I) Persons as such are to be absolutely free and dependent solely on their will. Persons, as surely as they are persons, are to stand with one another in a state of mutual influence, and thus not be dependent solely on themselves. The task of the science of right is to discover how both of these statements can exist together: the question that lies at the basis of this science is: *how is a community of free beings, qua free beings, possible?*

Until now we have demonstrated the *external* conditions of this possibility. We have explained (under the presupposition of these external conditions) how persons standing in a state of mutual influence, and how the sphere of their mutual influence (i.e. the sensible world), must be constituted. The proof of our propositions is based solely on the presupposition of such a community, which is itself grounded on the possibility of self-consciousness. Thus all the conclusions up to this point have been derived, by way of mediate inferences, from the postulate I am I; thus they are just as certain as this postulate. Our systematic path now leads us to a discussion of the *inner* conditions of such reciprocal interaction.

The point at which we left off is the point from which we shall now progress further: at the basis of all voluntarily chosen reciprocal interaction among free beings there lies an original and necessary reciprocal interaction among them, which is this: the free being, by his mere presence in the sensible world, compels every other free being, without qualification, to recognize him as a person. The one free being provides the particular appearance, the other the particular concept. Both are necessarily united, and freedom does not have the least amount of leeway here. – In this way, a common cognition emerges, and nothing more. Both [86] recognize each other in their inner being, but they are isolated, as before.

Present in each of the two beings is the concept that the other is a free being and not to be treated as a mere thing. Now if all their other concepts were determined by this concept, and if (since their willing is also part of their concepts) their actions were determined by this willing, then (if all their willing and acting were conditioned by the law of contradiction, i.e. if there were rational necessity here), they *would* not *be able to will* to affect one another arbitrarily, i.e. they could not do so at all; they could not *ascribe* to themselves the physical power to do so, and thus they would not *have* such a power.

Now obviously this is not the way things are. Each has also posited the body of the other as matter, as formable matter, in accordance with the following concept: each has ascribed to himself in general the capacity to modify matter. That is why each can obviously subsume the body of the other, insofar as it is matter, under that concept: each can think of himself as modifying the body of the other through his own physical power; and he can also *will* this, since his will is limited by nothing but his capacity to think.

But precisely because each is free (i.e. because each can make choices within the entire sphere of his efficacy), each can limit the exercise of his power, each can prescribe laws (and in particular the law that has just been indicated) for such exercise. Thus, the validity of the law depends solely on whether someone is consistent or not. But consistency here depends on the freedom of the will, and it is not clear why someone should be consistent, when he *need* not be; it is just as unclear why he should *not* be consistent. The law would have to be directed towards freedom. – Here, therefore, is the dividing line between necessity and freedom within our science.

(II) It is not possible to provide an absolute reason why the rational being should be consistent and why it, in consequence of this, should adopt the law that has been established. But perhaps it is possible to offer a hypothetical reason. Now it can be demonstrated immediately that, if an absolute community [87] among persons, as persons, is to exist, then every member of such a community would have to adopt the above law. Persons reciprocally treat one another as persons only insofar as each exercises an influence on the other's higher sense, and therefore only insofar as each leaves it up to the freedom of the other to accept such an influence, but leaves the lower organ completely unaffected and unconstrained. Any other kind of influence cancels the freedom of the one who is influenced, and therefore cancels the community of persons as persons, as free beings. But now, as we have just seen, it is physically quite possible for each person to exercise an immediate influence on the material body of the other person. If a person in an enduring community *never* wills to exercise such an influence, then this is thinkable only if one assumes that he has accepted that law and thereby prescribed limits to the freedom of his will; and – since it is not possible to find a reason for limiting one's will in this way, other than that there should be a community among free beings as such – this is thinkable only if one assumes that the person has accepted this law for *this* reason and with this presupposition.

If it could now be shown that every rational being must necessarily will such a community, then the necessity of the postulated consistency could also be demonstrated. But that cannot be demonstrated on the basis of the premises established thus far. It has indeed been shown that, if a rational being is to come to self-consciousness – and hence if it is to become a rational being – then another rational being must necessarily exercise an influence upon it as upon a being capable of reason. These are reciprocal propositions: no influence as upon a rational being, no rational being. But that, even after self-consciousness has been posited, rational beings must continue to influence the subject of self-conscious-ness in a rational manner, is not thereby posited, and cannot be derived without using the very consistency that is to be proven as the ground of the proof.

Thus the postulate that a community among free beings as such ought to have an enduring existence appears [88] here as arbitrary, as a postulate that each could adopt simply by his own free choice; but if one adopts this postulate, one thereby necessarily makes oneself subject to the above law. (The rational being is not absolutely bound by the character of rationality to will the freedom of all rational beings outside him. This proposition is the dividing line between a science of natural right and morality, and it is the distinguishing characteristic of a pure treatment of natural right. Within the sphere of morality, there is an obligation to will this. In a theory of natural right, one can only say to each person that such and such will follow from his action. Now if the person accepts this or hopes to escape it, no further argument can be brought against him.)

(III) Let us assume that I have resolved with complete freedom, as this has been understood above, to exist in community with free beings, and – to make our argument clearer – to exist in community with a particular free being, C, as one free being with another. What have I posited thereby, and what have I not posited? We shall *analyze* this proposition.

I want to stand with C in a *community* of rational, mutual treatment. But a community is nothing without *several* beings. That is why I necessarily also think of the person C here, and in my concept of him I ascribe to him the same intention I have. – I myself have freely adopted this intention; in accordance with it, I think of C as free; I must also think of him as free in his adoption of the intention that I ascribe to him in my concept of him. Therefore, I necessarily posit our community as dependent also on the free decision of the other and therefore as contingent, as the result of a *reciprocal willing*.

I want nothing more than to stand with him in a *community* of rational treatment; this way of proceeding is to be mutual. We *both* want to treat each other in this way. He me, I him; I him, he me. Therefore, if *he* does not treat me in this way, then I have posited *nothing* in my intention; and if there exists nothing beyond [89] this intention, then I have posited nothing at all. I have not posited that I want to treat him as a free being even if he does not treat me as one; just as little have I posited that in that case I want to treat him as an unfree being and thus treat him as he treats me. With respect to these matters, I have posited neither the one nor the other; I have posited nothing at all. Just as *his* treatment of me does not fit under my concept, so too my concept, as it has been established, ceases to apply, and the law that I prescribed to myself through that concept, as well as the obligation I imposed upon myself, also cease to apply. I am no longer bound by them, and once again I am dependent solely on my free decision.

(IV) These are the results of what has been said so far: It is not possible to point to an absolute reason why someone should make the formula of right – limit your freedom so that the other alongside you can also be free – into a law of his own will and actions. This much is clear: a community of free beings as such cannot exist if each is not subject to this law; and therefore, whoever wills such a community must also necessarily will the law; and thus the law has hypothetical validity. *If* a community of free beings as such is to be possible, then the law of right must hold.

But even that condition, the community of free beings, is conditioned in turn by a common willing. No one can realize such a community with another by his own will alone, if the other does not have the same will and if he does not subject himself, in consequence of that will, to the law of right that is conditioned by it. If the other does not have this will (and the sure proof of this is that he treats the first person in a manner contrary to the law of right), then the first one is, by virtue of the law itself, absolved from adhering to that law. The law held only under the condition that the other behaved in accordance with the principle of right; this condition does not obtain: therefore the law, according to its own expression, is not applicable to this case, and if there [**90**] is no further law, as is presupposed here, then the first person is left simply and solely to his own arbitrary will: he has a right against the other.

The difficulty which, for the most part, has been left unresolved by previous treatments of the theory of right is this: how is it possible for a law to command by not commanding? how can a law have force by not being in force? how can a law encompass a sphere by not encompassing it? The answer is: all this necessarily follows if the law prescribes a determinate sphere for itself, if it directly carries within itself the quantity of its own validity. As soon as the law indicates the sphere to which it applies, it thereby simultaneously determines the sphere to which it does not apply; it explicitly holds itself back from saying anything about this sphere and making prescriptions with respect to it. – In relation to a particular person, I am absolved from adhering to the law requiring me to treat him as a free being, and the question of how I will treat him depends solely upon my free choice, or I have a right of coercion against him. These claims mean, and can mean, nothing other than: this person cannot, *through the law of right alone*, prevent my coercion of him (although he may well do so through other laws, by physical strength, or by appealing to the moral law). My coercion is not contrary to *this* law, and if the other person has nothing to appeal to but it, he must endure my coercion of him.[a]

(V) The applicability of the concept of right is now completely secured, and its limits have been precisely determined.

---

[a]   In his essay *On Perpetual Peace*, *Kant* brings the concept of a *lex permissiva*[8] to the attention of theorists of natural right. Such a law is one that carries within itself the quantity of its own validity. Insofar as such a law encompasses a particular sphere, it leaves free everything that lies outside it. The moral law is not of this kind. It does not posit a particular sphere for itself, but governs all acts of rational spirits; thus, the concept of right is not to be derived from it.

[8]   Permissive law. See n. 15, p. 13.

A sure criterion has been established for determining which sensuous beings are to have rights ascribed to them, and which are not. Everyone [91] who has a human shape is internally compelled to recognize every other being with the same shape as a rational being, and therefore as a possible subject of right. But everything that does not have this shape is to be excluded from the sphere of this concept, and there can be no talk of the rights of such beings.

The possibility of what is to be determined by the concept of right and what is to be judged in accordance with it has been demonstrated: the mutual influence of free and rational beings upon one another. It has been shown that such beings *can* have an influence upon one another without harming their character of being free.

The law of right, as a law in general, has been determined. It has been demonstrated that it is in no way a mechanical law of nature, but rather a law for freedom: for, physically speaking, it is just as possible for rational beings to treat each other without mutual respect for each other's freedom and by means of natural force alone, as it is for each to limit his power through the law of right. It has been demonstrated that, if this law is to hold in actuality, if it is to be carried out in practice, then everyone must continually and freely make it a law for himself.

The quantity of the applicability of this law has been determinately stated. It holds in general only under the condition and in the event that a community, a reciprocal influence among free beings as such, is to exist without harm to their freedom. But since the end of this community itself is in turn conditioned by the behavior of the person with whom one wants to enter into community, the law's validity for the individual person is in turn conditioned by whether or not the other person subjects himself to the law. But if the other does not subject himself to the law, then the law holds precisely by not holding, and it entitles the one who has been treated contrary to right to treat the offender as he wills.

[92] Third main division
Systematic application of the concept of right; or the doctrine of right

§8

Deduction of the subdivisions within a doctrine of right

(I) If reason is to be realized at all in the sensible world, it must be possible for several rational beings to exist alongside one another as such, i.e. as free beings.

But the postulated coexistence of the freedom of several beings – and this obviously means *enduring* coexistence in accordance with a rule, not merely coexistence here and there by chance – is possible only insofar as *each free being makes it a law for himself to limit his freedom through the concept of the freedom of all others.* For:

(a) the free being *can*, and has the physical capacity to, interfere with the freedom of other rational beings, or to annihilate it completely; but

(b) with respect to choosing from among all the things he can do, the free being is dependent only on his free will; thus if he does not interfere with the freedom of others, this would have to be the result of a *free decision*; and

(c) if within a community of rational beings such interference *never* occurs and *never* can occur, the only possible explanation for this is that all the free beings have freely made this way of acting into a *law* for themselves.

(The proposition just set forth is nothing more than the judgment of the philosopher who reflects on the possibility of a community of free beings, and should neither be nor mean anything more. *If* free beings as such are to coexist, then their coexistence can be thought only in the manner indicated; this [93] can be proved, and has been proved satisfactorily. The issue is not whether they are to coexist or whether the condition of the possibility of such coexistence (the law) occurs. Nor is it a question of who wills one thing or the other. – For now we can say only this much about the law-giver: It is nature that willed a plurality of rational and free beings to exist alongside one another in the sensible world, insofar as she produced a plurality of bodies that can be cultivated to possess reason and freedom. This does not mean that nature has understanding and a will; about that we are resigned to ignorance. Rather, it simply means: *if* one were to ascribe an understanding and a will to nature in her various operations, her plan could be none other than that free beings should exist alongside one another. Thus it would be nature that willed that the freedom of each individual should be limited by the possibility of the freedom of all others. But since nature wills that everyone should be completely free, she also wills that they freely impose this law upon themselves – that is, she wills that it be a law for freedom, not one of her mechanical laws. What kind of measures nature may have hit upon in order to achieve her end without harming the freedom of such individuals, will become apparent.)

First, we shall once again analyze the law that has been set forth.

(a) It is to be a *law*, i.e. no exceptions to it are to be possible; once it has been accepted, it is to command universally and categorically.

(b) In consequence of this law, everyone is to limit his *freedom*, i.e. the sphere of his freely chosen actions and expressions in the sensible world. Accordingly, the concept of freedom here is *quantitative* and *material*.

(c) One is supposed to limit one's freedom by the possibility of the *freedom* of others. Here, the same word (freedom) has another meaning, one that is merely *qualitative* and *formal*. Each is said only to be able to be free in general, to be a person: but the law, at first, says nothing about *how far* the sphere of each person's possible free actions is supposed to extend. No one has a right to an action [94] that makes the freedom and personality of another impossible; but everyone has a right to all other free actions.

Therefore, the first question is: what is entailed by the idea that someone is free in general, or is a person? Since here we are considering the content of this idea as a condition of the possibility of the co-existence of free beings, such content is to be called *a right*; and for the same reason, the conditions of freedom and personality will be set forth here only insofar as they can be violated by physical force.

This right, or these rights, are contained in the mere concept of the person as such and are therefore called *original rights*. The doctrine of original rights arises through the mere analysis of the concept of personality insofar as the content of this concept *could* be, but – in accordance with the law of right – *ought* not to be, violated by the free action of others.

The doctrine of original right will constitute the first chapter of our doctrine of right.

(II) The judgment that has just been established is *hypothetical*. If free beings as such are to exist alongside one another, then each of them must impose upon himself the law we have described. The antecedent (which we do not know to be posited or not) is conditioned by the consequent: *if* they are to coexist, then each must give this law to himself, and if they do not give it to themselves, then they cannot exist with one another. – Thus the only reason the philosopher has for assuming that there is such a law is the presupposition that these free beings are to co-exist.

From this, we can draw the following conclusions. The law is conditioned, and a possible being that might want to give the law to himself can – so far as we know, at least up to this point – give it to himself only as a conditioned law. Such a being adopts this law in order to attain the end that the law presupposes. Thus the rational being can subject itself to the law only insofar as this end is attainable; or stated otherwise, the law holds for the rational being only insofar as the end is attainable.

But now the end of existing with another person in a community of freedom is attainable only under the condition [95] that this other person has also imposed upon himself the law of respecting the first person's freedom, or his original rights. This law is completely inapplicable to my behavior with respect to someone who has not given this law to himself, since the end for the sake of which I was supposed to respect the other person's original rights no longer exists. Thus although I have subjected myself to the law in general, I am nevertheless not bound – in consequence of the law itself – to respect the freedom of this particular person. –

I think of myself as both subject to the law and not subject to it: I *think of myself* as subject to the law *in general* but as not subject to it in this particular case. In consequence of the former, I act *in accordance with right*, under the command of the law, and thus I possess a *right*; in consequence of the latter, I may violate the other person's freedom and personality, and my right is thus a *right of coercion*.

(a) Because the law is *conditioned*, and can be adopted only as conditioned, each person has the right to *judge* [*urteilen*] whether or not the law applies to a particular case. Here such judging – since it occurs with a view to the law of right – is *judging in a legal sense* [*ein Richten*]. Each is necessarily his own *judge* [*Richter*], and here – wherever a right of coercion exists – the one who has this right is at the same time the judge of the other against whom he has it; for the *right of coercion* is possible only on the basis of such a knowledge of right. But apart from this condition, no one is originally the judge of another, nor can he be. – The result of these inferences is: *there is no right of coercion without the right of passing legal judgment.*

(b) The person who is supposed to have the right of coercion must himself stand under the law and be thought of as having subjected himself to it; and as being someone about whom it cannot be proved – at least from his actions – that he does not obey the law. Otherwise, he may very well have the power to coerce another person, but never the right to do so, since such a right flows only from the law. Furthermore, one should pay attention to *the* character of the right of coercion, [96] namely, that this right flows only from the law's silence, from its general non-applicability to a particular case, and not in any way from a *command* of the law. This is why there is only a *right* to coerce, a right a person may or may not avail himself of, but by no means a *duty* to coerce.

From this deduction of the *right of coercion*, it is clear when such a right can exist: namely, when a person has violated the original rights of another. Therefore, once original rights have been set forth in the first chapter, it will become clear when they are violated. Nevertheless, for the sake of a systematic overview, it will not be superfluous to enumerate and clarify the cases in which the right of coercion exists; this will be done in the second chapter of the doctrine of right.

(III) The right of coercion in general, including every particular instance of it, has its ground; but everything that is grounded is necessarily finite and extends no further than its ground. Thus, if one can determine the limit of the applicability of the ground, one can also indicate the limit of what is grounded. The ground of my right of coercion is the fact that the other person does not subject himself to the law of right. By appealing to this ground, I simultaneously posit that I would have no right of coercion if the other person subjected himself to the law, and – expressed quantitatively – that I have such a right only to the extent that he does not subject himself to the law and that I have no such right at all if he does subject himself to it. – The right of coercion has its limit in the other's voluntary subjection to the law of right; any coercion beyond this limit is contrary to right. This general proposition is obvious at once. The only question (since we are propounding a real and not merely formal doctrine of natural right) is whether and how this limit can be found and determined in applying the law. A right of coercion does not exist unless an *original right* has been violated; but when there has been a violation, such a right surely does exist, and in this way the right of coercion can be demonstrated in every particular case. Furthermore, it is immediately clear that [97] anyone who wills that the right of coercion exist does not will the violation of an original right and, if such a violation does occur, he wills that it be undone and annulled. In view of this, the law's quantity would then also be *demonstrable every time*. In each case, the limit of the rightful use of coercion could be determined: it would extend to the point of complete restitution and complete compensation for the violation; it would extend to the point where both parties were returned to the condition in which they found themselves prior to the unjust violation. Thus the right of coercion, with respect to both its quality and quantity, would be precisely determined by reference to the damage suffered and would not depend on any further condition.

But – and this is a circumstance that recent treatments of the doctrine of right have for the most part overlooked – the right of coercion is by no means grounded simply on the fact that the other person fails to respect the law only in the present, particular case. Rather it is grounded first and foremost on the fact that – by his present violation – he makes it known that he has not made that rule into a universal law for himself. *One* action contrary to right, even after a series of rightful ones, proves that the rule of right is not an inviolable law for this person, and that until now he has refrained from unjust actions for quite different reasons. Now from this it becomes clear that no free being can live securely alongside him, since security can be grounded only on a law, and becomes possible only by being thus grounded; and thus the person who has suffered the violation acquires the right to annihilate completely the violator's freedom, to cancel altogether the possibility of ever again entering into community with him in the sensible world. Thus the right of coercion is *infinite* and has no limit whatsoever (a proposition that theorists of right have one-sidedly maintained at one moment, and one-sidedly denied the next), unless the violator accepts the law as such in his heart and subjects himself to it. But as soon as he accepts the law, the right of coercion ceases, for its duration was grounded solely on the duration of the other person's lawlessness; and from now on, any further coercion is contrary to right. In this respect the limit of the coercion is *conditioned.*

[98] Now how is the *condition*, the other person's sincere subjection to the law of right, to be given?

Not through his attestation of regret, his promise of better behavior in the future, his voluntary subjection to authority, his offer of compensation, etc., for these provide no reason to believe in his sincerity. It is possible that he has been moved to such behavior only by his present weakness, and that he is only waiting for a better opportunity to overpower the person he has violated; indeed, this is no less possible than that he is sincere and that a revolution has now suddenly occurred in his way of thinking. The person who has been violated cannot lay down his weapons and put his entire security at risk on the basis of such uncertainty. He will continue to exert coercion, but since the condition of this right is problematic, his right to continue exerting coercion is itself merely problematic.

By the same token, the first violator – if, perchance, he volunteered to provide compensation, which is unconditionally demanded by the law of right – will and must resist the coercion directed against him, because all of his freedom is threatened by it. Since there is always the possibility that, from now on, he might voluntarily subject himself to the rule of right as a law and never again undertake anything contrary to it, and since in that case the other's continuing coercion of him would be contrary to right, it follows that he may very well also possess the right to resist and to pursue the other until the other's freedom is completely destroyed: but *his* right to do so is also merely problematic.

Thus the factor that determines the limit of the right of coercion cannot be given – on an enduring basis and as a matter of right – in an external tribunal; the ground for deciding the issue lies within the conscience of each person. There is, so it seems, an irresolvable conflict of rights here. The ground for deciding the issue could be provided only *by the entirety of future experience.*

That is, if the first violator – after he is completely free again – were never again to undertake anything contrary to right, and if the person who was violated – after receiving restitution – were likewise to refrain freely from all further coercion, then [99] it would be reasonable to believe that the former had subjected himself to the law and that the latter had opposed him only in order to preserve his own rights (and therefore had never overstepped them). An experience of this kind would ground – on an enduring basis and as a matter of right – their mutual restoration of freedom, i.e. the abandonment of physical force by both sides.

But this mutual restoration of freedom – the peace between the two parties – is not possible, unless that experience has already taken place. For, in accordance with what was said above, no one can risk giving up his hard-won advantage over the other party by ignoring his legitimate suspicion and believing in the other's sincerity. *That which is grounded is not possible without the ground; and the ground is not possible without that which is grounded.* Thus we are caught in a circle. We shall soon see how, in such a case, one must proceed in accordance with the synthetic method, and we will see what – in the present investigation – the result of this method will be. But before doing so, we shall first take a closer look at what we have just discovered.

A right of coercion in general, as a universal concept, can easily be derived from the law of right; but as soon as one attempts to demonstrate how this right is applied, one gets entangled in an irresolvable contradiction. This is because the ground for deciding how to apply it cannot be given in the sensible world, but resides instead in each person's conscience. The right of coercion, as a concept that can be applied, stands in clear contradiction to itself, in that it is impossible to decide in any particular case whether the coercion is rightful or not.

Whether or not the wronged party himself can exercise the right of coercion depends on nothing less than an answer to the question of whether a genuine doctrine of natural right is possible, by which we mean a science of the relation of right between persons outside the state and without positive law. Since most theorists of right are content to philosophize formally about the concept of right, and – as long as their concept [100] is merely thinkable – care very little about how the concept can be applied, they very easily get around the question just posed. Here we have answered the first question – and thereby also the second – in the negative; and in order to be convinced of the undeniability of the present doctrine of right, one must come to see clearly that it is impossible for the wronged party himself to exercise the right of coercion (an impossibility that we have demonstrated here). Therefore, the proposition just established is of supreme importance for our entire doctrine of right.

The circle was this: the possibility of the mutual restoration of freedom between the two parties is conditioned by the entirety of future experience; but the possibility of future experience is conditioned by this mutual restoration of freedom. In order to eliminate the contradiction, these two elements will be synthetically united in accordance with the method demonstrated in the *Wissenschaftslehre*.[1] *The mutual restoration of freedom and the entirety of future experience must be one and the same*, or more clearly stated: the entirety of future experience that

---

[1] Fichte describes his synthetic method (the forerunner of Hegel's dialectical method) in §3 of the 1794 *Wissenschaftslehre* (*The Science of Knowledge*, pp. 111–13). The synthetic method proceeds dialectically by finding an apparent contradiction in one of its deduced concepts (or principles) and then searching for a "higher" (more complex) concept that is capable of resolving the contradiction without completely negating either of its poles. The clearest example of the method is found in §§1–3 of the same text. There Fichte first claims (§1) that the I is all of reality but then (§2) deduces a not-I that is opposed to it. The contradiction is resolved (§3) by introducing the concept of limitation (the idea that what is real need not encompass all of reality), which makes it possible (at least until the next contradiction is found) to grant both the I and not-I a degree of reality. This particular application of Fichte's synthetic method is discussed in more detail in Frederick Neuhouser, "The First Presentation of the *Wissenschaftslehre* (1794/ 95)," in *The Cambridge Companion to Fichte*, ed. Günter Zöller (Cambridge: Cambridge University Press, forthcoming).

both parties desire must already lie within and be guaranteed by the mutual restoration of freedom.

There is no doubt that this proposition had to be introduced; the only question is: how is what it requires possible?

First, it is immediately clear that, in consequence of what the proposition requires, the entirety of future experience – that is, the desired experience of the complete security of both – is to be made present in a single moment, the moment of their mutual restoration of freedom; and it is to be made present in a way that can be validated by external evidence, since neither party can know the inner dispositions of the other. Therefore, both would have to make it impossible, physically impossible, for themselves to violate one another further, and in such a way that the other party would have to see this impossibility and be convinced of it. Security for the future is called *a warranty, a guarantee*.

Thus the proposition above says: the parties must mutually guarantee security to one another; otherwise, they could no longer exist alongside one another, in which case one of them would necessarily have to be destroyed.

[101] The further question is: how is this guarantee possible? – The two parties were not able simply to lay down their weapons, because neither was able to trust the other. Therefore, they would have to place their weapons, i.e. their entire power, into the hands of a *third* party they both trust. They would have to commission this third party to repel whoever among them would violate the other. The third party would have to be capable of doing this, and therefore would have to *have superior power*. Thus this third party would exercise the right of coercion on behalf of both of them. – If the third party is to do this, they must give this party the authority to decide their present dispute as well as any dispute that could possibly arise between them in the future; that is, they would have to surrender to this party their *right to pass legal judgment* [*Recht des Gerichts*]. They must surrender this right to the third party without reservation, and with no right of appeal. For if one of them could guide the decision of their now common judge, then he would still be taking right into his own hands; but the other party does not trust him, and therefore cannot consent to such an arrangement. *Thus, both must unconditionally subordinate their physical power and their right to pass a judgment, i.e. all their rights, to that third party.*

(IV) *Thesis.* According to the law of right, the person's freedom is limited by nothing but the possibility that others alongside him can also be free and have rights. According to that law, a person is supposed to be permitted to do anything that does not infringe the rights of another, for the person's right consists precisely in this permission. Each person has the right to pass his own judgment on the limit of his free actions, and to defend this limit.

Antithesis. The same law of right implies that each person must completely and without reservation alienate his power and his capacity to pass judgments of right, if a rightful condition is ever to be possible among free beings. Through this, each person fully loses both the right to pass judgment on the scope of his rights and the right to defend them; each person thereby becomes [102] dependent on the knowledge and good will of the one to whom he has subjected himself, and thus ceases to be free.

This latter proposition contradicts the former. The former is the law of right itself; the latter is a correct inference drawn from that law. Thus, the law of right is in contradiction with itself. This contradiction must be canceled. The heart of the contradiction is this: within the province of the law of right, I can give up only so much of my freedom as is necessary in order that the rights of those with whom I enter into community in the sensible world can also exist. But now I am supposed to lay down all my rights and subject them to the opinion and authority of a stranger. This is impossible and contradictory, unless – in and through such subjection – all the freedom that properly belongs to me in my sphere, in accordance with the law of right, is secured.

Unless this condition is met, I cannot rationally subject myself to such an authority, and the law of right gives no one a right to demand that I do so. Thus I must be able to judge for myself whether this condition is met. My subjection of myself to the authority is conditional on the possibility of this judgment; such subjection is impossible and contrary to right if such a judgment is not made. Therefore, above all else, *I must subject myself with complete freedom.*

After having subjected myself, I no longer have a right to pass judgment on the scope of my rights (as has been expressly stated and proved); therefore, the requisite judgment must be possible and must actually be made *before* I subject myself. I am supposed to make the following judgment: "In being subjected, my rightful freedom will never be infringed; I will never have to sacrifice any more of that freedom than I would have had to sacrifice pursuant to the law of right and according to my own judgment." [103] Thus before I subject myself, I am to imagine the entirety of my future experience in the state of being subjected, i.e. I am to receive a guarantee that I will be completely secure within the limits of my rights.

First of all: *what* is supposed to be guaranteed to me? – The complete security of all my rights over against the one to whom I have subjected myself and – through his protection – over against all individuals with whom I might possibly enter into community. I ought to be able to see for myself that all possible future judgments of right that might be pronounced upon matters relating to me can turn out only as I myself would have to pronounce upon them in accordance with the law of right. Therefore, *norms* concerning these future judgments of right must be submitted for my inspection; it is in accordance with these norms that the law of right is applied to all cases that might possibly arise. Such norms are called *positive laws*; the system of such laws in general is called (positive) *law*.

(a) All positive laws stand, either more or less directly, under the rule of right. These laws do not and cannot contain anything arbitrary. They must exist precisely as every intelligent, informed person would necessarily have to prescribe them.

(b) In positive laws, the rule of right in general is applied to the particular objects governed by that rule. Positive law hovers midway between the law of right and a judgment of right. In positive law, the rule of right is applied to particular objects; in a judgment of right, positive law is applied to particular persons. – The civil judge has nothing to do other than to decide what happened and to invoke the law. If legislation is clear and complete, as it should be, then the judge's verdict must already be contained in the law.

The contradiction presented above has been canceled in part. When I subject myself to the law, a law that has been inspected and approved by me (which inspection is – as has been proved – the exclusive condition of the possibility of my being rightfully [104] subjected to it), I am not subjecting myself to the changeable, arbitrary will of a human being, but rather to a will that is immutable and fixed. In fact, since the law is exactly as I myself would have to prescribe it, in accordance with the rule of right, I am subjecting myself to my own immutable will, a will I

95

would necessarily have to possess if I am acting rightfully and therefore if I am to have any rights at all. I am subjecting myself to my will, a will that is the condition of my capacity for having rights at all; for if my will were different from this, it would be contrary to right, since the law is the only rightful will; and thus I would be entirely without rights, since only he who has subjected himself to the law of right can possess rights. Therefore, far from losing my rights through such subjection, I first acquire them through it, since only through such subjection do I show that I fulfill the exclusive condition under which someone has rights. Although I am subjected, I remain always subjected only to *my* will. I actually did exercise my right to be my own judge this one time, and I exercised it as applying to my entire life and to all possible cases; and the only thing that has been taken from me is the trouble of carrying out my judgments of right by my own physical power.

Result. One can rationally alienate one's power and ability to pass judgments of right only to the necessary and unbending will of the law, but by no means to the free and changeable will of a human being. The law of right requires only the former; only this kind of alienation is the condition of all rights. The latter alienation is not exactly contrary to the law, because right is not the same as duty, and so a person may in fact give up his rights; but this alienation does not follow from the law of right either.

(V) The contradiction presented above has been canceled in part, but only in part. The person who subjects himself was supposed to have been given a guarantee by the *law* for the future security of all his rights. But what is the law? A concept. How, then, is the law supposed to be brought to life, how is this bare concept to be realized in the sensible world? – We shall present the question from yet another angle.

To guarantee somebody the security of his rights [**105**] means: to make it impossible for those rights to be violated, and in such a way that the person must be convinced of that impossibility. Now through the subjection described above, the security of the subjected person is to be guaranteed, not only over against the one to whom he has subjected himself, but also over against all persons with whom he can ever enter into community; therefore, it is supposed to be completely impossible for the person's rights to be violated, and before he subjects himself, he is supposed to be able to convince himself of this complete impossibility. Now of course, this impossibility is contained in the will of the law; but the much larger question is: how, then, is the person supposed to be given *the* guarantee that the law, and only the law, will prevail?

The person is supposed to be secure before the law itself; therefore, it must never happen that the power of the law is used against him, except in those cases provided for by the law. Through the law, the person is supposed to be secure before all others: therefore, the law must constantly act where it is supposed to act. It must never rest once it has been awakened.

In short: *the law must be a power*: the concept of the *law* (from the preceding section of our investigation) and the concept of a *supreme power* (from the section immediately preceding that one) must be synthetically united. The law itself must be the supreme power, and the supreme power must be the law, both one and the same: and in subjecting myself I must be able to convince myself that this is so, that it is completely impossible for any force other than that of the law to be directed against me.

Our task is precisely defined. The question to be answered is: *how does the law become a power?* The power we are seeking does not exist immediately in nature; it is not a mechanical power (as was shown above), and human beings certainly have the physical power to perpetrate injustices. Thus, the power we are seeking must be one that depends on a will. But now this will is not supposed to be free, but necessarily and immutably determined by the law. [106] There can be no such will belonging to an individual – that is, a will on whose rightfulness every other person could always securely rely. Therefore, it must be that the will we are seeking would have power only in cases where it willed the law, and would have no power where it did not will the law; and so our task, defined more narrowly, is: *to find a will that is a power only when it wills the law, and is an infallible power when it does so*.

A supreme power over a free being could come about only if *several* free beings were to unite, for there is nothing in the sensible world more powerful than a free being (precisely because it is free and can reflectively and purposefully direct its power); and there is nothing more powerful than an individual free being except for several free beings. Their strength therefore would consist solely in their being united. Now their power is supposed to depend on the fact that they will the law, or right. Therefore, their *union* (upon which their power depends) would have to depend on the fact that they will the law, or right: their willing of right would have to constitute the only bond of their union. As soon as they willed what was contrary to right, their union and – along with that – their entire power would have to dissolve.

Now in every union of free beings it is necessarily the case that willing what is not rightful breaks the agreement. To say that a number of free beings become united means: they will to live with one another. But they cannot coexist unless each limits his freedom through the freedom of all the others. If a million human beings exist alongside one another, each individual may very well will for himself as much freedom as possible. But if the will of all were to be united into one concept as in one will, this will would divide the sum of possible freedom into equal parts, with the aim that all would be free together, and that therefore the freedom of each would be limited by the freedom of all the others.ª

[107] Thus right is the only possible basis for the unity of their wills; and since a specific number of human beings with specific inclinations, involvements, etc. exist together here, this means right as *applied to them*, i.e. their *positive law*. They will the law just as surely as they are all united. If even only one of them were to be oppressed, this one person would certainly not give his consent, in which case they would no longer all be united.

We have stated that the object of their agreement is their positive law, the law that determines the limits of the rights and freedoms of each

---

ª This is Rousseau's *volonté générale*, whose distinction from the *volonté de* [107] *tous* is by no means unintelligible.[2] All individuals will to keep as much as possible for themselves and to leave as little as possible for everyone else; but precisely because of this conflict in their will, the parts in conflict cancel each other out, and what remains as the final result is that each should have what belongs to him. If two people are involved in dealings with each other, it can always be assumed that each wants to gain an advantage over the other; but since neither of the two wants to be the disadvantaged one, this part of their will is mutually annihilated and their common will is that each receive what is right.

[2] Rousseau famously distinguishes the general will (*volonté générale*) from the will of all (*volonté de tous*): "There is often a great difference between the will of all and the general will. The latter considers only the common interest; the former considers private interest, and is only a sum of private wills. But take away from these same wills the pluses and minuses that cancel each other out, and the remaining sum of the differences is the general will" (Jean-Jacques Rousseau, *On the Social Contract*, ed. Roger D. Masters, trans. Judith R. Masters (New York: St. Martin's Press, 1978), II, ch. 3). Interpreters have traditionally found Rousseau's talk of pluses and minuses difficult to grasp, but Fichte offers a plausible reading of this passage that supports his own point here, namely, that the principle rational beings must agree on in the assigning of rights (their "common will") is equality of rights and freedom for all.

individual under particular circumstances. Now they need not articulate the will of this law explicitly, nor do they have to collect votes concerning it (which would result only in a very impure expression of that will). Anyone who knows their number, their involvements, their entire situation, can tell them what they all agree on. Their law is given to them by the rule of right and by their particular physical situation, just as a mathematical product is given by the two factors being multiplied; any intelligent being can attempt to find this law. In no way does the *content* of the law depend on arbitrary choice [*Willkür*], and the slightest influence of arbitrary choice upon the law makes it unjust and brings the seed of discord and the ground of future dissolution into this union. But the *form* of law, its binding force, is given only through the consent of individuals to unite with this particular group of people into a common being. Therefore, all are united only with respect to right and the law; [108] and whoever is united with all the others also necessarily wills right and the law. In such a union, every individual wills the same as all others. But as soon as two individuals are not united in their willing, then at least one of them is also not united with all the rest; his will is an individual will, and precisely for that reason it is an unjust will. If the will of the other party to this conflict of right agrees with the common will, then his will is necessarily right.

In such a union, there is no question that the just will – if it sets itself into action – will not always overpower the unjust will, since the latter is always only the will of an individual, but the former is the common will.

The only question is, how can things be arranged so that this common will is always active, and is always operative when it needs to suppress an individual will; so that, as a result, the physical powers of individuals relate to one another just as their wills relate to one another in the concept of their union; so that the individual powers are interwoven with the common power as one, just as – when the synthetic unity of the will of all constitutes one concept – the individual will is interwoven with the common will to form one will. This must follow necessarily and in accordance with a strict rule, for everyone who subjects himself is to be given a guarantee that is fully convincing to him; everyone is to be shown that it is absolutely impossible within this union for any power to take action against him other than that of the law, and that every other power will be immediately repelled by the law – that this does not depend in any way on chance or the good will of someone else, etc.; rather, the organization of the whole entails that the law must surely be exercised at all times.

The strongest and only sufficient guarantee that each individual can rightfully demand is that [**109**] society's very existence be bound up with the efficacy of the law.

In *general*, this is true simply by the nature of the case. If injustice were to become universal, society would necessarily have to dissolve and thereby perish. But if power is occasionally exercised beyond the bounds of the law, or if the law is inactive, the union does not necessarily break apart. Now this would be a poor guarantee for the individual – if it were the case that violence might be done to him personally and thus to other individuals as well, but that injustice could never be done to everyone all at once.

Thus the relation would have to be such that every single (even seemingly trivial) injustice against the individual necessarily entailed an injustice against all. How is this to be arranged? The law should necessarily be a deed, or fact.[3] It will always be a deed with complete certainty, if – conversely – the *deed* is *law*, i.e. if everything that any one individual is ever permitted to do in this union should become lawful simply because it is done by this individual this one time, and thus should be permitted to be done by anyone who desires to do it. In this kind of union, every injustice necessarily affects everyone; every transgression is a public offense; what was permitted to be done to me is from now on permitted to be done to every individual in the entire community, and thus – in order for even one person to be secure – the first business *of all* must be to protect me, to help me in securing my rights, and to punish what is not rightful. It is clear that this guarantee is sufficient – that through such an arrangement the law will always be operative but will never transgress its limit because, if it did, that transgression would be lawful for everyone.

It is clear that an individual who enters into such a union receives his freedom, though he also gives it up, and he receives his freedom precisely because he gives it up; that [**110**] all contradictions are dissolved by the concept of such a union and that the rule of right is

---

[3] To say that the law should necessarily be a deed (or fact) is to say that what the law commands should immediately and predictably become reality. The use of "deed" (*Tat*) is no doubt an allusion to Fichte's doctrine of the *Tathandlung* (see n. 1, p. 25), suggesting that the act of giving law ought to be a *Tathandlung*, an act of consciousness that at the same time constitutes reality.

realized because such a union is realized; that everyone who wills the rule of right must necessarily will such a union. – Thus the concept of such a union circumscribes the scope of our investigation. A more detailed analysis of this concept will be presented in the third chapter of the doctrine of right, *On the commonwealth*.

[111] FIRST CHAPTER OF THE DOCTRINE OF RIGHT
DEDUCTION OF ORIGINAL RIGHT

§9

How can an original right be thought?

It is possible to talk about rights only under the condition that a person is thought of as a person, that is, as an individual, and thus as standing in relation to other individuals; only under the condition that there is a community between this person and others, a community that – if not posited as real – is at least imagined as possible. What initially, and from a merely speculative perspective, are the conditions of personality become rights simply by thinking of other beings who – in accordance with the law of right – may not violate the conditions of personality. Now it is not possible to think of free beings as existing together unless their rights mutually limit each other, and therefore unless the sphere of their original rights is transformed into the sphere of their rights within a commonwealth. Therefore, it would be utterly impossible to reflect on rights merely as original rights, i.e. without considering the necessary limitations imposed by the rights of others. Nevertheless, an investigation into original rights must precede an investigation of rights within a commonwealth and must ground the latter investigation. Accordingly, one must [112] abstract from the limitations imposed by the rights of others, an abstraction that free speculation so readily engages in that it does so without even thinking, and only needs to be reminded of having done so. There is no difficulty, then, regarding the possibility of such abstraction.

What speculation needs to be reminded of and to have brought into focus is only *that* this abstraction has been made, and that therefore the concept it generates possesses ideal possibility (for thought), but no real meaning. If one disregards this point, one will arrive at a merely formal theory of right. – There is no condition in which original rights exist; and no original rights of human beings.[4] The human being has actual rights only in community with others, just as – according to the higher principles noted above – the human being can be thought of only in community with others. An original right, therefore, is a mere *fiction*, but one that must necessarily be created for the sake of a science of right. Furthermore, it is clear – and this must be repeated once again, though it has already been emphasized many times before – that the conditions of personality are to be thought of as rights only insofar as they appear in the sensible world and can be violated by other free beings (as forces in the sensible world). Thus there can be, for example, a right to self-preservation in the sensible world, to the preservation of my body as such, but by no means a right to *think* or to *will* freely. Moreover, it is clear that we do indeed have a right of coercion against someone who attacks our body, but definitely not against someone who disturbs us in our comforting beliefs or who offends us with his immoral behavior.

§10

Definition of original right

The principle of any judgment of right is that each is to limit his freedom, the sphere of his free actions, through the concept of the freedom of the other (so that the other, as free in general, can exist as well). The concept of freedom at issue here (which, as already stated above, has only formal meaning) yields the concept [113] of original right, that is, of that right that should belong absolutely to every person as such. We shall now discuss this concept more precisely.

With respect to *quality*, this concept is a concept of the capacity to be an absolutely first cause; with respect to *quantity*, what is comprehended under this concept has no limits at all, but is by its nature infinite, because what is at issue is only that the person is to be free in general,

---

[4] The assertion that human beings have no original rights must be understood to mean, at least, that in a state of nature original rights cannot be reliably enforced. Beyond this, Fichte might also be espousing the Hobbesean view that outside a state – in the absence of a sure guarantee that rights will be enforced – original rights do not give rise to genuine obligations to respect the freedom of others. This is suggested by his remarks to the effect that the obligation to respect others' rights is not absolute but conditional on having a reliable sign of their intent to respect one's own. See, for example, §12, III.

but not the extent to which he is to be free. Quantity stands in conflict with this concept as it has been put forth here as a merely formal concept. With respect to *relation*, the freedom of the person is at issue only insofar as the sphere of the free actions of others is to be limited in accordance with the law of right, because these others could make the required formal freedom impossible. This consideration determines the quantity [the scope] of the investigation. We are concerned here only with *causality* in the sensible world, as the only realm within which freedom can be limited by freedom. Finally, with respect to *modality*, this concept has apodeictic validity. Each person is to be free without qualification.

Original right is thus the absolute right of the person to be *only a cause* in the sensible world (and purely and simply never something caused).

§11

Analysis of original right

The concept of an effect – indeed, of an absolute effect – contains both of the following:

(1) that the quality and quantity of the action are fully determined by the cause itself;

(2) that the manner in which the object of the effect is affected, both qualitatively and quantitatively, follows immediately from the action's being posited; so that it is possible to go from one to the other: one can be immediately determined on the basis of the other, and both are necessarily known as soon as one is.

Insofar as the person is the absolute and final ground of the concept of his own efficacy, of his own concept of an end, the freedom that is expressed therein lies beyond the bounds of the present investigation, for that kind of freedom never enters the sensible world and cannot be restricted by anything within it. The will of the person enters the realm of the sensible world only insofar as it is expressed in a determination of his body. [114] Thus in this realm the body of a free being is to be regarded as itself the final ground of its own determination, and the free being – as appearance – is identical with its body. (The body is the I's representative in the sensible world, and where only the sensible world is being considered, it is the I itself. –) In everyday life we always think in this way: *I* was not there. He saw *me. He* was born, died, buried, and so forth.

Therefore:

(I) The body, regarded as a person, must be the absolute and final cause of its determination to exercise efficacy. The question of to what extent and according to which laws the body might be limited by its own organization is irrelevant here and does not enter into this account. The body *is* only what originally belongs to it. Yet – anything that is physically possible in the body must be permitted actually to be produced in it, if and only if the person wills it. The body must neither be set into motion nor restricted in its motion by any external cause; there must be absolutely nothing that immediately exercises an effect upon it.

(II) An effect in the sensible world that is made *possible* by the body's movement must infallibly follow from such movement. (Precisely *not* the movement that was merely thought or intended.) For if someone did not know the nature of things very well and did not accurately calculate his ability to act in opposition to their power of resisting him, then any resulting movement that is contrary to his intention is his own fault and he has no right to complain about anything outside himself. The only requirement is that the sensible world not be determined by an alien, free power that stands outside it and in opposition to the person's efficacy, for then the person would cease to be a free cause.

(III) But determining one's body purposively in order to affect a thing follows only on, and out of, a knowledge of the thing to be affected; thus, the free being is ultimately dependent after all. Now this point, in general, was already acknowledged some time ago and excluded from the present investigation. Efficacy and determinate knowledge reciprocally condition one another [115] and occupy the same sphere, as has been proved and explained above. One simply cannot will to produce effects beyond the givenness of objects; that would contradict the essential nature of reason: the person is free only in the sphere within which objects are given.

To describe this more precisely: it is within the sphere of the given and under the condition that something is given that one is free to leave the given as it is or to make it into something else – that is, as it ought to be in accordance with his concept of an end. The person is free to relate the manifold elements of the given reciprocally to one another, to determine them by means of one another, to adapt them to one another, and to arrange them into a whole that is purposive for him. If one of these pieces is missing, the person is not free and not dependent solely on his own will.

Now for this to be the case, it is necessary that *everything remain* as it was once known by the free being and posited in his concept (regardless of whether it is now specifically modified by him or not). What has not been modified but only thought by the rational being and brought into conceptual alignment with his world becomes modified, precisely by *not having been modified*. It is in consequence of his concept of the end of the whole (to which this particular thing is supposed to conform), that the person has not modified the thing, since it [already] conforms to his concept simply by virtue of its natural shape (and he would have modified it if it did not thus conform); or he has modified his end in accordance with the thing's natural characteristics. His refraining from a particular activity was itself an activity, a purposive activity, and thus a modification, even if not of this particular thing, but rather a modification of the whole to which this thing was supposed to conform.

Now on its own, nature – which stands under mechanical laws – cannot really bring about change in itself. All change is contrary to the concept of nature. What appears to us as nature's effecting change within itself occurs in accordance with its immutable [mechanical] laws, and would not appear to us as change at all – but would appear to be constant instead – if we knew those laws well enough. If the world we rely on in forming our ends [116] should change in accordance with those laws, then that is our own fault. Either we should not have counted on the permanence of that thing (if the laws in accordance with which the change takes place are too powerful for us), or else we should have forestalled the laws' effect through artifice and skill (if the laws are not too powerful for us). Only other free beings could have produced an unforeseeable and unpreventable change in our world, i.e. in the system of things that we have known and related to our purposes; but in that case, our free efficacy would be disrupted. – The person has the right to demand that in the entire region of the world known to him everything should remain as he has known it, because in exercising his efficacy he orients himself in accordance with his knowledge of the world, and as soon as a change occurs in the world he immediately becomes disoriented and impeded by the course of the world's causality, or he sees results completely different from the ones he intended.

(Here is the ground of all property rights. The part of the sensible world that is known to me and subjected to my ends – even if only in thought – is *originally* my property. (It is not, simply for that reason, my property *in society*, as we shall see more precisely in what follows.) No one can affect that part of the sensible world without restricting the freedom of my efficacy.[b]

Thus the old dispute is settled here: i.e. whether the right to property in a thing is grounded solely by the formation of the thing, or whether it is grounded already by the will to possess the thing. The dispute is settled by [117] synthetically uniting both opinions, as must be the case in a system that proceeds strictly in accordance with the synthetic method; it is settled by demonstrating that merely subordinating a thing to our ends, even without actually forming it, is always itself a kind of formation, because it presupposes that one has freely refrained from a possible activity, and has done so in accordance with an end. Moreover, as will be shown below, the formation of a thing yields a property right only insofar as the thing, in being formed, is subjected and remains subject to our ends. Thus the final ground of the right to property in a thing is the subjection of the thing to our ends.)

(IV) To say that the person wills that his activity in the sensible world should become a cause, means: he wills that there should be a perception that corresponds to his concept of the end of his activity; and this means (as is obvious and has been illuminated above more clearly) a perception in a future moment that follows generally (which is not to say immediately) on the moment of his willing.

It has already been noted that, if this is to be at all possible, then in the future (i.e. after either the person's active efficacy or his purposive omission of activity) the things must remain undisturbed and be left to their natural course; and the person, by willing to become a cause, must immediately will this as well. But we are abstracting from this here.

---

[b] Think, for example, of an isolated inhabitant of a desert island who sustains himself by hunting in the island's woods. He has allowed the woods to grow as they might, but he knows them and all the conveniences they afford for his hunting. One cannot displace or level the trees in his woods without rendering useless all the knowledge he has acquired (thus robbing him of it), without impeding his path as he pursues game (thus making it more difficult or impossible for him to acquire his sustenance), that is, without disturbing the freedom of his efficacy.

But it is also clear that, in order to be able to perceive – and to perceive in the way that has already been thought out, in accordance with a rule that is already known to him – the person would necessarily have to will that the present relation of the parts of his body to one another (i.e. his body itself) should endure and that the present relation of his body to himself as willer and knower should also endure; more specifically, the person would have to will that there will exist for him a future state and that it will follow from his present state in accordance with a rule known to him, the rule he took into account in exercising his efficacy. Thus it is through the will and only through it that the future is grasped within the present moment; [118] it is through the will that the concept of a future in general and as such first becomes possible; through the will, the future is not only grasped but also determined: there is to be a future *like this*, and in order for there to be such a future, I am to be a being of this kind. But if I am to be a being of this kind, then *I* must *be* in general.

(Here we are arguing from a willing of a particular kind of future existence to the willing of a future in general, i.e. of our wish to continue existing. We are claiming that we do will – originally and in accordance with the laws of reason, which in this context govern us even mechanically – to continue existing, not for the sake of continued existence in itself, but for the sake of a particular state of continued existence; we do not regard continued existence as an absolute end, but as a means to some end. This is obviously confirmed by experience. All human beings desire life for the sake of something; the nobler in order to go on doing, the less noble in order to go on enjoying.)

The person wills what we have been describing, just as surely as he wills at all, regardless of what he wills. Thus this particular willing is the condition of all willing; its realization, i.e. the preservation of our present body (which, in the realm of natural right, denotes the same as *self-preservation*), is the condition of all other actions and of every expression of freedom.

(V) Summarizing everything that has now been deduced: by virtue of his original right, the person demands that there be a *continuing reciprocal interaction between his body and the sensible world, determined and determinable solely by his freely constructed concept of such a world.* This concept of an absolute causality in the sensible world and – since this concept was equivalent to the concept of original right – the concept of original right itself has been fully exhausted, and nothing more can belong to it.

Accordingly, original right is an absolute and closed whole; every partial violation of it affects and influences the whole. Now if one wanted to introduce subdivisions into this concept, they could be none other [119] than those contained in the concept of causality itself, which we have already presented above. Thus, original right includes:

(1) the right to the continued existence of the absolute freedom and inviolability of the body (i.e. there should be absolutely nothing that exercises an immediate effect upon the body);

(2) the right to the continued existence of our free influence within the entire sensible world.

There is no separate right to self-preservation; for it is merely contingent that, in a particular instance, we happen to be using our body as a tool, or things as a means, for the end of securing the continued existence of our body as such. Even if our end were more modest than self-preservation, other persons would still not be permitted to disturb our freedom, for they are not permitted to disturb it at all.

But one should not lose sight of the fact that the entirety of our original right is valid not merely for the present moment, but extends as far into the future as we can comprehend with our minds and in our plans; therefore, our original right immediately and naturally includes the right to secure the entirety of our rights for all the future.

Original right returns back into itself and becomes a self-justifying, self-constituting right, i.e. an *absolute right*; and herein lies the proof that the scope of our investigation of original right is complete, for a comprehensive synthesis has come to the fore. I have the right to will to exercise my rights for all the future so far as I posit myself, because I have these rights: and I have these rights, because I have the right to will them. The right to be a free cause and the concept of an absolute will are the same. Whoever denies the freedom of the will must – in order to be consistent – also deny the reality of the concept of right; such is the case, for example, with *Spinoza*, for whom "right" denotes merely the power of the individual as he is *determined* and limited by all that is.[5]

---

[5] Baruch Spinoza (1632–1677), *Theological–Political Treatise* (1670), trans. Samuel Shirley (Leiden: E. J. Brill, 1991), ch. 16.

[120] §12

Transition to an investigation of the right of coercion through the idea of an equilibrium of right

According to the above, a right of coercion is grounded in a violation of original right, i.e. when a free being extends the scope of his free actions so far as to violate the rights of another free being. But the violator, of course, is also free and has a right to be free. The violator is entitled to original right, and – as was demonstrated above – original right is infinite. Yet it is supposed to be possible for the violator, by freely exercising his original right, to violate the rights of another. Therefore, if someone can violate a right by exercising his own original right, then original right must have a particular quantity that is determined by the law of right; and an answer to the question "when does the violation of a right give rise to a right of coercion?" depends on the answer to another question: "what quantity of freedom does the law of right determine for each person?"

Stated more clearly: if some exercise of freedom is *contrary to right* and thereby justifies the use of coercion, then the *rightful* exercise of freedom, i.e. of original right, must be restricted within certain limits; and one cannot specify which exercises of freedom are contrary to right without knowing which ones are rightful; each can be determined only through its opposite. If these limits can be specified, and if each person remains within them, then no right of coercion arises; in that case, right is the same for all, or there is an equilibrium of right. Before anything else, we must set forth the conditions of this equilibrium in order to prepare, ground, and provide a regulative principle for the investigation of the right of coercion that follows; for the right of coercion arises only where the equilibrium of right has been violated: and in order to define the former, one must know what is meant by the latter.

(I) Every relation of right is determined by this proposition: each person is to limit his freedom through the possibility of the other's freedom. We have already discussed what belongs to freedom in general and in [121] itself. If such freedom were infinite as described above, then the freedom of all – except for that of a single individual – would be canceled. Then freedom itself, even its physical existence, would be annihilated, and thus the law of right would contradict itself. This contradiction dissolves as soon as one sees that the law of right does not apply merely to one individual with the others excepted, but holds instead for all free beings without exception. If A ought to limit his freedom so that B alongside him can also be free, then B, in turn, ought also to limit his freedom so that A alongside him can be free, so that a sphere of free efficacy also remains for A. This proposition becomes more determinate if one realizes that A limits himself through the possibility of B's freedom, only under the condition that B likewise limits his freedom and that the law is null and completely inapplicable if this does not occur. The self-limitation of each is reciprocally *conditioned* by that of the other, at first only *formally* (i.e. with regard to the fact that it occurs as such at all). If both do not limit themselves, then neither of them does. This follows from the very nature of the relation and is sufficiently clear from what has been said above; but it remains too general; it is an empty concept, incapable of being applied. If one were to say to the other, "don't do that, it disrupts my freedom," why shouldn't the other answer him by saying, "and refraining from doing so disrupts mine"?

Thus the question to be answered is this: *how much* should each limit the quantity of his free actions for the sake of the other's freedom? How much freedom may be retained by one individual for himself and must be respected by the other, in order that the one can conclude that the other has any rights? Conversely, how much freedom must each individual grant to the other in his concept of him, and how much of the other's freedom must he respect in undertaking his own actions, in order that the other can conclude that the first one has any rights?

[122] The relation of right in general is determined by nothing other than the law of right that has been established. Thus the question just posed can be answered only on the basis of that law. But the law as it has been set forth is only formal and does not determine any quantity. The law posits only *the fact that*, but not *how much*. Thus either the whole law is completely inapplicable and leads only to an empty conceptual game; or the *how much* must follow from *the fact that*, and the former is posited simultaneously along with the latter.

To say that both are posited simultaneously means that the mere concept of the freedom of a being outside me simultaneously prescribes the quantity of the limitation I am to impose upon myself. – It is completely clear that the answer had to turn out this way if our concept was to be applicable: but it is somewhat more difficult to say what this proposition might actually mean, and how and why it might be true. We shall first analyze the proposition, which contains the three following elements.

(a) The actual – and not thought merely problematically, as possible – self-limitation of a free being is conditioned by his knowledge of a particular free being outside him. Whoever does not have such knowledge cannot limit himself, and a possible being that I do not know does not obligate me to limit myself.

If – as occurs in the deduction of original right – a person in the sensible world is thought of as isolated, then (*as long as* he does not know of any person outside himself) he has the right to extend his freedom as far as he wills and can, and – if he so desires – the right to take possession of the entire sensible world. His right is actually infinite (if original right can be an *actual* right at all), for the condition under which such a right would have to be limited is absent.

(b) The self-limitation of a free being is also fully determined, without further qualification, by his knowledge of another free being outside himself. His self-limitation is first of all [**123**] *posited* by such knowledge, as one might well acknowledge without any objection. Each person, as surely as he subjects himself to the law of right, must limit his freedom through the freedom of the other as soon as he knows of another free being outside himself. From the moment that the individual (whom we have posited as isolated) knows of a free being outside himself, he has to consider not solely and exclusively the possibility of *his* freedom, but also the possibility of the other's freedom. But we are also claiming more: his self-limitation is *determined* by his knowledge of the other; this knowledge solely and exclusively prescribes how far such limitation would have to go.

(c) In any case, my freedom is limited by the freedom of the other only under the condition that he himself limits his freedom through the concept of mine. Otherwise, he is lawless and has no rights [*rechtlos*]. Thus if a relation of right is to result from my knowledge of the other, then both the knowledge and the limitation of freedom it brings about must be reciprocal. Therefore – every relation of right between particular persons is *conditioned* by their reciprocal recognition of one another, and is also fully *determined* by such recognition.

(II) We shall apply this proposition to the individual cases that fall under it, first of all to the right to the continuing freedom of one's body.

According to the above, when a rational being perceives a body that is articulated so as to represent reason in the sensible world (when a human being perceives a human body), he must posit it as the body of a rational being, and he must posit the being that is presented to him by means of it as a rational being. In positing this body, he determines it as a certain quantity of matter in space, a quantity that fills this space and is impenetrable in it.

Now as a consequence of original right, the body of a rational being is necessarily free and inviolable. Thus a person who has knowledge of such a body must, in consequence of such knowledge, necessarily limit his freedom to an efficacy that is external to this [**124**] body and to the space it occupies in the sensible world. He cannot posit this body as a thing that he can arbitrarily influence and subject to his ends and thereby take into his possession; rather he can posit it only as something that limits the sphere of his efficacy. His efficacy can extend anywhere except where this body is. As soon as I have seen such a body and perceived it for what it is, then I have perceived something that limits the sphere of my efficacy in the sensible world. My efficacy is excluded from whatever space that body occupies.

But since this self-limitation depends on (1) the other likewise perceiving me and positing me just as I have posited him (which is necessary in itself), and (2) the other likewise limiting his freedom through his knowledge of me, just as I have limited my freedom; it follows that my limitation and the other's right are only *problematic*; and it is not possible to determine whether these two conditions have been met or not.

(III) When I posit the body of the being outside me as absolutely free in determining itself to exercise efficacy, and when I posit the being represented by such a body as a free cause in the sensible world, I must necessarily posit that this being wills that some effect in the sensible world correspond to his concept, and thus that he has subjected certain objects in the sensible world to his ends (in consequence of the concept of original right). And when this other perceives me, he must assume the same about me.

The objects that each of us has subjected to his particular ends would have to be mutually immune to interference by the other, if we knew which objects had been subjected to each other's ends. But since this knowledge remains internal to the consciousness of each one of us and is not manifest in the sensible world, it follows that the objects of right and the objects in relation to which we should limit ourselves are problematic.

The objects of right are problematic; however, it is not only the objects, but also right in general that is problematic, uncertain, and dependent on a condition that remains unknown, namely whether both parties reciprocally have rights in relation to one another. I am [125] obligated to respect the objects the other has subordinated to his ends only under the presupposition and to the extent that he respects the objects I have subordinated to my ends. Now he certainly cannot show whether or not he respects these objects, unless he knows what they are; and similarly, I cannot show whether or not I respect the objects he has subordinated to his ends, unless I know what they are. This lack of knowledge therefore makes it impossible to confirm that we are beings who possess rights in relation to one another.

(What is problematic is not only whether both parties are disposed to respect each other's property but even whether they are both disposed to respect the freedom and inviolability of each other's bodies. Thus, there is no real relation of right between them at all; everything is and remains problematic.)

We have already seen above that, as soon as the right of coercion comes into being, it is no longer possible for humans to live peacefully alongside one another without some kind of agreement. Here we find that this impossibility arises even earlier, prior to any right of coercion; it arises with the grounding of any reciprocal rights at all, as we shall now see in more detail. Namely:

(IV) The two parties cannot remain ignorant about which objects the other has subordinated to his ends, if their rightful coexistence is to be possible in accordance with a rule that guarantees it (rather than because of some mere contingency that might or might not obtain). For neither of them, from now on, can subordinate to his ends – and thereby appropriate – something that he has not already subordinated to his ends, without fearing that the thing might have already been appropriated by the other person he has now come to know about; and thus without fearing that his own appropriation of the thing might violate the other's rights. In fact, from the moment they come to know of one

another, neither can be secure even in his previously acquired possessions, because it is always possible that the other might appropriate one
of his possessions under the assumption that it is not yet possessed by
anyone, in which case it would be impossible for the deprived party to
prove that he is its owner; and indeed his own possession of the thing
might be *contrary to right* (even if it is *in good faith*), because the other
person might have actually been the first to subordinate the thing [126]
to his own ends. Now how is the issue to be decided? It is impossible for
both parties themselves always to know which of them was the first to
gain possession of the contested thing; or, if they could know this, the
ground for deciding the matter would depend on their consciences,
which is completely inadequate for establishing external right. An
undecidable conflict of right arises between them, a conflict of physical
forces that can end only with one of them being physically annihilated
or completely driven away. – Only by chance (i.e. if it should turn out
that neither of them ever desires to have what the other wants to keep
for himself) could they live together rightfully and in peace. But they
cannot let all of their rights and security depend on such chance.

If this mutual ignorance is not canceled, a rightful relation cannot
come to exist between them.

The issue of which are the objects of right and obligation is
problematic. In fact, whether there are any rights or obligations between
them at all is problematic. Whoever wills that right should exist must
necessarily will that this condition, which makes all right impossible, be
canceled. The law of right wills that right should exist; it therefore
necessarily wills that this condition be canceled. Thus, there is a right to
insist that this condition be canceled. A person who does not want to
cancel this condition demonstrates by that very fact that he does not will
that right should exist and does not subject himself to the law of right;
he therefore becomes devoid of rights and justifies the use of unlimited
coercion against him.

(V) But *how* is this ignorance to be canceled? *That* every person has
subjected, and must have subjected, something to his ends is, as we have
demonstrated above, entailed by the concept of a person as a free cause
in the sensible world. Thus first of all, each person, as soon as he knows
that another person exists outside him, must limit what he possesses to
a *finite quantum* of the sensible world. If the person wanted to subordinate the entire sensible world exclusively to his ends, [127] then the

freedom of the other person now known to him could not also exist. But the other's freedom is supposed to be able to exist as well; thus this first person is obligated by right to leave something behind for the other person, as an object of his free efficacy. But *what* particular quantum each has chosen or wills to choose depends on his own freedom.

Furthermore, only the person himself can know what he has chosen, for his choice remains internal to his consciousness and is not expressed in the sensible world. Therefore, each would have to tell the other what he wills to possess exclusively for himself, for this is the only way to cancel the uncertainty that, in consequence of the law of right, ought to be canceled. Each is rightfully obligated to *determine* himself *inwardly* with regard to what he wills to possess; and the other has the right to coerce an undecided party to arrive at a fixed decision concerning what he wills to possess; for as long as the person remains undecided, neither right nor security can exist. Furthermore, each one is obligated by right to *declare outwardly* what he wills to possess; and the other has the right to coerce him to make this *declaration of his possessions*, because without it, likewise, neither right nor security can exist.

Thus, all relations of right between particular persons are conditioned by their reciprocal declaration of what they will to possess exclusively, and all relations of right become possible only through such declaration.

(VI) The claims declared by both parties are either compatible or in conflict with one another; the former if neither declares that he wants to possess what the other wants for himself, the latter if both make claims to the same thing. In the former case, the two are already in agreement; in the latter, their disagreement cannot be decided on the basis of right. For instance, it cannot be decided by appealing to an earlier appropriation of the thing; for neither can demonstrate that he was first to appropriate it, and so the claim to first appropriation is not valid for the purpose of external right. What grounds the right of possession in the court of external right (namely, a declaration of one's will to possess something) is identical on both sides; thus both parties possess an equal right.

Either: both must compromise [128] and yield in their demands until their claims are no longer in conflict, and thus until they reach the state of agreement that was posited in the first case. – But neither has the right to coerce the other to compromise and give in. For the fact that the other does not want to yield with respect to these particular objects does not mean that he refuses to subject himself to the law of right in general. He has chosen and declared a particular possession, and thus he has fulfilled his obligation to the law of right. Judging from his declaration, he is also willing to subject himself further to the law of right, if I will only let him have what he demands. He refuses to subject himself only to my will to possess this very thing, and this will of mine is a particular, individual will, not the will that belongs to the law of right (a will we both ought to share), and the law of right decides nothing concerning which of us ought to own the contested object.

Or: if they cannot compromise, then (since the contested right of both sides is identical) there would emerge an irresolvable conflict of right and – out of that conflict – a war that could end only with the death of one of them. Now since such a war, like all war, is absolutely contrary to right, they must (in order to prevent a war) turn over the decision concerning their conflict to a third party. They must unreservedly allow this third party to make judgments of right concerning the present case and must guarantee this party's decision-making power for the future; therefore, they must subject to this third party both their right to judge and their physical power: – this means, according to what was said above, that they must enter into a commonwealth with one another. Each of them has a right to this, namely a right to coerce the other either to compromise in good faith or to enter into a commonwealth with him – a right to coerce the other not to do one or the other, but to choose one of the two options – for otherwise, there would arise between them no relation of right, which, in consequence of the law of right, ought to exist.

(VII) Now if the two parties [129] have been in agreement from the start or have reached agreement by way of compromise (this is the only case relevant here, for later we shall discuss the contract concerning private property within the state), and assuming that each now rightfully possesses what belongs to him in consequence of their reciprocal and uncontested declaration, then what is the basis of their property right to the *particular* objects that happen to be theirs? It is evidently grounded in nothing other than the fact that their wills were not in conflict, but in agreement – in the fact that neither has made any claim to what belongs to the other. In saying, "*Only* this ought to be mine," the one is simultaneously saying (by way of limitation through opposition): "What is not included in my claim may be yours," and so, conversely, for the other. Therefore, their property right (i.e. their right to exclusive possession) is completed and conditioned *by mutual recognition* and does not take place without this condition. All property is grounded in the unification of several wills into one.

I am excluded from possessing a particular object, not by the will of another, but solely through my own free will. If I had not excluded myself, I would not be excluded at all. But I must exclude myself from something, as a consequence of the law of right. And so this is the only way things could have turned out, if each person originally has the right to own the entire sensible world but does not actually retain that right, and yet is to be, and to remain, free in this loss.

In order to clarify our position, we shall add the following.

(1) Only in the imagined context of original right do I acquire a possession simply by subordinating something to my ends. In this way, I acquire the possession as something valid *only for myself*; but it was not to be expected that I would make a claim against myself, that I would have a dispute with myself over a particular possession, – this is true, obviously, to the extent that I regard myself merely as a person within the sphere of natural right. The situation is different, of course, before the court of the moral law; there the human being is [**130**] divided against himself, so to speak, and does make judgments against himself.

But the proposition concerning possession in the context of original right had to be set forth, since the will to possess something is the *first* and *highest* condition of property; it is not, however, the *only* condition, and it must be further determined by another. As soon as the human being is posited as being in relation to others, his possession is rightful only if it is recognized by the other; and only in this way does his possession acquire an external, *shared* validity, a validity that – at this point in the analysis – holds only for him and for the other who recognizes it. Only in this way does the *possession* become *property*, i.e. something individual. An individual can exist only if it is distinguished from another individual; therefore, something individual can exist only if it is distinguished from another individual thing. I cannot think of myself as an individual without positing another individual in opposition to me: by the same token, I cannot think of anything as my property without at the same time thinking of something as the property of an other; and conversely, the same applies to the other. All property is grounded in reciprocal *recognition*, and such recognition is conditioned by *mutual declaration.*

(2) Thus property in a *particular* object – and not just the possibility of possessing something in general as one's own – is valid only for those who have recognized this right to property amongst themselves, and no further. It is always possible, and not contrary to right, that all the rest of the human species might have a dispute with me and might want to reclaim a share of what this other or these few others have recognized as mine. Thus no property is certain, no property is thoroughly secure for the purpose of external right, unless it is recognized by the entire human species. Securing this recognition seems to be an immense problem, and yet it is easily solved and actually has been solved for a long time by the present constitution of humankind. The commonwealth, and therefore every individual citizen joined within it, recognizes and guarantees the property of each person who lives within it. [131] The states that border this commonwealth or state recognize its property, i.e. the property of all individual citizens within it. In turn, the states that border these states recognize their property, and so on. Thus, even if the distant states have not recognized the property of the state within which *I* live (and thus indirectly my property), they have nevertheless recognized the property of the states that immediately border them. These states and their citizens cannot enter my state's territory without passing through and making free proprietary use of the territories that lie between my state and theirs, and this they are not permitted to do, in consequence of their recognition of the bordering state's territory. Therefore, since the earth is an absolute, closed, interrelated whole, all property on earth is indirectly recognized by virtue of the immediate, mutual recognition between neighboring states. – Of course, in a state of war all relations of right cease to exist; and the property of all the individual states at war becomes uncertain: but then again, the condition of war is not a rightful condition.

(VIII) If the two parties' harmonious declaration still leaves something unassigned (as is to be expected, since it is impossible for the two of them to enclose the entire sensible world and divide it between themselves), it is the property of neither (*res neutrius*).[6] This requires no special declaration; anything not included in the declaration of the two is excluded from it, and by virtue of being excluded, it goes from being

---

[6] Literally, thing that belongs to neither. Fichte uses the term to refer to a thing that a particular group of persons (here a group of two) regards as ownerless, even though the thing may in fact have an owner unknown to them.

determined to being undetermined (even if, for instance, it is still unknown to both parties at the time of their mutual declaration and is discovered only later). A thing of this kind, which is ownerless *for them* (*res neutrius*), can well become the possession of a third party and be subordinated by him to his ends; but since the two know only of each other and know nothing of a third party, they cannot take account of this unknown, merely possible third party in their considerations.

One or the other of the two parties might later decide [**132**] to subordinate a part of what is unassigned to his ends and thereby take possession of it. Since it is not part of the property he has recognized as belonging to the other, it seems that he is fully justified – in consequence of his original right – in taking possession of it. But now if the other, who for the same reasons has the same right, were also to take possession of the object, who is to decide this new conflict of right? Thus in order to prevent such a conflict from arising, a declaration and recognition must take place in connection with the parties' expansion of their possessions, as is the case in their initial acquisition. This second declaration and recognition, as well as all possible subsequent ones, are subject to the same difficulties that affected the first; both parties can will to possess the same thing, and both have the same right to will to possess it. It is always possible that this problematic right of both might give rise to an irresolvable conflict of right and to a war that can end only with the death of one or both of them. Thus the relation of right achieved thus far between them is not yet determinate and complete, and there is still no enduring state of peace between them.

Now for this reason, the indeterminacy cannot remain, and the two parties cannot let all their rights and their future security depend on this new contingency, i.e. the mere fact that neither desires what the other wishes to have or that they voluntarily reach agreement. Therefore, as in the parties' initial unity in a relation of right, it is necessary to establish a determinate rule concerning their future appropriation of things.

It is not just prudent and expedient to do this; rather, the law of right absolutely *requires* it, because otherwise no complete and secure relation of right would be established, no lasting peace would be concluded between them. Therefore, each has the right to coerce the other to agree to some rule that will be valid for both in their future appropriation of things.

What kind of rule could this be? The act of *declaration* [133] determines which particular object has been appropriated; it is through the act of *recognition* that the owner obtains the other person's consent (which is required for the right to property). The latter can precede the declaration, i.e. recognition can take place once and for all, in a moment when the two sides are peacefully united. But the declaration of future appropriation cannot take place at this moment of initial unity; for then it would be an actual appropriation of objects, not a future one. The objects would already be assigned (rather than unassigned and assignable only in the future). Therefore, it is the recognition, not of what is already assigned, but of what is assignable, that must occur in advance, i.e. the parties must reciprocally bind themselves to the rule that each will immediately recognize as the other's property whatever he declares as his possession in the realm of what has not yet been assigned.

In consequence of this contract, the one who simply makes his declaration first would acquire the full property right merely by his declaration, for the other is already bound in advance by the contract to give his consent. With this, temporal priority grounds a claim of right for the first time, and it does so merely in consequence of a voluntary agreement (but one that is necessary in the context of right). The formula of right: "*Qui prior tempore, potior jure*,"[7] which until now had no validity before the external court of right, has been justified. Another formula of right: "an ownerless thing falls to the one who is first to take possession of it" (*res nullius cedit primo occupanti*) has been more clearly determined and delimited here. Within the context of external right, there is no absolutely ownerless thing. An ownerless thing comes to exist for the two contracting parties (*res neutrius*) only by their mutual declaration and their excluding themselves from the thing. Such a thing is only problematically *res nullius*,[8] until an owner steps forward to claim it. (The thing is only *res neutrius per declarationem*;[9] the thing *cedit, ex pacto, primo occupanti et declaranti*.[10])

An irresolvable conflict of right is still possible, and the relation of

---

[7] Priority in time gives preference in right.

[8] Ownerless thing. *Res nullius* differs from *res neutrius* in that the former has no owner at all, whereas the latter might in fact have an owner who is unknown to a group of persons, for whom it then constitutes a *res neutrius*. See n. 6, p. 118.

[9] A thing that belongs to neither by declaration.

[10] Passes by agreement to the first who possesses it and declares it to be his.

right [134] is not yet fully secured, as long as there is nothing to ensure that a person's declaration will follow as quickly as possible upon his taking possession of the object, i.e. upon his perception of the object and his decision to keep it for himself. For what if, immediately after I have taken possession of an object, the other person (whom I seek out in order to declare my possession to him) comes along and takes possession of the same object, and now sets out to declare his possession to me? Whose property is it? In fact, this kind of conflict of right might often be irresolvable in the consciousness of the two parties – and certainly in the courts of external right – because neither can prove that he was the first. Thus in spite of all the care they may have taken, both parties, once again, would be in danger of falling into a war with one another.

Thus, the acts of taking possession and declaration must be synthetically united; or even more stringently, in the act of occupation the occupied object must become determined such *that the other cannot perceive the object without simultaneously perceiving that it has been taken possession of.* The object itself must make the declaration: therefore, the two parties must agree upon signs for designating their acts of appropriation. This, and precisely this, is necessary in order to prevent the possibility of further conflicts of right; therefore, there exists a right to coerce the other to abide by such signs. – These signs are signs only to the extent that the two parties have agreed upon them and made them signs. Thus they can be whatever the parties want them to be. The most natural way to designate one's property in land is to separate it from other land by fences and ditches. This makes it impossible for non-rational animals to enter the land, and it reminds rational beings that they ought not to exercise their capacity to do so.

(IX) A conflict of right could also arise concerning the surrender of property (*derelictio dominii*). Here it is immediately clear that one's initial property (which [135] became property through declaration and recognition) can be surrendered only through the owner's declaration that he no longer wants to possess it; and that – whatever else may happen – each person must always assume that the other wants to continue possessing what he has previously appropriated, as long as he has not expressly stated that he no longer wills to do so. That which is grounded extends only as far as the ground: now the property we have been discussing is grounded solely in a declaration, and thus it cannot be annulled unless the declaration is also annulled. But a declaration is annulled only by a contrary declaration. The abandoned property thereby becomes ownerless for both parties and stands under the rule of right concerning ownerless objects, indicated above. – Property that is acquired after initial acquisition (*dominium acquisitum*) is acquired in accordance with the sign that the parties have agreed upon for designating a thing as property, and it is annulled as soon as this sign is annulled, all according to the rule: that which is grounded does not extend further than the ground. – One could argue that, once the other has seen the sign, he knows that the designated thing is owned by someone. The owner can now remove the sign, in order not to continue something that is superfluous; or perhaps the sign might get old and disappear on its own. But this is precisely why it can never be proved that the other has actually seen the sign that designates the thing as property. He might never have come across the object at all; or if he did come across it, he may have paid no attention to the sign because the object did not interest him. Therefore, the sign is never superfluous, but rather is a ground of right that continues to be necessary; and if the owner removes the sign or allows it to fall into ruin, he is to be regarded as having surrendered his property right.

(X) By entering into this particular contract concerning property, the two parties mutually prove to each other that they are subjecting themselves to the law of right, since this contract can be entered into only in consequence of this law: and hence they prove to each other that they are beings who have rights. [136] Therefore, through this contract, the inviolability of their bodies (which had remained problematic until now) simultaneously acquires its sanction as well and becomes a categorical right. Of course, this right requires no special agreement; for its *extent* is not under dispute here, but is given when one simply perceives a human body. *That* there is such a right (which had been problematic before) has now been decided by the parties' agreement to this contract. Our inquiry has returned back into itself; that which was first and had been problematic before has now become categorical as a result of the inquiry's own course of development, and so the investigation is fully exhausted.

With respect to the limits of their free actions in relation to each other, both beings have now been completely determined and, as it were, mutually constituted for each other. Each has his own determinate position in the sensible world; and there is no possibility of a conflict of right if they both maintain their respective positions. An equilibrium of right has been established between them.

(XI) The proposition that has been synthetically established here – i.e. that the law of right, which in itself is merely formal, may materially determine the scope of each person's rights – has been confirmed by its general applicability. My relation of right to a free being is immediately determined for me simply through my perception of him, i.e. the relation is posited as something that has to be determined: the law of right presents me with this absolute task – either freely to determine this relation of right, or to let the state determine it.

Thus, we have answered the most important question of a doctrine of right: how can a merely formal law of right be applied to determinate objects?

[137] SECOND CHAPTER OF THE DOCTRINE OF RIGHT ON THE RIGHT OF COERCION

§13

Our entire argument in the deduction of an equilibrium of right turns in a circle; if one reflects on this circle, one will see that a rightful state of affairs – the possibility of which the argument was supposed to demonstrate – once again becomes impossible; and the concept of right still seems to be empty and devoid of all application.

For each of the rational beings that we posited as mutually perceiving one another, it was problematic: whether he could count on the security of his rights in the other's presence, and thus whether the other also had rights; or whether he was to be driven away by physical force outside his sphere of influence. This doubt was supposed to have been resolved through the fact that the two of them together determined and mutually recognized the scope of their respective rights; for such determination and recognition supposedly demonstrate that they are subjecting themselves to the law of right.

But their mutual security does not depend only on the fact that they agreed to a rightful state of affairs between themselves; rather, it depends on the fact that in all their future free actions they will govern themselves in accordance with this agreement. [138] Therefore, this agreement presupposes that each trusts that the other will keep his word, not merely now and again, or when it seems beneficial for him to do so; rather, it presupposes that each will trust that the other has made keeping his word an inviolable law for himself. Now a person could not give his word as something he intends to keep, nor could he actually keep it in the future, unless he has willed that there be a relation of right between himself and the other, i.e. unless he has subjected himself to the law of right.

Therefore – what is supposed to prove the other's capacity for having and respecting rights, namely, subjecting himself to the law, proves this only if one already presupposes what was to be proved; without this presupposition the proof has neither validity nor meaning.

One must take this point seriously in order to have a precise understanding of the entire inquiry that follows. The security of the two parties is not supposed to depend on a contingency, but on a near-mechanical necessity that excludes every possible exception. There can be such security only if the law of right is the inviolable law of both parties' wills; and if both are not mutually convinced that this is the case, no agreement can provide such security, for the agreement they make can be effective only if they have subjected their wills to the law of right. There are various reasons why the parties might be motivated to enter into an agreement without intending to keep their word. Or, both parties might enter into an agreement that they honestly intend to uphold and they might be sincerely committed to living with one another in a rightful state of affairs; but then later (perhaps lulled and misled by the mundaneness of their peace, relieved of the fear that might have partly motivated their good-faith agreement, and completely sure that the other is weak) one or both might have a change of heart. As soon as one of them thinks that such insincerity or change is possible, he can no longer rest easy but must always be on his guard and [139] prepared for war; he thereby puts the other (who might have still been sincere about the agreement) into a similar position, arousing the other's distrust as well. Each thereby acquires the right to terminate his peace with the other and to rid himself of the other, for the possibility of the coexistence of their freedom has been eliminated. Their contract is completely destroyed, since that which grounded it, their mutual trust, has been eliminated.

Result. The possibility of a relation of right between persons in the sphere of natural right is conditioned by mutual honesty and trust. But mutual honesty and trust are not dependent on the law of right; they cannot be brought about by coercion, nor is there a right to do so. It is not possible to coerce someone to have an inner trust in my honesty, because such trust has no outward expression and therefore lies outside the sphere of natural right. But I cannot even coerce someone not to express his distrust of me. For if he indeed distrusts me, such coercion by me would force him to give up all concern for his security, and therefore all his freedom and rights; I would thereby be subjecting him to my arbitrary judgments of right and to my power, i.e. I would be subjugating him to my control, which no one has a right to do.

§14

The principle of all laws of coercion

As soon as honesty and trust between persons who live together have been lost, mutual security and any relation of right between them become impossible, as we have seen. It is impossible to convince the parties that their mutual distrust is groundless, since such conviction could be based only on a good will that is firm and completely secured against all wavering and weakness; this is a trust that hardly anyone can place in himself, let alone in another person. Once honesty and trust have been lost, they cannot be re-established; [**140**] for either the insecure position of both parties persists and their distrust is communicated to each other and intensified by the caution that each sees the other using; or else war breaks out between them, which is never a rightful state of affairs, and in the midst of such a war each will always find sufficient reason to doubt the other's disposition to act in accordance with right.

Now neither party is concerned with the other's good will in itself, i.e. formally regarded. In this matter, each stands before the judgment seat of his own conscience. The two parties are concerned only with the consequences, i.e. the content, of the other's will. Each wills, and has the right to will, that the other undertake only those actions he would undertake if he had a thoroughly good will; whether or not such a will is actually present is beside the point. Each has a claim only to the other's *legality*, but by no means to his *morality*.

But now it is neither possible nor right to institute an arrangement under which a mechanical force of nature would keep people from engaging in wrongful actions. First, such an arrangement is impossible, because the human being is free and for that reason able to resist and overcome any natural force. Second, such an arrangement is contrary to right, because it would turn the human being into a mere machine in the sphere of right and would make the freedom of his will count for nothing. Therefore, the arrangement we are looking for would have to be directed *to the will itself*; it would have to enable and require the will to determine itself and will only those things that can co-exist with lawful freedom. – It is easy to see that this had to be the answer to our question; but it is a bit more difficult to understand how such an answer will be possible.

The free being posits ends for itself with absolute freedom. It wills because it wills, and its willing of an object is itself the ultimate ground of such willing. Above, we defined the free being in just this way, and it must [141] remain so defined: if the free being were understood otherwise, I-hood would be lost.

Now if things could be arranged so that the willing of any unrightful end would necessarily, and in accordance with an ever-operative law, result in the opposite of what was intended, then any will that is contrary to right would annihilate itself. The fact that one willed something would be the very reason one could not will it; any will that is contrary to right would be the ground of its own annihilation, just as the will in general is the ultimate ground of itself.

It was necessary to present this proposition in its full, synthetic rigor, since all laws of coercion, or penal laws, (the entirety of penal legislation) are grounded on it. We shall now analyze this concept, in order to clarify it.

The free being posits an end for itself. Let us call this end A. Now it is certainly possible that A might be related to other ends as a means, and that these ends, in turn, might be related to still other ends as a means, and so forth. But no matter how far one takes this chain of reasoning, one must still ultimately assume that there is an absolute end that is willed simply because it is willed. All ends that can serve as a means are related to this absolute end as parts of an absolute all-encompassing end, and therefore are themselves to be regarded as absolute ends. – To say that someone wills A is to say that he demands that something corresponding to the concept of A be given in perception as existing. Thus his concept of A's real existence, or his willing that A should exist, is his motive for willing A. A person, as surely as he at the present moment desires A and wishes above all else that A should exist, just as surely abhors the opposite of A and regards it at the present moment as the most feared of all evils.

Now if the person were to foresee that in attempting to bring about A, its opposite would necessarily follow, then – precisely because it is the existence of A that he wishes or desires, and thus abhors the opposite of A – he could not will to realize A; he could not will A, precisely because he wills it; and our problem [142] would then be solved. The strongest and currently dominant desire would provide its own counter-weight, and the will would annihilate itself. It would maintain and bind itself within its limits.

Therefore, if an arrangement could be found that would operate with mechanical necessity to guarantee that any action contrary to right would result in the opposite of its intended end, such an arrangement would necessitate the will to will only what is rightful; such an arrangement would re-establish security, after honesty and trust have been lost, and it would render the good will superfluous for the realization of external right, since a bad will that desires other people's things would be led – by its own unrightful desire – to the same end as a good will. An arrangement of the kind we have been describing is called a *law of coercion*.

There exists, in general, a right to institute such an arrangement. For the law of right dictates that reciprocal, rightful freedom and security ought to prevail. Although freedom and security could prevail as a result of honesty and trust between persons, no law can bring about honesty and trust so that they could be relied upon with certainty; therefore, freedom and security must be realized through the only means that guarantees they will be realized in accordance with a rule: and this means is nothing other than the law of coercion. Therefore, the task of instituting such an arrangement belongs to the law of right.

Finally, this law of coercion does not infringe upon the freedom of the good will or its full dignity. As long as someone wills only what is rightful for the sheer sake of its rightfulness, no desire for what is not rightful will arise in him. But now, as we have seen, the law is directed only towards a desire for what is not rightful; the law finds its motivation in this desire alone, and applies to a person's will only by means of it. Only by desiring what is not rightful do we, as it were, give the law something that enables it to seize and restrain us. Therefore, whenever this desire is not present, the law of coercion is not operative, and it is [143] completely canceled as far as the will is concerned; the law is not our motive for acting or not acting, because another motive has already brought rightfulness into existence. No external law is given to someone who is righteous; he is completely liberated from such a law, and liberated by his own good will.

But – and this is the second possible case that a law of coercion is concerned with – one might inflict an injury without willing to do so, as a result of negligence or carelessness. In such a case, the law of coercion we have been describing (which is grounded on and directed at the will to cause injury, or rather the will to promote one's own advantage by injuring another, and – as we have just seen in another context – ceases to apply when such a will is not present) has no influence and offers no protection. But now from the point of view of the injured party, a loss inflicted out of carelessness is no different from one inflicted by a bad will, and fear of this kind of loss leads to the same insecurity and anxiety as the fear of intentional, hostile assaults. Therefore, the arrangement we have been describing does not yet sufficiently ground security. Arrangements must be made to protect against carelessness as well.

All inattentiveness is reducible to the fact that the human being *has no will at all* in cases where he necessarily ought to have one and where – just as certainly as he is taken to be a rational and free being – he is counted upon to have one. He has constructed for himself absolutely no concept of his action, but has acted mechanically, as chance has driven him to act. This makes it impossible to live in security alongside him; and it makes him into a product of nature that one would have to bring to a state of rest and inactivity, but for the fact that one neither can (because the person still has a free will as well) nor may do so (because the person's freedom must be altogether respected). – In order to make it possible for others to live alongside him in security, the human being ought, by means of his free will, to direct the expressions of his physical power towards an end he has reflected on: and in connection with the freedom of others, the following rule can be laid down for him:

[144] *He must exercise precisely as much care not to violate the rights of others as he does to prevent his own rights from being violated.* The proof of the validity of this rule is the following: the ultimate final end the law

sets for me *is mutual security*. The end contained in the law is that I not infringe the other's rights, just as and to the same degree that it contains the end that the other not infringe mine; and as long as both of these ends are not equally ends of my will, my will is not rightful and I am incapable of entering into a secure, peaceful relation with the other.

The question is, how are things to be arranged so that the person will come to have a will when he ought to have one, or – as we have more clearly defined the proposition in our rule – so that he takes as much care to ensure the other's security against himself as he does to ensure his own security against the other?

To begin, we shall examine the first formulation of the problem, precisely because it is the more difficult one and thus makes our investigation most interesting: how are things to be arranged in order to bring about a will in someone?

Something that has no will at all is not a free and rational being, which contradicts our presupposition. The persons we are considering here do have wills, and in addition, the particular direction of their will is known; they have declared the objects that, by means of their will, they have subjected to their ends (i.e. their property). The arrangement we are seeking would have to begin with this will, which certainly does exist, and produce out of it a will that does not exist but is nevertheless needed in order to make mutual security possible; i.e. the satisfaction of the will that the parties do possess would have to be made to depend on their having the other will that they ought, but perhaps do not want, to possess. – To illustrate: I surely do have A as my *end*. Now, if I am to live with the other in a relation of right, I would also have to have B as my end, yet it is doubtful that I always will. But the willing of B will surely be produced in me, [**145**] if it is made into a condition of attaining end A. I am then forced to will B, contrary to my good will, since without it A (which I do will) would become impossible. Let A stand for the end of asserting my own rights; let B stand for the end of not infringing the other's rights. Now if a law of coercion operates with mechanical necessity to ensure that any infringement of the other's rights becomes an infringement of my own, then I will exercise the same care to ensure the security of the other's rights as I do to ensure the security of my own, since through this arrangement the other's security against me becomes my own security. In short, any loss the other suffers as a result of my recklessness must become my own loss.

And now for a comparison. In the first case, the will strayed beyond its limits; it sought something that belonged exclusively to the other, but treated this thing as something to be used for its own advantage. It is precisely this over-extension of the will that the law makes use of in order to drive the will back into its boundaries. – In the latter case, the will did not extend far enough, that is, it was not at all concerned with what belonged to the other, as it should have been. The law makes use of the care that the will rightfully takes to maintain what is its own in order to induce it to fill out its proper limits. Therefore, under the direction of the law of coercion, the effect of one's caring for one's own security is the opposite of the effect intended, i.e. caring for one's own security always has the effect it ought to have in order to maintain an equilibrium of right. Thus the concept of a law of coercion, which aims to secure this equality of rights for everyone, is fully exhausted.

§15

On establishing a law of coercion

The law of coercion is supposed to function so that any violation of rights will result inevitably and with mechanical necessity (so that the violator [146] can foresee it with complete certainty) in the same violation of the violator's own rights. The question is, how can such an order of things be brought about?

As the matter itself shows, what is needed is an irresistible coercive power that will punish the violator. Who is supposed to establish such a power?

This power is posited as a means for establishing mutual security when honesty and trust do not exist (and under no other circumstances). Thus one can will such a power, only if he wills this end (mutual security in the absence of honesty and trust), but he must also will this end necessarily. Now it is the contracting parties we have posited who will this end; therefore, they and only they can be the ones who will the means. In willing this end (and in this alone) their wills are united: thus their wills must also be united in their willing of the means, i.e. they must make a contract among themselves to establish a law of coercion and a coercive power.

Now what kind of power is this supposed to be? – This coercive power is guided by a concept and aims at the realization of a concept (indeed a concept that is constructed through absolute freedom), namely the concept of the limits posited by the two contracting parties in their contract concerning their efficacy in the sensible world; therefore, this power cannot be a mechanical power but must be a free one. Now such a power (one that would unite all these requirements within itself) is not posited apart from their own power, as determined by their common will. Thus the content of the contract they make to establish a right of coercion between themselves is this: *both will to deal with the one of them who has wronged the other by applying the law of coercion to him with their united power.*

Now if a case arises where there exists a right of coercion, the violator must be one of the two parties. It is contradictory to think that the violator might counter his own violation with his own powers; for in that case he would have refrained from perpetrating the violation, there [147] would have been no violation, and the right of coercion would not have arisen. Thus the violator could promise only that he would not resist the other's coercion, but voluntarily submit to it.

But this, too, is contradictory, for – in accordance with our presupposition – the violator (regardless of whether he wronged the other intentionally or out of negligence) has a steadfast will to keep what is his. Indeed, the law of coercion aims exclusively at such a will. In the first case (i.e. if the wrong is intentional) it is directed even at the will to take possession of what belongs to the other; and it is precisely this will that the coercion is supposed to thwart. If the violator were to submit voluntarily to the coercive force, there would be no need to use such force against him; he would have voluntarily abandoned his wrongful act, and thus would not have the kind of will that the law of coercion presupposes. (A duty *to allow* oneself *to be coerced* is contradictory. Whoever allows himself to be coerced is not coerced, and whoever is coerced does not allow himself to be.)

But nevertheless it would have to be this way; from what other source could a superior power for enforcing rights come (since we must ascribe equal physical strength to the two persons)? Therefore, the same person whose promise not to interfere with others' property could not be trusted and who then actually failed to keep his word, would have to be trusted to keep the contract regarding coercion and to submit voluntarily to the penalty affecting his own property. –

Then, if the transgressed party enforces his own rights and if the transgressor must fully submit, his hands bound, to the transgressed party's judgment and its implementation, who will guarantee to the transgressor that the transgressed party will not either intentionally exceed the limits of the law of coercion or make a mistake in applying it to the present case? Therefore, even the party being penalized would have to place an unheard of and impossible trust in the other's rightfulness, impartiality, and wisdom, [148] at a time when he no longer trusts the other at all. This is, without a doubt, contradictory.

Therefore, such a contract, as we have presented it here, is contradictory and simply unrealizable.

Such a contract could be realized only if the injured party were always the more powerful one – but only up to the limit dictated by the law of coercion deduced here – and then were to lose all power when he reached that limit; or – in accordance with the formula presented above – only if *each party were to have exactly as much power as right.* Now as we have also seen above, this occurs only within a commonwealth. Thus, the right of coercion can have absolutely no application apart from a commonwealth: otherwise, coercion is always only problematically rightful, and for this very reason it is always unjust actually to apply coercion, as if one had a categorical right to it.

(Accordingly, there is no *natural right* at all in the sense often given to that term, i.e. there can be no rightful relation between human beings except within a commonwealth and under positive laws. – *Either* there is thoroughgoing morality and a universal belief in such morality; and furthermore, the greatest of all coincidences takes place (something that could hardly occur, even if everyone had the best intentions), namely, the claims made by different human beings are all compatible with one another. In this case the law of right is completely impotent and would have nothing at all to say, for what ought to happen in accordance with the law happens without it, and what the law forbids is never willed by anyone. – For a species of perfected moral beings, there is no law of right. It is already clear that humankind cannot be such a species, from the fact that the human being must *be educated* and must *educate himself* [*sich erziehen*][11] to the status of morality; for he is not moral by nature, but must make himself so through his own labor.

---

[11] This is the same term Fichte used in §3 to characterize the summons that one free subject must address to another if self-consciousness is to be possible. See n. 5, p. 38.

Or – the second possibility – there is no thoroughgoing morality, or at least no universal belief in it. In this case the external law of right exists, but [**149**] can be applied only within a commonwealth. Thus, natural right disappears.

But what we lose on the one side, we recover on the other, and at a profit; for the state itself becomes the human being's natural condition, and its laws ought to be nothing other than natural right realized.)

[**150**] THIRD CHAPTER OF THE DOCTRINE OF RIGHT
ON POLITICAL RIGHT [*STAATSRECHT*], OR RIGHT
WITHIN A COMMONWEALTH

§16

Deduction of the concept of a commonwealth

The problem that we were left with, that we could not solve, and that we hope to solve through the concept of a commonwealth, was this: how to bring about a power that can enforce right (or what all persons necessarily will) amongst persons who live together.

(I) The object of their common will is *mutual security*; but since, as we have assumed, persons are motivated only by self-love and not morality, each individual wills the security of the other only because he wills his own, willing the other's security is subordinate to willing one's own; no one is concerned whether the other is secure against oneself, except to the extent that the other's security is the condition of one's own security against the other. We can express this briefly in the following formula: *Each person subordinates the common end to his private end*. (This is what the law of coercion reckons with; [**151**] by linking the welfare of each in reality to the security of the welfare of all others, the law of coercion is meant to produce this reciprocity, this necessary conjunction of the two ends, in the will of each individual.)

The will of a power that exercises the right of coercion cannot be constituted in this way; for, since the private will is subordinated to the common will only through coercive power, and since this coercive power is supposed to be superior to all other power, the private will of the coercive power could be subordinated to the common will only by its own power, which is absurd. Therefore, the coercive power's private will must already be subordinated to and in harmony with the common will, and there must be no need to bring about such subordination and harmony, i.e. the private will of the coercive power and the common will must be one and the same; the common will itself, and nothing else, must be the private will of the coercive power, and this power must have no other particular and private will at all.

(II) Thus, the problem of political right and (according to our proof) of the entire philosophy of right is *to find a will that cannot possibly be other than the common will.*

Or, in accordance with the formula presented earlier (one that is more in keeping with the course of our investigation), the problem is: *to find a will in which the private and the common will are synthetically united.*

We shall solve this problem in accordance with a strict method. Let us call the will we are seeking X.

(a) Every will has itself (in the future) as an object. Everything that wills has self-preservation as its final end. The same goes for X; and so self-preservation would be *the private will* of X. – Now this private will is supposed to be one with the common will, which wills the security of the rights of all. Therefore, X, just as it wills *itself*, wills *the security of the rights of all.*

(b) *The security of the rights of all* is willed only through the harmonious will of all, through the concurrence of their wills. *It is only in this regard* that *all* agree; [152] for in all other matters their will is particular and directed to their individual ends. In accordance with our assumption of universal egoism (which the law of coercion presupposes), no individual, no single part of the commonwealth, makes this an end for himself; rather, only *all* of them, taken as a whole, do.

(c) Thus X would itself be this *concurrence* of all. This concurrence, as surely as it willed *itself*, would also have to will the security of the rights of all; for it is one and the same as that security.

(III) But such *concurrence* is a mere concept; now it should not remain so, but ought rather to be realized in the sensible world, i.e. it ought to be brought forth in some particular external expression and have effect as a physical force.

For us, the only beings in the sensible world that have wills are human beings. Therefore, this concept would have to be realized in and through human beings. This requires:

(a) That the will of a certain number of human beings, at some point in time, actually becomes harmonious, and expresses itself or gets declared as such. – The task here is to show that the required concurrence does not take place of itself, but rather is based on an *express act* of all, an act *that takes place in the sensible world and is perceptible at some point in time and is made possible only through free self-determination.* Such an act is implied by a proof already presented above. That is, the law of right says only that each person should limit the use of his freedom through the rights of the other, but it does not determine how far and to which objects the rights of each ought to extend. These latter determinations must be expressly declared, and declared in such a way that the declarations of all are harmonious. Each person must have said to all: I want to live in this place, and to possess this or that thing as my own; and all must have responded by saying: yes, you may live here and possess that thing.

Our further investigation of this act will yield the first section of the doctrine of political right, *on the civil contract* [*vom Staatsbürgervertrage*].

[**153**] (b) That this will be established as the steadfast and enduring will of all, a will that each person – just as certainly as he has expressed this will in the present moment – will recognize as his own so long as he lives in this place. In every previous investigation it was always necessary to assume that such willing for the entire future is present in a single moment, that such willing for all future life occurs all at once. Here, for the first time, this proposition is asserted with justification.

Because the present will is established as valid for all time, the common will that is expressed now becomes *law*.

(c) This common will determines both how far the rights of each person ought to extend, in which case the legislation is *civil* (*legislatio civilis*); and how a person who violates these rights in one way or another ought to be punished, in which case the legislation is criminal or penal (*legislatio criminalis, jus criminale, poenale*). Our investigation of this will yield the second section of the doctrine of political right, on *legislation*.

(d) This common will must be equipped with a power – and indeed a superior power, in the face of which any individual's power would be infinitely small – that will enable it to look after itself and its preservation by means of coercive force: *the state authority*. This authority includes two elements: the right to judge, and the right to execute the judgments it has made (*potestas judicialis et potestas executiva in sensu strictiori*,[12] both of which belong to the *potestas executiva in sensu latiori*[13]).

(IV) The common will has actually expressed itself at some point in time, and – by virtue of the civil contract that has been reached concerning it – has become universally valid as law.

In accordance with the principles established thus far, there can be no difficulty at all in seeing what this universal will will be, with regard both to the determination of each individual's rights, and to the penal laws [*Strafgesetze*]. But this will is still open-ended and has not yet been set down anywhere, nor has it been equipped with any power. The latter must occur if this will is to endure and if the previous [154] insecurity and war of all against all are to be prevented from returning again soon. The common will, as a mere will, is realized, but not yet as a power that can preserve itself: and therefore the final part of our problem remains to be solved.

The question seems to answer itself.

That is, those who are thus joined together, as physical persons in the sensible world, necessarily possess power of their own. Now since a person can be judged only by his actions, so long as no one transgresses the law, it can be assumed that each person's private will concurs with the common will, and thus that his power is part of the power of the state. Each person, even if he were privately to develop an unjust will, must always fear the power of all, just as they all must also fear his power, because they can know nothing of the unjustness of his will, which has not yet shown itself in actions. The power of all (which is to be assumed to have been declared in favor of the law) keeps each individual's power within its boundaries; and therefore there exists the most perfect equilibrium of right.

But as soon as someone transgresses the law, he is thereby excluded from the law, and his power is excluded from its power. His will no longer concurs with the common will, but becomes a private will.

Similarly, the person who has been wronged may not participate in executing the common will: for precisely because he has been wronged, his will that the offender pay compensation and be punished is to be regarded as his private will, not the common will. Now according to our presupposition, his private will is kept within its limits only by the

---

[12] Judicial power and executive power in the narrower sense.
[13] Executive power in the broader sense.

power of the common will. If he were now to be given control over this power for the purpose of executing what (we are assuming) is his private will, then this, his private will, would no longer be limited by the power of the common will, which contradicts the civil contract. Therefore, only a *third party* could be the judge, because this party (it is to be assumed) takes an interest in the entire conflict [155] only to the extent that the common security is endangered, since no private advantage can accrue to this party, regardless of who is allowed to keep the contested possession; therefore, it is to be assumed that the third party's will concerning this conflict is nothing other than the necessary, common will and is entirely free from influence by its private will, which remains completely silent and finds no application. –

(V) But it is always possible for the third party – out of some inexplicable preference for one of the parties, or because some benefit actually does accrue to it, or even out of error – to pronounce an unjust verdict and to carry it out in alliance with one of the parties to the suit. These two would then be united in an unjust alliance, and the superior power would no longer reside on the side of the law. Or to express this in more general terms:

In a situation of the kind just posited, it is possible for several persons to unite against one or against several weaker ones, in order to oppress them with their common power. In such a case, their will is indeed a will they share as oppressors, but it is not the common will, since the oppressed have not given their will to this arrangement: the oppressors' shared will is not the common will that had previously been made into law, a will to which those now being oppressed had also consented. It is therefore not the will of the law, but rather a will directed against the law, though one that possesses superior power. As long as it remains possible for such an alliance to exist, contrary to the law and on the side of injustice, the law does not have the superior power it ought to have, and our problem has not been solved.

How can such an alliance be made impossible?

According to our presupposition, each individual wills the common end, or right, because he wills his own private end; each desires public security because he desires his own security. Therefore, it is necessary to find an arrangement whereby individuals could not ally themselves against others without [156] surrendering – in consequence of some infallible law – their own security.

Now it is obvious that, given this kind of alliance, if it is possible once for a group of people within the state to unite against individual citizens and oppress them, then it is possible a second and third time as well; therefore anyone who now allies himself with the oppressors must fear that, in accordance with his own maxim, his turn may also come to be oppressed. However, it is still possible that everyone might think: but that won't happen to me; I, for one, will be clever enough always to manage to be on the side of the stronger, and never on the side of the weaker.

It is necessary to make this thought utterly impossible. Each person must be convinced that the oppression and unrightful treatment of *one* citizen will result with certainty in the same oppression and treatment of himself.

Such certain conviction can be produced in a person only by a law. Therefore unjust violence, by virtue of having occurred once and in a single case, would have to be made *lawful*. If something has occurred just once, then – precisely because it has occurred – everyone would have to have the full right to do the same thing. (According to the formula stated above: every deed that is allowed to occur would necessarily have to be made into a law, and so the law would then necessarily have to become a deed.)

(This proposition is grounded in the very nature of what is at issue here. The law is the same for all; therefore, if the law allows one person to do something, it must necessarily allow all to do it.)

But this proposal cannot be carried out: for if it were, the law itself would cancel out right and justice for all time. For precisely this reason, the law of right cannot imply that such injustice is to be declared just; rather, it can imply only that such injustice must absolutely not be allowed to occur in a [157] single case, for allowing such injustice to occur in a single case would necessarily result in its being legitimized, not only in thought, but also in reality. How this is to be arranged will soon become clear, when we return to take a closer look at the concept, presented above, of the law's power. We shall soon see how this must happen, when we return to take a closer look at the principle presented above.

We have said that the state's coercive power can preserve itself only on the condition that it be continually efficacious; therefore, it will be destroyed forever if it is inactive even for a moment; it is a power whose *existence at all* depends on its *existence, or expression, in every single case*: and since this order of things cannot come into being on its own (at least not uninterruptedly and in accordance with a rule), it would have to be established by a fundamental law of the civil contract.

The required order of things gets established through the following decree: the law shall have absolutely no validity for future cases until all previous cases have been decided in accordance with it: no one shall be granted relief under a law until all previously aggrieved parties who have pursued their claims under the same law have been granted relief; no one shall be punishable for an offense under a law, until all previous offenses under the same law have been discovered and punished. – But since law in general is really only one law, it cannot pronounce anything in its particular applications, if it has not first resolved all the previous claims arising under it. Ensuring that previous claims have been resolved would have to be the job of the law itself: in doing so, the law would be prescribing a law to itself; and a law of this kind, one that returns into itself, is called a *constitutional* law.

(VI) Now if this order of things involving the administration of public power is itself secured by a law of coercion, then universal security and the uninterrupted rule of right will be firmly established. But how is this order itself to be secured?

[158] If – as we are still assuming here – the populace as a whole [*die ganze Gemeine*] administer the executive power, then what other power is there to force them to live up to their own law concerning the chronological order in which the executive power is to be exercised? Or, what if the populace, out of good intentions and devotion to the constitution, lived up to that constitutional law for a while, but because they were unable or unwilling to grant relief to someone who had been aggrieved, the administration of justice came to be suspended for a time? In such a case, the resulting disorders would soon become so great that the populace, out of necessity, would act contrary to their own constitution and would have to quickly pounce upon new offenses, before punishing the old ones. This standstill in the laws would be the populace's punishment for their laziness, negligence, or partisanship; and how should the populace be forced to inflict this punishment upon themselves and to endure it? – The populace would be their own judge in the administration of justice. Out of convenience or partisanship, the populace would allow many things to go unpunished, as long as the

resulting insecurity did not progress too far; and if the insecurity were to increase and make itself felt by the majority, then they would pounce, with an unjust and passionate harshness, on those offenders who have been emboldened by the previous leniency and who now expect the same leniency in their own cases, but who are unfortunate enough to be offenders precisely at this time, when the populace are being roused to act. This would continue until the resulting terror became widespread, the populace fell back into a slumber, and the cycle began all over again. This kind of constitution, the *democratic* one in the truest sense of the word, would be the most insecure there could be, since one would have to fear not only the violent acts of all the others just as he would outside the state, but also, from time to time, the blind fury of an enraged mob that acts unjustly in the name of the law.

Thus our problem has still not been solved, and the condition of human beings under the constitution just described is as insecure as it would be without a constitution. The real [**159**] reason for this is that the populace are simultaneously both *judge and party* in the administration of right.

This formulation suggests how the problem is to be solved. In the administration of justice, judge and party must be separated, and the populace cannot be both at the same time.

The populace cannot be the party being judged in this kind of proceeding. For, since the populace are, and ought to be, supremely powerful, a judge would never be able to carry out his verdict against the populace by force. The populace would have to submit voluntarily to his verdict. But if they do so, then they value justice above all else; and if we were to assume this about them as a general rule, there would be no need for a judge, and the judge would not in fact be one, but only an advisor. If the populace do not will right, then they will not submit to it, since they cannot be coerced; they will reproach the bearer of the unwelcome verdict for being blind or disloyal, and they will remain, as before, their own judge.

To summarize: the judgment as to whether state power is being applied in accordance with its proper end must be made in accordance with some law. In this matter, the same person (whether physical or mystical) cannot simultaneously be both the judge and the party being judged. But the populace (who, in a legal matter such as this, must be one or the other) cannot be a *party*; therefore – and this is the important conclusion we draw here – the populace cannot administer public power, because, if they did, they would have to present themselves as a party before a higher tribunal.

(It is crucial that one be convinced of the conclusiveness of the reasoning just presented, for it contains, so far as I know, the very first strict deduction, based on pure reason, of the absolute necessity of representation within a commonwealth.[14] Moreover, it shows that representation is not just a beneficial and prudent arrangement, but one that the law of right demands absolutely, and that democracy in the sense explained above is not just an impolitic constitution, but entirely opposed to right. [160] The claim that the populace cannot be both judge and a party at the same time might not give rise to much doubt, but perhaps our other claim will, namely, that whoever administers public power must be made absolutely accountable. Yet this claim follows from everything we have said thus far. Every individual who enters into the state must be convinced that it is impossible for him ever to be treated contrary to the law. But being treated thus is a possibility if whoever administers the law cannot himself be made accountable for what he does.)

Therefore, the populace would have to alienate the task of administering public power; they would have to transfer it to one or several particular persons who would nevertheless remain accountable to them in administering it. A constitution in which the one who administers public power is not accountable is *despotism*.

It is, therefore, a fundamental law of any constitution that accords with reason and right that the *executive power* (which includes within it, as inseparable, the judicial power and the executive power in the narrower sense) and *the right to oversee and judge how such executive power is administered* (which I shall call the *ephorate* in the broadest sense of the word) are to be separate; and that this right to oversee and judge is to remain with the populace as a whole, but the executive power is to be entrusted to particular persons. Thus no state may be governed *despotically*, or *democratically*.

---

[14] This use of "representation" derives from Kant's use of the term in *Perpetual Peace* (p. 101). According to Kant, a representative government is one in which executive authority is not exercised by the people as a whole but delegated to a smaller group of individuals, who then become the people's "representative" in executing the law. Defined in this way, representation is the direct opposite of democracy "in the proper sense of the term." See n. 16, p. 14.

(Much has been said concerning the separation of powers (i.e. of the *pouvoirs*, the parts of one and the same public power). It has been said that the legislative power must be separated from the executive power; but this statement seems to contain something indeterminate in it.

It is true that, for each particular person, particular positive law becomes *law* and binding with respect to its *form*, only insofar as the person subjects himself to the law, i.e. only insofar as he declares: I want to live in this particular state, which includes this particular people, this land, these means of livelihood, and so forth. But the *content* of law, at least of civil law (other branches of legislation will be discussed separately), comes from the mere assumption that [161] these particular human beings, in this particular place, want to live alongside one another *in accordance with right*; and each person subjects himself to the law by declaring: I want to live with you people, and to do so in accordance with *all* the just laws that might ever be given in this state. Since those who administer the executive power are charged with presiding over right in general and are responsible for seeing to it that right prevails, it must be left up to them to care for the means by which right is to be realized, and therefore even to draft the ordinances themselves, which are not really new laws, but only more determinate applications of the one fundamental law, which states: these particular human beings are to live alongside one another in accordance with right. If those who hold power apply this fundamental law incorrectly, disorders will quickly develop for which they will be accountable; and thus they will be compelled to issue just laws, ones that every rational person could approve.

Separating the judicial from the executive power (the latter understood in the narrower sense of the word) is completely futile, and is possible only in appearance. If the executive power must carry out the verdict of the judicial power without any opportunity to object, then the judge himself holds unlimited power in his hands, and the two powers only seem to be separated in the two persons. But of the two, the one who carries out the verdict has no will at all, but only physical power directed by an external will. But if the executive power has the right to veto the verdict, then it is itself a judicial power – it is indeed the ultimate judicial power – and the two powers, once again, are not separate. – According to our investigation, the executive power (in the broadest sense of the word) and the ephorate are to be separate. The former includes the entire public power in all its branches; but with respect to how such power is administered, the executive power must be made accountable to the ephorate (the concept of which is still far from being fully defined here).)

According to the usual classification, the executive power is entrusted [162] either to one person, as in a lawful and rightful *monarchy*, or to a body of persons organized under a constitution, as in a *republic* (in the narrower sense of the word): or to be more precise, the executive power is always held by a corps of persons, since one person can never do everything on his own. Thus the only difference between a monarchy and republic is that, if there is no unanimity within the corps of persons, the dispute is settled either by the unappealable decision of a life-long president (the monarch), or by some collective voice, such as a majority vote. In the latter case, the perpetual president is a mystical and often mutable person (i.e. those whose voices constitute a majority of votes and who decide the dispute without the possibility of appeal are not always the same physical persons).

Further, those who administer the executive power are either elected or not. In the former case, either *all* or only *some* are elected. In a *democracy* (in the narrower sense of the word, i.e. a representative, and therefore rightfully constituted, democracy), they are elected directly by the populace. If *all* persons in authority are directly elected by the populace, it is a *pure* democracy; if not, it is a *mixed democracy*. In an *aristocracy*, the corps of those who hold power can also vote to fill their own vacancies; if they fill all their own vacancies, it is a *pure* aristocracy; if they fill only some of them (such that the people elect some of the magistrates directly), it is a *mixed aristocracy*, or an *aristo-democracy*. It is also possible for a perpetual president of the government to be elected, in the case of an *elective kingdom*.

In all these cases, the vote is taken either from the entire populace (such that every citizen is eligible to vote) or only from a part of it. Thus the right to vote is either limited or unlimited. The only true limitation of the right to vote is when eligibility is based on birth; for, if each citizen can attain any office within the state, but [163] can ascend to the higher ones only step by step from the lower ones, then the vote is not absolutely, but only relatively, limited. But if the right to vote is absolutely limited and eligibility to vote is based on birth, then the constitution is a *hereditary aristocracy*; and this brings us to the second possible scenario mentioned above, namely that the representatives are not personally elected.

That is, it is possible for the representatives to be such by birth; either they attain their status as representatives solely by birth (as does the crown prince in every hereditary monarchy); or they are, by virtue of their birth, at least the only ones eligible to vote for the highest state offices (as is the nobility in general in monarchies, and the patricians in particular in hereditary–aristocratic republics).

It is through the law (i.e. through the original will of the populace who give themselves a constitution), that each of these regimes obtains the force of right. All are rightful regimes as long as an ephorate is present; and all can produce and maintain universal right within a state, as long as the ephorate is efficacious and properly organized.

The question concerning which governmental constitution is best suited for a particular state is not a question for the doctrine of right but for politics; its answer depends on which constitutional form will enable the ephorate to function most strongly.

In cases where an ephorate has not yet been established, or where – because the majority are still barbarians – it cannot be established, hereditary representation is the most advantageous form. This is because someone who holds power unjustly and fears neither God nor any human tribunal, will at least fear the revenge that – because of all his wrongs – will pile on top of his (perhaps innocent) descendants and, in accordance with the necessary course of nature, come crashing down on them with complete certainty.

(VII) The persons to whom the populace have offered the execution of public power must have accepted it, and must have made themselves accountable for [164] how they administer it before the tribunal of the populace; otherwise, they would not be representatives and power would not have been transferred to them.

Their acceptance of public power must be voluntary, and both parties (the populace and representatives) must reach a good-faith agreement about it. For, although the law of right requires that there be public power as well as persons who are expressly appointed to administer it; and although there therefore exists a right to coerce each person to agree to the establishment of such power; nevertheless, the law of right says nothing about which particular persons should be given this power.

Here we shall follow the very same reasoning we followed above in our examination of the contract concerning private property. Since the law of right cannot be applied at all unless a public power has been established, and since such a power cannot be established unless it is transferred to particular persons, it follows that there is a right to coerce each person to give his particular consent to the appointment of these persons; further, there is a right to coerce each person to decide (in the event that he is elected) whether he will accept the office or not. The election (and here this means the determination of how in general the representative positions in this state are to be filled, i.e. the entire section of the constitution dealing with this issue) must be established through the absolute *agreement of all*. For, although there is also a general right to coerce each person to enter into a civil constitution, there is no right to coerce a person to enter into any particular one. Now since a state becomes a particular state by virtue of both the persons who hold power and by the law that establishes how they are to be elected, no one has a right to force someone else to recognize as his own the representative or representatives that the first person has recognized. If people cannot agree about which representatives are to be recognized, the larger and therefore stronger group will lay claim to the territory in which they live, and the others (since they can no longer be tolerated in the same territory) will have a choice: either to join the majority, in which case the vote [165] becomes unanimous; or to leave the territory and thus no longer count themselves as belonging to this union, in which case the vote, once again, becomes unanimous. Since, in general, a contract becomes inviolable and irrevocable when (but *only* when) a rightful relation would not be possible without it, this also holds for the contract in which the state transfers executive power to particular persons, and which we shall call the transfer contract [*Uebertragungscontract*].

Once a person has accepted public power, he may not give it up unilaterally, but only with the consent of the populace, because if his position cannot be suitably filled, his resignation might, at the very least, interrupt the rule of right or even cause it to cease altogether. Similarly, the populace may not unilaterally cancel their contract with him: for the job of administering the state is his position within the state, it was allocated to him as his possession; and insofar as he holds this possession pursuant to the transfer contract, he has no other; this is what was allocated to him, when all the citizens were allocated their property; therefore if the populace were to cancel the contract unilaterally, there could not be any *rightful relation* between him and the commonwealth. But if he willingly accepts such a cancellation and comes to an agreement with the populace concerning compensation, then he may do so.

Furthermore – since, under this contract, the one who administers public power makes himself accountable for seeing to it that right and security prevail, he must inevitably insist on having the power (and the free use thereof) that he deems, or ever will deem, necessary for achieving that end; and such power must be granted to him. He must be granted the right to determine what each person should contribute towards promoting the state's ends, as well as the right to apply this power entirely according to the best of his knowledge and conviction. (We shall soon see the extent to which this power must nevertheless be limited.) Therefore, the power of the state must be placed [166] at his free disposal, without any limitation, as is already implied by the concept of state power.

Public power must be used to secure right for all individuals in all cases, and to thwart and punish injustice. It accepts responsibility for doing so, and any undiscovered violation will have the most unfortunate consequences for the state and for public power itself. Therefore, those who administer public power must have the power and the right to keep watch over the citizens' conduct; they have *police power* and *police legislation*.

The foregoing account already implies that in the civil contract, each person has unreservedly subjected his own judgment concerning right to the judgment of the state and to the administrator of state power (now that we have posited such an administrator); and therefore that the administrator of state power is necessarily a judge whose decisions cannot be appealed.

(VIII) Now to which law of coercion is this highest state power itself to be subordinated, so that it can always bring about right, and nothing but right?

We said above in general: it must be physically impossible for the public power, or, in this case, those who administer it, to have a will other than the will of right. We have also already indicated above how, in general, this is to be achieved. Their private end, i.e. the end of their own security and wellbeing, must be linked to the common end and must be attainable only if the common end is attained. They must be incapable of having any interest other than that of promoting the common end.

Right is merely *formal*; therefore, those who administer public power must be incapable of having any *material* interest whatsoever in their verdicts, any interest in how their verdicts turn out in this or that case. The only thing that can matter to them is that their verdicts accord with right (and certainly not how their verdicts might sound).

[167] Thus first of all, they must be completely independent of all private persons in all of their private ends (i.e. with respect to their needs). They must have an ample and secure income, so that no private person can do them any favors, and so that any inducement they might be offered will come to nothing.

In order not to be led astray into partisanship, those who administer the executive power must have as few friendships, connections, and attachments among private persons as possible.

Above we presented the following principle, aimed at securing equal right for all individuals in all cases: the law shall make its judgments in chronological order and shall not decide any future case until it has dealt with the earlier ones. Now once a regular judicial institution has been established (one that is always at work, perhaps with several things at once); and since some disputes concerning right may be easier to decide than others; and since it is of the utmost importance to avoid delays in the administration of right; it follows that this principle, as presented above, must cease to apply. But this judicial institution must always be able to prove that it is actually at work investigating all of the claims brought before it: furthermore, it is absolutely necessary that a definite time be fixed (according to the type of dispute at issue) within which each claim must be fully dealt with; otherwise, the law would lose its force (as implied by the principle stated above). Without these requirements, it would be completely impossible to tell whether everyone has really been treated rightfully; and no one could ever complain that he has been denied his rights, since the judge could always silence him by saying that his claim will be dealt with in the future.

But the following is a sure criterion for determining whether right is being administered as it should. The judgments and procedures of those who hold public power may never contradict themselves; they must always handle a new case in the same way they handled a similar case in the past. Each of their public actions must be made into an inviolable law. This commits them to doing what is right. They can never will to proceed unjustly, [168] for if they did, they would have to do the same from now on in all similar situations, in which case the most obvious insecurity would soon result. Or, if they are later forced to deviate from their first maxim, everyone will immediately see that they proceeded unjustly.

In order to enable people to judge whether right is being administered as it should, all the proceedings of those who hold state power, along with all the circumstances and reasons for their decisions, must, without exception, be fully publicized – at least after each case has been closed. For in certain cases involving the police, state power might have to be exercised in secret, in order to ensure public safety (for which those who hold public power are accountable to the populace). Those who administer public power must be granted this much, but once public safety is ensured, their proceedings may no longer remain secret. And public safety is ensured, once their verdict has been pronounced and carried out.

(IX) If those who hold power administer their office according to the laws we have been describing, then right, justice, and security will prevail, and each person, on entering the state, will be fully guaranteed what is his. But since honesty and trust cannot be presupposed, how will those who hold power themselves be forced to adhere to these laws? This is the final issue to be addressed in solving the problem of a rational state constitution.

The executive power has the last word in judgments concerning right; its final judgments cannot be appealed; no one *may* (since such unappealability is the condition of any relation of right whatsoever) and no one *can* (since the executive branch has superior power, relative to which all private power is infinitely small) invalidate the executive power's judgments or prevent them from being carried out. Presumptive right, which is constituted as certain right, has spoken in the person of the judges, who have been declared infallible. Upon their judgment, every case must come to an end and every verdict must be carried out infallibly in the sensible world.

There are only two situations that clearly prove that the constitution has been violated: (1) where the law [169] has not been brought to bear on a particular case within the prescribed amount of time; and (2) where those who administer public power contradict themselves or must commit obvious injustices in order not to contradict themselves.

Furthermore, it has been proved that only the populace can sit in judgment of those who administer the executive power. But there is a difficulty here: where, and what, is "the populace"? Is it anything more than a mere concept, and if it is supposed to be more, then how is it to be realized?

Before the tribunal of public power – and since this tribunal continues to exist without interruption and without end – all the members of the state are only private persons, and not the populace; each is always subordinate to the superior power of the state. Each person's will is only his private will, and the common will is expressed only through the will of the superior power. The populace, as such, do not have a separate will and cannot actualize themselves as the populace, until they have detached their will from the will of the executive power and retracted their declaration that the executive power's will is always their own.

But how can this happen? No private person has the right to say: the populace ought to convene, all individuals who until now have been private persons ought to come together and be the populace; for if this individual's will does not accord with the will of those who hold public power (a will that still does represent the common will), then the individual's will is a private will, one that contradicts and rebels against the common will and thus one that constitutes a rebellion and must immediately be punished as such. But the will of this individual will never accord with the will of those who hold public power, and those who hold public power will never want to convene the populace. Those who hold public power either know that their administration is just, in which case it would completely contradict the original common will if, in the absence of an emergency, one were to disturb individuals in their private affairs and interrupt the administration of right; or else they [170] know that they have acted contrary to right; in which case it is implausible that they will surrender the power that they still hold and will themselves call the populace together to be their judge. Thus, they continue to be their own judges; there is no higher judge for them to fear, since the very existence of such a judge depends on their decision to call the populace together; and the constitution remains, now as before, despotic. – In sum: only the populace can declare themselves to be the populace; and thus – before they can declare themselves to be the populace – they would have to convene as the populace, which, as one can see, is contradictory.

There is only one way to eliminate this contradiction: *The constitution must specify in advance the circumstances under which the people shall come together as the populace.*

The most obvious scenario is that such a constitutional law could prescribe that the people assemble on a regular basis at certain, specified times, so that the magistrates could give them an account of how the state is being administered. Such an arrangement is feasible in small states (especially republics), where the population is not widely dispersed, and thus where they can convene easily and without taking up much time, and also where the state administration is simple and easy to assess. But even in small states, this momentous legal proceeding tends to lose its dignity when people become too accustomed to it; also, individuals will have time to prepare in advance for it, the usual result of which is that the private will of scheming, ambitious parties will prevail over the common will. But in a state of considerable size – and in several respects it is better for states not to be small – a constitutional law of this kind would not even be feasible. For, even abstracting from the fact that, in a large state, the above-mentioned abuses would occur only more extensively and with greater danger, regular assemblies would necessarily take up people's time and interfere with their private lives, so that their concern to protect themselves from such disruptions would itself become the biggest disruption of all.

Therefore, it is possible to establish the following principle: *The populace must never be convened except when it is necessary; but as soon as it* [**171**] *is necessary, they must come together immediately, and be willing and able to voice themselves.*

It will never be necessary for them to convene (and they will also never want to convene), unless right and the law have ceased to function altogether; but in that case they must, and surely will, convene.

In a rightfully ordered state, right and law in general must be linked to the rights of each individual; therefore, the law must be completely nullified wherever it has clearly failed to function as it ought (i.e. if a case has not been resolved within the specified amount of time, or if power has been applied in a contradictory manner, or if some injustice or violation is otherwise obvious).

But now who is to judge whether the law has thus failed? Not the populace, for they are not convened; not the state authorities, for they would then be judges in their own case. Even less can it be the person who believes that he has suffered injustice, for then he, too, would be judge in his own case. Therefore – *the constitution must establish a particular power expressly for the sake of judging whether the law has failed to function as it should.*

This power would have to oversee continuously how public power is administered, and thus we can call it the *ephors*.

The executive power is accountable to no one other than the assembled populace; thus the ephors cannot sit in judgment of those who hold public power; they must, however, constantly observe how state business is conducted. They therefore have the right to make inquiries wherever they can. The ephors may not block the judgments of those who hold public power, for such judgments cannot be appealed. Neither may the ephors themselves issue a verdict in a particular case, for the magistrative authority is the only judge in the state. *Thus the ephors have absolutely no executive power.*[c]

[172] But they do have an *absolutely prohibitive* power; not to prohibit this or that *particular* verdict from being carried out, for in that case they would be judges, and the executive power would not be unappealable; but rather to nullify henceforth all administration of right whatsoever; to suspend public power completely and in all of its parts. This nullification of all enforcement of right I shall call *state interdict* (by analogy to interdict within the church. The church long ago invented this infallible device to enforce the obedience of those who need her.).

Therefore, it is a principle of any rational and rightful state constitution that an *absolutely negative* power is to be posited alongside the *absolutely positive* one. Since the ephors hold no power at all and the executive power holds an infinitely superior power, one might well ask how the former, on the basis of their command alone, can coerce the latter to suspend its operations. But this coercion will come of its own accord. For the publicly announced suspension of the executive power

---

[c] In this respect, the ephorate (in the narrower sense of the word) that has been deduced here on the basis of pure reason is completely different from the ephorate in the [172] Spartan constitution, from the state inquisition of Venice, and the like. The *people's tribunes* in the Roman republic bear the closest resemblance to the ephorate discussed here.

is simultaneously an announcement that, henceforth, anything decided by the executive power is invalid and unenforceable as a matter of right; and it is only natural that, from that moment onward, parties whose claims have been denied by the executive power will no longer submit to its judgments, and – by the same token – parties who have won their cases before the tribunal of the executive power will no longer rely on its judgments.

Furthermore, the interdict declares that those who had previously administered the executive power are merely private persons and that all their orders commanding the use of power are unenforceable as a matter of right. From the moment of the interdict onwards, any use of power based on their command is an act of resistance against the common will as declared by the ephors, and is therefore an act of rebellion and must be punished as such, and so – as we shall soon see – will be punished with absolute certainty.

Can the magistrates [173] expect to incur a more severe punishment for resisting the ephors' interdict, than they would incur if their case is brought before the populace? This cannot be, for in the latter case, the highest possible punishment awaits them anyhow. However, if they resist the ephors' interdict, they are treating their case (a case they could still win) as a lost cause; and so by resisting the interdict they already incur – even before the reasons for imposing the interdict can be examined – the highest possible punishment, one they still might have been able to escape. Thus the magistrates are not likely to resist.

The announcement of the interdict is at the same time a call for the populace to convene. The populace are compelled, by this the greatest misfortune that could befall them, to assemble immediately. The ephors are, by the nature of their role, the accusing party, and they have the floor to state their case.

To say that the populace ought to convene does not mean that every person from every part of the (perhaps very extensive) state is supposed to gather in one place (which might be completely impossible in many cases); rather, it means only that everyone is to take part in the proposed investigation, which can certainly be discussed in every city and village of the realm, and that everyone is to cast his vote concerning it. How this is to be arranged so that the result truly reflects the common will, is a question for politics and certainly not for the doctrine of right. But, for a reason we shall indicate below, it is necessary in this kind of proceeding that, here and there, large groups of the people actually do come together in one place.

Whatever the populace decide becomes constitutional law.

Therefore, it is necessary first of all for the populace to decide that the interdict announced by the ephors is formally valid as a matter of right – regardless of what they think about the content of the dispute – and that any resistance to it is to be punished as a form of rebellion. If they should decide otherwise, they would be annulling the entire interdict, and thus also nullifying the ephorate's very efficacy, and therefore, in essence, nullifying the ephorate itself, assigning to themselves [**174**] a superior power with no accountability, i.e. the populace would be establishing a despotism, which is contrary to the law of right and altogether unlikely. They will not do this, because what is right is bound up with what is advantageous to them.

Furthermore, as regards the content of this proceeding, the judgment of the populace will necessarily be just, i.e. in accordance with the original common will. If they acquit a magistrate who, according to the ephors' charge, had allowed a deed to go unpunished (and there can and must be no doubt concerning the *facts* of the case, and the ephors must see to it that there is none), they would be deciding thereby that such a deed ought never to be punished, but is instead a rightful action, i.e. one that can be done to any one of them as well. If the executive power is accused of acting in a contradictory manner or committing an obvious injustice and if the populace says that there is no such contradiction or injustice, then the populace thereby make the executive power's dubious or apparently unrightful maxim into a fundamental law of the state, in accordance with which each of them also wants to be treated. Therefore, the populace will doubtlessly reflect on the matter very carefully and strive to avoid rendering an unjust verdict.

The losing party, whether the ephors or the executive power, will be guilty of high treason. If the ephors' accusation turns out to be ungrounded, they will have interrupted the administration of right, which is the commonwealth's most important business; if the executive power is found guilty, it will be because it has used the power of the state to stifle the administration of right.

No one will think it excessive that the executive power can be held liable for high treason; but perhaps it might seem so in the case of the ephors. One could argue that it seemed to them that the law was in danger; they acted according to their conscience and simply made a mistake. But the same can also be said of those who hold executive power, and the following answer applies in both cases: a mistake here is just as dangerous as a bad will, and the law must seek to prevent such mistakes just as vigilantly [175] as it suppresses bad wills. The wisest among the people ought to be elected as magistrates; and especially old, mature men as ephors.

Besides, before announcing any interdict, the ephors will probably negotiate with those who hold power, to try to get them to discontinue or correct their injustice voluntarily and without causing a stir; and by doing this, the ephors will automatically become thoroughly acquainted with what is really involved in the case.

The people's decision is retroactively valid; judgments based on maxims that have been rejected by the people's decision shall be annulled, and persons who have been harmed by such judgments shall be restored to their previous positions; but they shall be restored without detriment to other parties, who acted according to a presumptively valid, albeit now discredited, law of right. Compensation must be provided by the judges who caused the harm. The reason the people's decision is to be valid retroactively is that the losing party was not allowed to appeal against the judge's verdict, since it was necessary to presume that the judge's will agreed with the true, common will: the judgment's validity was grounded on the presumption that the judgment was lawful. Now it turns out that the opposite is the case: this ground no longer obtains, and so neither does the grounded. It is as if the judgment had never been pronounced.

The positive and negative powers – the executors and the ephors – are the parties to be judged before the assembled populace; therefore, they themselves cannot be judges in their own case and do not belong to the populace, who in this context can now also be called *the people* [*das Volk*]. – The ephors bring the suit, as noted above, and so are the accusing party; the executors are accountable for the charges, and so are the defendants.

(To what extent are the magistrates a part of the people? This question, like many others, has been raised before in general terms, and so people have answered it in a general, and therefore [176] one-sided way, because they failed to define the specific circumstances under which they wanted the answer to apply.

154

Here is the answer. Before the magistrates were elected, they were not magistrates; they were not at all what they now are; they were something different and therefore were part of the people. If magistrates are born as representatives, like a crown prince, then they never were part of the people. Before being elected to state office, persons born into the aristocracy or nobility are private persons and part of the people. They are not magistrates, but only eligible (exclusively eligible) to be elected as such. Since those who are born into the aristocracy and nobility might be biased in favor of the executive power, the constitution must include safeguards to ensure that their voice does not detrimentally influence the decisions of the common will; how this is to be done is a question for politics.

Just as soon as the magistrates have been elected, even before they have accepted their positions, they are no longer part of the people, for they are now negotiating with the people; and in such negotiations, they and the people are two different parties. If they clearly declare that they do not accept the office offered to them, they return to being part of the people.

But if they do accept the office offered to them, they are forever excluded from being part of the people.

In accepting responsibility for public security and right, the magistrates put their own person and freedom at risk, and so they must not merely be able to ratify legislation; they must have a decisive *negative* vote (a veto); i.e. the transfer contract must give them the option of saying: we do not want to rule in accordance with such laws; but then the people must also have the option of saying: if you do not want to rule in accordance with laws that we judge to be good, let someone else rule.

With the completion of the transfer contract, the populace automatically become subjects; and from that point onward, the populace as such no longer exist; the people are not a people, not [177] a whole, but only an aggregate of subjects: and the magistrates, too, are no longer part of the people.

If, with the announcement of the interdict, the populace convene in the manner described, then the magistrates, as we have shown, are parties in the case and once again are not part of the people. If the magistrates win this momentous legal proceeding, they are magistrates once again and not part of the people; if they lose it, their only possible punishment is exclusion from the state, i.e. banishment, in which case, they again are not part of the people. Accordingly, the magistrates are never part of the people and are forever excluded from the people by the transfer contract.)

(X) The security of the whole commonwealth depends on the absolute freedom and personal security of the ephors. By virtue of their position, their job is to serve as a counter-weight to the executive authorities, who have been endowed with superior power. Thus, first and foremost, it must be completely impossible for the ephors to become dependent on the executive power in matters pertaining to their well-being, and so the ephors must be eminently well paid, as well paid as the executive power. Furthermore, as one would expect, the ephors will be exposed to the snares and threats of the executive power, and will have no defense other than the power of the populace, which, however, are not assembled. Therefore, the law must make them secure in their persons, i.e. they must be declared inviolable (*sacrosancti*). The slightest act of violence against them, or even only the threat of violence, shall be *high treason*, i.e. a direct assault on the state. Such an assault, encouraged or undertaken by the executive power, shall automatically count as an announcement of the interdict; for by assaulting the state in this way, the executive power clearly and directly severs its will from the common will.

Furthermore, the power of the people must exceed beyond all measure the power that the executive officials possess. If the power of the latter could even come close to counter-balancing that of the people, then – if the executive officials wanted to oppose the people – there would at least arise a war between them, something the constitution must make impossible. If the executive officials had superior power, or [178] if they could ever acquire it in the course of a war, they would be able to subjugate the people, which would result in unconditional slavery.

Therefore, a condition of the rightfulness of any civil constitution is that the executive power should never, under any pretext, acquire power that is capable in the slightest of resisting the power of the populace. Every end must be sacrificed to this, the highest possible end, the preservation of right in general.

Moreover, this is precisely why a principal maxim for a rational constitution (and it is necessary to make provisions for implementing this maxim) is that when the populace convene throughout the country – for instance, in the country's remote villages – they should assemble in groups that are large enough to muster adequate resistance against any possible attempts by the executive officials to oppose them; so that, as a result, once the populace declare themselves as the populace, a very formidable force will have already been mobilized.

(XI) An important question in this connection is: how is the people's decision to be determined? Must their decision be unanimous, or is a majority of votes sufficient, and do those in the minority have to submit to the majority?

As we have shown above, unanimity is necessary where the civil contract is concerned. Each person must declare for himself that he wants to enter into a commonwealth with this particular group of people for the purpose of maintaining right.

The situation was quite different when it came to the election of magistrates. Of course, the minority were not required to accede to the majority; but since they were the weaker party, they could be forced by the stronger party to leave this place (i.e. the place where the majority now want to realize the constitution they have designed), and to take up residence elsewhere. If the minority do not want to leave – and they will hardly want to do so – then they will have to let themselves be bound by the majority's opinion. This is because they would obviously be too weak to resist the majority. Therefore, our proof implies that [**179**] here, too, there must be a decisive majority, such that there is no chance that violence might break out and no need at all to fear a war (which is always contrary to right): thus the election of magistrates must not rest on a margin of just one or a few votes. Until it is possible to achieve a decisive majority, they will have to try to reach some agreement among themselves.

In deliberations as to whether the accused executive officials have proceeded rightfully or not, there cannot be – in accordance with our premises – a great diversity of opinions. First of all, the *deed* to be judged must be clear, and – given the nature of the issue – it will be. Then the only question is: is this just or not, should it be, for all time, lawful for us, or not? This question is to be answered briefly, and with a decisive "yes" or "no." Thus there can be only *two* opinions, affirmation or denial; a third option is not possible.

Now assuming that the citizens all possess at least ordinary, sound judgment, this question is very easy to decide and – as was already shown above – it is so directly related to the weal and woe of each individual that because of its very nature, it will always be answered with complete unanimity, such that one can assume in advance that whoever answers it differently from the majority either is partisan or lacks sound judgment. It will be incumbent upon the more sensible citizens amicably to correct those who lack sound judgment and to bring them around to accepting the general opinion. If they cannot be convinced, they will arouse the strong suspicion that they are partisan, and thus dangerous citizens. If they simply cannot agree with the majority's opinion, then, of course, they are not obligated to make their security depend on a law that they do not acknowledge as right: but by the same token, they can no longer live among a people that lets itself be judged in accordance with this law; they must [180] therefore emigrate from the state – without, however, any detriment to their property (to the extent that it is absolute property and can be taken with them, which shall be discussed in good time). Since emigrating may involve substantial inconveniences, it is hardly to be expected that anyone will undertake to do so unless he is firmly convinced that the majority's opinion will destroy general security, and so it is likely that people will accede to the majority's decision, so that the decision turns out to be unanimous. Thus in all cases, my theory, as always, assumes not the rightfulness of the *majority's* opinion, but only the rightfulness of *unanimity*; but I have claimed that those who do not want to submit to the overwhelming majority (which, in our case, could quite easily be set by the constitution at seven-eighths or even higher) thereby cease to be members of the state, thus making the vote unanimous. The main point not to be overlooked is this: the majority of votes, as we have shown, must come very close to being all the votes.

(XII) Under the constitution we have been describing, right, and only right, will infallibly and necessarily prevail, so long as the ephors do not unite with the executive power to oppress the people. This final and most challenging obstacle to a just constitution must likewise be removed.

The ephors ought not to be dependent on the executive power, and it ought to be impossible for the executive power to do favors for them. The ephors must not have any connections, relationships, friendships, or the like with those who administer executive power. The people will be on guard against such relations, and – if they were to arise – the ephors would immediately lose the people's trust.

Furthermore it is advisable, in fact almost necessary, that those who hold executive power be appointed for life, because they must leave behind their professions in order to serve; but it is equally [181] advisable that ephors be appointed only for a *determinate* period of time, since they do not need to give up their professions in order to serve. Retiring ephors must give to the incoming ephors an account of what took place during their term of office; if some injustice has occurred and continues to make itself felt, the new ephors are immediately obligated to call the populace together by announcing the interdict and to let the populace have their say concerning both the retired ephors and the executive officials. It is obvious that an ephor who has been found guilty is to be punished for high treason. – But to have administered the duties of the ephorate with honor entitles a person to enjoy for life the highest of honors.

The ephors must be appointed by the *people*, not by the executive power (which would obviously be inappropriate); nor can the ephors appoint their own replacements, because the new ephors are the judges of the outgoing ones, and if the outgoing ephors could appoint the new ones, they would be able to insure their own impunity. The constitution must determine the manner in which the ephors are to be elected. No one may petition to become an ephor; the kind of person who should become an ephor is one who has gained the attention and trust of the people (who, precisely in order to fulfill this sublime task of electing the ephors, will continuously notice their great and honest men).

(XIII) If, after these provisions have been made, the ephors should still ally themselves with the executive power in order to oppose the freedom of the people, then such could be possible only if – of all the country's exemplary men who have been elected over time to be ephors – there is not even one who did not become corrupt immediately upon taking office; and furthermore only if every one of these ephors could count on the corruption of all the others with such confidence as to be able to let all of his own security depend on it. This is impossible, or, if it is possible, one could easily conclude: a people so corrupt that those who are universally recognized to be the best among them are of such low morals, do not deserve a better fate than the one they are given. [182] But since a rigorous science must take into account even the most improbable of scenarios, the following advice applies to such a case.

Any private person who calls the populace together *in opposition to the will* of the executive power (which, as long as the populace are not convened, represents the common will) – and calling the populace together will always be contrary to the will of the executive power, because the latter, by nature, will never want to call the populace together – is, as shown above, a rebel (because his will is rebelling against the presumptive common will and seeking to amass a force against it).

But – and one should note this well – the people[d] are never rebels, and applying the expression *rebellion* to the people is the most absurd thing that has ever been said; for the people, both in fact and as a matter of right, is the highest authority, above which there is no other; it is the source of all other authority, and is accountable only to God. When the people assemble, the executive branch loses its power, both in fact and as a matter of right. A rebellion can only be a rebellion against a superior. But what on earth is superior to the people! The people can rebel only against themselves, which is absurd. Only God is above the people; therefore, one can say: if the people have rebelled against their ruler, then one must presume that the ruler is a god, which just might be difficult to prove.

Therefore, two scenarios are possible: *either* in such a case the people themselves rise up unanimously, perhaps provoked by violence too terrible to ignore, and pass judgment on the ephors and the executive officials. By its very nature, their uprising is always just – not only formally, but also materially – for so long as the insecurity and the poor administration of the state do not oppress them *all* and do not become universally harmful, every individual will look out only for himself and try to get by as best he can. No people have ever risen up in unison like a single man – nor ever will – [183] unless the injustice has reached an extreme.

Or, in the second scenario: one or more private persons will incite the state's subjects to constitute themselves as a people: these persons, of course, must be presumed to be rebels and – in accordance with presumptive right (as long as the populace have not yet constituted

---

[d] It should be understood that I speak of the *entire people.*

themselves) – will be punished as such by the executive power (assuming it can apprehend them), in accordance with the presumptive common will. But an unjust power is always weak, because it is inconsistent and because general opinion – and often even the opinion of those it uses as its tools – is opposed to it; and the more unjust it is, the weaker and more powerless it is. And so the more despicable the executive power is, the more likely it is that those who incite the people will escape their punishment.

Now the populace either will or will not rise up in response to the inciters' call. If they do, the executive power will dissolve into nothing and the populace will judge between the executive officials and the inciters, just as they would otherwise between the executive officials and the ephors. If the populace find that the call to rise up was well grounded, then the will of the inciters will be confirmed (by the will of the populace, declared after the fact) as the true common will; it will become clear that the inciters' will contains the *content* of right, and it will acquire the *form* of right (which it still lacks) from the assent of the populace. On account of their heart and virtue, the inciters will be the nation's saviors, and its unordained, natural ephors. By contrast, if the populace find that the inciters' call and accusations were ungrounded, then they are rebels, and will be condemned as such by the populace.

If the people do not rise up, this proves *either* that the oppression and public insecurity have not yet become sufficiently palpable, or that they really did not exist at all; *or* that the people have not yet awakened to will their freedom and to know their rights; that they are not yet mature enough to take up the great legal task assigned to them; and therefore, that they never should have been incited to rise up in the first place. [184] Those who incited the people are to be punished as rebels, in accordance with external right that is entirely legitimate, even though – according to internal right and before the tribunal of their own consciences – they may well be martyrs of right. As far as their intentions are concerned, they may be innocent; but as far as their actions are concerned, they will be punished as entirely guilty; they should have known their own nation better. If such a nation were to have risen up, the result would have been the destruction and nullification of all right.

The provisions presented here concerning the election of those who administer the executive power, the election of the ephors, and their duties, are laws pertaining to how the law is to be administered; and all the laws of this kind, taken together, are called the constitution. Thus in the third section of the doctrine of political right, we shall discuss *the constitution*.

(XIV) The constitution (and by this we obviously mean a rightful and rational one) is unchangeable and valid for all time, and it is necessarily posited as such in the civil contract.

For every individual must consent to the constitution; therefore, the constitution is guaranteed by the original common will. Each individual has entered into the state only under the guarantee that this *particular* constitution provides for his security. He cannot be forced to consent to another constitution. But since – in the event that another constitution were to be implemented nonetheless – an individual could not live under a government ruled by a constitution that he has not approved but rather would have to leave the state (which contravenes the original contract), it follows that the constitution may not be changed at all, if even only one individual were opposed to the change. Thus a change in the constitution requires *absolute* unanimity.

The difference between the absolute unanimity needed to change the constitution, and the relative unanimity deduced above, is this: relative unanimity may be achieved by excluding some individuals from the state in cases of emergency, but absolute unanimity may not be achieved in this way. With relative [185] unanimity, an individual's right to remain a citizen is contingent on his accession to the majority; with absolute unanimity, the right to remain a citizen is absolute.

We have said that a constitution that is rightful in general (i.e. insofar as it contains a constituted, but accountable, executive power as well as an ephorate) is unchangeable. – But within the general parameters of rightfulness, an infinite number of modifications are possible, and it is these further determinations that are changeable.

If a constitution is not rightful, it may be changed so as to be made into a rightful one: and no one is permitted to say, I do not want to give up the previous constitution. For the people's tolerance of a previous, unrightful constitution is excusable only if they had been ignorant about, or incapable of adopting, a rightful one; but as soon as the concept of a rightful constitution is available to them and the nation is capable of realizing it, everyone is obligated to accept it, for *right ought to prevail*.

The situation is different when it comes to improving and amending civil legislation. This occurs of its own accord. At first, the state was composed of a particular group of human beings, who pursued this and that particular trade, and the law was tailored to these particular circumstances. These groups grew in number, new means of livelihood arose – of course, none may arise without the state's approval – and so then the law had to change out of necessity, in order to remain suitable for this people, which has completely changed; and the executive power is responsible for seeing to it that the law is always suitable for the people.

(XV) The entire mechanism described here is necessary if a rightful relation among human beings is to be realized; but it is certainly not necessary that all of these motors and springs always operate externally and visibly. Rather, the more finely tuned a state is, the less these things will be noticed, because the state's quiet power, its inner weight, will eliminate in advance any possibility of its [186] having to operate externally. The state itself pre-empts its own action.

The most immediate task of the state is to settle disputes among the citizens concerning property. The more simple, clear, and comprehensive the law is, and the more certain its infallible execution, the less frequent such disputes about property will be, because everyone will be able to know rather precisely what does and does not belong to him, and will hardly undertake what he can see will be a futile attempt to appropriate another's property. If the few disputes that might yet arise out of error are settled correctly and in a manner that is intelligible to both parties, then crime will cease to exist. For what is the source of all crimes other than greed and the passions it arouses, or also poverty and need – neither of which would exist if the law kept careful watch over each person's property? How can crimes occur, once their sources are eliminated? Good civil law, if it is strictly administered, will completely eliminate the need to enforce criminal law. – Besides, who will dare to commit a crime if he knows with certainty that it will be discovered and punished? If these laws were enforced for only half a century, the concept of crime would disappear from the consciousness of the happy people who lived under them.

If the executive power has so little to do, it will have that much less of an opportunity to be unjust. Its rare exercise of power will be an act that inspires respect for both the people and itself; all eyes will be upon the executive power, and the respect it necessarily inspires in the nation will provide it with respect for itself (if there were any danger that it would not otherwise have any).

Likewise, the ephorate will never have to exercise its authority, because the executive power will always be just; there will never be any need to consider an interdict or a people's tribunal.

Therefore, if the concepts we have presented should cause anyone fear, or [187] if the idea of a people's tribunal should lead someone to imagine God knows what atrocities, here are two reasons why one should not be disturbed. First: only a lawless mob yields to excess, not a deliberative body that assembles under and in accordance with the law, and in conformity with a determined, formal procedure. Formal procedure – let it be said in passing – is one of human beings' greatest blessings. By forcing them to pay careful attention to certain details, formal procedures force human beings to take care in whatever they are doing. Anyone who wants to exempt humankind from all formal procedures does not have the good of humanity in mind.

Second: all of these provisions have been set up, not to be implemented, but to make the situations in which they would have to be implemented impossible. It is precisely where these provisions have been set up that they are superfluous, and it is only where they have not been set up that they are necessary.

[191] Foundations of Natural Right
According to the Principles of the *Wissenschaftslehre*: Part II, or Applied Natural Right

First section of the doctrine of political right
Concerning the civil contract [*Staatsbürgervertrag*]

§17

(A)

First of all, we shall analyze – and with greater care than has been necessary up to this point – the concept of a contract in general.

To begin with, a contract involves two persons, whether natural or mystical; these two persons are posited as each willing the same object as his exclusive property. – Therefore, the thing they contract about must be the kind of thing that can become a person's exclusive property, i.e. it must be the kind of thing that does not get changed when it becomes a person's property but (by virtue of its own essence and nature) remains as it was when a person thinks it in his concept of an end; furthermore, it must be the kind of thing that – if it remains the same as it was when the person thought it in his concept of an end – can be used only as exclusive property (see §11 (III)). If the first condition were not met, a contract would not be possible; if the second condition were not met, none would be necessary. For this reason, there can be no contract concerning a portion of air or light.

Furthermore, both parties must have the same right to the thing; otherwise, no dispute concerning right would arise between them; [192]

it is precisely this kind of dispute that the contract is supposed to mediate. Now, by their nature, all objects and all free beings who lay claim to such objects fit this description. Prior to the contract, the only right-based reason anyone can adduce as to why he ought to possess the disputed thing is his free and rational nature; but every free being can adduce this same reason. It is impossible for different persons to have a dispute over the ownership of their bodies; this is because it is physically impossible for more than one subject to make natural use of a human body, that is, to set a human body in motion through will alone; however, as we have shown, all free beings have an equal right to all the rest of the sensible world.

But it must be noted that in order for a contract to be possible it is not necessary that the two parties already, *in the present*, lay claim to the same possession; rather, it is necessary only that the two fear that such conflicting claims might arise *in the future*. But in order for a contract to be possible, one of these two scenarios must obtain; for otherwise, the spheres of the freedom of the two parties would be completely separate from one another, and would be regarded by them as such, in which case it would be entirely unnecessary to stipulate by contract what the spheres of their freedom ought to be. – For instance, if you and I are separated by a river we both take to be uncrossable, then it will not occur to either of us to promise the other not to will to cross the river and settle on the other bank. The river is posited for us, by nature herself, as the limit of our physical powers. But if the river were to become shallow enough to wade through, or if we should discover how to traverse it by boat, then – and only then – will it become necessary for us to make an agreement to limit our free choice.

This will of each party to possess this or that thing as his own property is the private will of each. Thus, first of all, a contract involves *two private wills*; since these private wills are directed at an object, they are to be called *material wills*.

Thus in order for a contract to be possible, both parties must will to enter into a contract concerning either their already conflicting claims or their claims that might possibly conflict in the future; [193] moreover, the two parties must will that each one of them, for his part, will yield in his claims to the disputed objects, until their two claims can co-exist. If only one of the two, or if neither, wants to enter into a contract, then no contract is possible and war will inevitably result. According to the law of right, the rational being is required to will to enter into a contract, and so there is a right of coercion that can force each person to do so. (Admittedly, this right of coercion can not actually be applied, since it is impossible to determine how far a person ought to yield in his claims.) This right of coercion exists, because a state of actual war, or even just a state of fear about a possible war, is not a rightful state of affairs: this has all been demonstrated above. – Thus the second requirement for a contract to take place is that *the wills of the two parties be united for the purpose of peaceably resolving their dispute over rights*: and since this unity of will determines the form of a contract, we shall call it *the formally common will*.

A further requirement for the possibility of a contract is that both parties limit the private wills they initially have to the point where these wills are no longer in conflict; what is required, therefore, is that each party, for his part, give something up, and will never to possess what the other wants to keep as his own. We shall refer to this unity of wills as *the materially common will*. In this materially common will, the private wills of both are united in a single common will. – The will of each of the contracting parties is now also directed at the other's property, property that perhaps it was not directed at before; each party's will is now directed at property that he may not have even known about before, since in order for a contract to take place it is not necessary that there already be an actual dispute over the objects, but only that the parties fear a possible dispute in the future; or alternatively, the will of each of the contracting parties is now also directed at property about which he has not yet made any decisions (even if he already did know about the property). Each party's will now extends beyond his own private end, but only as a *negative* will. Each person simply refrains from willing to have the things that the other wills; beyond this, each makes no decisions about what the other wills, other than that he does not want those things for himself. Because of this merely negative will, each is completely indifferent to whatever else might happen to the other's property – e.g. to whether it might be taken from the other by some third party. [**194**] Thus the important point here is that the parties' material will – to the extent that it is a common will – is merely negative.

Finally, the concept of a contract also implies that this common will is established as an enduring will, one that guides all future, free actions of the two parties; it is established as their law of right that will determine their future, rightful relation to one another. As soon as either of the parties goes even one step beyond his limit as specified in the contract, the contract is nullified, and the entire relation of right based on it is canceled.

One might think that in such a case the injured party has only to demand restitution, and that if this were simply provided, then the relation between the two parties would be restored. Now this is certainly correct if the injured party is satisfied with the restitution and wants to renew the contract with the offending party. But in order to understand what follows, it is important to realize that the injured party is not bound, as a matter of right, to be satisfied with such restitution, and that – to be perfectly consistent – the offense nullifies the relation of right between the two parties. We shall now prove this claim.

Before the contract existed, each of the parties had a complete right to anything that the other party wanted for himself, even those things that – as a result of the contract – were actually allotted to the other party. Even if one of the parties did not yet know at the time that a certain thing existed, he still could have learned of it later and subjected it to his ends. It is only through the contract that he lost his right to it. Now the contract exists only insofar as the parties continue to adhere to it; as soon as the contract is breached, it is nullified. But if the ground of something ceases to exist, then what is grounded also ceases to exist; and since the contract provided the only ground for each person's forfeiture of certain things, it follows that – when this ground ceases to exist – so too does each person's forfeiture of everything that belonged to the other. The two parties stand once again in the same relationship they were in before the contract existed.

[195] *(B)*

After these necessary premises, we now proceed to an examination of the civil contract in particular.

(I) There can be no rightful relation among persons without a positive determination of the extent to which each individual's use of his freedom ought to be limited; or, what amounts to the same thing: without some determination of property in the broadest sense of the word (i.e. insofar as it denotes not just the possession of real estate or the like, but a person's rights to free action in the sensible world in general).

Thus if the civil contract is to bring about a universal relation of right, each individual must reach agreement with all other individuals concerning the property – the rights and freedoms – he ought to have, as well as those he ought to leave untouched for the others and over which he ought to relinquish all of his natural entitlements. Every individual must be able to agree with every other individual, *as an individual*, about these things. Think of an individual at the moment of making such a contract; he is the first of the parties required for a contract. Now, in one general concept, bring together all those individuals with whom this first individual must, one by one, enter into a contract. This group of individuals constitutes all the rest – but *only as individuals*, for the first party must contract with them as individuals and as independently existing beings whose decisions are not influenced by anyone else. – What I am saying is that all of these individuals constitute the second party in the contract. Each individual has said to all of them: I will to possess this, and I demand of you that you give up your claim to have any right to it. And all of them have responded: we shall relinquish our claims on the condition that you relinquish your claims to everything else.

This contract contains everything that is required in a contract. First of all, it contains the merely private will of each individual to possess something as his own; without this, the individual would not have entered into the contract we are discussing here. (Thus, each citizen necessarily owns property. If the other citizens had not granted him anything, he would not have relinquished his claim to what they possess, for such [196] relinquishment must be reciprocal; therefore, he would not have entered the civil contract.) Our assumption here is that they all possess a formal will to enter into a contract. Each individual must have agreed with all the others, and all the others must have agreed with each individual, about the content of their possessions; otherwise, the contract would not have come to be, and no relation of right would have been established. – Each individual's will is *positive* only with respect to what he wills to possess for himself; with regard to everyone else's property, it is merely *negative*.

The proposition demonstrated above applies to this contract as well – namely, that each individual's property is recognized by every other individual, only so long as the first individual himself respects the other's property. The smallest violation of another's property nullifies the entire contract and entitles the injured party to take *everything* from the transgressor, if he can. *Therefore, each individual pledges all of his own property as a guarantee that he will not violate any of the others' property.*

I shall refer to this first part of the civil contract as *the citizens' property contract*. If one were to articulate the result of all the individual contracts that have been made, it would be their merely *material* will, the will that is directed towards objects and that determines the limits of the individuals' freedom. This will is what yields *civil law* in the narrower sense of the word; it constitutes the foundation of all the laws that might possibly be enacted in this state concerning property, acquisition, freedoms, and privileges, and it is inviolable.

Each individual has at one time *actually* expressed himself in the manner described, whether through words or actions, by dedicating himself publicly and openly to a particular occupation; and the state has agreed to it, at least tacitly.

Throughout this discussion we have been supposing that everyone enters into a contract with everyone else. Against this, someone might observe: since human beings necessarily go about their business within a particular, limited region, nothing more is required than for each individual to contract only with his three or four closest neighbors. Now [**197**] we have been assuming that this would not be sufficient. Thus our assumption must be that it is possible for anyone to come into contact with any other individual, and therefore that individuals do not remain enclosed within their own spheres, but rather have the right to live among one another and to encounter one another in any region of the state. We shall see later, and in more detail, that this is really the case. Here we are only making the following point: the requirement that the civil contract should be a contract of everyone with everyone implies that any territory on the surface of the earth – although such territory might in part, i.e. in a certain respect, be divided up among individuals – must nevertheless be, in a certain other respect (which the civil contract is to determine), a sphere where everyone can exercise his efficacy. And so the merchant should be allowed to travel about in order to peddle his wares; the herdsman to graze his cattle; the fisherman to cross the farmer's land to reach the riverbanks, and so on – all of which can be allowed only in consequence of the contract.

(II) But now the purpose of the civil contract is to ensure that the boundaries of each individual's exclusive freedom (where such boundaries are determined by the property contract or civil contract) are protected through the coercive power of physical force (since individuals neither can nor will rely merely on the good will of others).

Such coercive power has not been established if – as we have shown – the will of each contracting party remains merely negative in relation to the other's property. Therefore, since the contract we are describing is supposed to be a civil contract, there would have to be yet a second contract joined to the first (i.e. to the property contract); and in this second contract, each individual would promise to all the other individuals (who are still regarded as individuals) that he will use his own power to help them protect the property that is recognized as theirs, on the condition that they, for their part, will likewise help to defend his property against violation. We shall refer to this contract as the *protection contract* [*Schutzvertrag*].

This second contract is conditioned with respect to its content by the first. Each person can only promise to protect [**198**] what he has recognized as the other's right, whether this is an actual, present possession or a general entitlement to acquire a possession in the future (in accordance with a certain rule). But a person can by no means promise to assist the other if the other were to be involved in dealings not allowed by the first contract.

This second contract is distinguished from the first in that the person's will, which had been merely negative in relation to the other's property, now becomes a positive will. Each person not only promises – as he did in the first contract – to refrain from violating the property of everyone else, but now also promises to help protect everyone else's property against possible violations by any *third* party. It makes no sense for a person to promise to protect the other from oneself. If the first person simply refrains from transgressing against the other, then the other already has sufficient protection from him.

The protection contract, like every other contract, is conditioned. In the protection contract each person pledges to help protect all the others, on the condition that the others likewise protect him. The contract and the right it grounds dissolve if one party fails to fulfill the contract's conditions.

(III) The protection contract is distinguished from the property contract by the interesting fact that, in the latter, the parties promise merely to refrain from doing something, while in the former they promise something positive. Therefore, one can know at any time whether the property contract is being fulfilled, since it requires simply that the other party at all times *not* do certain things; by contrast, one cannot know equally well whether the protection contract is being fulfilled, since, according to it, the other party is supposed to do something that he cannot do at all times, and that he is not actually obligated to do at any time. – I shall explain myself more clearly with regard to this very important point.

The protection contract is a conditional contract concerning a positive performance, and as such – when viewed according to strict right – it can have absolutely no effect, but is completely null and empty. The protection contract could be formulated as follows: [199] "I will protect your right, under the condition that you will protect mine." By virtue of what does the one party obtain the right to the other party's protection? Evidently only by virtue of the fact that he *actually protects* the other party.

And if this is so, then, strictly speaking, no party would ever acquire a right to the other's protection. – For the sake of what will follow, it is important that this be clearly understood; and understanding it depends on understanding how this contract is conditioned. I am bound, as a matter of right, to protect you, only under the condition that you protect me. One should carefully consider what the latter clause means. It does not mean: "if you merely have the good will to protect me." For a good will cannot have any validity before the tribunal of external right; besides, a good will could change, and in general everyone has the right never to depend on the good will of others. This clause does not even mean: "if you have already protected me once before." For the past is past, and is of no help to me in the present; morality, gratitude, and other such good inner dispositions might well move me to compensate the other for his past protection; but what is to be grounded here is a claim of right. In the sphere of right, there is no way to bind human beings together other than through the insight: whatever you do to the other, whether good or bad, you do not to him, but to yourself. In the case at hand, this means that I would have to be able to see that, in protecting the other, I protect only myself; I do so either actually in the present, or else – if in the future I should need protection – his protection of me follows with absolute necessity from my having protected him. The former is impossible; for insofar as I do the protecting, I neither need, nor receive, protection; the latter is equally impossible; for the decisions of the other's free will cannot be foreseen with absolute certainty.

The discussion just presented is the clearest way of seeing the matter, but it can also be viewed from several other angles. [200] Either both parties to the protection contract are attacked at the same time: then neither can rush to the other's defense, since each has to look after himself. Or, one of them is attacked first. Then what prevents the other, who is called to come to his defense, from saying: "Our contract is a conditional contract; you acquire the right to my protection, only if you have protected me. Now you have not actually fulfilled this condition – the issue is not whether you could have fulfilled it or whether you have always possessed the good will to fulfill it (if only the opportunity had arisen for you to do so); rather, the only issue is this simple fact – you have not fulfilled the condition. But if the condition does not apply, then neither does the conditioned." This is exactly how the other, for his part, will argue as well; and so what is conditioned will never obtain, since the condition can never obtain. If the one party actually does help the other, the two may come into a relation of moral obligation, but not a relation of right.

For the sake of clarity, let us compare this contract, which is intrinsically void, with the right that is grounded in the property contract. In the property contract, the condition is merely negative on either side; that is, the condition is that each party refrain from violating the rights of the others. It is for this reason that it is always possible to fulfill this condition, and to show clearly before the tribunal of external right, that the contract's binding force is rightfully grounded. The condition is not something, but nothing; it is not an affirmation, but a mere negation, which can always occur at any point in time; and therefore what it conditions can also always occur at any point in time. I am always bound to refrain from violating the other's property, because thereby, and only thereby, do I rightfully prevent the other from violating mine.

If this part of the civil contract, i.e. the protection contract, is void, then the security afforded by the first part, i.e. the property contract, is also nullified. To be sure, as we have just shown, the rights grounded in the property contract continue to exist and can always be shown to exist; but whether someone wants to let himself be [201] bound by right depends on his good will. (This is because the contract that was supposed to justify a coercive power cannot ground even a single right.) Thus we remain, as before, in a state of insecurity and dependence on the good will of others, a will upon which we are neither inclined, nor obligated, to rely.

The difficulty we have just presented must be canceled: and once we solve it, the civil contract will be further – in fact, completely – determined. The crux of the difficulty is that it is always problematic whether or not a person fulfills the obligation he has incurred through the protection contract (and thus whether or not he imposes any obligation on the other). The difficulty would be canceled if things could be arranged such that the fulfillment of such obligations could never be problematic. And this would not be problematic, but certain, if each person's mere entrance into the state automatically entailed that he has already fulfilled protection contract; that is, if each person's promise and fulfillment of the promise were synthetically united, if *word and deed* were one and the same.

(What we have just proved concerning the protection contract in particular is valid for all contracts involving positive obligations, since our proof is based on the general character of any such contracts. Thus, by presenting the form through which the protection contract can become valid as a matter of right (i.e. when one's word itself becomes a deed), we are presenting a form that is valid for all contracts involving positive obligations, a form that, later in this treatise, we shall actually apply to such contracts.)

(IV) The mere existence of the protection contract ought simultaneously and directly to entail that any obligations existing under it have been fulfilled. How can this be arranged? Clearly, only as follows: when the civil contract is formed, a protective power (a power to which each person entering the contract contributes) is simultaneously assembled and posited by means of that very contract. By contributing to the protective power upon entering the state, each person would actually and immediately fulfill the obligations he has under the protection contract to all the others. Hence from that moment on and by virtue of his mere entrance into the state, the question of whether a person will fulfill his obligations under the protection contract would no longer be problematic, for the person [202] has already actually fulfilled them; and continues actually to fulfill them, so long as his contribution is contained as a part of the whole protective power in general.

Now how is this protective power to be established, and what actually takes place when it is?

In order to illustrate the important concept we are arriving at, let us return to the point at which we saw the individual as he entered into the contract with all the others. This individual is one of the contracting parties. As a condition of his entering the state, he is required to contribute to the protective power. But *who* requires that he make such a contribution? With whom does he actually negotiate about this, and who is the second party in this contract?

This second party demands protection; – for which particular individual, then, does this party demand protection? For no particular individual at all, and yet for all of them; that is, for every individual whose rights are violated; now every one of them may or may not be such an individual. Therefore, the concept of who is to be protected is in *oscillation* [*im Schweben*];[1] it is an indeterminate concept: and this is precisely how we get the concept of a whole that is not merely *imagined*, i.e. not merely produced by our thought, as was the case above (I), but rather the concept of a *real* [*reellen*] whole, one that is unified by virtue of the subject matter itself; it is not the concept of a bare "all," but of an "all-ness" or totality [*nicht bloß Aller, sondern einer Allheit*].

We shall describe this in more detail. A bare, abstract concept is formed entirely by a free act of the mind; so, too, with the concept of "all," which we presented above. The concept we have arrived at here is formed not just by an act of free choice, but by virtue of something real [*etwas Reelles*], by virtue of something that, however, is unknown and comes to exist only in the future, i.e. when the feared transgression actually takes place. No one ever knows who will actually be trans-

---

[1] In everyday German *schweben* can mean to hang freely in the air (to hover) or to go back and forth between two points (to waver or oscillate). Fichte introduces the term in the 1794 *Wissenschaftslehre* in his explanation of how the faculty of imagination, in its encounter with the check, or *Anstoß* (see n. 3, p. 32) produces the manifold of images that furnish the content for empirical intuition. In supplying the content of empirical intuition the imagination is said to oscillate (*schweben*) between subject and object; the imagination brings the two together in the sense that it is through its activity that the not-I first acquires empirical reality in relation to the I. The imagination's activity is characterized as an oscillating or wavering, because on its own – without concepts – it cannot yield a stable object of experience but only a set of fluctuating images (*The Science of Knowledge*, pp. 185, 194, 201–3). In the present context Fichte invokes the idea of oscillation in reference to a concept (that of who is to be protected by the protection contract) that is "indeterminate," or has no determinate referent. The connection between conceptual indeterminacy and oscillation is further articulated in the *Wissenschaftslehre nova methodo* (1796/99) (Breazeale, *Fichte: Foundations of Transcendental Philosophy*, pp. 360–1, 409).

gressed against; it can happen to anyone. Thus each individual can believe that this whole protective arrangement has been established solely for his benefit, and so will gladly make his own small contribution to it. It is also possible, however, for someone else to be transgressed against; but then the first individual's contribution [203] has already been woven into the whole and cannot be withdrawn. This indeterminacy, this uncertainty as to which individual will first be transgressed against – therefore this *oscillation* in the imagination – is the real bond that unites the different individuals. It is by means of this that all merge together into one, no longer united in just an abstract concept (as a *compositum*), but rather in actuality (as a *totum*). Thus in the state, nature re-unites what she had previously separated when she produced several individuals. Reason is one, and it is exhibited in the sensible world also as one; humanity is a single organized and organizing whole of reason. Humanity was divided into several independent members; the natural institution of the state already cancels this independence provisionally and molds individual groups into a whole, until morality re-creates the entire species as one.

The concept we have presented can be well illustrated by the concept of an organized product of nature, e.g. a *tree*. If each individual part of the tree were endowed with consciousness and a will, then each part, just as certainly as it wills its own self-preservation, must also will the preservation of the tree, since it can be preserved only if the tree is preserved. Now from the perspective of the individual part, what, then, is the *tree*? The tree in general is nothing other than a mere concept, and a concept cannot be harmed. But the part wills that *no* part among them all, regardless of which one it is, should ever be harmed, because the part itself would also suffer if any other part were harmed. – Such is not the case with a pile of sand, where each part can be indifferent to whether any other part is separated, trampled upon, or strewn about.

Therefore, what is to be protected is the whole that has come about in the manner just described. This whole is the second party to the contract that we have been seeking. Thus, the will that is declared in such a contract is not a private will at all (except temporarily, when it still relates to the individual contracting party, who – according to our presupposition – is first called upon to provide protection); rather, it is by its very nature a common will, since – in order to remain indeterminate – it can be nothing other than common.

[**204**] We have identified the point at which this whole becomes unified as a whole. But then how, and through which particular act of willing, has it come to be this whole? We realize perfectly well that this whole exists. But let us see with our own eyes how it comes to exist! – We shall stick to the perspective suggested earlier, i.e, the perspective from which we observe the individual in the act of negotiating, and our question will be answered right away.

In negotiating, the individual declares his will to protect – undoubtedly his will to protect the whole, as was required of him. He thus becomes a part of the whole and merges together with it; now unforeseeable contingencies will determine whether he will protect others or be protected by them. In this way, the whole has come to exist as a result of contracts among individuals, and it is made complete by all the individuals contracting with all other individuals, as with a whole.

This particular contract, by means of which alone the two previous contracts are protected and secured, and which makes all three contracts in their unity into a civil contract, shall be called the *unification contract.*

(V) In consequence of the unification contract, the individual becomes a part of an organized whole, and thus melts into one with the whole. Does the individual's entire being and essence become fully intertwined with the whole – or only partly so, such that in a certain other respect he remains free and independent?[a]

---

[a] Rousseau claims unconditionally: each individual gives himself up completely.[2] He arrives at this claim as follows. Rousseau assumes a right to property that pre-exists the civil contract; this right to property is grounded in the individual's formation of things. Now it is obvious that each individual must negotiate with all the others about his property, and that it can become his property *in the state* only if the others grant him possession of it; therefore, it is obvious that property is subjected to the decision of the common will, and thus that all property ceases to be property until such negotiations have been concluded. In this respect, each individual does indeed give up everything.

According to our theory, no individual can bring anything with him to the civil contract, for prior to this contract he *has* nothing. The first [**205**] condition of giving something up is that one already have received something. Therefore, this contract – far from starting with *giving* – ought to begin with *receiving*.

[2] Rousseau, *Social Contract*, I, ch. 6: "Properly understood, all of these clauses [of the social contract] come down to a single one, namely, the total alienation of each associate, with all his rights, to the whole community." (See also ibid., I, ch. 1.) Rousseau's view appears to be in direct conflict with Fichte's claim that citizens retain their original rights when entering the state, yet Fichte is correct to note that Rousseau's statement does not imply that his state provides no guarantee of personal property rights but only that property claims made in the state of nature are not valid unless compatible with the principles on which the social contract is based, the rights and freedom of all citizens. Presumably one of Fichte's aims in this note is to emphasize the similarities between his view and Rousseau's, despite what appears to be a fundamental disagreement.

[205] Each individual makes a *contribution* to the protective body: he votes to appoint magistrates, and to secure and guarantee the constitution; he makes his particular contribution in the form of abilities, services, products of nature, or – when transformed into the universal measure of a thing's value – money. But he does not entirely alienate himself or what belongs to him. For if he did, what would he still possess that the state, for its part, would promise to protect? The protection contract would then be only one-sided and self-contradictory, in which case it would have to be expressed as follows: all individuals promise to offer protection, while also promising not to have anything that could be protected. Therefore, the *protective body* is made up only of portions of what belongs to individuals. All individuals are included in the protective body, but only partly so. But to the extent that they are included in it, they constitute the state's authority (whose purpose is just to protect the rights of each individual), and they form the true sovereign. – Only in the act of making this contribution is each individual a part of the sovereign. In a free state, i.e. one that has an ephorate, even these contributions are ways of exercising sovereignty. But the idea of *what is to be protected* includes *everything* that everyone possesses.

The whole that has now been established cannot – according to the principle stated above – undertake to protect anything it has not recognized. Therefore, insofar as it undertakes to protect each individual's possessions, it also recognizes those possessions; thus, this real [*reelle*] whole of the state also validates the property contract, which above seemed to have been made by everyone only as individuals. The whole is the *owner* of all the possessions and rights of every individual, insofar as it regards and must regard any injury to such property or rights *as an injury to itself.* But insofar as the whole regards something as *subject to its free use,* [206] the state's property is limited to what each individual is obligated to contribute towards shouldering the state's burdens.

With respect to those things that he has not contributed to the state's ends, the individual is completely free; regarding these things, he is not intertwined with the whole of the body politic, but remains an individual: a free person, dependent only on himself. It is precisely this freedom that is secured for him by the state's power and for the sake of which alone he has entered into the contract. Humanity separates itself from citizenship in order to elevate itself with absolute freedom to the level of morality; but it can do so only if human beings have first existed within the state. But, insofar as the individual is limited by the law, he is a *subject*, subordinate to the state's protective power within the sphere left over for him. The contract was made with the individual only on the condition that he contribute to the whole: thus, the contract is canceled as soon as the citizen does not contribute. Thus each individual continually pledges all his property as a guarantee that he will contribute, and he will forfeit it, if he does not contribute what he owes. The whole, or the sovereign, becomes his *judge* (since he himself withdraws from participating in this whole), in which case he and everything he owns become subjected to the whole: and all this together constitutes the *subjection contract*, which, however, is merely hypothetical. Thus, if I fulfill my duties as a citizen continually and without exception (which obviously entails that, in relating to other individuals, I do not transgress the limits to my freedom prescribed by law), then, as far as my public character is concerned, I am simply a participant in this sovereignty, and, as far as my private character is concerned, I am simply a free individual, but never a subject. I would become a subject only if I failed to fulfill my duties. – If there is a penal law dealing with such cases (as one would expect), then the individual can pay a penalty for his fault, and thus retain the whole of his possessions by giving up a part of them.

And thus our investigation returns into itself; and the synthesis is complete.

[207] The civil contract is one that each individual makes with the real whole of the state, a whole that forms and maintains itself by means of the contracts that individuals make with one another; by virtue of the civil contract, the individual merges with the whole of the state as regards some of his rights, but receives in return the rights of sovereignty.

The two parties in this contract are the individual on one side, and the body politic on the other. The contract is conditioned by the free, formal will of both parties to enter into contract with each other. The material will concerning which the parties must reach agreement aims (from the one side) at a particular portion of property, and (from the other side) at the renunciation of all other property plus a particular contribution to the protective power. Through the contract, the citizen (for his part) acquires a secure portion of property, while the state receives from him a renunciation of all his natural rights to what others possess (which is necessary, if all the state's other citizens are to have rightful possession of their things), as well as a particular contribution to the protective power.

This contract is its own guarantee: it contains within itself the sufficient ground of its fulfillment, just as every organic being has within itself the complete ground of its existence. For any person, either this contract does not exist at all, or, if it does, then it binds him completely. Anyone who does not fulfill this contract is not a part of it, and anyone who is a part of it necessarily fulfills it entirely. If someone exists apart from this contract, then he stands outside every rightful relation whatsoever and is rightfully excluded altogether from any reciprocity with other beings of his kind in the sensible world.

Corollary

So far as I know, the only way in which anyone until now has conceived of the whole of the state has been by thinking of an ideal aggregation of individuals; and so true insight into the nature of this relation has been obstructed. By merely aggregating individuals, one can unite anything into a whole. In such an aggregation, the bond of unity exists only in our thought; and if we happen to think of the matter differently [208] (which is contingent on our free choice), then what had been united will be separated again, as before. One cannot comprehend the true unity, if one has not demonstrated the bond of the unity *apart from the concept.* (This is how we express ourselves from the empirical standpoint; from the transcendental standpoint, we would have to say: "if one has not demonstrated *that which rationally necessitates this unity.*") We have demonstrated this in our presentation. That is, in the concept of who is to be protected, all individuals merge into one, because of the inevitable indeterminacy concerning which individual will need visible protection, and – even more importantly – concerning which individuals benefit invisibly from the fact that the law holds bad wills in check, even before they break out into action.

The most appropriate image for illustrating this concept is that of an organic product of nature. This image has frequently been used in recent times[3] to describe the unity of the different branches of public

---

[3] Kant, for example, compares the state to an organism in the *Critique of Judgment*: "The analogy of . . . direct natural purposes can serve to elucidate a certain [kind of] association [among people], though one found more often as an idea than in actuality: in speaking of the complete transformation of a large people into a state, which took place recently, the word *organization* was frequently and very aptly applied to the establishment of legal authorities, etc., and even to the

power, but – so far as I know – it has not yet been used to explain the civil condition as a whole. In a product of nature, each part can be what it is only within this organic unity, and outside such unity, the part would not exist at all. Indeed, if there were no such organic unity, then absolutely nothing would exist, for without the reciprocal interaction of organic forces that keep each other in a state of equilibrium, there would be no enduring form at all, but only an eternal struggle of being and not-being, a struggle that cannot even be thought. Similarly, it is only within the unity of the state that the human being attains a particular place in the scheme of things, a fixed position within nature; and each person maintains *this particular* place in relation to others and in relation to nature only by existing in *this particular* unity. Apart from the state, human beings would experience only passing gratification, but never the least concern for the future; and even this passing gratification would be devoid of all rightfulness, because there would be others like us who had the same right to it. Nature constitutes herself by bringing all organic forces into a unity; humanity constitutes itself by bringing the free choice of all individuals into a unity. The essence of [**209**] raw matter, which itself can be conceived only along with organic matter and only as a part of the organic world-whole, consists in the fact that there is no part in it that does not contain within itself the ground of its own determinacy, there is no part in it whose moving force is not fully explained by its existence and whose existence is not fully explained by its moving force. The essence of organic matter consists in the fact that there is no part in it that contains within itself the ground of its own determinacy, there is no part within it whose motive force does not presuppose the existence of something outside it and whose own existence does not presuppose some motive force outside of it. The same relationship holds between the isolated human being and the citizen. The former acts merely in order to satisfy his needs, and none of his needs are satisfied except through his own actions; he is what he is externally only by virtue of himself. The citizen, by contrast, has various things to do and leave undone, not for his own sake, but for the sake of others; his highest needs are satisfied by the actions of others, without any contribution from himself. In the organic body, each part

entire body politic. For each member in such a whole should indeed be not merely a means, but also an end; and while each member contributes to making the whole possible, the idea of that whole should in turn determine the member's position and function" (p. 254n).

continually preserves the whole, and by doing so, is itself preserved; the citizen relates to the state in the very same way. And in fact, in the one case as well as in the other, this preservation of the whole does not require any special arrangement; each part, or each citizen, preserves only itself in the place that has been determined for it by the whole, and in the very act of doing so, it preserves the whole in this particular part: and precisely because the whole preserves each part in its place, the whole returns into itself and preserves itself.

[210] Second section of the doctrine of political right
On civil legislation

§18

On the spirit of the civil or property contract

(I) The contract described above concerning property in general, which constitutes the first part of the civil contract, grounds the relation of right between each individual and all other individuals in the state. It is therefore the foundation of what we call civil legislation, civil right, and so forth. Thus we need only give a complete account of this contract, in order to exhaust the object of our investigation in the present section, i.e. civil legislation.

As we have shown above, original right consists essentially in an ongoing reciprocal interaction, dependent only on the person's own will, between the person and the sensible world outside of him. In the property contract, a particular part of the sensible world is allocated exclusively to each individual as the sphere of his reciprocal interaction with it; and this part of the sensible world is guaranteed to each individual under these two conditions: (1) that he refrain from disturbing the freedom of all others in their spheres, and (2) that, in the event that these others are transgressed against by some third party, he will contribute towards their protection.

At first, a sphere for the exercise of his freedom, and nothing more, is allocated to him. This sphere contains certain objects, as determined by the freedom that has been granted to him. *Thus his right to have property in these objects extends as far as the freedom granted to him extends, and no further.* He acquires such objects only for a particular use; and it is only from this use, and from what might hinder such use, that he has the right to exclude everyone else. The object of the property contract is a particular activity.

[211] (Recall what was said above. According to the concept of original right, the first ground of all property is my having subjected something to my ends. – But to which ends? Each individual must address this question on entering the civil contract, and this contract must be thoroughly determinate and determining. Only this declared and recognized end in things, and nothing else, is guaranteed; and property in the objects extends only to the attainment of this end, as is immediately clear.)

(II) Now these ends can be quite varied, even with regard to the use of a single object, and so they can also be quite varied with regard to the use of different objects. The question is: can all of a citizen's possible ends be subordinated to one, single end?

The person, in undertaking an action, always presupposes his own continued existence; the end of his present action always lies in the future, and he is a cause in the sensible world only insofar as he moves from the present moment to future ones. Freedom and continued existence are essentially united, and whoever guarantees the former necessarily guarantees the latter as well. *The future is contained in present activity*.

Nature has destined the human being (the only being we are concerned with here) for freedom, i.e. for activity. Nature attains all of her ends, and so she must have provided for this end as well, and we have every reason to expect that she will actually attain it. Now what arrangements could she have made to drive the human being to activity?

If we assume that every human being wishes for something in the future, then nature would surely attain her end if she had arranged things so that the possibility of any future whatever for the human being *were conditioned by present activity*. Conversely, the necessity of *present activity* would be entailed by the wish for something in the future. The future would be conditioned by present activity; the future would necessarily be contained in present activity.

[212] But since there could be human beings who did not wish for anything in the future, and furthermore since the desire for continued existence remains completely ungrounded except by virtue of some

present activity (which is itself conditioned, in turn, only by the desire for future existence), nature's arrangement would be a vicious circle. Therefore she had to unite both sides in some third thing within the present, namely *pain.* When the human being's continued existence is endangered, present activity and the wish for, and possibility of, continued existence are connected to present pain. This pain is *hunger* and *thirst*, and thus we find that the need for nourishment alone is the original impetus – and its satisfaction the ultimate end – of the state and of all human life and conduct. This is true, obviously, only so long as the human being remains entirely under the direction of nature, and does not elevate himself through freedom to a higher existence: thus the need for nourishment alone is the highest synthesis, which unites all contradictions. Accordingly, the highest and universal end of all free activity is to be able to live. Everyone has this end; therefore, just as freedom in general is guaranteed, so too is this end. If this end were not attained, freedom and the person's continued existence would be completely impossible.

(III) And so we arrive at a more detailed description of the exclusive use of freedom that is granted to each individual in the property contract. To be able to live is the absolute, inalienable property of all human beings. We have seen that a certain sphere of objects is granted to the individual solely for a certain use. But the final end of this use is to be able to live. The attainment of this end is guaranteed; this is the spirit of the property contract. A principle of all rational state constitutions is that everyone ought to be able to live from his labor.

All individuals have entered into this contract with all individuals. Thus all have promised to all that their labor really ought to be the means for attaining this end, [**213**] and the state must make arrangements to insure this. (In a nation where everyone goes naked, the right to work as a tailor would be no right; or, if there were to be such a right, the people would have to stop going naked. "We grant you the right to make such products," means the same as "We obligate ourselves to buy such products from you.")

Furthermore, all property rights are grounded in the contract of all with all, which states: "We are all entitled to keep this, on the condition that we let you have what is yours." Therefore, if someone is unable to make a living from his labor, he has not been given what is absolutely his, and therefore the contract is completely canceled with respect to him, and from that moment on he is no longer obligated by right to recognize anyone else's property. Now in order to prevent property rights from being destabilized in this way, all the others must (as a matter of right and in consequence of the civil contract) relinquish a portion of their own property, until he is able to live. – As soon as someone suffers from need, that portion of others' property that would be required to spare him from such need no longer belongs to those others; rather, it rightfully belongs to the one in need. The civil contract must provide for such a repartitioning of property. This contribution of property to persons in need is just as much a condition of all civil justice as is a contribution to the protective body of the state, since such assistance to the needy is itself a part of providing the necessary protection. Each person possesses his own property, only insofar as, and on the condition that, all citizens are able to live off what belongs to them. If all are not able to do so, then each person's property ceases to be his own, and becomes the property of those who cannot live off their own. This happens, of course, always in accordance with some particular judgment by the state authority. The executive power is just as responsible for such repartitioning as it is for all the other branches of state administration, and the poor (those, of course, who have entered into the civil contract) have an absolute right of coercion to such assistance.

(IV) The principle that has been established is this: everyone must be able to live *off his labor*. Therefore, the ability to live is [**214**] conditioned by labor, and there is no right to be able to live, if this condition is not fulfilled. Since all are responsible for seeing to it that each person can live off his own labor and would have to subsidize him if he were unable to do so, they all necessarily also have the right to check and see whether each person in his own sphere labors enough to make his own living; and they transfer this right to the state power, which is ordained to look after the rights and affairs of the commonwealth. No one has a rightful claim to assistance from the state until he has demonstrated that he has done everything possible in his own sphere to look after himself and has still not been able to sustain himself. But since even in this case a person could not be allowed to perish, and since the state itself would be reproached for not having required the person to labor, the state necessarily has the right to oversee how each person manages his own property. Just as (according to our former principle) there ought to be no poor people in a rational state, so too (according to the present principle) there ought to be no idlers in it, either. A rightful exception to the latter statement will be discussed below.

(V) Thus the property contract includes the following actions within it. (a) All declare to all – and in making their guarantee, to the populace as a *whole* – how they intend to make a livelihood. This statement is valid without exception. Anyone who cannot declare this cannot be a citizen of the state, for such a person can never be obligated to recognize the property of the others. (b) All – and by virtue of the guarantee, this means the populace – allow each person to pursue this livelihood exclusively in a certain respect. There can be no occupation in a state without the state's permission. Each person must expressly declare his occupation, and thus no one becomes a citizen *in general*, but each enters into a certain class of citizen at the same time that he enters into the state. There may never be any indeterminacy about this. Each person possesses property in objects only insofar as he needs such property to pursue his occupation. (c) The end of all such labor is to be able to live. All – and by virtue of the guarantee, this means the populace – [215] guarantee to each person that his labor will attain this end; and in truth, they obligate themselves to provide all the means they can towards that end. These means belong to the full right of each person, which the state must protect. In this regard, the contract is as follows: each person promises to do everything he can in order to be able to live based on the freedoms and rights granted to him; conversely, the populace promise, on behalf of all individuals, to give him something more, should he still be unable to live. All individuals obligate themselves to contribute to such assistance, just as they have done for the purpose of providing protection in general; and thus the civil contract includes a provision for rendering assistance to those who need it, just as it entails the state's protective power. Accession to the former, like accession to the latter, is a condition for entry into the state. The state authority oversees this part of the contract, like all other parts of it, and it possesses the right of coercion, as well as the authority to force everyone to fulfill it.

§19

Comprehensive application of the principles thus far established concerning property

(I) The arrangement that nature has made in order to force us into free activity is the following.

Our body is an organized product of nature, and the organization within it endures without interruption, as is entailed (according to the proof presented above) by the concept of organization in general. But the business of organic nature in general can be accomplished in one of two ways: either raw matter is taken into the body and organized for the first time within it, or else something that is already organized is taken into the body and further organized within it. Furthermore, this business of nature can take place in two different ways: either nature herself sees to it that the materials to be organized are brought into the body's sphere of activity, or else nature counts on the body's own activity to bring these materials to itself or to bring itself to them. The latter is the case only with beings that are [216] articulated so as to be capable of free movement. Now since nature's artistry is evidently higher in the second member in each of these pairs, it would not be surprising if the issue of how the body is organized and the issue of whether it is articulated for free movement parallel one another: i.e. in bodies that are articulated for free movement, organization is possible only through the taking in of materials that are already organized, while bodies that are not articulated for free movement can be organized by taking in raw matter alone. Without getting involved in an issue that is entirely extraneous to our purpose here (namely, the question of why and according to which laws this is so), we shall be content simply to observe that this is the case. Plants are formed out of raw matter, or at least out of matter that is raw and non-organized for us; animals, by contrast, nourish themselves only from the kingdom of organized bodies. Anything that seems to be an exception to this rule is not. When animals swallow iron, stones, or sand (even when they do so out of natural instinct), it is not for the sake of nourishment (for these materials are not digested), but rather for the sake of expelling harmful ingredients from the body.

Now it is even possible for articulated creatures themselves to feed, in turn, on other articulated creatures, or to eat flesh. It seems that these creatures exist on a higher level of organization. The human being is obviously destined to take his nourishment from both kingdoms of organized nature.

(II) A condition of the continued existence of the state is that a sufficient amount of food be available; otherwise, human beings would have to end their association with each other and disperse.

All organization takes place according to natural laws, which human beings can only learn about and guide, but never change. Humans can subject parts of nature to the known conditions under which nature's laws apply, and they can be certain that such laws of nature, for their part, will not fail to apply; in this way, they attain the capacity to promote and increase organization in nature. And where several human beings want to live together in one place through freedom, which nature could not have anticipated, it is to be expected that [**217**] nature will need such assistance. If this is so, then promoting organization in nature is the very foundation of the state, since it is the exclusive condition under which alone human beings can go on living together.

First of all, it will be necessary to augment the plant kingdom, in order to feed human beings and cattle. By the laws of their nature, plants are bound to the earth, they grow out of it, and – as long as the process of their organization continues – they are tied to it. It is to be expected that some human beings will devote themselves exclusively to the production and care of plants, and a right to do so is to be granted to them, since the state's very existence is conditioned by the exercise of this right.

The process of organization progresses over time in accordance with certain laws, and nature may not be disturbed in carrying out these laws. Thus in order to achieve the intended end, it is absolutely necessary that every cultivated part of the plant kingdom remain exactly as the cultivator has known it to be, since he must rely on this knowledge in his further activities; thus it is absolutely necessary that the land that he cultivates be granted to him exclusively and for the purpose of such cultivation. Accordingly, we must first discuss:

(A) The agriculturalist's property in land

(1) Land is humanity's common support in the sensible world, the condition of humanity's existence in space and thus of its entire sensible

existence. The earth in particular, regarded as a mass, cannot be owned, for, as a substance, it cannot be subjected to any exclusive end that a human being might have; but according to what was stated above, it is contrary to right to exclude all other human beings from using a thing, without being able to declare what one's own use of the thing would be. (One might argue that the earth can be used for building houses; but [218] in that case, it has already been modified and is not being used as a substance, but only as an accident of a substance.) Therefore, the agriculturalist's right to a particular piece of land is nothing more than the right to cultivate products entirely by himself on this land, and to exclude everyone else from such cultivation and from any other use of this land that would conflict with his use of it.

Thus the agriculturalist does not have the right to prevent this piece of land from being used in some other way that is not injurious to his cultivation of it; e.g. mining or pasturing animals on land that has already been harvested but not yet re-seeded (unless he also has the right to raise animals on it). The state has the right to allow the miner to dig underneath land that has already been parceled out, and the agriculturalist has no right at all to object to such digging. This is all on the condition that the agriculturalist's field does not become unsafe or actually cave in because of such digging, in which case either the miner or the state (depending on what the relevant contract says about the matter) must compensate the agriculturalist.

Under the guarantee of the state, the land is divided up by individuals and designated by boundary markers, so that right can exist with *certainty*. Therefore, displacing a boundary marker is an immediate crime against the state, since it undermines right and gives rise to insoluble conflicts of right.

Every agriculturalist, if that is his sole occupation, must be able to earn his livelihood by laboring on his land. If, in spite of all his labor, he is unable to do so, then – since he cannot be anything other than an agriculturalist – a new distribution must be undertaken that increases his property, as required by the principles established above. Whether someone labors on his parcel of land at least enough to be able to earn his livelihood from it is subject to state supervision. The reason such state supervision extends even further than this will become apparent below.

The agriculturalist, as a citizen in general, must make his particular contribution to meeting the state's needs. [219] As far as we can tell up to this point, he cannot make such a contribution from any source other than the products of his fields. As long as he has not made this contribution, he has no property, for he has not yet fulfilled the contract through which something becomes his property in the first place. If he has made his contribution, then the contract requires the state to protect his remaining possessions against the transgressions of others; and at least as far as we can tell up to this point, even the state itself does not have the slightest claim to these remaining possessions. Therefore – only the agriculturalist's products constitute his absolute property; the very substance of those products belongs to him, in contrast to land, where only an accident of the substance belongs to him. (More precise modifications of this right to property will become apparent below.)

(The proposition that the products of my labor are my property – a proposition upon which some have sought to ground the right to property in general – is here confirmed. Some have criticized this as a principle of all property rights in general by objecting that one must first demonstrate one's right to undertake such labor in the first place. Within the context of the state it may very well be possible to demonstrate this; all persons with whom the individual engages in mutual, reciprocal interaction and thus with whom one exists in relations of right, have – through their consent – given him the right to such labor. It is only under this condition that the proposition indicated above is valid in the state; and since, in general, it is only within the state that something can be valid as a matter of right, it follows that this proposition can be valid at all only under this condition.)

(2) If anything grows wild on cultivated land, it is to be assumed that the owner of the land has subjected it to his end of cultivating the land, and thus it rightfully belongs to him. For this reason, it cannot belong to a stranger, since the stranger's disposing of the thing would interfere with the owner's free disposition of it on his own land, and thus would prevent the owner from achieving the end that is guaranteed to him.

(3) Uncultivated land is the property of the populace; for when the land was divided up, this land was not given to any individual. In the case of uncultivated land, one must carefully distinguish between the substance and its accidents. The substance, the land itself, is something the populace [220] have saved for the purpose of a future division, if such becomes necessary. The accidents, the things that grow wild on

the land, cannot be left on their own, for they would perish; and so it is appropriate that they be used up. It is most appropriate for the populace to use them for public purposes and thus to count them as part of the state's income, or to make them a matter of *royal prerogative [zu einem Regale]*.[1] In this way, they are a contribution made by everyone, even though no one pays a single penny. But the following is to be noted here:

(α) Things whose ownership is not expressly declared in the contract are the property of neither party; and within the state, they are not the property of any individual citizen (Part I, §12, VIII.). Therefore, the contract between individuals and the whole state must expressly determine whether all products growing in the wild (e.g. woods) should be counted as state property, or whether only some should, and which ones. (The right to the forests.) Anything that has not been designated is the property of no one, and belongs to the first person (and this obviously means the first citizen) who takes possession of it; for otherwise, the thing would waste away without being used. Since the land itself has not yet been subjected to anyone's ends, all must be allowed to tread upon it without restriction. (Fallen wood, wild berries, and so forth.)

(β) Whatever grows wild must always give way to the cultivation of the land, since more sustenance can be gained from the latter than from the former. Thus uncultivated lands must be divided up as soon as the needs of individuals make it necessary; and if someone wants to possess something as his own field, it may not be left uncultivated. Anyone is entitled to make use of the fruits of the land, only if the land is uncultivated. As soon as the land is cultivated, this right ceases to exist. When land is cultivated, the state is compensated for its loss of the benefits from it by the taxes levied on the newly formed fields. – This is certainly not meant to imply that all the forests ought to be uprooted, but only that the harvesting of timber ought to be carried on as a kind of agriculture, in which case rights that apply to cultivated land will apply to forests as well.

---

[1] *Regale* traditionally designates a royal prerogative granted (by a king) to an individual or group that gives its possessor exclusive rights to carry on certain profitable economic activities, such as the coining of money or postal services. Fichte uses this term to refer to similar prerogatives granted by the state, including rights to the use of mines, forests, and uncultivated land.

[221] *(B)*

Since we are talking about land, we shall also deal with the topic of *mining*, which we have already mentioned. The products of mining – metals, semi-metals, etc. – stand midway between organic natural products and raw matter; they constitute nature's transition from the latter to the former. The laws according to which nature creates these metals are either altogether undiscoverable or at least have not yet been understood well enough to allow us to produce them artificially, in the same way we produce crops (i.e. by guiding nature, through the use of our free will, in forming such products). The products of mining can only be found as already formed by nature, without any contribution from us. In principle, each individual must be free to say: "I want to search for metals," just as each is free to say: "I want to grow crops"; and the earth's interior could be divided up among miners, just as the earth's surface was divided up among agriculturalists. Each individual would then possess a portion of the earth's interior as his own property and for his own use, just as the agriculturalist possesses portions of the earth's surface as his own property and for his own use; and the metals that the miner finds would belong to him, just as the crops that the agriculturalist grows belong to him. But mining cannot be undertaken in this way, and for two reasons: first, because the results of mining are uncertain, for metals are not produced by the human's free will, and thus one can never be certain that he will be able to make a living from mining; second, because once a particular portion of the earth has been dug through, it cannot be dug through again. Mining must be undertaken by a standing and enduring association, which would not need immediate results and could wait patiently for the gains finally to be had from mining. For these reasons, no association is better qualified for this task than the state itself, which (as we shall soon see) has yet another, particular reason for acquiring metals. Therefore, property in land under the earth's surface [222] rightfully belongs to the populace, who allow such land to be worked on; and miners become wage laborers (about which we shall say more in greater detail below) who receive their pay, regardless of whether they discover a lot, a little, or nothing at all. Thus mines are *naturally a matter of royal prerogative*, like the forests.

The same principle applies to property rights in everything else that nature produces in this manner: precious stones, amber, and other rare stones that might be valued, as well as quarries, clay-pits, and sand-pits, etc. The state has the right to make these objects into a royal prerogative, and since the state itself takes responsibility for searching for them in sufficient quantities (it is obligated to do so, to prevent the public from complaining about not having enough), it also has the right to prohibit everyone else from doing so. If this were not done, and if someone wanted to undertake such work for his own livelihood as his particular occupation, then he would need the express permission of the state (since the state must be informed about how each person makes his living). The state can also grant someone the exclusive privilege to mine in certain districts, in which case no one else would henceforth be allowed to mine in those districts. Or finally, if neither of these is done, then such objects, which are the property of no one, belong to the first person who *happens* to find them. The main point here is that only an *expressly stated law* (i.e. an express declaration about how appropriation may take place, according to what was said above) – and by no means a *silent, assumed law* – can prohibit citizens from appropriating such objects.

In many places, quarries and the like are left to those who cultivate the land. In accordance with the principles stated above, the agriculturalist's right to these things is not based on his property in the land, but on the law's silence. If the kind and quantity of the materials to be got from such quarries are significant, then nothing prevents the state from appropriating the quarry and providing the agriculturalist with another piece of land as a substitute for his well-grounded right to an equally large and fertile field. Obviously, we are assuming here, as always, that the state's enrichment of itself through the use of royal prerogatives must benefit the individual citizens, [**223**] and that, as the state's wealth increases, the direct taxes on the citizens must decrease (provided that the state's needs do not increase in the same proportion).

(C)

There are also animals on the earth whose properties can be useful to humans and subjected to human ends, or even whose substance can be useful, since their flesh can be eaten, their hides can be used to make things, etc. First of all, if a person wants to make regular use only of the accidental properties of animals, then he must first bring the animal under his control; and since animals can be nourished and maintained only by organic matter, but – once an animal has been brought under human control – it is unlikely that nature alone will suffice to care for the animal, it follows that the person must assist nature in nourishing such animals, i.e. he himself must feed them, to the extent that he can. Since nature (as in the case of organic nature generally, and thus here as well) operates according to rules, it follows that my declared use of an animal for a particular end depends on my *exclusive possession* of it; it depends on the fact that only I nourish, tend, and care for it (and no one else does), and that, conversely, only I enjoy the benefits the animal can provide.

In principle, every individual has the same right to take possession of a particular animal as anyone else. Just as there is no reason *a priori* why this meadow ought to be mine rather than my neighbor's, so too there is no reason why only I ought to milk this cow rather than my neighbor. Thus one can acquire exclusive property in animals only through the property contract with the state.

But property in animals is not the same as property in a piece of land, which always remains in the same place and is clearly designated, once its location in space is designated; an animal does not remain in the same place but rather is able to move freely about. Thus what kind of sign should indicate that this particular [**224**] animal belongs to this particular person and to no one else?

(1) First, if not all, but only some, species of animals are to become the exclusive property of particular persons, then it is necessary, before all else, to specify which particular species may be owned as property at all, and which may not: so that anyone who happens to have a particular animal under his control can immediately know that, if the animal is not *his* property, then it is certainly the property of someone else (even if he does not know who the particular owner is). This happens insofar as the state has declared that this particular species of animal cannot be anything other than property. For example, if I have the right to hunt (about which we will say more below), then I may shoot a deer, because it is a deer, but I may not shoot a horse that I have not seen before. Why may I not shoot the horse, as I may shoot the deer? Because I know that a horse necessarily belongs to someone, even if I do not know who its owner is. However, if someone were to tame a deer, it would undoubt-

edly be his property. But then suppose that the deer runs away from him and I shoot it dead. Will anyone think that I bear the same responsibility as I would if I had shot the person's horse? Certainly not. The reason for this is that the horse, but not the deer, has been declared to be the kind of thing that can only be property. The owner's right remains intact (even if the animal should escape from his control) and is grounded on the original property contract, which specifies which animals in the state are always to be regarded as property. Such species are called *domesticated*.

The reason why precisely these particular animal species have been declared to be property resides in their fitness for serving human needs (because of their *properties*), their ability to be tamed, and their need of human care.

But one should not think that taming and care constitute the true ground of one's right to own them; [**225**] the true ground is nothing other than the contract; therefore, if new species of breeding animals (e.g. kangaroos or Italian buffaloes) were to be introduced into a state, then the right to own them would first have to be guaranteed by the state, sanctioned by a law, and publicly announced; for otherwise, the unfamiliar animal could be taken for a wild animal and treated as such. (The situation would be different if a person kept the animal locked up in his own yard, where it would become his property by virtue of its location, in accordance with the principles of a *householder's rights*, which we will discuss below.) Furthermore, the state has the complete right to forbid the keeping of certain animals, e.g. dogs that serve no purpose, or a menagerie of lions, bears, or apes.

(2) But then which particular owner owns this particular animal, which (because of its species) has been declared to be property in general? Two scenarios are possible. Either the animals remain on the land and under the immediate care of their owner, so that the owner can always declare them as his own. In this case, however, the owner's property right is still much too uncertain, since someone else can easily pass off a stolen or lost animal as his own, provided only that it is among his herd and on his land. Or, the animals of several owners are mingled and driven to pasture together; but then how can the owner prove which animals are his? Fortunately, in this situation animal instinct has partly made up for the legislator's neglect. A domesticated animal becomes accustomed to its stable and hurries back to it, and so a judge can decide

the matter by following the animal's own verdict. If, in such cases, no further disputes over ownership arise, it is due entirely to the simplicity and honesty of the common people, and perhaps to some of their superstitions as well. But then again – what can one do to prevent one's animals from being stolen other than to make sure that his stables are locked up, and how can one prove that theft has occurred? In a well-constituted state, shouldn't it be required that livestock be legally marked, and [226] that such markings be just as inviolable and subject to the law's protection, as the boundary markers of land? If this were done, confusion would hardly be possible, and theft would always be possible to prove. (It is certainly possible to mark animals in this way, as in the case of the army's horses.) Every sale, along with the marking on the sold animal, would have to be legally recorded, and thus the requisite security would be achieved.

(3) With other types of animals that can be owned, property in them is actually determined by the place the animals occupy, provided they are of the kind that can be confined to a particular place, and must be so confined if they are to serve our ends. Thus the place itself is given to the owner, so that he can maintain this particular animal there, and the animal is his property, insofar as it occupies this place (fish ponds, aquariums, and even bird-houses). If the fish is no longer in the fish pond, or the bird escapes from the bird-house, it is no one's property. (The carp remains property if it is in water bounded by solid land, e.g. if one were to dam up a stream to form a pond, because the carp does not reproduce in streams. But it is not property if it happens to enter a river, because then the owner could not prove that it is his property. The carp occupies a middle position between wild and domesticated animals; when in water bounded by solid land, it is tame, but in a river it is wild. Such is not the case with pike and similar fish.)

(4) Property is granted to persons only in connection with the end to be achieved by such property; this also applies to property in animals. Now the very substance of most animals is useful; their flesh can be eaten or at least various parts of their bodies can be used to make things; but at the same time, the properties of such animals are also useful (cows' milk, hens' eggs, the labor of oxen and horses, and so forth).

Thus the right to property in the *substance* of an animal may very well be restricted; whether there is such a restriction is a matter to be determined by the original contract and the laws grounded on it. Any such restriction would not [227] nullify or restrict property rights in general, which may very well extend to the properties of the animal, and so a person cannot argue: "If I cannot do what I want with my animal, then how is it really mine?" It is yours only in a restricted way, only for a particular use that the state permits. And so there could be a law requiring that a certain number of livestock always be maintained and that one may not slaughter any livestock falling below this number. If there is such a law, the state must have also made arrangements for producing the necessary fodder for the animals; for otherwise the state's laws would contradict themselves.

Animals reproduce and their offspring count as properties of themselves; and so humans may also make use of the offspring. Owning the parent animal automatically entails that one owns its full line of offspring (just as owning the first seed of corn entails that one owns all the corn that can be produced from it), since the owner has been granted the right to raise animals and grow corn. But increases in the herds may very well be limited to a certain number.

(5) Animals move about freely and feed on the products of the field; thus, if an animal causes damage to a field, there emerges the following conflict between the property rights of the agriculturalist and those of the animal-owner. The former will say: "Within the state, I have the right to cultivate this field, and its products are mine alone." And the latter will answer: "Within the same state, I have the right to raise animals, and it is their very nature (which the state clearly knows about), to move about freely to get their food." The state must settle this conflict by passing laws grounded in the original property contract, which either require only the one party (the animal-owner) to keep his animals under his supervision, or (what is fairer) also require the other party to put a fence around his field. Whoever neglects to observe the precautions the law commands not only must pay compensation for the resulting damages, but may also be fined as well. But if damages should still occur, despite their having taken all the precautions [228] commanded by law, then those damages are to be regarded as an accident for which neither party is liable, and the state must bear them.

(6) We have assumed that certain animal species are declared to be those that can *only* be property. They are called *domesticated* animals; animals that do not fall under this category (and for no reason other than the simple fact that they do not fall under it) are *wild* animals. i.e.

no one's property. It is precisely *these* species that are declared to be wild, because they cannot be domesticated, and because their properties cannot be subjected to human ends. However, insofar as their substance can be used (although such use may be possible only through the animal's death, since they cannot be domesticated), they are a good that the populace have not apportioned, and thus they are *common property*. Wild animals cannot become the property of an individual before the individual has captured them. Since these animals cannot even be kept within the state's boundaries and thus cannot be kept for future times (as uncultivated land can be), it is highly appropriate that one capture them wherever they are found.

Wild animals can be divided into two classes. In the first class, either the animals are confined to an element that has not been subjected to human ends (at least to the extent that humans do not live *in* or *off* the same element that the animals do), e.g. wild fish in water. Or, even if the wild animals live in and nourish themselves off the same element from which humans nourish themselves (i.e. the earth), the harm such animals cause to humans is still not very great (e.g. small birds certainly eat seeds and fruits, but, in turn, they also greatly reduce the number of harmful insects). How these wild animals should be treated, from the perspective of right, is not easy to answer. Fishing must be done (whereas bird-catching is not really necessary); and if it is to be done in an orderly fashion and thus not cease altogether because of irregular practice, the right to fish should be divided among individuals by way of particular zones, and should be assigned exclusively to such individuals. [229] Each individual who has been given a right to fish within a particular zone is to be regarded as every other owner (e.g. as someone who owns land for the purpose of growing crops). The principles stated above imply that these fishermen may not interfere with someone else's use of the same territory, if it doesn't harm their use of it (e.g. if a ship traverses their part of the river), or if it has been authorized to take place alongside their use (e.g. if someone else is authorized to grow crops on the river's banks).

The situation is different with the second class of wild animals, those that are harmful to humans and interfere with human ends. All animals that are properly called wild, especially the larger ones, belong to this class. The state has guaranteed each person – as that person's property – the security to achieve his ends, but especially the opportunity to grow crops, which are particularly vulnerable to being damaged by wild animals; and so it is the duty of the state to protect agricultural land from being ravaged by wild animals. The wilderness must always give way to civilization, and irregular occupations (whose capacity to provide sustenance for the population is unreliable) must give way to regular ones (whose capacity to provide sustenance can be depended on in advance). Thus every rational state ought to regard the wilderness primarily not as something useful, but as something harmful, not as an emolument, but as an enemy. The primary purpose of hunting is to protect the fields, not to take possession of wild game. Accordingly, the state would have to enlist those in its service to provide such protection, just as it must provide protection against robbers, fires, and floods. And thus there would also be no doubt that if a wild animal happened on to a field, the agriculturalist would have the right to kill it, without first calling on those who have been appointed by the state to hunt wild animals, just as a person whose house is on fire has the right to put it out without incurring complaints from the officials who have been appointed to put out fires.

But now since hunting also has significant benefits, one should not assume that the state must tax its subjects in order to pay for hunting; rather, it is to be expected that [230] hunting will pay for itself. Accordingly, the most reasonable approach is to give individuals the right to hunt (like the right to fish) as a form of property, determined according to particular zones. It should be noted and well understood that this does not automatically make the animals themselves into property; the animals do not become property until the hunter has killed them. Rather, it is the right to hunt in a particular zone that constitutes one's exclusive property. However, since the main reason the state allows hunting is to protect the fields, the hunter can keep his right to hunt only under the express condition that wild animals are actually kept from doing harm and, as the owner of that right, the hunter must compensate land-owners for any damage caused by wild animals within his zone. This follows without contradiction from the individual's contract with the state concerning his property and from the contract that the state must make with the hunter.

Only the hunter can have a reason to tend and care for wild animals. The hunter is permitted to do so, only if the wild animals do not interfere with the ends of civilization, which always takes priority over the wilderness, i.e. only if the wild animals remain in the forest. If someone were to kill a wild animal in the forest, he would be infringing on the hunter's property. If someone were to encounter a wild animal in his fields, he would be justified in killing it for the sake of preventing any harm. The state certainly does not guarantee the life of a wild animal, which does not constitute any possible end of the state; rather, it is only the animal's death that is a possible end of the state. A wild animal that has been killed belongs to the hunter who possesses the right to hunt in that zone. If, before it was killed, the animal caused any harm, then the hunter must pay for the harm done; even if the dead animal is worth nothing at all, the hunter must still pay for the harm it caused. But then does the hunter have any basis in right for complaining: "The killed animal could have produced many others, or I myself could have had the pleasure of killing it"? Such statements are contrary to all right and reason. The primary purpose of hunting is to protect civilization, and every other purpose is inessential. In relation to this purpose, the hunter is obligated to fulfill still other tasks [231] such as the extermination of predatory animals that are neither useful nor directly harmful to the hunter himself, e.g. chicken-hawks and similar birds of prey, sparrows, and even caterpillars and other harmful insects. (The hunter is already motivated to exterminate those wild animals that interfere with his own pursuit of game, e.g. foxes and wolves, etc.)

If the job of hunting were only a burden without any benefits, then the authorities themselves would have to do the job. But since hunting involves significant benefits for the hunter – and herein lies a problem, for, as a rule, a hunter can derive more benefits for himself, if he spends less time on his obligations to the state (and thus complaints about hunters are readily and commonly voiced) – it follows that hunting must be strictly supervised by the authorities. This is also why hunting cannot be done by the authorities themselves (even though, as noted above, they are responsible for seeing that the job gets done). Hunting involves certain emoluments; thus the authorities must give the job to someone else. If hunting were left in the hands of the authorities themselves, they would be both party and judge (in effect, bribed by the advantages and pleasures of hunting) in any case between themselves and the agriculturalist; and this would be contrary to all right. It would be terribly absurd if the authorities (which have no authority above them but are themselves the highest authority) were able to reap the benefits and pleasures of hunting by doing injustice to the agriculturalist.

(D)

All of the property rights described thus far deal with the possession of natural products as such, regardless of whether humans assisted nature in her production of them (as in agriculture and animal-breeding), or whether humans simply searched for the products that nature had already produced without any human guidance (as in mining, forestry, fishing, and hunting). Thus we shall designate this class of citizens by a single, general name: *producers*.

Now it is quite possible that these raw products still [232] need to be worked on in some specific, artificial way in order to be made suitable for human ends; and in the present, wholly empirical investigation, we shall rely simply on the fact that this is the case, without any further *a priori* deduction. It is to be expected that other citizens will dedicate themselves exclusively to working on these raw materials to prepare them for the ends of their fellow citizens. This implies a second class of citizens, which I shall call the *artists*, in the broadest sense of the word. The distinction between these two classes is clearly defined, and the designations, in themselves, are perfectly accurate. Those who belong to the first class leave nature entirely to herself; they do not prescribe anything to her, but simply subject nature to the conditions under which she may exercise her formative power. The producers who merely search for nature's products do even less than this. As soon as nature has done her job, the producers' work is over; the product is ripe, or the raw product is available. Now citizens from the second class enter the scene, and (unlike the first class) they no longer rely on nature's assistance, either because the product's own formative drive is already dead (by virtue of its ripeness), or else because they themselves must kill it for their own purposes. They configure the natural parts entirely in accordance with their own concept, and the moving force lies in *themselves*, not in nature. Something that is produced in this manner is called a product of art. Every thread the spinner spins is such a product. Now to be sure, the word *artist* has been used more specifically to refer to particular classes of these laborers. But this usage of language can do no harm to our usage, which is grounded *a priori* on a correct distinction and which we certainly need not generalize, but which we have asserted, out of necessity, only for the purpose of the present investigation.

A certain number of citizens must be granted the exclusive right to work in a certain way on certain objects. If their right is not *exclusive*, then they have no property. They have refrained from doing the work of others, but these others have not done the same for them. The property contract with them is one-sided; [**233**] it places obligations on them, but does not entitle them to anything. Thus it is null and void. A group of citizens who are exclusively authorized to work in a certain fashion on a certain product is called a *guild* [*eine Zunft*]. Abuses by guilds (the remnants of earlier barbarism and general incompetence) ought not to occur; but the guilds themselves must exist. The elimination of all restrictions on these occupations would directly contravene the original property contract.

The artist must be able to make a living from his labor, as stated in the proof given above. In general, we can distinguish two classes of artists: those who merely expend their labor but do not own the materials on which they work (*operarii*), and those who do own the materials on which they work (*opifices*). The state must guarantee to the former that he will have work to do, and to the latter that he will be able to sell his wares.

(Are individuals to be prohibited from making their own wooden shoes or linen coats? A person would think of doing so only under conditions of the most extreme poverty or in the most poorly organized state (i.e. he would have to have nothing he could exchange for these things, or else he would be making very poor use of his time and energies); otherwise, he would gain nothing, and lose quite a bit, if he were to make his own things. Therefore, legislation in a well-constituted state does not have to concern itself with this.)

The content of the contract between everyone and the artists is as follows: "You artists must promise to do work for us that is of sufficient quantity and quality, while we, in turn, promise to come only to you for this kind of work." If the guilds should fail to do good work, they will forfeit the exclusive right granted to them by the contract; thus the testing of those who want to enter the guild, i.e. those who want to be included in this contract, is a matter of everyone's concern. The ruler (or perhaps the guild itself on behalf of the ruler, acting as the government's partner in this administrative task) must calculate how many persons can make a living from each type of work, as well as how many workers are needed to meet the public's needs.

[234] If the artists in a particular line of work cannot all make a living from their work, then the state has miscalculated; it must make up for this miscalculation and provide the individuals with other ways of making a living.

(E)

However, the artist does not live off his work, but off the products. Thus there must always be a sufficient number of products available for the state's inhabitants (producers as well as artists) to live off, at least from one constitutional convention to the next.

Now the artist can ask for the producer's products, only in exchange for his own labor or his own finished articles; conversely, the producer can ask for the artist's labor or finished articles, only in exchange for his own products.

An exchange takes place, which the state must regulate, i.e. the state must arrange things so that the artist, in exchange for all of his labor or articles, receives the quantity of products he needs in order *to live during the time that he is making the articles.* Conversely, the producer, in exchange for all the products that he himself has not consumed (and according to the very same proportion indicated above), receives the particular articles he needs. – There must be a perfect equilibrium between raw products and finished articles.

There may not be more artists than can live off the products of the land. A barren earth does not allow for luxury. In that case, the people must learn to live within limits. (However, the scope of this principle is subject to severe limits, since the people can engage in foreign commerce; in the present context we are not considering this possibility, but are regarding each state as a self-sufficient whole. Since foreign commerce makes a people dependent and cannot be counted on to be steady and lasting, every state would do well to organize itself so as to be able to do without it.)

Each person must be able to acquire what he needs as quickly as possible. In order to facilitate exchange, the state needs people whose sole job will be to exchange things, i.e. *merchants.* The right to work as a merchant is [235] granted exclusively, as a form of property within the state, to a certain number of people (and the state must calculate what this number should be).

The merchants must be able to make a living. Moreover, all commerce is to be supervised by the state (about which we will soon say more).

Contracts of exchange between people – regardless of whether they involve labor or things, and regardless of whether they were formed directly between producers and artists, or were mediated by the merchants (the various types of contracts have been summarized in the formula: *do, ut des*; *facio, ut facias*; *do, ut facias*; *facio, ut des*)[2] – are guaranteed by the state. The state will see to it that they are fulfilled, for such contracts absolutely must be valid, if a relation of right between co-existing human beings is to be possible. The state cannot guarantee what it does not recognize, and so it must pass laws that determine which contracts are valid and which ones not. A contract formed *in violation of* the law is not valid. A contract formed *apart* from the law is not valid *as a matter of right*; instead, such a contract must be judged in terms of morality and honor. The validity of any contract derives immediately or mediately (i.e. by means of positive law) from the law of right, in accordance with the principle: anything whose non-existence would make every relation of right impossible is absolutely valid as a matter of right.

Now in this exchange of products for finished articles and labor, there is naturally a decisive advantage in favor of the producers. The producer can live, at least for the most part, without the artist's works, but the artist cannot live without the producer's products. Now as part of the civil contract, the artist has been promised that he will be able to make a living off his labor, i.e. that he will always be able to acquire the *appropriate* products (based on the standard already indicated above) for his labor. Thus, in consequence of the civil contract, the producer is obligated to sell his products. But now according to what we said above, his products are his absolute property, and so he must be at liberty to sell them for as much as he can. However, based on what we have just demonstrated, he must not be allowed to do so. Therefore, it is necessary to set a *maximum price* for foodstuffs and for the raw products most commonly used in making finished articles. [236] Now if the producer does not want to sell at this price and if the state does not have

---

[2] I give that you may give; I do that you may do; I give that you may do; I do that you may give. This formula expresses the four classes of contract recognized in Roman law.

the right to use physical force to make him sell, then the state must at least be able to coerce his will. The state can best achieve this end by selling from its own storerooms, which it can very easily do (since, as we stated in our theory above, the farmers must pay taxes to the state in the form of products). The artist is certainly not in a position to put pressure on the producers to any great extent, for he always needs foodstuffs. (I am speaking here about states constituted in the manner described above, and not those constituted in the usual manner, those that require farmers to pay their taxes in cash and thus often make it very easy, especially as tax deadlines approach, for those with cash to squeeze the farmer's products out of him.)

However, it is necessary to draw a distinction between the finished articles that the producer cannot do without, and those that he can. – Included in the first category are tools for cultivating the land (i.e. all that is involved in producing or finding the products), warm clothing for harsh climates, and shelter. As with the producer's products, it is necessary to set a maximum price for these things. In order to be able to enforce its law, the state must also keep in its storerooms agricultural tools, as well as the basic necessities for clothing; the state must also employ masons and carpenters who can build houses for it, if need be. The producer can do without mere luxury items, if they are too expensive for him. The enjoyment of them is not guaranteed to him. (The state must see to it that articles that are dispensable – especially those that can be obtained only through foreign commerce and whose availability over time is unreliable – do not become indispensable. The best way to do this is to impose very heavy taxes on such articles. The purpose of such measures must not be to bring in a lot of revenue, but to bring in *none* at all. If a lot of revenue is brought in, the taxes should be raised even higher. But the state should not do this too late, i.e. after [237] such articles have already become needs because of the state's prior neglect, and after the citizens' enjoyment of them has become more or less guaranteed because of the law's prior silence.)

(F)

We are caught in a contradiction.

Thesis. In consequence of the civil contract, the state guarantees that, once a citizen has fulfilled his duties of providing protection and support, he will have an absolute, unrestricted property right to the remainder of his possessions. Each citizen must be permitted to destroy, waste, discard, or do whatever he wants with his own things, so long as he does not use them to inflict positive harm on others.

Antithesis. The state constantly lays claim to this remainder (i.e. to the producer's products, and to the artist's labor and finished articles) in order to make possible the necessary exchange of goods; and it does so in accordance with the following principle, contained in the civil contract: "Each person must be able to live off his labor, and must labor in order to be able to live." Thus the property contract contained in the civil contract contradicts itself. The property contract and one of its immediate implications stand in contradiction.

Once we find the reason for this contradiction, the contradiction itself is resolved. The state lays claim to this remainder, not with respect to its *form* (as a remainder and as property), but rather for the sake of its *substance*; the state lays claim to it, because it is something that is needed to sustain life.

Thus in order to solve the contradiction at its foundation, it is necessary to distinguish between the *form and substance* of the remainder. The state must be able to control the *substance* without touching the *form*.

Without making a show of unnecessary profundity here, I shall resolve the matter without further ado. There must be a bare form, or mere sign, of property that signifies everything that is beneficial and useful in the state, yet without itself being the least bit useful, for if [238] it were useful, the state would be justified in claiming it for public use.

Such a form or sign is called *money*. The use of money must necessarily be introduced into the state. And this is how the difficulty noted above is resolved. The producer may not keep his products, but must give them up. But are they not his absolute property, guaranteed by the state? – The producer is not to give them up for free, but in exchange for finished articles. But right now he does not need any finished articles, at least not the ones you are offering him. And so he receives *money* for them. – The same also applies to the artist.

The state is responsible for supplying the producer with finished articles in exchange for his products, and for supplying the artist with products in exchange for his finished articles. But neither of them currently wants, in exchange for what he has, an equivalent amount in what the other has to offer – and so each receives, in exchange for what he has, a sign of its value in the form of money. It is as if each one's commodity is being kept in storage for him. And as soon as one wants to have the commodity in actuality, he must be able to acquire it in exchange for the mere sign of it. At any time, each person must be able to acquire, in exchange for his money, anything whose enjoyment in general the state has guaranteed; for every piece of money in the hands of a private person is a sign of the state's indebtedness.

The sum of money circulating within the state represents everything that is marketable within the state. If the amount of money remains the same but the amount of what is marketable increases, then the value of the money increases proportionally; if the amount of what is marketable remains the same but the amount of money increases, then the value of the money decreases proportionally. Thus, if a state is considered in isolation, it does not matter whether there is more or less money in it; such an increase or decrease is only illusory. A larger amount of money has no more value than a smaller amount, since both still represent the same thing, namely the sum total of what is marketable within the state; and a particular portion of all the money in circulation will always only buy the same, corresponding portion of the state's sellable goods.

[239] As we have seen, the very concept of money implies that the substance of the money, as such, is completely useless to human beings. The value of this substance must be based simply on general opinion and agreement. Each person must merely know that every other person will recognize it as the equivalent of the corresponding portion of what is marketable within the state. In this regard, *gold* is a very good kind of money; for the true value of gold, its usefulness, disappears into practically nothing when compared to its imaginary value as a sign. *Silver* is not nearly as good as a kind of money, for it is intrinsically very useful for making things. Because gold and silver are rare, and because a state cannot make more gold and silver at will, these materials have become money *throughout the world.* *Paper and leather money* are the best kinds of money for an isolated state (if ways can be found to prevent private persons from counterfeiting it), since the value of their substance, when compared to their artificial value, is nothing at all. Even if a state were to increase the amount of its paper or leather money at will (which would be very easy to do), there would be no harm, since (as

noted above) the value of money stands in direct proportion to how much of it there is. But since nowadays all civilized states, at least, carry on foreign commerce, and since foreigners are not likely to accept that a state's money can have the same value if the amount of this money can be arbitrarily increased *ad infinitum*, it follows that paper and leather money (even within the state itself) will be much less desirable than gold and silver, which have the same value both inside and outside the state. This will be all the more pronounced, the more commodities the state has to import, and the fewer it has to export, in exchange for its national currency.

The state alone has the authority to coin money, because only it can guarantee to everyone the value of this money. For this reason, the mines are necessarily a royal prerogative.

Citizens pay taxes with their products or finished articles. Obviously, they can also pay with money, since money is the [240] state-authorized sign of all things. However, each person, if he wishes, should also be at liberty to pay his taxes in kind; for this is the original arrangement. For the sake of equality and uniformity, the amount of these taxes to be paid must be defined in terms of natural goods; for the value of a particular piece of money can fluctuate greatly. If taxes are paid with money, the amount to be paid is the current market cost of those goods that serve as the standard for determining the taxes. However, in the state we have been describing, where a maximum price is set for the citizens' primary needs, the value of money will not fluctuate much.

What remains after taxes have been paid is, in consequence of the state contract, pure property. But since, in consequence of the same contract, the state has the right to force each person to share his property with those citizens who need it, everyone receives *money* in its place. And this money is *absolute, pure property, over which the state no longer has any rights at all.* Every piece of money I possess is simultaneously a sign that I have fulfilled all of my civil obligations. With regard to such money, I am completely free of the state's supervision. Taxes on the mere *possession of money* are completely absurd. All money, by its very nature, has already been allotted to its possessor.

Supplies that one has purchased with money for one's private use (but by no means for commercial use, which stands under state supervision), and in general any furniture, clothing, or valuables for one's own use, are likewise absolute property, and for the same reason noted above.

(G)

In consequence of the civil contract, the state is responsible for protecting and guaranteeing the security of property in money and the like (in short, all absolute property). But now all these things, and especially money, are such that property in them can in no way be described by reference to particular persons. (The fact that I, and no one else, own the field that lies between this and [**241**] that plot of land and is indicated by such and such boundary markers, should be written down in the record books of my municipality; and if any dispute should arise about it, the record books will decide the matter right away. But how is it possible to signify that I, and no one else, own this particular thaler? All thalers look alike, and should look alike, because they are supposed to change owners without any further formality.)

Furthermore, the state cannot keep track of how much cash and the like each person has. Even if it could, it ought not, and the citizen need not tolerate any attempt to do so; for in this respect, he is entirely beyond the state's supervisory authority. Now how should the state protect what it does not know, what it is not supposed to know, and what is by its nature completely indeterminable? The state would have to protect it in an indeterminate, i.e. general, way. But for this to happen, the property to be protected would have to be connected to and inseparably associated with something determinate, which – since the right to such determinate property is unique and attributable to it alone – would have to be expressly posited as the *paradigm of all absolute property*, which even the state may not violate or subordinate to its supervisory authority. This determinate property would have to be visible, recognizable, and determinable by reference to the person of the owner.

This determinate property with which the indeterminate property is associated, can be of two kinds. (This distinction is drawn from a distinction pertaining to the indeterminate property to be determined.) First, the state has granted to each person (assuming he has paid his taxes) the *use* of the goods he himself has built, made, or purchased. Thus a person's immediate, state-sanctioned use of something signifies and defines a piece of property within the state. If someone makes immediate use of something, it is to be assumed that it belongs to him until the contrary is proven; for in a well-administered state, it is to be assumed that a person simply would not be able to make use of something if doing so were contrary to the will of the law. But if someone makes immediate use of a thing, [242] then that thing is associated with the person's body. Therefore, whatever someone has in his hands or on his body belongs to him; and in this way, the thing is adequately signified as his. Money that I have in my hand, pay out, or carry in my clothing, is – like the clothing with which it is associated – *mine*. (The Lazzaroni[3] always carry all their absolute property on their bodies.)

But second, it has been noted: my absolute property is not only that of which I make immediate use, but also that which I designate for future use. Now I cannot be expected or required always to carry all my absolute property on my body. Therefore, there must be some kind of surrogate for my body, by virtue of which anything associated with it – simply because it is thus associated – is designated as my property. Such a surrogate is called a *house* (housing in the broadest sense of the word: the room someone has rented, the maid's dresser drawers, baggage entrusted to the postal system, and the like). My house as such stands directly under the protection and guarantee of the state, and so everything in it stands indirectly under that protection and guarantee. The state guarantees against violent intrusions into my house. But the state does not know, and ought not to know, what is in my house. Thus the particular objects in my house, as such, stand under my own protection and absolute dominion, as does everything that I do in my house – assuming, of course, that the effects of my actions do not go beyond its walls. The state's supervisory authority extends to the lock on my door, and my own authority takes over from there. The lock on my door is the boundary line between state and private authority. That is why locks exist: to make self-protection possible. Within my house, I am sacred and inviolable, even as far as the state is concerned. In civil matters, the state may not apprehend me in my house, but must wait until it finds me on public ground. However, in the doctrine of criminal legislation, we shall see how this *right over one's house may be lost*.

My house determines what my absolute property is. [243] If a thing

---

[3] The Lazzaroni take their name from the Italian word for beggar or idler, which itself derives from the name of the Biblical beggar Lazarus. The name was originally applied to the lower classes of Naples by the Spanish, against whom the Lazzaroni revolted in 1647. In 1797–8 they supported the Bourbons in their struggle against the revolutionaries.

has made its way into my house (obviously, with the state's awareness and consent), then it is my absolute property. In the context of the constitution described here, the fact that I have a house and things within it is sure proof that I have fulfilled my obligations to the state: otherwise, and before I have done so, I have no house; for the state will first take from me what I owe it.

(H)

If I am the absolute master and protector in my house (in the most precise sense of the word, i.e. in my room, if I do not have my own house), then everything that enters it stands under my dominion and protection.

No one may enter my house without my consent. – Even the state cannot force me to permit someone to enter, for even the state may not enter without my consent. In our houses, we no longer stand under the supervision and guarantee of the state, but under our own, and so personal security in our relations with each other depends on good faith and trust. What happens in the house is a private matter, which a person can forgive; what happens in public is a public matter, where the transgressed party's forgiveness can in no way acquit the transgressor. In our houses we have a tacit contract with one another concerning the mutual security of our bodies and goods. Whoever breaches this contract based on good faith and trust is *dishonorable*, i.e. he disqualifies himself from ever being trusted again. (A deep-seated ethical sense, existing from time immemorial and in all nations, has decided this. In all nations it has been considered dishonorable for a host to insult a guest, or a guest to insult a host, in the house. In all nations, thievery inside the house has been considered more disgraceful than violent robbery in public. The latter is at least as harmful as the former, and so this general opinion could not be based simply on self-interest. The real difference is this: an act of robbery is flagrant; it is a force that openly sets itself against another force that does not trust it. [**244**] Theft, by contrast, is cowardly, since it makes use of another's trust in order to harm him.)

Everything in the house, e.g. cash, furniture, food, etc. (excluding food in the case of merchants), is beyond the supervisory authority of the state, and property in these things is not directly guaranteed. All contracts concerning such things are based on good faith and trust. – (Unless, as part of the contract, someone declares himself to be a merchant and wants the matter to be guaranteed by the state; this must be an option for anyone who does not trust the other, and the state must pass laws concerning it.) If I lend money to someone based on his word, but he does not keep his word and defaults on the loan, then the state will not help me: and rightfully so, for our contract was not formed under the guarantee of the state, and I cannot prove, as a matter of right, that he owes me a debt. By contrast, if I receive a bill of exchange from him, then – since the state has declared that such a bill will suffice, as a matter of right, to prove his debt – our contract is formed under the guarantee of the state, which then owes me its protection. If contracts based on mere good faith and trust are broken, the state will not help the injured party, but the person who breaks such contracts is dishonorable.

A citizen's *honor* consists in others' belief that he is faithful and trustworthy in cases where the state cannot guarantee anything, for where it does provide guarantees, everything is a matter of coercion (in which case good faith and trust are irrelevant).

The state has neither the right nor the power to command citizens to trust one another; for it itself is constructed on the premise of universal mistrust. Even the state is not to be trusted, as we have shown in our discussion of the constitution as a whole.

Conversely, the state has no right to prohibit trust in general. It does, however, have a perfect right to prohibit transactions within its jurisdiction from being based merely on good faith and trust, and [245] to nullify anything that would otherwise follow from such transactions as a matter of right. For if such transactions were allowed, widespread confusion would ensue, and the state would not be able to make any guarantees to private persons concerning rights that it did not know about. A field, a garden, or a house can be sold only under the state's supervisory authority; for the authorities must always know who the true owner is. But since the state may not at all interfere with or keep track of what people do with their absolute property (for individuals must be allowed to discard, destroy, etc. their absolute property), then why should it not also allow transactions involving absolute property to be based on good faith and trust? Therefore, people must be allowed to lend cash and cash equivalents apart from the state's supervisory authority.

But now the state is nevertheless supposed to protect every citizen's absolute property. What can it do to protect it against dishonorable deeds? Nothing more than *to warn all citizens against people who are known to be dishonorable.*

The state's right and duty to do so is grounded in the property contract: the state must protect the citizens against all dangers; but dishonorable actions pose a grave danger. Thus to the extent that it can, the state must make dishonorable deeds impossible. The punishment for those dishonorable deeds discussed here shall be infamy. (And only for such deeds; for the state cannot change people's opinions, especially if they are grounded in human nature, such as those at issue here. *Voltaire,*[4] for example, suggests that dueling be punished with infamy. This is impossible, for human beings cannot be made to regard as dishonorable someone who risks his life to the same degree that his opponent does (although one may very well think that he is foolish); just as, by contrast, everyone regards treacherous murder as dishonorable.) But the state cannot *prohibit* someone from trusting a dishonorable person. Whoever wants to do so must be allowed to do so at his own risk.

No one has the right to demand that the other trust him or that the state force the other to trust him. Trust is [246] earned and freely given. But everyone does have the right to demand that he not be declared dishonorable unless he has done something to deserve it. Being trusted by others is a significant good that a person might possibly earn and that depends on the others' uncoerced good will. A person may not be robbed of this possibility; if someone should try to do so, a lawsuit can be brought against him.

Thus *the right to honor* in the state is really only the right not to be declared dishonorable unless one has done something wrong. The state has guaranteed this right by virtue of the fact that – in consequence of the law of right – both the state as a whole and individual citizens have refrained from interfering in the natural course of events and public opinion concerning honor. This is a purely negative right.

---

[4] François Marie (Arouet Voltaire) (1694–1778) was a leading figure of the French Enlightenment and a defender of human rights. He was the author of philosophical works, plays, poetry, novels, and historical treatises. His criticism of duels is of a piece with his general opposition to feudalism and the ethos on which it was based.

(1) Concerning the right to personal security and inviolability

The freedom and absolute inviolability of each citizen's body is not expressly guaranteed in the civil contract, but is always presupposed as part of each citizen's personality. The very possibility of the contract and of everything one might contract about is based on such freedom and inviolability. One cannot push, assault, or even detain a citizen without interfering with the use of his freedom and diminishing his life, wellbeing, and free activity. Blows and wounds cause pain; but everyone has the right to be as well as he can, so far as nature allows him. Other free beings may not interfere with him in this regard. An attack upon a person's body is an injury to *all* of his rights as a citizen; and so it is certainly a crime within the state, since the exercise of all of his rights is conditioned by the freedom of his body.

In all public areas – and any area outside the house, e.g. an open field, is a public area (the garden is usually counted as part of the house and falls under its rights) – I am always under the protection and guarantee of the state. An attack upon my person [247] in a public area is a public crime, which the state must investigate and punish as part of its official duties (*ex officio*, i.e. without requiring a special complaint), and the private persons involved cannot settle the matter on their own.

But in our houses we do not stand under the protection or jurisdiction of the state, although the house itself does. Thus any forcible intrusion into the house, whether by day or night, is a public offense, and is governed by the rules pertaining to such offenses. But whoever comes into my house without having had to break in or to *break open a lock*, has entered with my consent and on mutual good faith and trust between us. (For this reason, knocking on a person's door has become customary and ought not to be abolished, and saying "*Come in!*" confers upon a person the right to enter). I have allowed him into my house, because I did not think he would forcibly attack me or my property; otherwise, I would not have let him in.

But supposing now that he does forcibly attack me (whether his attack is upon my property or directly upon my person, or both): if, say, I defend myself against his first attack with my own person, can I then still expect and demand the state's protection?

First of all, the state does not know what goes on in my house; it does not have the right publicly to know about it, or to act as if it did. If the state is to know about it, then I myself would have to notify it, as a state, in accordance with the rules of right, i.e. I would have to file a lawsuit. (The statement, "Where there is no plaintiff, there is no judge," applies here, and only here; but it does not apply to offenses that take place in public areas. Taverns, cafés, and the like – in short, any place where anyone is welcome for the purpose of spending their money – are public areas, where commerce takes place. Our states often extend that rule of right, which applies only here, much further than they should.) If the parties themselves want to reach their own good faith agreement on the matter, then the state has no right to inquire into it.

But then is the state obligated to take up lawsuits and administer right concerning private offenses, and on what ground? Here is why it is: in consequence of the [248] civil contract, the state must protect me (even when I am in my house) and everything in my house; however, it may not do so directly (for that would contravene my right), but only indirectly (only in a general and indeterminate way). Direct protection would contravene my right, for in order to protect me directly, the state would have to keep track of what goes on in my house, which would contravene my right. Now if I surrender this right by voluntarily informing the state about what goes on in my house, then I would be voluntarily subjecting to the state's direct jurisdiction what had previously been subject to it only indirectly. What I voluntarily place under the state's jurisdiction acquires all the rights of what stands immediately under its guarantee. – Of course, the penal law would have to take account of such an arrangement and make it known, so that no one expects immunity for certain offenses, only to find out afterwards that he was mistaken.

But with this resolution we have gotten ourselves into a serious difficulty, namely: if someone is killed in his house, he cannot file a suit. One might say that his relatives will do so. But what if he has none, or what if the relatives themselves have killed him? – The state has no jurisdiction over what occurs in the house; and so there is, especially in the latter case, no protection or law against murder in someone's house. In fact, legislation that enables only the transgressed party, so long as he is alive, to sue the transgressor, gives every transgressor an incentive to end the matter by simply killing anyone he fears might sue him.

Things cannot be this way. Therefore, reason must yet have a specific solution for this situation. Let us look for it.

If the murdered person were alive, he could either file a suit or pardon the transgressor. He has been killed contrary to right; he ought still to be alive, and the state knows nothing of his death, for he was killed outside its jurisdiction. Thus, the state still has to ask what he resolves to do in this situation; therefore, in accordance with perfect, external right, it is to be assumed that, as far as the state is concerned, his will continues to exist. The murdered person has [**249**] not determined his will in this matter; but it is determined, declared, and guaranteed by the general will of all the citizens, *regarded as individuals and subjects* (i.e. not by the common will of the state which in this situation judges, decides, and guarantees, but does not will, demand, or sue). – (In our section on testaments, we shall further discuss how the deceased person's last will is guaranteed by the general will of individuals, a concept that is entirely new in our investigation. This general will of all individuals (the public) and the guarantee it provides come to exist where all individuals have a reason to determine that the deceased person had a will and that his will is enforceable, since, in a similar situation, they themselves would necessarily want to have a will and have it enforced.) Now how is the general will to determine the murdered person's will? The general will declares that his will would have been to file a suit. There ought to be someone who represents this general will with respect to the deceased person's last will – someone who serves as the *plaintiff*, a kind of public prosecutor; for the state does not, and cannot, really know about the murder. Every private person has the right to see that this public prosecutor does his duty. Everyone has the right to inform him about such matters and to bring a suit against the prosecutor himself, if he fails to prosecute the transgressor.

Each private person must not only have the right but must himself also be obligated, to report what he knows about such transgressions. If someone does not do so, he himself is punishable, in which case the prosecutor will prosecute him. In this branch of public power, the state is obligated to concern itself with the death of its citizens and how they die. Dying is a public act. Doctors must be under state supervision. And therefore, contrary to what was suggested above, it is in the transgressor's interest to preserve the life of the transgressed party. For as long as the latter is alive, he can pardon the transgressor; after he is dead, the transgressor falls into the hands of the public and its representatives, and for the sake of its own security, the public cannot pardon him.

[250] The right of self-defense belongs in this part of our treatment, and we shall now discuss it.

No one has the right to defend with his own body *property that is marked by the state as his* in such a way that the life of both the transgressor and the defender are inevitably endangered. For after the fact he can always prove his ownership and regain his property, and the transgressor can always be punished (e.g. if someone were to plow up another's crops). However, a person does have the right and duty to gather together witnesses and evidence to prove who the transgressor was.

By contrast, everyone has the right to defend (even by endangering the transgressor's life) unmarked property, i.e. property whose ownership is indicated only by the fact that someone has it on or near his person, or in his house. – Here one may not ask, "What is money, when compared to life itself?," for an answer to that is always a judgment about what is good, rather than what is right. Each person has the absolute right not to have anything taken from him by force and to employ any means to prevent that from happening. – If I protect my property with my own person, then any forcible attack upon my property is also an attack upon my person. If the attack is upon my person from the very outset, then I obviously have the same right of self-defense. This right is grounded in the fact that the state's help is not immediately available although I must be defended right away, since what is being attacked is *irreplaceable property.*

This also implies limits on the right of self-defense. I have this right only to the extent that the state cannot defend me; thus the fact that the state cannot defend me must not be my own fault, and I am obligated as a matter of right and so far as I am able, to make it possible for the state to defend me. I am obligated to call upon the state for assistance as soon as I am in danger; I do this by *crying for help.* This is absolutely necessary, and it is the exclusive condition of the right of self-defense. This condition must be specified in the law and impressed upon the citizens from their earliest youth so that they become accustomed to it. For what if [251] I should murder someone and then say: "He attacked me, and I was able to save my own life only by killing him"? The murdered person cannot accuse me of lying; and so there is nothing to prevent me from claiming that he attacked me, even if I myself were the attacker. In this way, everyone's security would be seriously endangered.

But if I have called for help, then I can prove as much; or at least the opposite could not be proved against me, in which case I would have the presumption of innocence in my favor. (Under the Law of the Twelve Tables,[5] if a person was robbed, he had a right to kill the thief if the thief offered resistance. And rightfully so in the case of unmarked property; for no one can be obligated to allow something to be taken from him unless it is possible for him to prove, after the fact, that he was its rightful owner. With unmarked property a person had the right to reclaim the stolen items by force. But now if the thief defended himself, then his attack became an attack upon the person's own body and life, and – once again – the person had a right to defend himself at the risk of killing the thief. But in such a case the law required him to cry for help. And once again, rightfully so; for the first law could apply only under this restriction. By crying out for help, the person has enabled himself to enlist the public as a witness to his innocence, or to get sufficient help to disarm and subdue the thief, and thus free himself from having to kill the thief in order to keep his property.)

An attack upon unmarked property occurs either in a public place (in the sense of the word explained) or in my house. In the first case there is no difficulty in applying the principles just established. In the second case no one – neither a private person nor even the state itself – has the right to enter my house. But by crying for help I give the state and everyone else the right to enter my house, and I thereby subject to the state's direct protection what had previously been subject only to its indirect protection. My cry for help is equivalent to filing suit, and so it constitutes a relinquishment of my right over my house.

Anyone who hears a person crying for help is [252] obligated by the civil contract and as a matter of right to come to the person's aid, in accordance with the principles outlined above. *For all individuals have promised to protect all other individuals. And a cry for help is an announcement that there is danger that cannot, at present, be remedied by the representative of the protective power (the state).* Therefore, a person's cry for help transfers back upon every individual not only the right, but also the civic duty, to offer immediate protection. If a person can be shown to have heard but not heeded someone's cry for help, he is punishable, for he has acted contrary to the civil contract; and the laws must take

---

[5] The Law of the Twelve Tables (lex duodecim tabularum) was the earliest written law of Rome. It was confirmed by the Roman assembly in approximately 450 BC.

this into account. Such assistance in an emergency is not just a *duty of conscience or a Christian duty*; it is an *absolute civic duty*.

Those who have come to offer assistance need not, and may not, do anything more than separate the combatants and stop them from further violence; by no means are they to decide the issue between the parties. If the ground of something ceases to exist, then what it grounds also ceases to exist. But those who have come to render assistance have an immediate right to offer protection because there is a *present* danger. But now this danger has been eliminated by their presence; and so they can now await the assistance of the state, which is the only rightful judge between the combatants. (E.g. it would be a barbaric act, both contrary to right and punishable, if a mob were to beat a thief who had already been apprehended. As soon as the danger to life or property has passed, the authorities are once again the sole protector and judge.)

There is yet another kind of self-defense, based on an alleged *right of necessity*, the theory of which we shall now discuss. This right is said to exist when two free beings find themselves in a situation – not because one has attacked the other, but out of sheer natural causality – where one can save himself only if the other dies and where both will die if one is not sacrificed for the other. (This situation includes that famous and wonderful plank, talked about in the schools, which is too small to carry both of the shipwreck survivors clinging to it; recently this plank has been transformed, for greater comfort, into a [253] lifeboat with the same features. We have clearly defined the issue by means of concepts and so can dispense with such examples.)

Great pains have been taken to solve this question of right, and various answers have been proposed, all because the principle that underlies every judgment of right has not been thought through with sufficient precision. – The main problem for a doctrine of right is: how can several free beings as such co-exist? In asking about the manner of such co-existence, one assumes that such co-existence, in general, is possible. But if this possibility no longer exists, the question of how it is possible (i.e. the question concerning right) is entirely inapplicable. But this is the case here, given our explicit presupposition. Here there is no positive right to sacrifice the other's life in order to save my own, but neither is it a violation of right to do so; i.e. I do not violate any positive right of the other if I sacrifice his life to save my own; for what is at issue here is no longer a matter of right at all. *For both of us* nature has rescinded the right to live; and the decision as to which of us shall live depends on physical strength and free choice. But since both of us must nevertheless be regarded as standing under the law of right (a law that we will once again, after the fact, be subject to in our relations to others), this right of necessity can be described as the right to regard oneself as entirely exempt from every law of right. (We have just said: the decision as to which of us shall live depends on free choice. Now any free choice not determined by the law of right stands under a higher law, namely, the moral law; and this law may very well prescribe a course of action in this case. And so it does. "Do nothing at all," says the moral law, "but instead leave the matter to God, who certainly can save you if it is His will, and to whom you must surrender yourself if it is not." But this is not part of our treatment here, which deals only with right.)

After the right of self-defense has been exercised, whether in [254] response to an attack or a natural contingency, the one who has exercised it owes the state an explanation. For this person has subjected himself to the state's laws for all time and wants to continue to be regarded as subject to them; but now in this case he has exempted himself from those laws, since no law of right could apply under the circumstances. It is incumbent upon him to show that the law of right did not apply. Anyone who does not voluntarily present himself before a judge creates a presumption of guilt against himself. It is to be presumed that the last will of the dead person is that the case be investigated. Thus it is the duty of the public prosecutor described above to file suit: either (1) to bring the responsible party to court, if he has not already appeared on his own, in which case – if it can be shown that nothing prevented the person from appearing earlier – his evil deed is already half-proven (for why would he avoid going to court, if he is confident that his actions were just?); or (2), if the responsible party has appeared voluntarily, to represent his adversary in court. The defendant is not obligated to provide positive proof that his really was a case of self-defense; for even in the most justified cases, it will be difficult to furnish such proof, since cases of self-defense happen suddenly and unexpectedly. As long as there is no negative proof that it was not a case of self-defense, that is sufficient to suspend court proceedings against him. For the person is not entirely acquitted, if he cannot positively prove that he acted in self-defense and if others might in the future come up with incriminating evidence against him. – In our section on the doctrine of criminal justice, we shall say more about this simple suspension of court proceedings.

Thus the citizen's property and honor have been clearly defined, and they, along with the citizen's life, have been rendered sufficiently secure; it is impossible to conceive how they could be made more secure.

[255] *(K)*

Here we shall examine the acquisition of property, which, as we shall soon see, automatically includes a discussion of the disposition of property.

Here we shall discuss property acquisition only in the truest sense of the word, i.e. acquisition that actually increases a person's wealth, or that at least alters its nature, given the two kinds of property there are, relative and absolute. We do not mean property acquisition in the sense of an exchange of one thing with a particular value for something else of the same value – or in the sense *of commerce*, the essentials of which we have already discussed above and which is not really acquisition, but only exchange. Similarly, we do not mean original acquisition, which would be at the same time an acquisition for the state, i.e. an increase in its own wealth. Such acquisition stands directly under the conditions of the original property contract. Here we are talking only about the complete transfer of property from one citizen to another – and thus about a genuine matter for civil legislation, which is our sole concern here – whereby the state's property remains unchanged and only the relation between citizens changes; that is, the complete transfer of property to a citizen who previously did not own this property at all or did not own it in the amount that he now has.

Property has a double nature: absolute property, which is not subject to state supervision (e.g. money and similar valuables), and property that stands directly under state supervision (e.g. fields, gardens, houses, civil licenses, etc.).

If each of these types of property is exchanged for the other, i.e. if a sale takes place, then each person acquires a type of property he did not have before, and so an analysis of such a transaction belongs to the present discussion. – There is no question about whether such a sales contract must take place under state supervision (by the courts), and under its guarantee. The state does indeed have [256] jurisdiction over property, protects it, and allocates it to particular persons; thus the state must know who the particular property owners are. No one is the rightful owner of an object unless he is recognized by the state.

The only thing about which there could be a question is the extent to which the state is obligated to give its consent to every agreement between private persons concerning property, and the extent to which it may withhold its consent and render a contract invalid.

First of all, the state's rightfully grounded aim concerning the property allocated to citizens for their own use is that it be used for the purpose of meeting the state's needs. Thus, a person who buys property must be obligated to use it, and must be in a position to be able to use it, e.g. he must be able to understand and engage in agriculture if he has purchased farmland, or to understand and practice the profession for which he has acquired a license; otherwise, something would be taken away from the state. – The question of whether someone can buy houses with the intention of razing them to the ground depends on the law's particular provisions, which must be guided by the circumstances.

Furthermore, since a seller's cash proceeds (which are, by nature, absolute property) are not at all subject to state supervision, but since the state must see to it that he has a secure means of subsistence, the sale can take place only if it will not jeopardize the seller's livelihood or render him a burden to the state. This can be arranged if: either the seller retains a so-called partial interest [*Ausgedinge*] in the house or land that he has sold; or his capital gain from the sale is safely invested under the state's supervision. The seller is not the absolute owner of his money, because it is his only means of subsistence, and he is responsible to the state for being able to provide for his own livelihood. It is obvious that anyone who sells something, just like anyone who buys something, gives up one kind of property by acquiring another.

[257] A second type of acquisition and disposition of property is the absolute type, whereby a person acquires property without, in turn, giving any equivalent to the person who had disposed of that property: *gifts* and *testaments*. – We shall begin with gifts.

Either relative or absolute property can be given as a gift. A gift of relative property, just like a contract concerning relative property, is valid only if the transaction takes place under the supervision of the courts. – But a gift of absolute property is valid simply insofar as it changes hands from donor to donee. Thus there can never be a dispute as to whether a gift of absolute property has been accepted or not. A gift of relative property is invalid if the donee did not accept it before the courts; a gift of absolute property is invalid if the donee simply did not accept it, or did not declare his intention to do so.

The same condition that applies to the sale of property also applies to gifts. The donor must keep enough property back for his own subsistence.

A person who has given a gift has no right to demand that it be returned; for the contract makes the donee its rightful and unrestricted owner.

A testament [*Testament*] is the means by which something is given away after the donor's death. The crucial question here is: how can the decedent's will [*Wille*] be binding upon the living? The concept of right applies only to persons who can and actually do stand in reciprocal interaction with one another in the sensible world. Thus at first glance, the deceased person has no rights: and so his property reverts to the state, which has the first claim to it, given that no individual may lay claim to property without the state's permission. But it is quite possible that a person, while still living, may harbor wishes pertaining to others after his death. It is often a real advantage to the person if those who are to benefit from his wishes firmly believe they will be fulfilled after his death; e.g. it is a considerable [258] good to him while alive to receive better care, devotion, and love from those who are to be his heirs. In short, this belief in the validity of testaments is a benefit to the living, who may very well have a right to this benefit. The matter can be understood only from this point of view. The issue here has nothing to do with the rights of the deceased (they have no rights), but only the rights of the living.

Wherever human beings have a need to believe in the validity of testaments, they will make provisions for it in their property contract. Thus this belief will be guaranteed for all. – But one must not lose sight of the fact that any such agreement about testaments is optional, i.e. a relation of right can exist among human beings without it, as we have seen above. Disputes concerning the rights to a decedent's property need not ever arise. The state is there to take possession of it. (If a contract is an indispensable condition of the relation of right among human beings, then it is necessary. But the contract concerning testaments is not of this kind: and for this reason, I say that it is optional.)

But any such belief concerning the validity of testaments can arise only if testaments are valid according to a law, i.e. valid without exception. Thus if all want to guarantee this belief to themselves, they must also will such a law; and so the state will have a law: "Testaments shall be valid." And so, for their own sake, all guarantee the validity of the decedent's last will. By guaranteeing this, they also guarantee the validity of their own last will; the decedent's rights are bound to the rights of the citizens who survive him. It is not *the decedent's* will, but the universal will, that binds the living whose interests are affected, and especially binds the state, which otherwise would have a right to inherit the decedent's property. Therefore, in the contract concerning testaments, the state as the common will (*volonté générale*) is the one party, and the universal will (*volonté de tous*) is the other.[6]

The representative mentioned above, as the representative of the will of all, is responsible for administering testamentary rights. In such matters, he serves as prosecutor before the state authority [**259**] and must see to it that testaments are properly executed. Unlike other magistrates, he does not stand under the executive power's supervision, for the executive power is an interested party in such matters (but he does prosecute his cases before the executive power, and would have to be punished by it if he failed in his duties); rather, he stands immediately under the people's supervision. Any private person who notices him failing in his duties must have the right to file suit against him. In such a case, by the way, it will not be necessary for strangers to get involved, since interested parties will be directly involved.

Testaments ought to be drawn up under the supervision, and with the consultation, of this magistrate, and with the consultation of *witnesses*. These witnesses represent the public, which, as we have shown, has an interest in making sure that testaments are honored. –

That testaments are rightfully valid is entirely optional: thus the *extent* of a person's right to pass on property by means of a testament is also entirely a matter of free choice, and depends solely on the disposition of the universal will, i.e. of the legislator; however, express provisions must be made, i.e. laws must be passed, concerning the extent of this right. The legislator, who must take account of the state's particular circumstances, is responsible for determining whether there

---

[6] See n. 2, p. 98.

should be provisions for the non-testamentary inheritance of property, and the extent to which such provisions should limit a person's free disposition of property (his *legacy*). There is only one *necessary*, *a priori* restriction on such free disposition, and it is the same one that applied to gifts in general: namely, the decedent's survivors – e.g. his widow – must have enough to live on, and his children must be brought up (i.e. taught how) to earn their own livelihood. Testamentary freedom may not be so broad as to override these provisions, since the state, after all, is responsible for seeing to it that the decedent's survivors are provided for.

No methods of acquisition, other than those indicated here, may be permitted within a state. And so our analysis of property is entirely complete.

[260] §20

On penal legislation

Thesis. If a person violates any part of the civil contract, whether willfully or out of negligence (i.e. where the contract counted on him to act prudently), then, strictly speaking, he loses all his rights as a citizen and as a human being, and becomes an outlaw with no rights at all [*wird völlig rechtslos*].

Proof. In consequence of the concept of right in general, a person has rights only under the condition that he is fit to live in a community of rational beings, i.e. only under the conditions that (1) he has made the rule of right into an inviolable law for all his actions, and (2) his consciousness of that law can actually determine all his free, external actions (i.e. insofar as they fall under the law). If someone willfully violates the law, then he has not fulfilled the first condition; if he violates it out of negligence, then he has not fulfilled the second. In either case, the condition of the person's capacity to have rights (his fitness to live in a society of free beings) ceases to exist; and if the condition ceases to exist, then so does the conditioned: his capacity to have rights. Such persons cease to have rights.

The civil contract, as such, does not alter this state of affairs. All the positive rights that a citizen has are conditioned on his not threatening the rights of any other citizens. Once he does so (either because he intentionally wills what is contrary to right, or because he is negligent), the contract is nullified. The rightful relation established by the civil contract between him and the other citizens ceases to exist; and since, apart from this contract, there is no other relation of right or possible ground for such a relation, it follows that there is no longer any relation of right at all between them.

Every offense results in the offender's exclusion from the state (the criminal is *outlawed and set free as a bird* [*wird Vogelfrei*]; i.e. his security is guaranteed as little as that of a bird [*Vogel*]; *ex lex, hors de la loi*[7]). His exclusion from the state would have to be executed by the state authority.

Antithesis. The sole end of state authority is the mutual security of the rights of all in relation to all others; [261] and the state is obligated only to employ those means that suffice for achieving this end. Now if it could achieve this end without completely excluding all offenders, then it would not necessarily be bound to impose this punishment for violations from which it can protect its citizens by some other means. In such cases, there would be no reason to exclude the offender; but admittedly (so far as we have seen), there would also be no reason not to exclude him. The decision would be a matter of free choice. But now it is just as much in the state's interest to preserve its citizens (provided only that doing so is consistent with the state's primary end), as it is in each individual's interest not to suffer the loss of all rights for every single offense. So from every perspective there is good reason, in all cases where there is no risk to public security, to impose alternative punishments for offenses that, strictly speaking, merit exclusion.

This can be arranged only through a contract of all with all, which would subsequently become the norm for the executive power. The content of this contract would be as follows: All promise to all others not to exclude them from the state for their offenses (provided that this is consistent with public security), but rather to allow them to expiate their offenses by some other means. We shall refer to this contract as the *expiation contract* [*Abbüßungsvertrag*].

This contract is useful for all (for the state as a whole) as well as for each individual citizen. Under it, the whole obtains both the prospect of preserving citizens whose usefulness outweighs their harmfulness, as

---

[7] Outside the law.

well as the *obligation* to accept their expiation; the individual citizen obtains the *perfect right* to demand that some expiation be accepted in place of the more severe punishment that he deserves. The citizen has a right – a very useful and important right – to such expiation [*abgestraft zu werden*].

The expiation contract becomes a law of the state, and the executive power is obliged to honor it.

(I) As we have shown, the expiation contract extends [**262**] only so far as is compatible with public security. Beyond that, it is contrary to both right and reason. In a state where it exceeds this limit, right would not exist, i.e. such a state could not adequately guarantee public security, nor could it oblige anyone to enter or remain in it.

Punishment is not an absolute end. The claim that it is (whether stated explicitly or through propositions that implicitly presuppose such a premise, e.g. the unmodified, categorical proposition that "he who has killed, must die") makes no sense. Punishment is a means for achieving the state's end, which is public security; and its only purpose is to prevent offenses by threatening to punish them. The end of penal law is to render itself unnecessary. The threat of punishment aims to suppress bad wills and bring about good ones, in which case punishment will never be necessary. Now if this end is to be achieved, each citizen must know with complete certainty that the law's threatened punishment will inexorably fall upon him for any offense he commits. (Thus punishment also exists to set an example, so that all are fully convinced that the penal law will be infallibly executed. The law's first aim was to prevent the criminal from committing a crime. Since this goal was not achieved, the state's punishment of the criminal serves another purpose: to prevent other citizens, and to prevent the criminal in the future, from committing the same offense. Thus the exercise of penal justice is a public act. Anyone who learns that an offense has been committed must also learn of its being punished. It would be a manifest injustice to those who are tempted in the future to violate the same law, if they were prevented from knowing that previous offenses had actually [**263**] been punished. Out of ignorance, they would expect to escape punishment themselves.)

The material principle of positive punishment within a state has already been presented and demonstrated above (§14). Every individual must necessarily put at risk precisely the same portion of his own rights and freedoms (his property in the broadest sense of the word) as he is tempted to violate of others' rights, whether out of selfishness or negligence. (The punishment must be equal to the offense: *poena talionis*.[8] Let everyone know: the harm you do to the other is not harm to him, but only to yourself.) The spirit behind this principle, as we have also seen, is this: there must be an adequate counterpoise [*ein hinlängliches Gegengewicht*] to unjust wills and negligence.

Whenever this principle is applicable, the expiation contract can apply; and then, as we have seen, public security can be guaranteed. Therefore, an answer to the question, "How far does the expiation contract rightfully extend?" depends in part, but only in part – we shall see later why this is so – on an answer to the question, "To what extent can there be an adequate counterpoise to bad wills and negligence?"

(II) Such counterpoise may or may not be possible, by reason of *either* the very nature of the matter *or* the particular condition of the subject whom the penal law aims to influence.

First, let us consider reasons pertaining to the nature of the matter. A person who is tempted to commit an offense is to be deterred from acting on his will by the fact that he wills some content. Therefore, if the law is to have any influence on him, his will must actually be directed at that content. His will must be *materially bad*, a selfish will that desires other people's property. The same goes for cases of negligence. A negligent person is to be compelled to take care not to harm others, by means of the fact that he is at least careful enough not to bring the same harm upon himself. [264] In cases of negligence, there is sufficient deterrence if the offender is simply required to compensate the other, for it is assumed that the other's property has been completely destroyed by the negligence so that it is of no value to the perpetrator or anyone else; in cases of intentional wrongdoing, the transgressor must not only return the property to its rightful owner, but must also pay, as an additional punishment, a fine equal to its value.

(Here is where the theory of counterpoise can be fully clarified. If the robber is required only to return what he stole, then his only punishment will be to have labored in vain. In committing the crime, he had to know that he might get away with it (for otherwise, he certainly would not have committed it, and would have simply spared himself the

---

[8] Punishment of like for like.

trouble of laboring in vain), and so his calculation was as follows: "Either I will be caught or not. If I am, then I will merely have to return what was not mine in the first place; if I am not, then I will gain what I stole. In either case, I cannot lose." But if his punishment is equal to the offense, then his loss if he is caught will be equal to what his gain would have been if he were not. Thus he will risk committing the crime only if the probability of his not being caught outweighs that of his being caught. But this should not be the case in a well-governed state.)

The principle of counterpoise is, by its very nature, inapplicable if the person's will is *formally* bad, i.e. if he causes harm, not in order to gain some advantage, but only for the sake of causing harm. Such a will is not deterred by punishment equal to the offense: a malicious, vindictive person will gladly suffer the loss, as long as his enemy is also harmed. If no other way can be found to protect the person's fellow citizens against such a formally bad will, then any offense arising from such a will is to be punished by exclusion from the state.

First of all, this is a situation where the person's disposition and intentions in committing the offense are relevant, and the punishment must take account of them. If this is all that scholars of right [265] have in mind when they want to base their judgments of right on the moral significance of the offense, then they are completely correct. But if they are talking about some allegedly one, true, and pure morality, then they would be terribly mistaken. When it comes to morality, no human being can or ought to judge another. The only purpose of civil punishments, and the sole criterion for determining their severity, is the possibility of public security. A person who harms public security simply for the sake of harming it is to be punished more severely than someone who harms it for personal gain, but not because his offense displays a higher degree of immorality. Morality is unitary and does not admit of degrees: it is to will duty simply because it is discerned as duty. Thus one may talk about degrees in a person's aptitude for morality, in which case, who would want to say that a person whose offense at least manifests vitality and courage is therefore more depraved than someone who acts merely for personal gain? Rather, such a person is to be punished more severely because the fear of a more lenient punishment, i.e. punishment equal to the offense, is not sufficient to deter his offense.

Thus the question arises: how can one know and prove in a manner that is valid for external right when a person has violated the law simply to cause harm and thus which principle of punishment ought to be applied to him?

If a person can demonstrate that he needed the property he stole, that he needed it for specific purposes, and that he actually used it for such purposes, then it is to be assumed that he committed the offense for personal gain. If he cannot prove these things (e.g. if he did not take or even intend to take the other's property for his own use, but instead destroyed it to no one's benefit), then a further uncertainty arises. That is, unintentional harm (which does not result in benefit to the offender) and intentional, malicious harm are very similar as far as external appearances are concerned. How are they to be distinguished? [266] There are two criteria for identifying intentional harm, one external and the other internal. The external criterion applies if it can be shown that the person freely undertook certain actions in the past that can only be understood as a means for causing harm. If a person claims that the harm he caused was unintentional, then he must *be able to prove* that *his free action* had *a completely different end*, which was only accidentally related to the harm caused to the other. The need for such positive proof cannot be waived. If a person cannot provide it, his malicious intent is as good as proven. However, it is always possible for a peculiar alignment of circumstances to make it seem that the person acted out of premeditated malice, even if he did not. Therefore, one must consider the internal criterion as well; namely, whether the person had any enmity towards the injured party, whether there were any disputes between the two, etc.; or whether the person accused of malice ever did anything previously to warrant such suspicions about him. – Now what is to be done if, after all the circumstances have been weighed, the suspicion can neither be proved nor convincingly disproved (which is quite possible)? Many scholars of right recommend that the milder sentence be imposed in such a case; but such leniency towards a guilty party is a great hardship and injustice to the commonwealth. If someone simply reflects carefully on the matter, he will come up with the right answer on his own. The investigation into the matter has not been brought to an end, and could not be brought to an end based on the evidence available thus far; the evidence adduced thus far has neither convicted nor acquitted the accused, and so the judge, too, ought neither to convict nor to acquit him. At any rate, he indisputably deserves, and for now must suffer, punishment for negligence. But as regards his allegedly bad will, he should be allowed to go about interacting with others so that they can get to know him better and perhaps come up with the missing proof. For a more or less extended period of time (depending on the circumstances), the state authorities should keep him under special surveillance (though without infringing on his freedom), for there is no other way to observe his cast of mind. They [267] shall watch to see whether what is in dispute might later give rise to facts that will decide the case – what succeeds an event is often just as good or even better than what preceded it, at revealing the truth of the event, especially if the authorities let the suspected party, fully convinced that no one is watching him, go about his business for a time and let him freely pursue his intentions. They will watch to see whether his future actions confirm or refute the suspicions about him. If the suspicions are confirmed, the proceedings against him are to be renewed; if they are refuted, then after a period of time specified by law he shall be fully and formally acquitted. Such a suspension of judicial proceedings has already been suggested above, in our analysis of the right of self-defense, and it is generally recommended in cases where suspicion is unproven. In a well-governed state, no innocent person should ever be punished; but neither should an offense ever go unpunished.

It must still be noted that the law must explicitly announce that any harm done to another merely for the sake of causing harm will be punished more severely than the same injury done for personal gain. Everyone must have prior knowledge of the law under which he is punished; otherwise, the punishment would contain an element of injustice. Moreover, the end of the penal law (deterrence) can be achieved only if everyone is familiar with the law. The state must pass explicit laws specifying what kinds of carelessness will be punished as violations of right, and thus specifying the care one should take so as not to harm others in certain cases and while undertaking otherwise permitted actions; this obviously means equitable laws that are appropriate to the circumstances. If a person observes the care commanded by law, he is to be acquitted. If harm occurs in spite of his care, it is to be regarded as an accident of nature to be borne by the injured party, or, depending on the circumstances, as something for which the state authorities must provide compensation, if [268] they are responsible for it either through a defect in the law or negligence by the police.

The excuse that the offender was not in control of his reason because he was acting *out of anger or drunkenness* does indeed acquit the offender of charges of intentional, malicious willing; but this excuse, far from minimizing the offense, actually adds to it from the perspective of rational legislation, assuming that the accused is frequently in such a condition. For a single, illegal action might be nothing but an exception in an otherwise blameless life. But if someone says: "I often get so angry or so drunk that I lose my self-control," he is admitting that he regularly turns into an animal and thus is incapable of living in society with rational beings. He must forfeit his freedom until it is clear that he has reformed; or else he must be excluded from the state without mercy. Our laws show far too much leniency, especially in regard to the excuse of drunkenness; and so the laws dishonor themselves. If a nation or a class within a nation cannot renounce this vice, the laws certainly cannot prevent someone, if he so desires, from drinking himself into oblivion in his own house with those who want to keep him company, provided only that they all remain enclosed there until they have regained their senses; for in such a case, the state will take no notice of their condition. But whoever is found in such a condition on public property can legitimately be imprisoned.

The threat of a punishment equal to the offense is inapplicable by reason of the subject's condition if the subject has nothing to lose because he owns nothing other than his body (*capite censi*).[9] – In such cases, no one should complain about injustice by saying: "If a wealthy man steals (a crime he has absolutely no need to commit), he risks nothing more than losing his wealth, of which he probably has more than enough; but if a poor man steals (a crime which he may be led to by severe need), his punishment is to be more severe." This objection [269] would rest on an entirely false presupposition, as if the state were the moral judge of human beings and punishment had to match the moral depravity of the crime. The state's only aim with such a law is to protect property. But the threat, "What you steal from the other will be subtracted from your own possessions," will have no effect on someone who owns nothing. For such a person will think: "I'd like to see someone try to take something from me," which is exactly what one does hear in states that have not done anything about this problem and

---

[9] Literally, counted by head. It refers to the lowest class of Roman citizens, those who were counted only by head (rather than by what they owned).

are not even entitled to do anything about it (since they fail to supervise the administration of property or guarantee subsistence rights to the poor). Thus there must be some other way for the state to protect its citizens against such a person. We shall see below whether this must be accomplished by exclusion from the state, or whether there is some way in which the poor might escape exclusion.

(III) The will to act in direct opposition to the law and its power cannot be deterred by the principle of counterpoise. The most that can and should be done is that the law should simply maintain its authority as established; but in opposing this kind of criminal will, the law cannot be made twice as severe for all or twice as powerful (with the use of everyone's resources). That would amount to punishing everyone for the offense of a single individual. Therefore, because of the very nature of the matter, punishment equal to the offense is inapplicable here; so no punishment can expiate the offense.

One can commit this crime against the state in two ways: either *indirectly against the state in the person of its citizens, insofar as the offender violates the citizens and hence also the contract to which the state itself is a party*; or *directly against the state itself, by means of rebellion or high treason*.

We shall first explain how one can commit this crime against the state indirectly. The civil contract involves, first of all, a contract concerning property between every individual and every other individual, a contract that the state as such (understood as all the individuals woven together into an organized whole) does not enter into, but rather only guarantees. But the civil contract also involves a contract between [270] every individual and the state itself (in the specified sense), in which the state promises each citizen that it will always and everywhere protect *his absolute property, body, and life*, once he has fulfilled his duties as a citizen. The state has completely excluded itself from this absolute property and renounced all claims to it; the state has no rights but only duties with respect to this absolute property. The state becomes a *party* separate from the citizen and is directly answerable to the citizen if his property is ever violated. Now if an individual violates this contract, e.g. by breaking into someone's house (and not just by stealing something in the house, for this is a private crime that can be pardoned, or – in the event that it is punished – can be punished with punishment equal to the offense) or by injuring a fellow citizen's body or life, then he is thereby directly assaulting the state insofar as he is violating *its* contract and (to the extent he is able) making the state break its word, and nullifying its contract with the injured party. – In this situation, the state itself becomes a party in opposition to the injured person and thus would be drawn into a lawsuit with him, for it had promised, but failed, to protect him and his property. It is the criminal who has put the state in this position; therefore, he has assaulted the state itself, and so the principle indicated above applies to him: he is to be declared an outlaw without rights.

One can commit this offense against the state *directly* by means of *rebellion* or *high treason*. Rebellion occurs when one tries to amass or actually does amass a power against state authority, and then uses it to resist that authority. High treason occurs when one makes use of a power conferred upon him by the state for the purpose of impeding or destroying the state's own ends; or also when one fails to use such a conferred power to promote the state's ends, thereby using the nation's trust to frustrate its purposes. Failing to use authority is just as dangerous to public security as misusing it, and so is equally punishable. It makes no difference to us citizens whether you [271] use the power conferred upon you to commit your own offenses, or simply fail to use such power and thereby allow others to commit offenses. In either case, we are oppressed. Once a person has accepted a position of public power, the nation expects him to use the power conferred upon him to realize its ends; and so the nation makes no other provisions for achieving them. If the person had only declined the position to begin with (which he had every right to do), then the nation would have had to seek someone else to fill it; but by accepting the position and failing to live up to it, he has now made it impossible for someone else to do so.

Only private persons can rebel; only those who hold public power are capable of high treason.

(IV) All the kinds of offenses presented thus far merit absolute exclusion from the state, since the only kind of expiation we know thus far (i.e. punishment equal to the offense) is inapplicable to them. – But the question remains whether there might not be some means of expiation other than punishment equal to the offense. If there were, then – for the reasons given above – these means should be introduced where possible.

Let us first consider the case of a poor man who steals something for his own use, but then, once the stolen item is used up, has nothing with which to provide compensation and pay the penalty; should he really be punished by exclusion from the state? There is a solution under which the favor granted by the law [of expiation] may be conferred upon him as well. He has property in his skills and powers, and therefore must *work off* both the compensation and his punishment; it is obvious that he must do so immediately, for before he has worked off what he owes, he is not a citizen (as is the case with any punishment, for – strictly speaking – when a person commits a crime, he forfeits his rights as a citizen). Only after he has fulfilled his punishment does the convicted person becomes a citizen once again. Moreover, this work by him must necessarily take place under the state's supervision. Therefore, he forfeits his freedom until he has suffered the punishment. – (This punishment is that of a *workhouse*, which is to be clearly distinguished from a *disciplinary or correctional penitentiary*, [272] about which we shall say more below.) This work satisfies the law of punishment equal to the offense, but it is also a punishment that (so long as the police do not hide the criminal from public view) will most likely deter other people from committing such crimes in the first place.

If the criminal's will is *formally* bad, or if he commits a crime directly against the state, then – given his current disposition – it is simply impossible to tolerate him any longer within society. It is absolutely necessary that he be punished by exclusion, which both the law of right and the end of the state have already pronounced against him.

But it is not absolutely necessary that he *persist* in his current disposition. Therefore, as an alternative to exclusion (which is, without a doubt, justified in the present context), it may very well be possible to establish a second contract regarding expiation, one that states: all citizens promise to all others that they will give them the opportunity to make themselves fit to live in society once again, if in the present they are found to be unfit; and (what is also entailed by this contract) that they will accept them back into society, after they have reformed. – Such a contract is both optional and beneficial; but its benefits are available to everyone, and so through it the criminal acquires a *right* to attempt to reform himself.

First of all, the punishment established by this contract is an expiation in place of complete exclusion from the state, and so it is a favor granted to the criminal as a matter of right. But one can relinquish his right; and *everyone* is free to choose *which favors to accept or reject*: in rejecting this favor, the criminal declares himself an incorrigible scoundrel who scorns discipline and is to be expelled from the state immediately. Let no one think that granting this favor allows the criminal to escape punishment, or that giving him this choice will frustrate the law's purpose, which is [273] to deter crime. If a state and neighboring states are rationally constituted, then exclusion from the state is the most terrible fate a human being can encounter, as will become clear below; and it is unlikely that someone would choose exclusion, or – in considering whether to commit a crime – would find comfort in the idea that he can opt for exclusion, should his crime be discovered. – (One should note that, even in cases where the punishment is equal to the offense, the guilty party must freely submit to the punishment, for such punishment is also a favor granted to him as a matter of right. But in such cases, it is highly unlikely that someone would choose the loss of everything he has – which is an immediate consequence of exclusion – over the loss of only a part of it.)

Furthermore, this second expiation contract spoke of *reform*, but certainly not the *moral* reform of one's inner disposition. For in such matters, no human being is the judge of another. Rather, it spoke only of *political* reform, reform of the manners and maxims of a person's actual behavior. Just as a moral disposition is the love of duty for duty's sake, so is a political disposition, by contrast, the love of oneself for one's own sake, concern for the security of one's person and property; and the state can without hesitation adopt as its fundamental law: love yourself above all else, and love your fellow citizens for your own sake. In the hands of the penal law, this love of oneself above all else becomes the very means by which the citizen is forced to leave the rights of others undisturbed, for any harm he does to another is harm he does to himself. This concern for one's own security is what drove human beings to enter the state, and whoever lacks such concern has no reason to remain in it. It is only by virtue of such concern that each citizen gives to the state the guarantee required of him, and that the state maintains control over him. If a person has no concern for his own security, the law loses all influence over him. A person can fail to have such concern in one of two ways: either by transcending it through pure morality and forgetting his empirical self in the final end of all reason, [274] in which case the penal law has no role to play, since such a person will automatically observe political justice as a matter of duty; or by remaining beneath that concern and being too coarse and barbarous to care at all about his well-being, in which case the penal law will have no role to play, and he is simply unfit to live among others. A person's political reform consists in his coming to care once again about his own security.

Anyone who has caused harm for the sake of causing harm has exhibited not only inner malice (about which the state does not pass judgment), but also a savagery of manners and an extraordinary lack of concern for himself. If tenderness and mildness were to replace such savagery, if the guilty party would just start caring about his own security (to which lengthy punishment and its various evils will probably drive him), then he could be allowed back into society. The same goes for anyone who has attacked the property or person of another. Such a person is wild and untamed. And in the former case, he also exhibits an untamed desire for other people's property. Let him only learn to love and value what is his, and to direct his attention to protecting it. Someone who takes good and orderly care of his possessions is never a thief or robber; only a dissolute squanderer becomes such. – The rebel may often be a well-intentioned, though misguided, dreamer. Let him correct his concepts and discover the benefits of a civil constitution in general, and of his own state's civil constitution in particular; then he might become one of the state's most upright citizens. – It is only the traitor who has acted both dishonorably and disloyally; the people can never again trust him with public office. He is accustomed to wielding power and giving orders, and will not be easily satisfied with a life of quiet obscurity and modest, private affairs. But that would depend on whether he could be made to have sufficiently lower expectations. This might be difficult to do: but who would want to claim that it is absolutely impossible? (After all, Dionysius became a schoolmaster in Corinth.[10]) The primary rule in this regard is that one should neither despair of their reform, [275] nor cause them to despair of it – and furthermore, that they should have some degree of satisfaction with their condition, as well as the hope to improve it. Both of these aims can be achieved, in part, if they have freely chosen their condition in place of exclusion from the state; if they have given

---

[10] Dionysius II (395–343 BC) became ruler of Syracuse in 367. In 344 he was defeated by Timoleon and taken to Corinth, where he is said to have supported himself as a school teacher.

themselves the task of reform. They will have confidence in themselves because the state has confidence in them.

But these institutions for reform must also be prudently arranged. First, they must be actually separated from society and established according to the spirit of the law. The state has full responsibility for any damage caused by someone who, at the time, is being excluded from society. Therefore, these persons have lost all their freedom. However, if a person is to reform himself, and if his efforts at reform are to be subject to judgment, then he must be free. Therefore, a chief maxim is: such people must be free within necessary limits and must live in society among themselves. – They shall get nothing without having worked for it. It would be a grave error if these institutions were to provide for the prisoners' needs, regardless of whether or not they did any work and if idleness were to be punished by the most degrading treatment (physical blows), rather than by its own natural consequence, privation. Furthermore, all the proceeds of their labor, minus the costs of their upkeep, must remain theirs. Similarly, their property in the state (if they have any) is to be held for them in trust by the state, and they should know this. These institutions should teach them the love of order, labor, and property; but how is that possible, if neither orderliness nor labor does them any good, and if they cannot keep their own property? They must be both subject to, and free of, supervision. As long as they do not violate the law, this supervision must be unnoticeable; but as soon as they violate the law, they must immediately be punished for their violation.

(In order to establish such institutions, the state can use remote territories, or uninhabited islands and coasts, if it is a maritime state. And in [276] land-locked countries, aren't similar islands to be found in large rivers? Any state that resists such measures because of the cost does not deserve a response. For what is the purpose of state revenues, if not to achieve such ends? Furthermore, if these institutions are prudently arranged and if each person is given a job he has learned to perform, then the costs will not be so terribly high. A person who is able to support himself living alone will be all the more able to do so living together with others, and something will remain for covering the cost of the state's supervision. Of course, if funds are repeatedly mishandled in such institutions, they will be costly to maintain.)

The end and condition of the state's maintenance of these criminals is *reform*. Therefore, they must actually reform; otherwise, what is conditioned, the state's patience, will cease to exist. It would be very prudent if the criminal himself were allowed to determine, in accordance with the degree of his depravity, the length of time of his reform – but with the proviso that he would later be free to extend it in accordance with a certain standard. But each criminal must be given a peremptory term for reform, in accordance with his particular crime. As we have already emphasized above, the sole issue here is political and not moral reform; only deeds, not words, can determine whether such reform has taken place. Under such an arrangement, then, it will not be difficult – especially if the state's supervision is gradually relaxed as prisoners show signs of reform, so that their true disposition can develop more freely – to determine whether their dissoluteness has been replaced by a love of diligence and order, their savagery replaced by a milder sensibility. Of course, those appointed to make such determinations are to be sensible, conscientious men, who are held responsible for the future lives of these persons.

Those who have been reformed shall return to society and be reinstated in full to their previous positions. [277] Through their punishment and their subsequent reform, they have become fully reconciled to society. If the state regards these institutions as a genuine means for reform, and not merely as a means of punishment, and if it returns to society only those who have been truly reformed (and not those who have just been detained for a period of time and perhaps worsened by poor treatment), then even the general public would trust, rather than distrust, them.

Those who have not reformed within the peremptory term are to be excluded from the state as unreformable.

These institutions should also serve as punishment, and, as such, should deter crime. Loss of freedom, separation from society, and strict supervision are dreadful enough to anyone who is now free; further-more, there is no reason why the fate of prisoners cannot be portrayed to those on the outside as even more severe than it actually is, or why one cannot introduce distinctions between prisoners and non-prisoners that will frighten the latter, but will not be evil in themselves and will not make the prisoners more savage, e.g. distinctive clothing or shackles that do not cause pain or restrict the prisoners too much. The prisoner will become accustomed to such treatment, and it will make an appro-priate impression on those outside.

(V) The only crime that does not allow of any attempt to reform the criminal, and that therefore must be immediately countered with absolute exclusion from the state, is *intentional, premeditated* murder (not murder that arises incidentally out of some other act of violence). The reason for this is as follows: if someone has committed murder, then others must worry that he may well do it again. But the state has no right to force anyone to risk his life. Thus the state could not force anyone to supervise a murderer, who would have to be granted a certain degree of freedom if he is to reform; nor [278] can it force the other prisoners, who are being detained for the purpose of reforming, to tolerate a murderer in their midst.

(I have said: the state has no right to *force* someone to risk his life. But everyone has the right to risk his life voluntarily. Thus if there are associations and charitable organizations that want to try, despite the danger, to reform even murderers, they must be permitted to do so, but only if they can ensure that the murderer will not escape. For reasons that will become apparent below, it would be good if such associations did exist.)

Now what is to be done with those who are absolutely excluded from the state, either because they were murderers and there was no attempt to reform them, or because they refused to subject themselves to any such attempt; or because the attempt at reforming them failed? This is by far the most important issue to be investigated in a theory of punishment. Through our investigation, we hope to eliminate a great many confusions; and we shall not just make assertions (as is customary), but offer proof instead.

(a) Declaring someone to be an outlaw devoid of rights is the most serious thing the state, as such, can do to any rational being. For it is by virtue of the civil contract that the state is the state for each individual. Thus the furthest the state can go is to declare the contract null and void. From then on, both the state and the individual are absolutely nothing to each other, since apart from the civil contract there is no relation of right for them; there is no relation at all between them, they are nothing to each other. Whatever the state does beyond this, it does apart from any right based on the contract, and – since there are no positive, determinate, and determinable rights apart from those based on the contract – apart from any right at all.

(b) But now what follows from someone's having been declared to be an outlaw devoid of rights? The completely arbitrary treatment of the person thus condemned. It is not that one *has a right to treat him in this way*, but there is also no *right against it*; therefore, the condemned person is declared to be a [279] thing, a piece of livestock. – One cannot say: "In relation to the animal I have a right to slaughter this animal" (even though one does have that right in relation to other citizens in the state); but nor can one say: "I do not have this right." The issue here has nothing at all to do with rights, but only with physical strength. There is still quite a leap from the merely *negative* proposition, "there is no reason against it," to the *positive* one: "there is a reason for it." – The same goes for someone who has been absolutely excluded from the state. Within the context of (*external*) *right*, there is no reason at all why the next person who comes along and gets the idea in his head should not arbitrarily apprehend, torture, and kill him; but nor is there any reason why he should do so.

(c) If someone wants to do so, and actually does so, what would happen? Not punishment by the state, for the condemned person has no rights; but the perpetrator would earn everyone's contempt, infamy. Whoever tortures an animal for the pleasure of it, or kills an animal without any purpose or benefit, is held in contempt as an inhuman barbarian, is shunned and abhorred, and rightfully so. How much more so if someone should do the same to a being that, in spite of everything, still has a human countenance! Thus one refrains from treating the condemned in this manner, not because he has any rights, but rather out of respect for oneself and for one's fellow human beings. (The issue here has absolutely nothing to do with the moral aspect of such a deed, but only with its consequences in society.)

(d) What role does the state play in this regard? First, in relation to the condemned, the state is no longer the state; it no longer exists for him. For all expiation is based on a reciprocal contract. The state, for its part, has the right to impose such expiation; a person who has violated the law, for his part, has the right to demand that his punishment not exceed such expiation. But exclusion from the state is based not on the civil contract, but on the fact that it is annulled. The two parties are no longer anything to each other, and if the state kills the criminal, it does so not *as a state, but as the stronger physical* power, as a mere [280] force of nature. The state's reasons for not killing him are the same as those of the private person; it is not because of the outlaw's rights, for he has none, but rather because of its respect for itself, as well as for its citizens and other states.

But there is one possible reason that might lead the state to kill the criminal; namely, that it is the *only* way to protect itself against him. Since there is no countervailing reason, this reason is decisive here. Then the criminal is a harmful animal that is shot dead, a raging torrent that is dammed up; he is, in short, a force of nature that is overcome by the natural force of the state.

The criminal's death is not a form of punishment, but only a means to ensure security. This gives us the entire theory of the death penalty. The state as such, as judge, does not kill the criminal; it simply cancels the contract with him, and this cancellation is its public deed. If, afterwards, the state also kills the criminal, then it does so not by virtue of its judicial authority, but through the police. As far as legislation is concerned, the person judged is annihilated; he is delivered over to the police. This takes place, not in consequence of any positive right, but out of necessity. That which can be excused only on the basis of necessity is not honorable; thus, like everything that is dishonorable yet necessary, it must be done with shame and in secret. Let the wrongdoer be strangled or beheaded in prison! Because the contract has been broken (which is very fittingly portrayed by the breaking of the staff), he is already dead as a citizen and obliterated from the memory of the other citizens. What is physically done to the wrongdoer is no longer of concern to the citizens. It is immediately obvious that no one may be killed unless the civil contract has first been canceled.

(What can reason say about the public spectacles that accompany executions or about the practice of publicly displaying the bodies of executed criminals, and so forth – just as savages hang the scalps of their slaughtered enemies on their walls around themselves?)

The criminal's death is something incidental, and thus cannot be announced in the law; but exclusion from the state is announced in the law. Naturally, it [281] is possible that exclusion may well lead to death. That is why exclusion – but only exclusion – must take place publicly, in fulfillment of the law.

To make the death penalty more severe by means of torture is barbarism. The state then becomes a savage, gloating, vengeful enemy that tortures its enemy before killing him, so that he will feel death (*ut mori se sentiat*).

(It is sometimes necessary to supplement the arguments of reason by appealing to actual events. Here is a very famous one. In the Roman republic, a person who had forfeited his life (in the state) (*capitis damnato*[11]) was given the option of being exiled. Only if he posed a danger, as in the case of Catiline's co-conspirators,[12] would the Romans kill him; but then only in prison, not publicly. The consul Cicero was exiled, not because these conspirators were executed, but because their verdict was decided – contrary to the proper form of the law – in the senate, and not brought to the people's tribunal; thus Cicero was rightfully exiled.[13])

(e) In connection with the killing of criminals, there is a further issue to be considered here, which – even though it is not actually a juridical issue – must not be overlooked. That is, the moral law absolutely prohibits intentional killing in every case (and not merely *endangering* the life of another for the sake of some end commanded by reason). Every human being is to be regarded as a means for promoting the end of reason. No one can give up the belief that the other – no matter how corrupt he may presently be – can still be reformed, without giving up his own end as necessarily established for him by reason. A rigorous proof of this claim is furnished in a system of morality, where it is called for. Thus a private person may never kill; he must sooner put his own life at risk. Not so for the state, considered here as a police power which, as such, is not a moral person, but a juridical one. The regent may indeed be permitted, and can in certain [282] cases be morally obligated, to put his own person in danger *qua* human being; but he may not endanger the lives of others, and still less the life of the state, i.e. the life, security, and the rightful constitution of all.

(f) Thus the execution of unreformable villains is always an evil, although a necessary one, and so one of the state's tasks is to render it unnecessary. Now what is the state to do with condemned criminals, if it is not supposed to kill them? Life terms for criminals are burdensome to the state itself; and how could the state require the citizens, as such, to

---

[11] One condemned to capital punishment.

[12] Lucius Sergius Catilina (108–62 BC), also known as Catiline, organized an abortive conspiracy against the rulers of Rome in 63 BC. He and his co-conspirators were sentenced to death in the same year, and those who could be caught were strangled in prison. Catiline himself died in a struggle against the government's attempts to crush the insurgents.

[13] Marcus Tullius Cicero (106–43 BC) was exiled from Rome in 58 BC on charges of executing Catiline's followers without a legal trial (see previous note).

bear these costs, which do not serve any of their possible ends, since there is no hope for the criminal's reform and return to the state? There is nothing to do other than to banish the criminal for life – not deport him; deportation is a disciplinary measure, and the state has supervision of those who are deported. If it is feared that the criminal might return, he should be branded indelibly, but as painlessly as possible, for the state must not appear to engage in torture (as it also seems to do, for example, in flogging those who have been banished). Nor is branding a form of punishment, but rather a means to ensure security, which therefore devolves upon the police.

The question, "What is to become of those who have been branded and kicked out of the state?" is asked not by the citizen, but by the human being. Let them go into the wild and live among animals; such has happened, by accident, to human beings who were not criminals, and anyone branded under the constitution described here is incorrigible.

Remark. Against our theory of punishment in general, and our theory of the death penalty in particular, it has been claimed that there is an absolute right of punishment,[a] according to which judicial punishment is regarded not as a means, but as itself an end, [283] which is said to be grounded on a categorical imperative that is itself not further examinable [*unerforschlich*]. By relying on what is supposedly unexaminable, this theory allows its proponents to exempt themselves from the need to prove their claims and so to charge those who think differently with sentimentality and an *affected* humanitarianism and to label them sophists and shysters [*Rechtsverdreher*]; this is completely contrary to the equality (*of reasons*) and freedom (to express opinions *supported by reasons*) that are well known and rightfully demanded in the sphere of philosophy. The only exceptional part of this system, which gives it some

---

[a] Even the popular Herr *Jacob*, in his philosophical doctrine of right, already concurred, several years in advance, with the great, though not infallible, man to whom I refer above.[14] Jacob is well aware and is undoubtedly himself in the best position to know that Kant's theory involves several unresolved difficulties; but Jacob still cannot disagree with it, and hopes that, with time, it will turn out to be true. That time has now come.

[14] Ludwig Heinrich Jacob (1759–1827) was the author of *Philosophical Doctrine of Right, or Natural Right* (1795). The "great though not infallible man" is, of course, Kant, who defends the death penalty, and a retributivist account of punishment generally, in *The Metaphysics of Morals* (pp. 105–9). The part of *The Metaphysics of Morals* in which Kant discusses punishment, the "Doctrine of Right," appeared in January 1797, before the publication of Part II of Fichte's *Foundations* in autumn of the same year.

plausibility, seems to me to be this: it is said that "one has never heard of anyone who was sentenced to death for murder complaining that he was dealt with too severely and wronged; everyone would laugh in his face if he said this."[15] Now apart from the issue of laughing in the person's face, this statement is so true that if someone guilty of a bloody crime were himself to be killed by a power that was, in itself, entirely unjust and ignorant of his guilt, then the guilty person himself (if he remembered his own crime) along with anyone else who knew of his guilt, would have to conclude that he had not been treated unjustly. It is completely true such that we are forced to conclude: in a moral world-order, governed by an omniscient judge in accordance with moral laws, if a person is treated according to *the same* law that he himself established in treating others, then no injustice is done to him. This conclusion, which forces itself upon all human beings, is based on a categorical imperative. Thus there is absolutely no dispute about whether *a murderer* has been treated unjustly, if he, too, should lose his own life in a violent manner. But an entirely different question to be answered would be: from where does a mortal get the right of this moral world-order, the right to render the criminal his just deserts? and it was this purely juridical [**284**] question that the noble *Beccaria* (who was certainly not unfamiliar with that kind of moral judgment) had in mind.[16] Whoever ascribes this right to a worldly sovereign will surely be required (as Kant's system was) to say that the sovereign's rightful title to it is *unexaminable*; to derive the sovereign's authority from God; and to regard the sovereign as God's visible representative and every government as a theocracy.[17] For in Jewish theocracy, the principle, "He who sheds blood shall have his own blood shed in turn; an eye for an

---

[15] Kant, *The Metaphysics of Morals*, p. 107.

[16] Cesare Bonesano de Beccaria (1738–1794) was an Italian philosopher and criminologist who was greatly influenced by Rousseau. He wrote *Essay on Crimes and Punishments* (1764), a pioneering study of penal laws in which he advocated the abolition of torture and the death penalty.

[17] Kant does claim that the origin of supreme political authority is unexaminable (*unerforschlich*) for a people "in a practical respect," but by this he means not that the normative source of such authority is unknowable – for that is the people's will – but only that the historical origins of a particular state should not be examined by its citizens with the aim of proving its illegitimacy. Similarly, he endorses the saying "All authority is from God," but adds that it is merely a way of expressing the (true) claim that "the presently existing legislative authority ought to be obeyed, whatever its [historical] origin" (*The Metaphysics of Morals*, p. 95). Neither of these points is presented by Kant as directly relevant to the death penalty.

eye, a tooth for a tooth,"[18] was entirely fitting. This premise, however, would still be in need of proof.

Now, furthermore, claims of this kind are completely out of place in a system of right where legislative authority is ascribed to the people, and where the legislator cannot at the same time be regent;[19] therefore, one must assume that they are fragments of a very early version of Kant's system that have found their way to us out of sheer chance.

(VI) Whoever maliciously attacks an innocent person's honor automatically forfeits his own, for he makes himself unworthy of anyone else's trust. – Since the state owes compensation to the innocent victim anyway, it will publicize the offender's deed, and, as is proper, will let public opinion run its course.

Pillories and stocks are means for sharpening the public's sensibility and for making dishonor tangible for it. They must be as painless as possible (unlike, for example, the spinning pillory box [*die Trille*]); they are a punishment in themselves, and should not be combined with any other punishments if the crime does not by its nature involve dishonor. An offender who is being reformed is not dishonorable; and one who is being banished is not concerned with honor, for he is exiting the state. The punishment of dishonor is to be added only in cases where the nature of the crime entails it, e.g. in the case of burglary.

(VII) Reparation must always be made. The victim looks directly to the state for it, since the state, in the [**285**] civil contract, guaranteed him protection against all injuries; and the state looks to the criminal for it, so long as the criminal still owns something. It is clear from this that the victim is not required to bear the costs of investigating the crime. For why else does he pay his taxes? And the state can look to the criminal for reparations. If the criminal is excluded from the state altogether, all of his property is confiscated anyway.

A person who has suffered harm to his body and health must be cared for at the state's cost. It is the least – but only possible – compensation that can be given him for his irreparable loss.

(VIII) As we have seen, there are in general two entirely different kinds of punishment, one grounded on a contract and the other

---

[18] Gen. 9:6; Exod. 21:24; Matt. 5:38.

[19] In *The Metaphysics of Morals* Kant locates the source of legislative authority in "the united will of the people" (p. 91), but, unlike Fichte, he insists on a separation of the state's legislative and executive powers (pp. 93–4). See also n. 16, p. 14.

grounded on the absolute nullity of the contract. It is immediately clear that the citizen is obligated to subject himself to the first kind of punishment, without being coerced to do so, for such punishments are – in a certain, other respect – also his rights. It is also clear that he may, quite justifiably, be forced to consent to such subjection, since even harsher punishments are possible, and since he continues to pledge all the property he still owns as a guarantee of his subjection. He must voluntarily make himself available to any investigation of his possible wrongdoing, and he can be punished for failing to do so. Thus there is absolutely no reason for the state to seize his person.

In contrast, a guilty party cannot provide a guarantee, if his deeds qualify him for exclusion from society altogether, or for temporary exclusion in a correctional penitentiary; for (in the first case) he has lost all his rights categorically, and (in the second case) problematically (in the event that he does not reform). Therefore, in these situations, the state must seize the very person of the guilty party. The state's right of coercion begins with a person's relative property; if that property does not suffice for compensation, it extends to his absolute property; and if the guilty party does not willingly pay what he ought, then the state's right of coercion breaks into his house and – if even his house has been forfeited – it ultimately extends to his person.

[286] Third section of the doctrine of political right
On the constitution

§21

(1) *Regulative Principle.* That science that deals with a particular state as (empirically) determined by contingent characteristics and that considers how the law of right can best be realized in that state, is called *politics*. The questions of politics have nothing to do with our science, the doctrine of right, which is purely *a priori*, and they must be carefully separated from it.

All the questions that one might pose concerning the specific determination of the one and only rightful constitution are political questions. This is because the concept of a constitution that we have presented here completes the solution to the problem posed by pure reason: how can the concept of right be realized in the sensible world? And so with this concept, the science is closed. In this way the constitution is determined *a priori*. Now if it is to be determined any further, this is possible only by means of empirical data. We shall indicate which specific questions are possible, and prove that answers to them are grounded in the contingent situations of the peoples they govern.

(a) The first thing proved in the doctrine of the constitution was the principle that state power must necessarily be transferred, and certainly cannot remain in the hands of the populace. The question that arises from this, first of all, is whether state power should be transferred to one or to many (the question of the *forma regiminis*, as Kant calls it in his essay *On Perpetual Peace*[1]), whether the state, in regard to the persons who hold power in it, ought to be a monarchy [*Monokratie*] or an aristocracy. For democracy, in the terms being discussed here, is not an option.

Both forms of government are in accordance with right; thus choosing between them [287] is a matter of prudence. I shall briefly mention the reasons that would govern such a choice: the many are likely to be wiser, since they modify their opinion by deliberating with one another, but that is precisely why they are likely to act more slowly as well; furthermore, the ephorate will not have as powerful an influence over them, since everyone tends to shift blame onto others and to consider himself immune from it, since it is the majority that is to blame. A government with a perpetual president is more likely to err, but power functions more efficiently in his hands; and responsibility, which rests on his shoulders alone, also affects him more profoundly. Thus, in a monarchy, the government has more power and life. Therefore, the choice between the two types of government may come down to this: where the government requires more power (because the people are not yet accustomed to rigorous lawfulness, or because their relation to other peoples is not rightful and lawful), a monarchy is preferable. A republican constitution is to be preferred, however, where a rightful constitution has already exerted its influence and brought about the situation described above, such that the law exercises its influence by means of its sheer inner weight. Regardless of whether the highest regent is an individual or a whole body of people, it is easy to see that all subordinate officers must be appointed by this highest regent, and just as easy to see that they are subject only to its commands and judgments. For only the highest authority is responsible to the nation, and its only responsibility is to see to it that right and justice prevail in the state. But it cannot take

---

[1] In treating what he calls the question of *forma imperii* (usually translated "form of sovereignty"), Kant distinguishes three such forms – autocracy, aristocracy, and democracy – according to whether supreme (executive) authority in a state is exercised by an individual, by several persons, or by the entire citizenry ("Perpetual Peace," pp. 100–1). (When Kant discusses democracy in more detail (p. 101), it becomes clear that what is at issue for him in this classification is executive authority rather than the authority to make laws, which can only reside in "the united will of the people" (*The Metaphysics of Morals*, p. 91).) Fichte means to respond here to Kant's discussion of the *forma imperii*, but he mistakenly refers to it as the question of *forma regiminis* (form of government). For Kant the latter question concerns the distinction between republican and despotic regimes, which turns only on whether the executive and legislative powers in a state are separate.

on this responsibility if its choice of the persons through whom it shall administer justice is restricted, or if these persons are not completely subject to it.

(b) A second question is whether it is better for the people to elect their indirect representatives[2] (as in a rightfully constituted democracy, discussed above: §16, VI), or for the representatives to appoint their own successors, or even for there to be a hereditary succession. Regarding the appointment of the ephors, the question has already been decided above, in general and for every case, [288] based on the absolute principles of right. Thus the question remains open only with regard to the appointment of those who administer the executive power. And here the answer depends on empirical facts, in particular on the cultural level of the people, which is achieved only through prior legislation that has been wise and just. A people that is to elect its own regents must already be very cultivated: for, according to the principles stated above, the election must be *unanimous* if it is to be universally valid. But only *relative* unanimity is required; so there is always a danger that a part of the minority will either be excluded or given a regent against their will. But the constitution must prevent any basis for schisms and party factions among the citizens. Now as long as the people have not yet attained this high degree of culture, it is better – once and for all time – that even the right to elect regents be alienated (which, of course, can happen only through absolute unanimity) and that a fixed plan for the succession of regents be established for all time. In a republic the regents may elect their own successors; if the ephorate is sufficiently effective, it will be of the greatest importance to them to conduct this election with the utmost care. In a monarchy it is difficult to imagine who ought to elect the monarch other than the people, which – as stated above – should not vote. Therefore, the monarch could not be elected at all, but would have to be determined by birth. Beyond this, hereditary succession has other advantages as well, which make it advisable to institute, e.g. that the prince is completely cut off from the people and thus is born and dies without having any private connections with them.

(c) A question might arise concerning the conditions of the transference contract to be made with those who administer the executive power – concerning their personal rights, freedoms, and incomes, as

---

[2] It should be recalled that Fichte uses "representatives" to refer not to representative legislators but to those who execute the law; see n. 14, p. 141.

well as the sources of revenue to be available to them. But a judgment about that is purely empirical. The issue of where the revenue for public ends (including, of course, the livelihood of those who hold state power) [289] should come from, or the *principle of finances*, has already been given above and applied to particular cases as they arose. Everyone must contribute in proportion to his need for protection, and the protective power must be proportionate to the citizens' need for protection; this yields a determinate standard for assessing how much the citizens ought to be taxed – since citizens' need for protection is certainly subject to change, so too is their level of taxation. The regent, insofar as he holds supreme power, cannot be required to pay taxes, but could very well be sued in a people's court to account for his administration of tax revenue, if, for instance, the ephor were to bring a case against him; for it is a part of public right that subjects pay taxes only for the state's needs, and not for other, arbitrary ends.

(d) One might ask about the *constitution of courts*. It has been shown that the executive power also occupies the highest seat of judgment, beyond which there can be no further appeal. Based on what was said above, it is clear that this highest power will appoint lower judges, who will make judgments in its name that can be appealed before the highest power, to whom they are answerable. Thus the only remaining question concerns the *form* of a judicial investigation, or legal proceeding.

Legal proofs are conducted like all other proofs; and so the main resources for a legal proceeding are logic and healthy common sense in general. We have observed (where it was necessary to do so, in conjunction with the substance of the questions of right themselves) where positive proof is needed to convict a party, and where he is acquitted through negative proof (namely, that nothing could be proven against him). As a rule, the plaintiff has the burden of providing positive proof. This is the case even if the state is the plaintiff, for then it is not the judge, but rather a party to the suit. But the state is the judge as to whether sufficient proof has been provided.

However, *the swearing of oaths* as a means of proof gives rise to some concerns. Either the swearing of oaths is regarded only as [290] a ceremonial guarantee and the external formalities associated with it serve only to eliminate all frivolity and to make people reflect on the importance of such a guarantee (the presupposition here being that someone who is capable of publicly making a false statement will just as well swear a false oath); or else one assumes that an oath is more than a ceremonial guarantee, and that the same person who has no hesitation about publicly giving false testimony would have scruples about swearing a false oath. In the first case, it could be asked how the other party (if the dispute is a matter of civil law) or how the entire commonwealth (if it is a public issue) could be obligated as a matter of right to believe this guarantee and allow the judge's decision to depend on it, since the state itself is grounded on the premise of universal mistrust. In the second case, there is – in addition to this concern – a more important one: for if a person thinks nothing of publicly making a false statement, then what kind of belief might be capable of preventing him from confirming the same falsehood under oath? Since he does not fear being guilty of mere untruthfulness, he must believe that appealing to God as a witness is a supernatural, inscrutable, and magical way to incur God's wrath if he should swear to a falsehood. Now this is doubtless the true nature of superstition, which is entirely contrary to moral religion. In this case, the state would be counting on such immorality to persist, and – since it has made its own security depend on it – the state would have to promote such immorality with all its energy, which is absurd. Thus the swearing of oaths can be understood only as a ceremonial guarantee; and it can take place only if, in a private suit, the one party voluntarily allows the case to depend on such a guarantee by the other. *Volenti non fit injuria.*[3] In a public matter, oaths can never be used; for the regent cannot [**291**] compromise any of the commonwealth's rights. But if the laws are administered with sufficient care so that transactions requiring public sanction never take place without it; if the police power is vigilant enough; if judges have not only abstract formulas in their heads, but also good, common sense as well, then oaths will never be necessary.

(e) Furthermore, a question might arise about how the people can be assembled for the election of the ephors or – if an interdict has been pronounced – for the trial of those who administer the executive power. Regarding the election of the ephors, it is obvious that the ephors currently in office must announce the election, oversee it, collect the votes, and determine its result. (How many ephors there are is a matter

---

[3] No injury is done to a willing person. This maxim expresses the legal principle that someone who willingly exposes himself to a known danger cannot claim compensation for injuries that result from having done so.

for politics and will depend on the size of the populace, their level of culture, and the degree of order to which they are accustomed. If there is a high degree of culture and order, a smaller number of ephors will suffice.) But obviously, as already stated above, they are to do so without guiding the election (since new ephors are their future judges) or allowing any interruption in the ephorate. Particular men (syndics) must be chosen by the people from amongst the people themselves to collect the votes in a people's court (since the ephors themselves are a party in such a vote).

(2) Thus the only remaining issue we need to investigate in our pure doctrine of right is the *police* – its essence, duties, and limits.

First of all, what is the police?, i.e. its concept must be deduced. The state as such stands in a reciprocal contract with its subjects as such, in consequence of which both sides incur rights and duties. We have already identified the connecting link between the state and its subjects in those cases where the subjects can, and will, file suit against the state. But we have also touched on many matters about which the subjects cannot file suit, since such matters have to be officially supervised by the state. Thus in these matters, there must be a special connecting link between the executive [292] power and the subjects, and the *police* is just this link. It is through the police that the mutual influence, the ongoing reciprocal interaction, between the state and its subjects first becomes possible. Accordingly, the police is one of the absolutely necessary requirements of a state, and an account of the police in general belongs to a pure doctrine of natural right.

The state has a twofold relation to its subjects. On the one hand, it has duties to them, namely the duty to protect them as per its contract with them; on the other hand, it has rights, namely the right to require that they fulfill their duties as citizens and obey the laws. Instances where such duties or rights arise are mediated by the police; in both cases it is the mediating link between the state and its subjects. Just as a judicial verdict relates to positive law in connection with citizens, so the police relates to the positive law in connection with state authority. The police power makes it possible for the law to be applied.

First of all, let us consider the state's *duty to protect*, which is carried out by the police. One might think that, when it comes to such protection, each citizen will himself remind the state of its duty and demand the protection stipulated in the contract. But often an injury that has already occurred cannot be compensated for, and the end of the state is more to prevent injuries to its citizens than to punish them once they have occurred. The first branch of police power consists in *institutions for protection and security*.

Each citizen must be able to travel throughout the state's entire territory freely and secure from all accidents, as part of his right to cultivate the land, to acquire goods, to engage in trade and commerce, etc., or – if he doesn't do any of these things – as part of his right to enjoy his absolute property as he wishes. The more people there are living in one place, the more effective the measures must be for protecting them against possible attacks. Thus armed guards and patrols are needed, even on the highways, if they happen to be unsafe. These subordinate civil servants have absolutely no judicial authority, but they do have the authority to apprehend suspicious persons. They themselves are [293] to be held responsible, on pain of severe punishment, for any harm that occurs in the regions entrusted to their care.

Ensuring the safety of the citizens' lives and property requires that police superintendence extend to the *roads and streets*. The citizen has a right to demand good roads and streets, for the state has guaranteed him the ability to carry on his business in the quickest and most convenient manner possible, or – even if his travel is only for pleasure – to enjoy his rightfully acquired property in the manner most pleasing to him. As a part of this police power, warning signs should be posted in places that are unsafe. If, in the absence of any such warning, someone were to suffer harm, he would be entitled to demand compensation from the state; for the state has guaranteed his safety *in all activities not prohibited by law*. If a person ignores such a warning, he must bear the harm on his own, but without being subject to further punishment, since each person is master of his own body. Another task of the police is to insure that certified, state-approved doctors are available. (The process of approving doctors is best handled by medical faculties, who are the most competent judges in the matter and who should be seen in this role as a branch of the government, just as the guilds are in their examination of peers for admission to the guild.) The police should oversee pharmacies as well. Quackery and dabbling in cures must be prohibited *for those who want to practice it but not for those who want to avail themselves of such services*, if they can be found in a state that prohibits their practice; for each person is master of his own life.

As regards absolute property, the police must conduct night patrols to protect against violent break-ins. It must also protect against the danger of fire, and make provisions for issuing quick warnings and extinguishing fires when they occur. It must also keep watch over rivers and canals and provide protection against floods and the like. All these provisions are the state's absolute duty, in consequence of the civil contract; they are not mere acts of charity.

These provisions pertain primarily to what the state *itself* must do. Now furthermore, in consequence of its duty to protect, the state has the right to give the citizens certain laws that [294] aim to protect their fellow citizens against injury, facilitate the provision of public security, and aid in tracking down guilty parties. These are called *police laws*; they are distinguished from genuine civil laws by the fact that the latter prohibit *actual injuries*, while the former aim at preventing the *possibility* of injury. The civil law prohibits actions that, in and of themselves, violate the rights of others, e.g. burglary, robbery, attacks upon the body or life of another, etc., and everyone finds such prohibitions just. Police law prohibits actions that, in and of themselves, do not harm anyone and appear entirely neutral, but that make it easier for someone to injure others and make it harder for the state to protect potential victims or track down those who are responsible for their injuries. Ill-informed people tend to regard these prohibitions (the non-observance of which does not harm anyone) as unjust, and to doubt the state's right to issue them. (Thus, if one looks closely, one sees that *academic freedom* is conceived by many as an *exemption from all police laws*, although there really should be a police power in academic institutions.) But the right and duty to pass such laws are clearly entailed by the state's police authority. Let me clarify the matter with an example: it is obvious that no one's rights are violated if someone bears arms in public; for how can others be harmed by what I carry on my own body? But it does make it much easier for me to harm someone else, and therefore – in my opinion – the state would have a perfect right to prohibit citizens from carrying all weapons and even from having them in their houses, if it could only be sure that none of its citizens would ever face a situation in which they had to use them in self-defense. (And so in the Roman republic citizens were prohibited from bearing arms in public; and a military commander expecting to be honored for a victory was required to remain at the city limits (*ad urbem*) until the day of his triumphant entrance, or, if he insisted on entering the city sooner than that, he was required to lay down his arms and forgo the honor of a victory parade.) But [295] the state surely does have the right to prohibit the possession of certain weapons, e.g. air-powered rifles. Such weapons are never necessary for self-defense. If someone has the right to possess such a weapon, why should he shy away from firing it? It is simply an instrument for committing murder. Now it certainly does not follow that if someone has one, he will actually use it to commit murder. Murder is prohibited by *civil law*. But having one makes it quite easy for someone to commit murder, and if that is not his purpose, then he does not need precisely this weapon; therefore, he should not even have it in the first place: such possession is prohibited by *police law*. If there were a prohibition against being on the street at certain hours of the night without a light, that would be a police law, and its intention would be to make it easier for everyone to be seen at night. No one is harmed if a person happens to be on the street without a light; but in the darkness it would be quite easy for that person to cause harm, and it is just this possibility that ought to be eliminated. If someone violates a police law, he has only himself to blame for the troubles that might befall him as a result, and he may be punished for it as well.

The principal maxim of every well-constituted police power must be the following: *every citizen must be readily identifiable, wherever necessary, as this or that particular person.* Police officers must be able to establish the identity of every citizen, which can only be accomplished as follows. Everyone must always carry an identity card with him, issued by the nearest authority and containing a precise description of his person; this applies to everyone, regardless of class or rank. Since merely verbal descriptions of a person always remain ambiguous, it might be good if important persons (who therefore can afford it as well) were to carry accurate portraits in their identity cards, rather than descriptions. No one will be allowed to take up residence in any place without first disclosing, by means of his identity card, his identity and last place of residence. Below we shall see a remarkable example of what can be achieved with the use of such identity cards. But in order not to prevent citizens from enjoying even the innocent pleasure of remaining anonymous, [296] police officers must be prohibited – on pain of punishment – from demanding to see identity cards out of mere whim or curiosity, but may do so only when it is necessary to verify the person's identity;

in which case – if it should become an issue – they must be required to justify why it was necessary.

The state does not know what goes on inside a person's house; but it does have the authority to supervise what happens on the street that a person must, after all, traverse in order to enter his house. Therefore, citizens cannot assemble inside a house without the police knowing about it; and the police have the power, as well as the right (since the street is subject to their authority), to prevent such an assembly, if it arouses their suspicion. If so many people assemble that public security is threatened – and any assembly can pose such a threat if it is strong enough to resist the armed power of local authorities – then the police shall demand an explanation of their intentions, and watch to make sure that they actually do what they claim to be doing. In such a situation, a person's right over his house ceases to exist; or, if the owner of the house does not want that to happen, then the group must assemble in a public building. The situation is the same when people gather in the streets, in marketplaces, and so on: the police have the right to prevent, or to oversee, such gatherings. And so the state must issue laws saying that, depending on the circumstances, not more than a certain number of people may assemble without first having announced their assembly and its purpose to the police, so that the police may take the appropriate measures.

There are still two questions to be answered concerning the protection of absolute property, namely: how is it possible to prevent the counterfeiting of both bills of exchange and money? I am all the more happy to go into these matters, since it will allow me to present some examples of how even the seemingly impossible is very easy for a good police force.

[297] First of all, bills of exchange. I mean actual bills of exchange (whose value belongs to anyone who happens to possess them), and not mere assignations that designate a particular recipient. In large trading centers, especially at fairs, a bill of exchange may very well change owners several times in a single day. The persons through whose hands it has passed may not know one another. Now, it is true, a merchant is unlikely to accept a bill of exchange unless he knows the issuer and recognizes the signature on it. But signatures can be forged; and the simple fact is that counterfeit bills of exchange are actually produced and accepted, so it must be possible to defraud people with them. Now,

sooner or later, when the bill makes its way back to the alleged issuer, the forgery will be discovered. But how then is it possible to identify and apprehend the forgerer, so that he can be held responsible for the loss he has caused? Under the police power being described here, this does not pose even the slightest difficulty.

The names of those through whose hands the bill has passed will always be marked on the back of it. But under the usual way of doing things, a person can give a false name. As soon as one begins to look for him, he is nowhere to be found. According to our suggestion, anyone who transfers a bill of exchange (assuming that the recipient does not already know exactly and personally who he is) would have to present his identity card in order to show that he is this particular person, where he can be found, etc. The recipient of the bill has a duty to look at the identity card and to recognize the transferor accordingly. On the back of the bill of exchange, next to the name of the transferor, he will simply add the words: *with an identity card from such and such an authority*. The recipient will have to write down only two more phrases, and it will take just a minute or two longer to look at the person and his identity card; but otherwise, the matter is just as simple as before. Now if the bill of exchange turns out to be a counterfeit, and if an investigation points to a particular person, then where is he to be found? Given the [298] constitution of our police power, no one is allowed to leave one locality (he can be stopped at the city gate) without specifying the place he intends to travel to, which will be noted in the register of the place and on his identity card. He will not be received anywhere other than the place noted on his identity card. And if he should leave that place, the very same rules would apply again, and so there will be a continuous record of his whereabouts. But what if the person is a foreigner, or what if a citizen travels to a foreign land? States with police powers, especially commercial states, must agree upon some kind of arrangement whereby defrauders can be tracked down in all countries. Identity cards of states that are not party to this arrangement will not be recognized, and so citizens of such states will be denied the right to offer bills of exchange. This will undoubtedly force commercial states to accept such an arrangement. But, someone might object, it is possible to make counterfeit identity cards, and this would completely undermine the success of these measures. Our response is: the possibility of such counterfeiting must itself be eliminated, and there are undoubtedly adequate means for doing so, e.g. the use of paper or parchment that is manufactured exclusively for identity cards (as was done in the case of the French *assignats*), kept under the exclusive control of the highest authorities, manufactured under their supervision, and distributed to lower authorities who must keep an account of the paper that is used up. But cannot one counterfeit this paper itself? Even the French *assignats*, mentioned above, were counterfeited in spite of such precautions. They were indeed, because counterfeiting satisfied substantial interests (monetary gain as well as political animosity) and because the same piece of counterfeit paper could be used a hundred times over. In the situation we are considering, a piece of counterfeit paper can be used to make only *one* passport; and who would go to such great lengths, and perfect so many different skills, for that? The most one could achieve would be to circulate a valuable counterfeit bill of exchange. But would all [299] the requisite cost and effort – let alone the risks – really be worth it?

As for the second point, the counterfeiting of coins – the state guarantees the value of money. Anyone who accepts a piece of money as authentic does so on the word of the state, whose seal is stamped on it; thus the state is responsible to each citizen for the authenticity of money. Anyone who, *through no fault of his own*, is defrauded by means of counterfeit money must, as a matter of right, receive compensation from the state and receive authentic money in place of the counterfeit.

But under what conditions is a person defrauded *through no fault of his own*? Under what conditions is it reasonable to think that he could not distinguish the counterfeit money from the real? It is part of a citizen's education to know what real money looks like, and only where *several* persons have been defrauded is it reasonable to conclude that the counterfeit money could not be distinguished from real money.

Therefore, one of the state's immediate interests, and a branch of its police power, is to prevent the counterfeiting of coins, and to discover it wherever it exists. How can it accomplish this? Not by asking people where their money came from (as with bills of exchange), for no one can say who gave him this or that piece of money. However, if a substantial amount of money is involved, the person may very well know who gave it to him, in which case it does make sense to ask him about it. But in general, the police must act in advance to prevent such counterfeiting, by watching over the materials that could be used to make counterfeit coins (something it must learn from chemistry) and prohibiting the distribution of these materials (like poisonous substances) unless it knows the name of the person who wants them (*verified by his identity card*, of course) and the use to which they shall be put. The state can do this all the more easily, since it owns the mines, as shown above. Let it have a monopoly over metals, alloys, and other similar materials, and let it not distribute them to retailers without [**300**] knowing to whom and for what purpose they are to be distributed.

In addition to the duties of protection noted above, the executive authority also has the right to see to it that the laws (both civil and police laws) are obeyed. It must take responsibility for any offense committed within the state's territory, and it must apprehend the offender. But in order to oversee the laws in this way, it is obvious that the state does not need any special institutions; rather these functions must be included in the protective institutions we have been describing. For if someone is *acting unjustly* and overstepping the law, it follows that someone else is in need of *being protected*.

The exclusive condition of the law's effectiveness and of the entire apparatus of the state is that every citizen know in advance and with absolute certainty that, if he violates the law, he will be discovered and punished in the manner clearly prescribed. If a criminal can count on a high degree of possibility that his crime will not be discovered and punished, what will deter him from committing it? And then – even though we might have the wisest of laws – wouldn't we still be living in the previous state of nature, where everyone does as he pleases and we remain dependent on the good will of others? And then it would also be manifestly unjust to punish with the law's full rigor the few who happen to get caught. For in seeing others around them go unpunished, did they not have reason to think that they, too, would escape punishment? How could they be deterred by a law that they couldn't help but regard as invalid? The derisive observation made by ordinary people everywhere concerning our state constitutions – that a person is punished not because of his crime, but because he was caught – is fitting and just. The requirement that the police, as servant of the law, apprehend every guilty party without exception is absolutely necessary.

[**301**] Those who have heard my lectures have expressed doubt as to whether such a requirement can be fulfilled, and I cannot expect that my readers will react any differently. If such doubts were well grounded, I would not hesitate to conclude that the state itself and all right among

human beings would be impossible. Every so-called state is nothing other – and never will be anything other – than the oppression of the weaker by the stronger under the pretense of right, so that the stronger may use the weaker as they please; and in being oppressed, the weaker may in turn – as far as they are able – take advantage of those who are even weaker than themselves: and public right is nothing other than the theory of how unjust the stronger can be without harming their interests, as *Montesquieu*[4] ironically describes it. But is there any good reason to doubt that this requirement can be fulfilled, and where does this doubt come from? It comes from failing to adhere to the concept of the state as it has been established here, and failing to regard it as the concept of an organized whole within which alone these parts can exist and apart from which they simply could not exist in another whole; it arises from the fact that, in thinking of the individual parts, one always imagines our ordinary states. It is no wonder that these parts now fail in every regard to conform to our concept. In our ordinary states it would indeed be impossible to carry out the requirement that everyone who violates the law be apprehended, or, if it could be carried out – if, for example, an existing state were to employ some of the policing methods that we have mentioned here – then doing so would be an injustice that the people could not tolerate for long and that would only hasten the state's demise. For if disorder and injustice prevail from the top down, the government cannot continue to exist unless it also allows a good deal of disorder to exist below (so long as such disorder does not affect the government itself).

[302] The sole source of every evil in our makeshift states [*in unsern Nothstaaten*] is *disorder* and the impossibility of bringing about order in them. In our states the only reason why finding a guilty party often involves such great and insurmountable difficulties, is that there are so many people the state fails to care for, and who have no determinate status [*Stand*] within it. In a state with the kind of constitution we have established here, every citizen has his own determinate status, and the police know fairly well where each one is at every hour of the day, and what he is doing. Everyone must work and has, if he works, enough to

---

[4] Charles de Secondat Montesquieu (1689–1755) was a French political philosopher who helped found modern political science. He is best known for his highly influential *The Spirit of the Laws* (1748), in which he attempted to discover the principles that explain the development of diverse laws and customs throughout the world.

live on: there are no vagabonds (*Chevaliers d'industrie*), for they are not tolerated anywhere within the state. With the help of the identity cards described above, every citizen can be identified on the spot. In such a state crime is highly unusual and is preceded by a certain unusual activity. In a state where everything is ordered and runs according to plan, the police will observe any unusual activity and take notice immediately; and so, for my part, I do not see how either the crime or the criminal can remain hidden.

It should also be noted here that the police power, as we have been describing it, requires neither spies nor secret agents. Secrecy is always petty, base, and immoral. If someone dares to do something, he must dare to do it before the eyes of the whole world. Besides, *to whom* is the state to give such a dishonorable task? Should the state itself encourage dishonor and immorality and make them into a duty? For once the state authorizes some of its citizens to act in secrecy, who can guarantee that these citizens will not make use of that secrecy to commit crimes?

Besides, why should the state want to observe its citizens secretly? So that the citizens will not realize that they are being observed. And why should they not realize that they are being observed? Either, so that they will reveal without inhibition what they think about the government and what they are planning against it, and [303] thus become their own traitors; or, so that they will reveal what they know of other secret, illegal activities. The first is necessary only where the government and its subjects live in constant war with one another, where the subjects are unjustly oppressed and are striving to regain their freedom (as they have a right to do in a state of war). The second is necessary only where the police in general are so insufficiently watchful that something could have been kept secret from them. Neither reason applies in the state we have been describing here. The chief of police in Paris, who wanted his secret police to wear uniforms, became the laughing stock of a corrupt people and saved his life through such a simple policy. In my opinion, he showed healthy, uncorrupted judgment. In the state we have been describing here, police officers can wear uniforms. They are just as much honorable witnesses to innocence as they are accusers in the event of a crime. How could rectitude possibly fear and hate the eye of such watchfulness?

[304] Outline of family right
(First appendix to the doctrine of natural right)

FIRST SECTION
DEDUCTION OF MARRIAGE

Remark

Just as above we first had to deduce the necessity of the existence of several rational beings alongside one another, as well as their relation to the sensible world, in order to have an object to which the concept of right could be applied; so too we must here first get acquainted with the nature of marriage, and we must do so by way of a deduction, in order to be able to apply the concept of right to it with some degree of understanding. Just as rational, sensible beings and their sensible world do not first come to be through the concept of right, so too marriage does not first come to be through the concept of right. Marriage is by no means merely a juridical association, as the state is; it is a natural and moral association.

Therefore, the following deduction is not juridical; but it is necessary in a doctrine of right, so that one will have some insight into the juridical propositions to be established later.

[305] §1

Nature has grounded her end of reproducing the human species in a natural drive that is found in two distinct sexes, a drive that seems to exist only for its own sake and to aim at nothing other than its own satisfaction. This drive is itself an end of our nature, but for nature in general it is only a means. While human beings aim only at satisfying this drive, nature's end is fulfilled through the natural consequences of such satisfaction, without any further help from them.

Later, of course, the human being can learn, by experience and abstraction, that this is nature's end, and he can make it his own end through moral refinement of the way he satisfies this drive. But prior to experience and in his natural condition, the human being has no such end; rather, his ultimate end is simply to satisfy his drive; and things had to be this way, if the fulfillment of nature's end was to be assured.

(Here I shall only briefly explain why nature had to split up the two distinct sexes, the union of which is necessary for the species' reproduction; for an investigation into this does not really belong here.

The highest level of the formative power found in organic nature is the power to form a being of one's own kind, and this power is necessarily operative whenever the conditions of its efficacy are given. Now if those conditions were always given, nature would be in a state of perpetual flux from one shape to another, and no shape would ever remain the same. There would be eternal becoming, but never any being; and then even flux would be impossible, since nothing would actually be that could pass over into something else; this is an unthinkable and self-contradictory thought. (This is the same condition I referred to above as the struggle of being and not-being; §17B, V, Corollary.) Under these conditions nature is impossible.

If nature were to be possible, the species had to have some [306] organic existence other than its existence as a species; but it also had to exist as a species, so as to be able to reproduce itself. In order for this to be possible, the species-forming power had to be divided up and split into two perfectly matching halves, as it were, whose union alone would constitute a self-reproducing whole. In being divided this way, the species-forming power forms only the individual. It is only the individuals (in their union and their capacity to be brought into union) that exist, and only they that form the species; for in organic nature, *to be* and *to form* are one. The individual *has an enduring existence* only as a tendency to form the species. It is only in this way that rest and a cessation of power entered into organic nature, and – along with such rest – determinate shape; it is only in this way that it became nature at all, and this is why this law of the separation of the two generative sexes necessarily pervades all organic nature.)

§2

The specific determination of this natural arrangement is that, in the satisfaction of the sexual drive or in the promotion of nature's end (in the actual act of procreation), the one sex is entirely active, the other entirely passive.

(A reason can also be given for this more specific determination. The system of the totality of conditions for generating a body of the same species had to be fully united somewhere and – once set into motion – had to develop in accordance with its own laws. The sex that contains this system is called, throughout all of nature, the *female* sex. The only thing that could be separated from it was its first, moving principle; and it had to be separated, if nature was to have any lasting shape. The sex that contains this principle (in isolation from the matter to be formed) is called, throughout all of nature, the *male* sex.)

§3

The character of reason is absolute self-activity: [**307**] mere passivity for its own sake contradicts reason and completely annuls it. Thus, it is not at all contrary to reason for the first sex to have as an end the satisfaction of its sexual drive, for it can be satisfied through activity: but it is absolutely contrary to reason for the second sex to have the satisfaction of its sexual drive as an end, for it would then have mere passivity as its end. Thus, either the second sex (even in its potential) is non-rational, which contradicts our presupposition (namely, that they are supposed to be human beings); or else this potential, because of its particular nature, cannot be developed, which is self-contradictory, since nature would then contain a potential that it did not really contain; or finally, the second sex can never have the satisfaction of its sexual drive as an end. Reason and such an end completely annul each other.

But now the female's sexual drive, and its expression and satisfaction, are indeed part of nature's plan. Thus, the female sexual drive must appear in a different form, and – in order to be able to coexist with reason – it must appear even as a drive towards activity, indeed as a characteristic natural drive towards an activity unique to this sex.

Since the entire theory that follows depends on this proposition, I shall try to put it in its proper light and prevent any possible misunderstanding of it.

(1) The topic here is *nature* and a *natural drive*, i.e. something that (as long as the two conditions – reason and sexual drive – are present) woman, left entirely to herself and without *exercising her freedom*, will find in herself as something given, original, and incapable of being explained by reference to any of her previous free actions. This is certainly not to deny the possibility that woman might either sink below her nature, or through freedom elevate herself above it, even though elevation-above is itself not much better [**308**] than sinking-below. Woman sinks *below* her nature if she degrades herself to a condition of irrationality. In that case, the sexual drive can enter consciousness in its true form and become the intended end of her action. Woman raises herself *above* her nature if she does not aim at satisfying her sexual drive (either in its unrefined state or as it exists in a well-constituted female soul) as an end, but rather understands such satisfaction as a mere means towards another end posited by freedom. If this end is not to be a completely reprehensible one (as it would be, for instance, if her aim were to become a "Mrs." and thereby gain a secure livelihood, in which case her personality would be made into a means for gratification), it can be none other than nature's own end: that of having children, which even some women claim to be their end in satisfying their sexual drive. But since a woman could have achieved this end with any man whatsoever, the principle of having children does not explain why she chose *precisely this man*, and so it follows that she must admit, as the most tolerable yet plausible explanation, that she chose this man simply because he was the first that she could have, which certainly does not imply a great deal of self-respect on her part. But even setting aside this questionable circumstance, is it feasible that the end of having children in general could underlie a woman's decision to live with a man? A keen observer of human nature may well doubt whether such a clearly thought-out end will lead to its goal and whether children will actually be begotten on the basis of the concept of begetting them. – The reader, I hope, will forgive me for speaking so frankly in my effort to expose, in all their starkness, some dangerous sophistries, which have been used to perpetuate and palliate the denial of people's true aims.

Allow me to illustrate the entire situation by means of an image: the second sex, in accordance with nature's arrangement, exists at a level below that of the first; it is the object of a power of the first sex, and it had to be so if the two were to be brought together. But at the same time, the two as moral beings are supposed to be equal. This was possible only because [**309**] an entirely new level, one completely lacking in the first sex, was introduced into the second. This level is the form under which the sexual drive appears to the second sex (which appears to the man in its true form).

(2) Man can acknowledge his sexual drive and seek to satisfy it without giving up his dignity; I mean man in his original condition. A man who, though he has a loving wife, could still make sexual satisfaction his sole end is a coarse human being: the reasons for this will become clear below. Woman cannot acknowledge this drive. Man can court; woman cannot. If she did, it would constitute the most severe self-contempt. A negative answer to a man's courting says nothing more than: I do not want to submit myself to you; and this answer can be tolerated. A negative answer to a woman's courting would mean: I do not want to accept your submission to me; and this answer, without a doubt, is unbearable. Reasoning based on the concept of right is of no use here; and if some women are of the opinion that they must have the same right to seek a spouse as men, one can ask them: who is contesting that right, and why don't they therefore avail themselves of it? It is as if one were to ask whether the human being might not have the same right to fly as the bird. Let us, rather, allow the question of right to rest until someone actually flies.

This one difference between the sexes is the basis of every other difference between them. This natural law of woman gives rise to feminine modesty, which does not exist in the same way in the male sex. Coarse men even brag about their sexual exploits; but even amidst the worst profligacy into which the second sex has sometimes sunk and through which she has far exceeded the depravity of men, one has never heard of women doing so. Even the prostitute prefers to profess that she engages in her shameful business for financial gain, rather than out of sexual desire.

[310] §4

Woman cannot acknowledge that she surrenders herself, and – since, in the rational being, something is only insofar as the rational being is conscious of it – woman cannot surrender to sexual desire for the sake of satisfying her own drive. Since she must nevertheless surrender herself on the basis of some drive, this drive in her can be none other than the drive to satisfy the man. In this act she becomes the means for another's end, since she could not be her own end without giving up her final end, the dignity of reason. She maintains her dignity – even though she becomes a means – by freely making herself into a means, on the basis of a noble, natural drive, that of *love*.

Love is thus the form under which the sexual drive manifests itself in woman. But love is self-sacrifice for the sake of another, not on the basis of a concept, but as the result of a natural drive. Mere sexual drive should never be called love; that is a gross abuse of language, which seems to aim at making us forget everything noble in human nature. In my opinion, nothing at all should be called love other than what I have just described. In the man, it is not love, but the sexual drive, that exists *originally*. In him, love is not an original drive at all, but only one that is *imparted* and *derived*, one that is *developed* solely in connection with a loving woman; and in the man, love takes on a completely different form, as we shall see below. Love, the noblest of all natural drives, is innate only to woman; it is only through woman that love comes to exist among human beings (like other social drives, as we shall see below). In woman, the sexual drive took on a moral form, because in its natural form it would have completely annulled morality in her. Love is the innermost point of union between nature and reason. It is the only juncture where nature penetrates into reason and is therefore the most excellent of all that is natural. [311] The moral law requires one to forget oneself in others; love surrenders itself altogether for the other.

Allow me to give a brief summary: the sexual drive neither manifests itself nor resides in an uncorrupted woman; only love does, and this love is woman's natural drive to satisfy a man. It is, to be sure, a drive that urgently demands to be satisfied. Its satisfaction, however, does not consist in the woman's sensual satisfaction, but in the man's; for the woman, the only satisfaction is of the heart. Her only need is to love and be loved. It is only in this way that the drive to surrender oneself acquires the character of freedom and activity, which it must have in order to be able to co-exist with reason. There is probably no man who does not sense the absurdity of reversing things and attributing to man a similar drive to satisfy a woman's need. He can neither presuppose such a need in her, nor think of himself as an instrument of such a need, without feeling shame unto the innermost depths of his soul.

This is also why, in sexual union, the woman is not in every sense a means for the man's end; she is the means for her own end, that of satisfying her heart; and she is the means for the man's end only to the extent that we are talking about sensual satisfaction.

It would be a dogmatic error if one were to pretend to find deceptiveness in this, the woman's way of thinking, and if one were to say, for instance, "So woman aims to satisfy her sexual drive after all, only covertly." Woman sees no further, and her nature extends no further, than love: thus she *exists* no further. It means nothing to her that man (who neither possesses nor ought to possess female innocence and who is able to acknowledge everything) might dissect and analyze this drive. *For her*, this drive is simple, for woman is not man. If she were a man, one would be right to regard her as deceptive; but then she would not be *she*, and everything would be different. Or does anyone, perhaps, want to unearth the basic drive of female nature as a *thing in itself?*

[312] §5

By making herself into a means to satisfy man, woman gives up her personality; she regains her personality and all of her dignity, only by having surrendered herself out of love for this one man.

But if this sentiment should ever come to an end, and if the woman were destined one day to stop regarding the man she has satisfied as the most lovable of all his sex – if she could even conceive of this as a possibility – such a thought would make her contemptible in her own eyes. If there is any possibility that he might not be for her the most lovable of his sex, then – since she nevertheless gives herself only to him, out of the entire male sex – one has to assume that she does so only because nature has covertly driven her to make do with the first one to come along, which, without a doubt, would be a thought that dishonors her. Therefore, as surely as she surrenders herself while retaining her dignity, she must necessarily believe that her present sentiment can never end but is eternal, just as she herself is eternal. She who surrenders herself once, surrenders herself forever.

§6

A woman who surrenders her personality while retaining her human dignity necessarily gives to her beloved everything she has. If she were not to surrender herself completely but held back even the smallest thing for herself, she would thereby demonstrate that what she has held back is more valuable to her than her own person; and that, undoubtedly, would be a serious devaluation of her person. Her own dignity rests on the fact that, as surely as she exists and lives, she belongs completely to her husband and has unreservedly lost herself to and in him. What follows from this, at the very least, is that she cedes to him her property and all her rights, and takes up residence with him. Henceforth she continues to live and be active only in union with him, only under his purview and in his endeavors. [313] She has ceased to live the life of an individual; her life has become a part of his (this is fittingly indicated by the fact that she takes her husband's name).

§7

The man's position in the relationship is as follows. The man – who can acknowledge everything that is part of the human being and therefore who finds within himself the entire fullness of human nature – surveys the entire relationship as the woman herself never can. He sees an originally free being freely and with unrestricted trust subject herself unconditionally to him. He sees that she makes not only all of her external fortune, but also her inner peace of mind and her moral character (if not its very existence, then at least her belief in it) completely dependent on him: for the woman's belief in herself and in her innocence and virtue depends on the fact that she must never stop respecting and loving her husband above all others of his sex.

Just as the moral potential inherent in the woman expresses itself through love, so the moral potential inherent in the man expresses itself through *magnanimity*. He wants first and foremost to be master [*Herr*]; but he divests himself of all his power in relation to someone who trustingly surrenders to him. Remaining strong in the face of someone who is subject to him is fitting only for an emasculated man, one who has no power against resistance.

In consequence of this natural magnanimity, the man is, first of all, compelled by his relationship with his spouse to be worthy of respect, for her entire peace depends on her being able to respect him above all else. Nothing kills a wife's love more irrevocably than a husband's baseness and lack of honor. Thus the other sex will forgive our sex for everything except cowardice and weakness of character. The reason for this is by no means her selfish dependence on our protection; it is simply [314] because women feel that, while their destiny requires them to be subject, they cannot subject themselves to a sex that is cowardly or weak.

The wife's peace depends on her completely subjecting herself to her spouse and having no will but his. Since he knows this, it follows that, without denying his nature and dignity, i.e. his masculine magnanimity, he must do all that he can to make such subjection as easy as possible for her. Now he cannot achieve this by letting his spouse be master of him, for the pride of her love consists in her being and appearing to be subject to him, and in her not knowing otherwise. Men who subject themselves to the mastery of their wives thereby make themselves contemptible even to their wives, and rob them of all marital happiness. Instead, he can achieve this only by discovering her wishes and fulfilling them as if they were his own will, which is what she, if left to herself, would most want to have done. This is not merely a matter of satisfying her whims and fancies for the sake of satisfying them; at issue is a much higher end, that of making it easier for her always to love her spouse above all else, and of maintaining her innocence in her own eyes. A wife whose heart remains unsatisfied by obedience that involves no sacrifice, cannot fail, for her own part, to seek to discover in return the higher, hidden wishes of her husband and to fulfill them through sacrifices. The greater the sacrifice, the more complete is the satisfaction of her heart. From this arises marital *tenderness* (the tenderness of their feelings and of their relation). Each of the two wants to give up his own personality so that only the personality of the other prevails; they each find their own satisfaction only in the satisfaction of the other, and the exchange of hearts and wills is complete. It is only in union with a loving woman that the masculine heart opens itself to love, to a love that gives of itself without restraint, and loses itself in its object; it is only in marital union that the woman learns magnanimity, [315] conscious self-sacrifice in accordance with concepts: and thus with each passing day of their marriage the union becomes more intimate.

Corollaries

(1) In the union of the two sexes (and therefore, in the realization of the *whole* human being as a perfected product of nature), but also only in this union, is there to be found an external drive towards virtue. The man's natural drive of magnanimity compels him to be noble and honorable, because the fate of a free being who has surrendered herself to him in full trust depends on it. The woman's innate modesty compels her to observe all her duties. She cannot compromise reason in the smallest matter, without coming to suspect that she has compromised reason in the most important matter, and that she does not love her husband – the most unbearable thought for her – but rather is using him only as a means to satisfy her sexual drive. The man in whom there still dwells magnanimity and the woman in whom there still dwells modesty are capable of every refinement, but they are on the sure path to all the vices if the one becomes depraved, and the other shameless, as experience invariably confirms.

(2) This also answers the question: how can one lead the human species from nature to virtue? I answer: only by reproducing the natural relation between the two sexes. There is no moral education of humankind, if it does not begin from this point.

§8

A union of the kind described is called *a marriage*. Marriage is the *perfect union* of two persons of each sex that is grounded upon the sexual drive and has itself as its own end.

It is *grounded* upon the sexual drive in both sexes for the investigating philosopher; but it is [316] not necessary that either of the two persons who want to marry acknowledge this. The woman can never acknowledge this, but can acknowledge only love. Moreover, the continuance of the marriage is in no way contingent upon the satisfaction of this drive; the end of satisfying this drive can disappear altogether yet the marital union still endure in all its inwardness.

Philosophers have felt obliged to explain what the end of marriage is and have answered the question in very different ways. But marriage has no end other than itself; it is its own end. The marital relation is the most genuine mode of existence, as required by nature, for adult human beings of both sexes. It is only in this relation that all of the human faculties can develop; apart from it, many – indeed the most remarkable – aspects of humanity remain uncultivated. The necessary mode of human existence, marriage, can no more be explained by reference to some sensuous end than human existence in general can be so explained.

Marriage is a union between *two* persons; *one* man and *one* woman. The woman, who has given herself entirely to one man, cannot give herself to a second, for her own dignity depends on her belonging exclusively to this one. The man, who must govern himself in accordance with the will and slightest wish of this one woman so as to make her happy, cannot govern himself in accordance with the conflicting wishes of several. Polygamy is predicated on men's belief that women are not rational beings like men, but only tools for the man, lacking a will or rights of their own. Such is, indeed, the doctrine behind the religious law (of Islam) that permits marriage to more than one wife. This religion has drawn one-sided conclusions (but obviously without being clearly aware of its own reasons) from the fact that the destiny of feminine nature is to be passive. Polyandry is completely contrary to nature, and therefore extremely rare. If it were not sheer bestiality, and [317] could be based on any presupposition at all, it would have to presuppose that there is absolutely no reason and no dignity to reason.

By its very nature, the marital union is inseparable and eternal, and is necessarily entered into as eternal. The woman cannot assume that she will ever stop loving her husband more than any other of his sex, without forfeiting her feminine dignity; the man cannot assume that he will stop loving his wife more than any other of her sex, without forfeiting his masculine magnanimity. They give themselves to each other forever, because they give themselves to each other completely.

§9

Thus marriage is not an artificial custom or arbitrary arrangement, but is rather a relation in which the spouses' union is necessarily and completely determined by nature and reason. I say that it is completely determined, i.e. nature and reason permit only the kind of marriage described and absolutely no other union of the two sexes for the purpose of satisfying their sexual drives.

The task of establishing or determining marriage does not belong to the law of right, but rather to the much higher law of nature and reason, which – through their products – first provide a domain for the law of right. Regarding marriage simply as a legal association leads to inappropriate and immoral ideas. Perhaps people were led into that error by the fact that marriage does indeed involve the living together of free beings, like everything else that is determined by the concept of right. But it would be bad if this form of living together could not be grounded and ordered by anything higher than laws of coercion. A marriage must first exist before one can talk about marital right, just as human beings must first exist before one can talk about right in general. The concept of right is as little concerned with where marriage comes from, as it is with where human beings come from. Only once marriage has been deduced, as we have just done, is it time to ask to what extent the [318] concept of right can be applied to this relation, which disputes concerning right could arise concerning it, and how they ought to be decided; or, since we are teaching a real doctrine of natural right, which rights and duties the visible administrator of right, *the state*, has with respect to marriage in particular and concerning the reciprocal relationship between the two sexes in general. We shall now enter into this investigation.

SECOND SECTION
MARITAL RIGHT

§10

The substance of all rights is personality, and the state's first and highest duty is to protect the personality of its citizens. But now the woman loses her personality and all her dignity if, in the absence of love, she is forced to subject herself to a man's sexual desire. Therefore, it is the state's absolute duty to protect its female citizens against such coercion. This duty is not grounded in any particular, optional contract, but in the very nature of the matter, and is immediately contained in the civil contract; this duty is as sacred and inviolable as that of protecting citizens' lives (at issue here is the inner, moral life of female citizens).

§11

The female citizen can be subjected to such coercion directly, by means of physical force, in which case it is called *rape*. There can be absolutely no question as to whether rape is a crime. In rape, one attacks the woman's [319] personality, and therefore the substance of all her rights, in the most brutal of ways.

The state has the right and duty to protect its female citizens against such violence, by means of both police supervision and the threat of punishing those who perpetrate it. This crime manifests, first of all, the perpetrator's brutality, which makes him completely incapable of living in society. Intensity of passion does not excuse the crime but makes it more serious. Anyone who cannot control himself is a raging animal; since society has no means of taming him, it cannot tolerate him in its midst. Moreover, this crime manifests an unbounded disdain and disregard for all human rights. In some systems of law, rape is punished by death, and if a particular system of law regards itself as justified in imposing the death penalty at all, it would be completely consistent for it to impose the death penalty for rape as well. In accordance with my system, I would favor the correctional penitentiary: for, although rape is equal to murder in its disregard for human rights, it is still possible for other men to live together in a penitentiary alongside rapists.

As everyone realizes, the crime of rape does not allow for restitution. For how could one ever replace the unfortunate woman's ability to know that she will be giving herself, inviolate, to the man she will one day love? But there must be some restitution to the extent that such is possible; since the rapist cannot give his victim, and she cannot accept from him, anything other than property, I would favor the solution that he give her all his property.

Unmarried women, as we shall see below, stand under the authority of their parents, while married women stand under the authority of their husbands. Thus it is the parents or the husband who would be the plaintiff in any case that might arise. If the woman were unmarried and the parents did not want to file a suit, then the woman herself could do so; but not if she is married, for a woman is subject to her parents only conditionally, but she is subject to her husband altogether unconditionally.

[320] §12

Or, the female citizen is subject to such coercion *indirectly*, through the moral force of her parents and relatives, since they can induce her, through harsh treatment or persuasion, into a marriage against her inclinations. There can be no doubt that harsh treatment aimed at inducing a woman to marry should be forbidden and punished. In any other context persuasion is not an offense, but it clearly is here. In other situations one asks, "Why did you let yourself be persuaded?" But this question does not arise here. The inexperienced and innocent daughter knows nothing of love, knows nothing of the whole relationship being proposed to her, and so she really is being cheated and used as a means for her parents' or relatives' end.

Coercion by persuasion is the most harmful kind, and far more offensive than the physical force discussed above, at least in its consequences, if not also in form. In the case of rape, after all, the woman regains her freedom afterwards. But with this kind of coercion, she is usually cheated for her entire life out of the noblest and sweetest of sentiments, that of love, and out of her true feminine dignity, her entire character; she is completely and forever degraded to the status of a tool.

Thus there can be no question as to whether the state has the right and the duty to protect its young female citizens, through stringent laws and careful supervision, against this kind of coercion. The only question concerns the following: an unmarried daughter stands under the authority of her parents (as we shall see later); they are her legal guardians and court of first instance. It is they who would have to file a complaint about coercion inflicted upon her. Now it is absurd to think that they should file suit against themselves; for if they wanted the power of the state to prevent them from coercing her, they surely would have refrained from doing so on their own.

But we shall also see that a daughter [321] emerges from her parents' authority when she marries. The issue here, at any rate, is marriage. The parents themselves, who want to coerce her to marry, regard her as marriageable; and so in perfect accord with sound reason, the law could prescribe that the daughter becomes rightfully independent of her parents from the moment that they suggest marriage to her, and that after that she must watch over her rights herself. The state's final verdict in this matter, and thus the law's prescription, would have to be that parents who thus abuse their authority and quash their child's human rights for the rest of her life, should be stripped of that authority; and the daughter should be taken from them, along with the property that is due her, and placed under the direct protection of the state until she gets married. But since (notwithstanding this legal prescription) there is always a danger that a young, inexperienced daughter accustomed to blind, filial obedience would find it difficult to file suit; and since it is absolutely crucial that daughters not be coerced into marriage, state authorities could have the right to begin official proceedings in such cases, even if there is no pre-existing suit.

§13

Things are entirely different with the male sex. First, a man cannot be coerced in the true sense of the word into consummating a marriage, for that contradicts the very nature of the matter. It means very little if a man should be persuaded to marry, since in men genuine love does not precede marriage in any case, but arises only as a result of it. However, a man cannot tolerate a woman's being coerced to marry him, if he understands what his true interest is. That would violate his rights as a human being, since it would deprive him of the prospect of a happy marriage, which he has a right to demand. Love will surely come afterwards, many parents say. This may be quite likely in a man, if he obtains a worthy spouse; but it is very doubtful in a woman, and it is terrible [322] to sacrifice and degrade an entire human life for this mere possibility.

The result of what has been said is: marriage must be entered into with absolute freedom, and the state, in consequence of its duty to protect individual persons and especially the female sex, has the duty and the right to keep watch over this freedom in marriages.

§14

Because of its supervisory authority over freedom in marriage, the state must recognize and certify every marriage its citizens enter into.

Every marriage must be juridically valid, i.e. the woman's rights as a human being must not be violated; she must have given herself with a free will, out of love, and without being coerced. Every male citizen must be required to prove this to the state; otherwise, the state would have the right to suspect him of using force and to investigate him. But he cannot appropriately prove this except by letting his wife legally declare her free consent, in a *wedding ceremony*. The bride's "I do" really says nothing more than that she has not been coerced. All the other obligations arising from the marriage follow directly from the fact that they are entering into *one marriage*. What the man's "I do" might mean will become clear later. That he has not been coerced is shown by his leading the wife to the wedding ceremony. Since marriage is grounded on and exists only through morality, it is quite reasonable that marriages are entered into under the watch of those who are supposed to be the people's moral teachers, i.e. the clergy; but to the extent that the wedding ceremony has juridical validity, the clergyman is an officer of the state. And so consistories actually do regard themselves as *clerical courts* in such matters, and they are quite right to do so.

It is incomprehensible how the state and, in this context [323] especially, the clergy (who serve as legislators here) should have the right to prohibit marriages between persons who are to a certain extent related. If nature herself abhorred such a union, then the state and the clergy would not have to pass a law against it; but if nature has no such abhorrence, then they cannot base their law upon it. It is understandable how a nation could believe that its deity might be angered by such marriages, among other things. And if that is the case, the state has no right to *mandate* such marriages (just as it has no right in general to mandate a marriage between two particular persons), since it may not obligate its citizens to act contrary to their (albeit mistaken) consciences. But the state has just as little right to *prohibit* such marriages. Someone who believes that the deity will be angered will refrain from marrying a relative in any case; someone who does not believe this, or who is willing to take the risk of incurring the deity's anger, will be punished by the deity anyway (assuming that the nation's belief is true). Leave it up to the gods themselves to take their own revenge for the insults hurled at them. The priests have nothing to do but to conscientiously admonish and warn the nation, and to *announce* (as mere *expounders of the law*) to those who want to believe them which degrees of relatedness are prohibited between spouses, and which divine punishments shall be imposed upon violators.

There is no conceivable reason why those who do not believe in the deity's anger, or who are willing to risk incurring it, should be bound by other people's beliefs, except the following: punishment for the violators' sins might affect the innocent as well. But this is an evil and pernicious superstition, which can play no role in the state's legislation, and which cannot justify restricting the natural rights of others.

But independent of all religious reasons, could there still be political reasons for regarding certain marriages as impermissible? The best account of this, it seems to me, comes from Montesquieu (*De l'esprit des lois*, book 26, chapter 14).[1] It has always been the natural role of fathers to guard their children's innocence, in order to keep [**324**] their bodies as safe, and their souls as pure, as possible. Constantly occupied with this concern, fathers had to steer well clear of doing anything that could lead their children astray. For the same reason, they also had to try instilling in their children an abhorrence to any union between brothers and sisters. This is also the source of the prohibition of marriages between cousins. For in the world's earliest ages, a man's children all remained under his roof, and the children of two brothers thought of themselves as siblings.

Two remarks here. First, the preservation of chastity within families was the proper concern of fathers; but by no means was it a matter for civil legislation (as if one family's lack of chastity would actually violate another family's rights) or for police legislation (as if a family's lack of chastity could make such a violation more likely). Those who were not much concerned about chastity in their families could be *reminded* and *taught about* it by the nation's more cultivated members; but as a state, they certainly could not pass a *law* concerning it. If the ground of something ceases to exist, then what is grounded also ceases to exist. In this context, the ground is the cohabitation of certain related persons.

---

[1] Much of the rest of this paragraph is a paraphrase of claims made in Book 26, ch. 14 of *The Spirit of the Laws*.

As far as marriages between parent and child or between two siblings are concerned, this ground can never cease to be. As far as marriages between cousins, or between an uncle and his niece, or between brother-in-law and sister-in-law, etc. are concerned, this ground – their cohabitation – rarely applies in the present state of human affairs.

It is through sexual intercourse that a marriage is truly consummated; only through it does the wife subject her entire personality to the man and show him her love, which is the starting point of the entire marital relationship described above. Where intercourse has occurred, the couple is assumed to be married. (Only later shall we determine this proposition more clearly and consider its implications.) Where no intercourse has occurred, the couple can have any other kind of relationship, but not true marriage. Thus an *engagement to be married*, whether public or secret, does not constitute [**325**] a marriage; and a broken engagement is certainly not to be regarded as a divorce. But a broken engagement may very well be the basis of a right to demand compensation. The innocent party has to be returned to his or her previous condition, to the extent that such is possible. Even the *wedding ceremony*, if it precedes the consummation of the marriage (as is in accordance with proper mores), does not constitute marriage; rather it only bestows advance juridical recognition upon a marriage that will be entered into only later.

§15

The husband and wife are united in the most intimate way possible. Their union is a union of hearts and wills. Thus it is not to be assumed that disputes concerning right can arise between them. For this reason the state need not pass laws governing the relationship between the two spouses, for their entire relationship is not juridical, but a natural and moral relation of the heart. The two are one soul, and so the assumption is that they will not be at odds with one another or take each other to court, any more than a single individual would take himself to court.

As soon as any such dispute arises, their separation is already accomplished, and so their juridical divorce (about which we shall say more later) can follow.

§16

The concept of marriage entails the wife's most limitless subjection to her husband's will, not because of juridical, but moral, reasons. She must subject herself for the sake of her own honor. The wife does not belong to herself, but to her husband. By recognizing marriage (i.e. this familiar relationship grounded not in the state but in something higher) the state from now on ceases to regard the wife as a juridically distinct person. The husband represents her entirely; from the state's point of view, she is completely annihilated by her marriage, in consequence of her own [326] necessary will, which the state has guaranteed. In the eyes of the state, her husband becomes her guarantee and her legal guardian; in all things, he lives out her public life, and she retains only a domestic life.

The husband's guarantee for the wife is self-explanatory, for it is entailed by the nature of their union; what its limits are, we shall see below. But there is no harm if the husband also makes a separate declaration of this guarantee, and expressly pledges himself to be his wife's guarantor. The man's "I do" in the wedding ceremony can be seen as his assurance of this guarantee, and his "I do" makes sense only under this condition.

§17

The concept of marriage entails that the wife, who surrenders her personality, also gives her husband ownership of all her property, and all the exclusive rights she has within the state. In recognizing a marriage, the state simultaneously recognizes and guarantees the man's ownership of his wife's property – not *over against his wife* (for the assumption is that no disputes concerning right can arise between them), but rather *over against all other citizens*. In relation to the state, the man becomes the sole owner of both the property he already owns, and that which the wife transfers to him. His acquisition of her property is unrestricted; for after all, only he continues to exist as the sole juridical person.

Either the wife's property has already been declared, made known to the state, and recognized by it prior to the marriage, in which case it is simply transferred to the husband; or else it is given to her by her parents only at the time of the marriage, in which case it is declared only now by the spouses, and it is only now that their ownership of these objects is guaranteed by the state. In accordance with the proof given above, the state need not take account of their absolute property, their money and valuables. But since divorce is a future possibility, and in order to repartition their property, as would be necessary (we shall say more about this later), the state must know the value [327] of what the wife has brought to the marriage, or must at least have some way of ascertaining it, when and if it becomes necessary. Towards this end, it is sufficient if the wife's family keeps documentation on the matter, or if a sealed document is deposited with the courts.

The concept of marriage likewise entails that the husband and wife share a residence and their labors – in short, that they share a life together. The two appear to the state as only one person; if one of them does something with their common property, it is as if both of them did it. But the husband alone takes care of all their public, juridical activities.

§18

There is no need for a law of the state governing the relationship between spouses: there is just as little need for a law governing the relationship between them and other citizens. Later I shall explain my views on laws against adultery insofar as they seem and are expressed as if they are laws about property, and ought to protect a man's possession of his wife, and a wife's possession of her husband. Just as the state regards the spouses as one juridical person (represented outwardly by the husband) and their property as the property of one person, so every individual citizen is obligated to regard them in the same way. In any dispute concerning right, other citizens must deal with the husband; no one can do business directly with the wife. All that follows from this is that the spouses are responsible for making their marriage known to their nearest associates; this is necessary also for moral reasons, in order to prevent the scandal that would arise on account of relationships that are illegal or thought to be illegal, and so this is best done through the clergy.

§19

Originally, i.e. in accordance with his merely natural inclinations, the man certainly aims at satisfying his sexual drive. [328] But when he learns, either before getting married or after, through reflection and instruction, and in his actual dealings with honorable persons of the female sex (especially his mother), that woman harbors love within herself and is supposed to surrender herself only out of love, then even his merely natural drive becomes ennobled. Even he ceases to seek mere enjoyment and wants, rather, to be loved. Once he knows that woman makes herself contemptible if she gives herself without love, and that her desire is a degrading one, he will not let himself be used as a means for this base sensuousness. He must necessarily have contempt for himself, if he is forced to regard himself as a mere tool for satisfying an ignoble drive. It is on the basis of these principles that one should judge the effect a wife's adultery has on the husband.

A wife who gives herself to another man, does so: *either* out of true and complete love. But in that case, since her love by nature will simply not admit of being divided, she has ceased to love her husband, and so her entire relationship with him is annulled. Moreover, even though she claims that love excuses her, she has degraded herself, for, if she is still capable of morality, her prior union with her husband must now appear to her as ignoble and bestial, for the reasons given above. If she still allows the sham of her previous relationship with her husband to continue, then, once again, she completely degrades herself. She allows it to continue, either out of sensuous desire or for the sake of some external end. In either case, she uses her personality as a means for a base end and thereby makes even her husband himself into a means. – *Or*, in the second scenario, she surrendered herself to the other man out of sensuous desire: in this case one must also assume that she does not love her husband, but rather uses him only to satisfy her drive; and this is completely beneath his dignity.

Thus the wife's adultery invariably nullifies the entire marital relation; and a husband [329] cannot stay with an adulteress without degrading himself. (This has been manifest in the universal sentiment of every nation that has even the slightest degree of culture. Everywhere, a man who tolerates his wife's dissoluteness is treated with contempt and labeled with a specific term of abuse. This is because he sins against honor, and shows himself to be ignoble and base.)

A man's jealousy is characterized by contempt for the unfaithful woman. If his jealousy is of any other kind – if, for instance, it has the character of envy or resentment – then the man makes himself contemptible.

§20

A husband's adultery reveals his ignoble disposition, if the woman with whom he commits it surrenders herself to him, not out of love, but for some other end; in that case, enjoyment is his only aim. Or, if she gives herself to him out of love, his adultery constitutes the greatest injustice against her. For in committing adultery with her, he is implicitly claiming that he can fulfill all the duties of marriage, show her unlimited magnanimity, and take infinite care to satisfy her, all of which he is unable to do.

Now if a man commits adultery only in order to satisfy his sexual drive, his behavior is certainly ignoble, but not automatically fatal to his character, as it would be for a woman. But if his only aim in committing adultery is enjoyment, his wife can easily conclude that his relationship to her is no different, and that all she had previously taken to be his tender magnanimity is nothing other than his sexual drive, which would have to make her feel very degraded. In addition, a loving wife will find it very painful to know that the same sacrifice she made for her husband should belong to another woman besides herself. (This is why a wife's jealousy is characterized by envy and hatred for the rival woman.) Thus it is quite possible that a man's adultery will cause his wife's heart to turn away from him; but it is absolutely certain that it [**330**] will cause her to become bitter about their relationship, and this is contrary to the magnanimity he owes her.

Therefore – a husband's adultery does not necessarily nullify the marital relation, as a wife's necessarily does – but it is possible that his adultery will nullify it, in which case the wife is degraded in her own eyes. An adulterous husband is just as guilty as an unfaithful wife; one could even say that he is more so, since his adultery damages his magnanimity, and this reveals that his soul is base. The wife can forgive him; and a noble, worthy wife will surely do so. But the fact that she has something to forgive is oppressive for the husband, and even more so for the wife. The husband loses his courage and his power to be head of the marital relation, and the wife feels oppressed in not being able to respect the man to whom she has surrendered herself. Thus the relationship between them becomes rather inverted. The wife becomes the magnanimous one, and the husband can hardly be anything other than the submissive one.

This is manifest in common opinion as well. A wife who knows of her husband's dissoluteness and tolerates it is not treated with contempt; on the contrary, the more placid and wise she is in the face of his adultery, the more she is respected. Thus the assumption is that she should not seek legal redress. Where does this opinion, which is so deeply rooted in the human soul, come from? Merely from our laws, and merely from us men? But this opinion is shared even by women who complain about these laws. It is also based on the fundamental differences between the two sexes, as indicated above.

§21

In order to be able to make a well-founded judgment concerning the civil consequences of adultery and of the divorce that might result from it, we must first investigate the relationship of the state and law to the satisfaction of the sexual drive outside marriage.

The state has a duty to protect the *honor* of the female sex, i.e. to ensure, in accordance with what was said above, that she is not forced [331] to give herself to a man in the absence of love; for her honor is a part, indeed the noblest part, of her personality. But everyone also has the right – i.e. there is nothing in *external* right opposed to it – to sacrifice one's personality. Just as everyone has an unlimited, external – not internal, moral – right to one's own life, and just as the state cannot pass a law against suicide: so too woman, in particular, has an unlimited, external right to her honor. She is externally free to degrade herself to the level of an animal, just as the man must be externally free as well to have ignoble and base thoughts.

If a woman wants to surrender herself out of mere lasciviousness or for other ends, and if a man can be found who is willing to do without love, then the state has no right to stand in their way.

Thus the state, strictly speaking – though we shall see later what its remaining responsibilities are – cannot pass laws against prostitution and adultery, and cannot impose punishments for these activities. (Moreover, this is actually how things are originally arranged in Christian states. Offenses of this kind are punished, not as violations of civil law, but as violations of moral law, and they are punished by the association responsible for moral coercion, namely the church. The chief punishment for such offenses was always a fine imposed by the church. It is not our task here to examine the rightfulness of these procedures, for our topic is not the church but the state. For example, the income that the papal coffers receive from profligate women represents great consistency in inconsistency. It is actually the church that must grant its approval to this way of life, for otherwise no one would be permitted to engage in it; and the money given to the church is the fine paid in advance for the sins yet to be committed.)

§22

A relationship based on self-interest, and whose final end is to satisfy the sexual drive, [332] may be lasting and public. In that case, it is called *concubinage*, and it is made public (at least to an attentive police force) through the fact that the couple cohabits.

For the reason given above, the state cannot forbid concubinage. However, it must first make sure that the woman has not been coerced, but has voluntarily entered into this admittedly shameful contract. The woman must declare this; however, not with pomp and ceremony, since it is not a dignified relationship, and not to moral teachers, but rather to certain police officials, whose duty it is to deal with unseemly matters.

Furthermore, the state must be aware that this union is not a marriage, even though it has the external appearance of being one. It does not have the juridical consequences of marriage; the man does not become the woman's guarantor and legal guardian. The bond between them can be dissolved as soon as one of them wants it to be, and without any formality. The state has not guaranteed this bond. Nor has it guaranteed the conditions of the contract between them; and the woman acquires no rightfully binding claims upon the man, for the following reason. One acquires a rightfully binding claim, only if one engages in an occupation that the state recognizes and certifies. Now the state certainly cannot prohibit the occupation engaged in here, for it is beyond its right to do so; but nor can the state certify it, since it is an immoral occupation. Therefore, if the man refuses to keep his word, he will certainly show just how base he is, and – it is to be hoped – will incur the universal contempt of others; but the woman cannot file a legal complaint against him, and will be turned away by the courts.

§23

Or else – in the second scenario – satisfaction of the sexual drive outside marriage is not accompanied by cohabitation.

As a first possibility in this scenario, the woman [333] can subject herself to the man's will without him paying or promising to pay her (regardless of whether it be money, valuables, or even a favor); or in the absence of any express acknowledgment that her subjection is not out of love. In such a case it is to be assumed that she has subjected herself out of love. It is obvious that she has not done so for financial gain; and one should never assume, without proof, that she has done so out of lasciviousness, for this is contrary to woman's nature. Before drawing such a conclusion, one would have to prove explicitly that she is known for giving herself to everyone. But the woman's subjecting herself out of love is the ground of marriage. Thus a marriage has actually been consummated between these two hypothetical persons, even without explicit marriage vows. And any vows they might have exchanged only confirm what is already obvious.

The only thing lacking is public recognition of the marriage: the wedding ceremony. The state unconditionally owes this to the woman; for it owes it to her to protect her honor, as the right of her personality. On the assumptions made here, she herself has not compromised her honor; therefore, the state may not compromise it. The man can be coerced into having a wedding ceremony. He is not being coerced into marriage, for he has, in effect, already entered into it; rather, he is being coerced only into making a public declaration of it. If he manifests an insurmountable aversion to such a declaration, or if there are other grounds that make it difficult for the marriage to last, e.g. their complete inequality in social class, then he can be divorced after the marriage ceremony, and this divorce will be handled in accordance with the laws of divorce in general, which we intend to discuss in a moment. The woman and children are to bear his name, and she is to be regarded without qualification as a divorced woman.

(True inequality in social class entails that they will have unequal levels of education, that their entire systems of ideas will be utterly dissimilar, and that one of them will be out of place in the social circles to which the other must belong. This will make a marriage – a complete unification of heart and soul, a [334] true equality of the two persons – absolutely impossible. The relationship will inevitably become a concubinage, whose end is merely to satisfy self-interest (in the one party) and the sexual drive (in the other). The state can never allow such a relationship to pass itself off as an enduring marriage or recognize it as such. But by nature there are only two different social classes: one that cultivates its body alone for manual labor and one that cultivates primarily its mind. Any marriage between members of these two classes is a true *mésalliance*; and there are no classes other than these two.)

The second possibility is as follows: it can be proved of the woman who has surrendered herself to the will of this man that she has also done the same with others, either before or after giving herself to this man, or that she has surrendered herself to this man for a price. In the latter case, it must be clearly shown that she has expressly set this price on her personality and surrendered herself only after, or in the expectation of, receiving payment. The mere fact that on other occasions she has accepted gifts from her lover proves nothing against her virtue. But if this can be proved of her, then she is a dishonored woman, and is not entitled to protection from the authorities; for they cannot protect an honor that does not exist but has instead been forfeited by the woman herself.

Prostitutes (*quae quaestum corpore exercent*[2]), who make this into their sole occupation, cannot be tolerated by the state within its borders; the state must expel them from the country, and this without harming their freedom to do with their bodies what they will (as we have just derived it), for the following, very simple reason. The state must know how each person makes a living and must give each person the right to pursue his occupation. Whoever cannot declare his occupation to the state has no civil rights. Now if a woman should declare to the state that she makes her living from prostitution, the state would have a right to regard her

---

[2] Who make their living with their bodies.

as insane. *Propriam turpitudinem confitenti non creditur*,[3] is a correct rule of right. Thus it is as if she had declared no occupation at all, and [335] *it is for this reason* (provided that she does not consider some other occupation) that she is to be expelled from the state. In a well constituted state, this situation is not likely to arise. In such a state, each citizen is reasonably well cared for. If, in addition to their officially declared occupations, citizens have other occupations that do not constitute their fixed stations in society, the state will ignore these avocations. The question of force cannot arise here, since these avocations are not a public matter, as concubinage between regularly cohabiting persons is. The state knows nothing of these irregularities and so has not guaranteed men the enjoyment of these dishonorable pleasures, as it has, for example, guaranteed its citizens the ability to travel in the streets in peace and comfort. Thus supervising the health of these prostitutes is not a branch of police power; and, I admit, I regard such supervision as unworthy of a rightfully ordered state. Let those who want to be licentious bear the natural consequences of their licentiousness. Nor, obviously, does the state guarantee the contracts that citizens make regarding such things. A prostitute cannot file a complaint concerning such matters.

§24

Let us apply these principles to adultery. The state can just as little pass laws or impose punishments to prohibit adultery, as it can prohibit any other extramarital satisfaction of the sexual drive. For whose rights are supposedly violated by adultery? Those of the husband whose wife commits it, or those of the wife whose husband commits it? Is marital fidelity, then, an appropriate object for a law of coercion? It is certainly regarded as such in these laws. But in fact, marital fidelity is grounded on a union of hearts. This union is entered into freely and cannot be coerced; if *it* ceases to exist, then being coerced into *external fidelity* (which would only be possible through physical coercion) cannot be rightful, but is contrary to right.

---

[3] One who confesses to his own vice is not to be believed.

[336] §25

If the relationship that ought to exist between spouses and that constitutes the essence of marriage (boundless love on the part of the woman and boundless magnanimity on the part of the man) is nullified, the marriage between them is thereby canceled. Therefore – *spouses divorce each other out of free will, just as they became united out of free will.* If the ground of their relationship is canceled, their marriage no longer exists (even if they remain together); rather, their cohabitation can only be regarded as concubinage: their union is no longer its own end, but instead has an external end, usually some temporary advantage. Now no human being can be expected to engage in something as ignoble as concubinage: therefore, the state cannot expect persons whose hearts have grown apart to continue living together.

From this it would follow that the state has absolutely nothing to do in cases of divorce, other than to require that divorces be declared to it, the authority that originally recognized the union. After divorce, the juridical consequences of the marriage necessarily cease to obtain, and so the state must be notified of divorces, so that it can take the appropriate juridical measures.

§26

But now most of our states do indeed presume to exercise judgment as to what is right in cases of divorce. Are they completely wrong in that; and if not, what is the basis of their right?

This is the basis: the spouses to be divorced might ask the state to assist them with their divorce, in which case the state must decide whether or not it ought to do so. This would imply that *any judgment the state makes in matters of divorce is nothing other than a judgment of right concerning what assistance it ought to offer.* We shall go through this in detail.

[337] §27

Either both spouses agree to get divorced and also agree about the division of their property, so that they have no dispute concerning right; in this case they have absolutely nothing to do other than to inform the state about their divorce. The matter has already been settled between them; the object of their agreement is the object of their natural freedom, and strictly speaking, the state has no reason even to inquire about the reasons for their divorce.

If the state inquires about why we are divorcing, it is not actually the state that asks, but rather the church as a moral body. Now the church is completely right to do so. For marriage is a moral union, and so the divorcing spouses might want to justify their divorce to representatives of the moral body, the church, to which they hopefully still want to belong; they might also want to hear the church's teachings and moral advice. Moreover, it will be perfectly appropriate if the clergy tried to dissuade the couple. However, it is important to note that the clergy has no right to coerce the couple into explaining their reasons for divorce or into following the church's advice. If the two should say: "We want to follow our own consciences," or "Your reasons do not move us," then the clergy must leave the matter as it is.

Result: the consent of both parties dissolves the marriage juridically, with no further questions asked.

§28

If one of them does not consent to the divorce, then their informing the state about it is not merely a declaration but also a request for its protection, and this is where the state exercises its judgment concerning right.

What could the party wanting the divorce possibly request from the state? If a husband files for divorce against the will of his wife, his request implies that the state ought to expel the wife from his house. If a wife files for divorce against [338] the will of her husband, then – since a husband cannot be expelled from the house (because it belongs to him as the family's legal representative), while the wife, since she wants to leave, could probably do so – her request, I say, implies that the state ought to force the husband to provide her with some other place to live.

Now according to what laws should the state decide these matters?

§29

Consider a case in which the husband files for civil divorce because of his wife's adultery. In accordance with what was stated above, it is contrary to a husband's honor to continue living with such a woman, and their relationship can no longer be called a marriage, but is concubinage instead. But the state cannot force any human being to do what is contrary to his honor and moral sentiments. Thus in this case, the state's duty of protection requires that it release the husband from his wife. For what reasons, then, could the wife want to continue living with him? One cannot presume that she loves him, and so it must be for other ends. But the husband cannot let himself be made into a tool for her ends. What was said above entails that, if the husband does not file for divorce, the state has no right to inquire about his wife's adultery and effect the divorce against his will, for adultery is not a matter for civil legislation.

Even the church sees no honor in exhorting the husband to stay with the adulteress and in admonishing him to forgive her. For the church cannot advise him to do what is dishonorable and immoral, which is obviously what their continued cohabitation would be in this case.

Now consider a case in which the husband files for civil divorce because his wife does not love him. Either the wife will admit this. In that case, the state must release the man from his wife; for love alone is the ground of a rightful marriage, and where there is no love, [**339**] the relationship is merely concubinage. But for what reason could a wife demand to continue living with a man whom, by her own admission, she does not love? It would have to be for external ends, and the husband cannot let himself be made into a tool for such ends. – Or else, the wife refuses to admit that she does not love him. In that case, the state cannot make an immediate decision, but must carefully scrutinize this marriage, until the spouses reach an agreement, or until a compelling reason for divorce clearly and demonstrably manifests itself. The state acquires a right to scrutinize this marriage (a right it does not otherwise have with respect to any marriage) because it has been made the judge of an unclear situation that cannot be clarified without such scrutiny. (As a result of the husband's filing for divorce, what was only indirectly subject to the state's protective power has now become directly subject to it.)

The wife's refusal to fulfill what has rather crudely been labeled her "conjugal duty" proves that she does not love her husband, and to that extent it constitutes rightful grounds for divorce. Love begins with the wife's subjection to her husband, and this subjection constitutes the enduring expression of her love. I said, "*to the extent* that it proves that she does not love her husband": for if it can be proved that she has an illness or some other physical impediment, her refusal does not prove that she does not love her husband. In that case, the husband's filing for divorce would be ignoble beyond all comprehension. But what if his thoughts really are so ignoble? The state cannot become the handmaid of his base way of thinking; on the other hand, such a man is not worthy of a fine woman, and it is to be hoped that she will be able (especially through the clergy's encouragement) to consent to the divorce in exchange for compensation. In that case, both parties would consent and the state's only task would be to announce the divorce, and so there would no longer be a question about the state's role in it.

If the wife becomes the subject of a criminal investigation and the state apprehends her, then the [340] circumstances themselves separate her from her husband: the state itself takes her away from him. Otherwise the husband is her legal guardian. But he cannot be her guardian in a criminal – and therefore exclusively personal – matter. She becomes independent, and is thus separated from him. If she is found innocent, she returns to her husband's dominion. If after having been found guilty and punished, her husband wants to take her back, he may do so; but no one can force him to do so, for she has dishonored him.

§30

Consider a case in which the wife files for a juridical divorce because of her husband's adultery. According to what we have said above, it is certainly possible for the wife to forgive her husband, and it is not dishonorable – in fact, it is honorable – for her to do so. Therefore, it is advisable to try to dissuade her from divorcing him and even to encourage her to wait a while before taking action (for instance, by living apart). But if she insists on getting divorced, it must be granted to her; for only she herself knows her heart, and only she can decide whether her husband's infidelity has completely destroyed her love for him. Forcing a woman to remain subject to her husband after her love for him has been destroyed would be contrary to the state's first duty to the female sex.

In general, if a wife seeks a divorce, then – whatever her complaint may be – the state is always obligated to grant it to her if, after an attempt has been made to dissuade her, she still insists on it. In this matter the other sex must be given an advantage. The reason is as follows: in suing for divorce, a wife might not prove anything against her husband; but with regard to herself, she proves that she does not love him, and in the absence of love, she should not be forced to subject herself to him. But because a woman sometimes does not rightly know her own heart, and may very well love her husband more than she realizes, an attempt should be made to dissuade her, and she should postpone any action by living apart from him for a while.

A wife's suit for divorce on account of her husband's failure to perform his conjugal duty, [341] is a dishonor to her sex and a sin against nature. One can only regard it as barbarism if the state – or even the church on the state's behalf – accepts such a suit. Moreover, experience confirms that women themselves are ashamed to seek divorce on such grounds, and that they usually do so only as a pretense. The state should just let them openly acknowledge that they do not like their husbands.

A criminal investigation of the husband does not necessarily entail divorce. The relationship here is entirely different from one in which the wife is the subject of a criminal investigation. For the husband must always represent both himself and his wife in court. However, a criminal investigation of the husband constitutes perfectly valid grounds for the wife to file for divorce, for she cannot respect a criminal. But if she wants to stay with him, and wants to share his fate and make it easier for him to bear, then – to the extent that the laws allow – she is completely free to do so.

Malicious desertion – i.e. desertion in which the deserted spouse is not informed about the other's departure or the reasons for it – may be the ground of a spouse's suit for divorce. In that case the divorce is automatic, for the deserting spouse is to be regarded as having already effected the divorce. But the deserted spouse files for divorce, and so both have consented to it.

§31

When a couple divorces, what is to be done about their property?

Since my principles regarding this matter depart from the commonly accepted ones, I ask my readers to reflect carefully on the grounds for deciding the issue.

The wife subjects her personality, along with all of her property, to her husband. He can repay her love only if he, likewise, subjects all of his property, along with his person and freedom, to her; but with one difference, namely that he maintains external control over the whole. The unification of their hearts necessarily entails the unification of their property, under the [342] control of the husband. Their two properties become one.

This bond is now severed; but if the ground of something ceases to exist, then what is grounded ceases to exist. *Prima facie*, the spouses would have to be returned to the positions they occupied before the marriage; they would each have to get back what they contributed to the common pot.

But (and this observation drastically alters our result) the two have for some time – presumptively through one will and as a single subject – managed, enjoyed, augmented, and consumed this property. The effect of their joint management cannot be nullified; this effect necessarily is and remains an effect for which they are both responsible. One cannot go back and calculate things in such a way that one party could say to the other: "You needed this or that, which I did not; and I earned this or that, which you did not." For if the two had a true marriage, the needs of one were also the needs of the other, and the earnings of one were also the earnings of the other; the two were presumed, from the perspective of right, to be only one person. An individual person does not negotiate, settle accounts, and go to court with himself, and so neither can the spouses. But now, of course, this relationship is canceled, and things will be different from now on; but until their divorce, this is how things were, and the effect of this relationship cannot be nullified.

But now the external condition of this effect is the amount of property each brought to the marriage, and this means not just property in cash, but also in rights and privileges. (The internal conditions of this effect, i.e. each spouse's diligence and conscientiousness, are precisely not to be calculated.) The total property that the couple owns at the time of their divorce, as effect, would have to be divided in proportion to the amounts that each brought to the marriage. As we noted earlier, there must be some way of proving in court how much each has contributed to the marriage. Imagine, for example, that the wife contributed one-third, and the husband two-thirds, of their total property when the marriage began. The amount of their total property at the time of the divorce is to be [343] measured and divided according to that proportion, so that the divorced wife gets one-third of it, and the man two-thirds. The woman does not simply get back the amount she brought to the marriage, but rather that amount minus her share of the total loss (if the whole amount has decreased), or plus her share of the total gain (if the whole amount has increased). It is exactly like a business partnership. Other provisions contained in the law regarding the division of marital property may well have their political reasons, but they are not just.

The question of how the custody of children should be allocated between the divorced spouses can be answered only later, when we examine the relationship between parents and children.

THIRD SECTION
IMPLICATIONS OF THE RECIPROCAL RELATION OF RIGHT
IN THE STATE BETWEEN THE TWO SEXES IN GENERAL

§32

Does the woman have the same rights in the state as the man? It might seem laughable that this question is even being asked. For if reason and freedom are the only ground of a person's capacity to have rights, how could there be any difference in the rights of the two sexes, which possess the same reason and freedom?

But as long as human beings have existed, a rather different view seems to have been universally accepted, and the female sex seems to have been treated as inferior to the male sex in the exercise of her rights. Such universal agreement must have a deep-seated reason, and if there ever was a pressing need to discover that reason, there certainly is in our day.

Assuming that the other sex [344] has really been treated as inferior to the first sex with regard to rights, it simply will not suffice to explain such treatment by reference to woman's inferior mental and physical capacities. Especially with respect to their mental powers, women and their advocates would respond: "First, we are not given a proper education, and the male sex assiduously denies us access to educational resources. Second, your claim is not even entirely correct, for compared to most of the men who are the pride of their sex, we can just as well show you women who, based on a fair assessment, would be their equal. Finally, even if this inequality were established, it could never entail such a decided inequality of rights, for one perceives a great diversity of mental and physical capacities also among men, yet without allowing such oppressive conclusions concerning the reciprocal relation of right among them."

Hence, before all else, it is necessary to investigate whether women really are treated as inferior, as some of them and – even more so – some of their self-appointed advocates claim. In our presentation, one point will follow after the other.

§33

The question of whether the female sex is as entitled to every human and civil right as the male sex could be asked only by someone who doubted that women are full human beings. We have no doubt about that, as is clear from the principles established above. But there could still be a question as to whether and to what extent the female sex *can even will* to exercise all its rights. In order to answer this question, we shall examine the various situations a woman might be in.

§34

As a *rule* – we shall consider the exceptions below – [345] the woman is either still a *virgin*, in which case she stands under her father's authority, as does an unmarried young man. In this, the two sexes are perfectly equal. They are set free by their marriage, with respect to which both are equally free: or, if one of the two is to be favored, it ought to be the daughter. She absolutely may not be forced into marriage – not even through encouragement or persuasion – although this is more advisable in the case of the son, for the reasons indicated above.

Or, the woman is *married*, in which case her own dignity depends on her being and appearing to be completely subject to her husband. One should note well – this follows, in fact, from my theory as a whole, and has been expressly mentioned on several occasions, but it is perhaps not superfluous to emphasize it yet again – the wife is not subject to her husband such that he has a *right of coercion* over her; she is subjected through her own enduring, necessary wish to be subjected, and this wish is the condition of her morality. She may well take back her freedom, if she *willed* to do so; but that is the very point: she cannot rationally *will* to do so. Since their union is now universally known, she must will to appear to everyone she knows as completely subject to her husband, as completely lost in him.

Therefore, in consequence of her own necessary will, the husband is the administrator of all her rights; she wills her rights to be asserted and exercised only insofar as *he* wills them to be. He is her natural representative in the state and in society as a whole. This is her relationship to society, her *public* relationship. She cannot even think about exercising her rights directly on her own.

As far as the *domestic* and *inner* relationship is concerned, *the husband's tenderness necessarily gives back to her everything she has lost, and more.* The husband will not give up her rights, for they are his own rights; if he were to give them up, he would harm himself and dishonor both himself and his wife in the eyes of society. The wife also has rights concerning [346] public affairs, for she is a citizen. In states where the citizen has a vote concerning public affairs, I take it to be incumbent on the husband not to vote without having discussed the matter with his spouse and modified his opinion as a result of their discussion. Thus he will present to the people only the result of their shared will. In general, the father of a family – who looks after the rights of his spouse and children as well – must have more influence and a weightier vote in the commonwealth than someone who represents only his own rights as an individual. How this should be arranged is a matter to be investigated by politics.

Thus women actually do exercise their right to vote concerning public affairs, only they do not do so directly on their own, since they cannot will to do so without forfeiting their female dignity. Rather, they do so through the appropriate influence (grounded in the nature of the marital union) that they have on their husbands.

(This is also confirmed by the history of all great revolutions. Either they were instigated by women, or guided and significantly modified by women.)

Remark. Now if this must be conceded without objection, what do women and their advocates really demand? What is it, then, that has supposedly been taken from them, and that they now demand to have back? The rights themselves? They are most fully in possession of rights. It can only be the outer appearance that they lust after. They not only want to have an influence, but want it to be known that they have had an influence. They not only want their wishes to be actualized but also want it to be known that *they, precisely they*, have actualized their wishes. They seek celebrity during their lives, and after death in history.

If this alone is and can be their goal, then they and their complaints are to be rejected without hesitation; for they cannot even raise such complaints without having renounced all their [347] womanly merit. Very few of those who raise these complaints do so in earnest. They have been persuaded to utter such wonderful words (which they cannot even contemplate without dishonoring themselves) by a few misguided men who themselves, for the most part, have not deemed a single woman worthy enough to be made into a lifetime companion and who, as compensation for this, want to see the entire sex, in one lump sum, immortalized in history. Even a man whose actions aim chiefly – or even only incidentally – at glory will destroy the merit of his actions, and sooner or later, but inevitably, their glory as well. Women should be thankful that their station in life makes them immune to such suspicions about them. But more importantly, women who seek glory sacrifice the congenial modesty of their sex; and nothing can be more repulsive to woman's modesty than her being made into a display. Vanity and the thirst for glory are contemptible in a man, but in a woman they are corrupting; they destroy that modesty and that devoted spousal love on which her entire dignity depends. A rational and virtuous woman can be proud only of her husband and children, but not of herself, since she forgets herself in them. In addition, those women who seriously do envy men for their celebrity find themselves caught in a very easy-to–dispel delusion regarding the true object of their wish. Woman necessarily wants the love of some man, and in order to arouse it, she wants to attract the attention of the male sex. This is a natural disposition, and it is perfectly innocent in an unmarried woman. But these women count on fortifying the charms of their own sex (in which they perhaps do not have enough confidence) by using the same means that men use to get each other's attention, and they regard glory as just a new means to capture men's hearts. If they are married women, then their goal is as contemptible as their means is perverse.

[348] §35

If the husband is unable or unwilling to make an appearance at a national assembly, there is nothing to prevent his spouse from appearing in his place and casting their shared vote (but always as *her husband's vote*). (She could not cast it as her own without separating herself from her husband.) For if the ground of something ceases to exist, then what is grounded also ceases to exist. Now the wife could not vote, because the husband cast their shared vote. If he does not do so, then she herself can cast it.

This also gives us the principles for assessing the cases of widows, divorced women, and women who have never married but who nevertheless do not stand under paternal authority.

None of these women is subject to a man; thus there is absolutely no reason why they themselves should not exercise all civil rights, as men do. They have the right to cast their vote in the republic, as well as the right to appear in court and pursue their case. If, because of natural modesty and shyness, they want to appoint a legal guardian for themselves, they must be allowed to do so; and how they arrange matters with their guardian is up to them. If they do not want to appoint a legal guardian, there is no rightful basis for forcing them to do so.

§36

Everyone in the state should possess property and manage it himself in accordance with his own will; hence, so should the single woman. This property need not consist in absolute property, money, or valuables; it can also consist in civil rights and privileges. There is no reason why women should not possess these as well. A woman can own fields and carry on agriculture. (Her lack of physical strength is no obstacle to this. Experience shows that women, too, are certainly [349] capable of plowing, sowing, and the like. Among the Teutons, women carried on agriculture entirely on their own. And if there is something a woman cannot do by herself, she can certainly have it done for her by her servants, as actually does happen.) She can harvest other products. She could also pursue an art or handicraft, as long as it is suited to her abilities. She can pursue commercial trade, if she understands it. (Now all of this is actually done in our states, especially by widows, who carry on the business of their deceased husbands. There is no reason why this could not also be done by female citizens who have never married.)

§37

The only thing women cannot do is hold public office, and for the following simple reasons: A public official is completely and thoroughly accountable to the state, in accordance with the proof given above. Either he is accountable to the people, if he himself is the state's highest authority; or, he is accountable to this highest authority, if he has been appointed by it and entrusted with a part of its power. Thus he must be completely free and dependent only on his own discretion; otherwise, his accountability would be self-contradictory and unjust. But now a woman is free and dependent only on herself, only so long as she is unmarried. Thus the state could transfer an office to her, only on the condition that she promised never to marry. But no woman can ever rationally make such a promise, and the state cannot rationally accept such a promise from her. For a woman's destiny is to love, and love arises in a woman on its own, independent of her free will. But if she loves, it becomes her duty to marry; and the state may not prevent her from exercising that duty. But if a female public official marries, only two scenarios would be possible. Either she does not subject herself to her husband with respect to her official business, but remains entirely free in that regard; and this would be [350] contrary to her female dignity. In that case, she could not say that she has fully given herself to her husband. Moreover, what then happens to the firm boundaries between her public office and private life? What could remain of her public office that did not have a certain influence on her private life? Or, she does subject herself to her husband with respect to her official business, as nature and morality require her to do. In that case, he would become the public official and he alone would be accountable. The office would become his by marriage, like all the rest of the wife's property and rights. But the state – if its offices are real offices and duties, not merely sinecures to be enjoyed – cannot tolerate this. It must know and test the skillfulness and character of the person to whom it transfers an office, and cannot allow a person who has been chosen only by love to be imposed on it.

§38

The fact that women are not destined for public office has another consequence, which their advocates mention as a new grievance against our political institutions. That is, women, quite naturally, are not educated to adminster what they never ought to administer, and they are not sent to schools and universities. Thus they claim that their minds are neglected, that they are cunningly kept in a state of ignorance because of men's envy, and that they they are denied access to sources of enlightenment. We shall examine this accusation from the ground up.

One who is a man of learning by profession does not study only for himself; formally, *as* a man of learning, he does not study for himself at all, but for others. He may become a sexton, or state official, or physician, in which case his aim is to put his learning directly into practice. That is why he also learns the form of what he learns (i.e. how it is practiced), and he learns it precisely insofar as this form is present while he is learning. Alternatively, he may become a teacher of future men of learning, at a school or university, in which case his aim is to communicate to others what he has learned and [**351**] to augment it through his own discoveries, so that the culture will not come to a standstill. Therefore, he must know *how* this stock of learning is discovered and developed out of the human soul. This is precisely what women can have no need for, since they ought to become neither the former nor the latter. Only the results of intellectual culture are relevant to human usage, and women obtain these results in society: within each class of society, women obtain the result of the entire culture of that class. Thus what they envy us for is external and inessential, merely formal; it is the husk: because of their position and our social inter-course, they are spared the trouble of first having to work their way through this form, and they are immediately given what is essential. They could not do anything with the form, anyway: women are not and cannot become accustomed to regarding the form as a *means*, for one learns to do this only by making use of the form. Thus women regard the form as an *end* in itself, as something wonderful and excellent on its own. And this is also the reason why truly learned women – I am not talking about women whose reasoning is based simply on healthy common sense, for such women are highly respectable – almost always become pedants.

In order to avoid being misunderstood in any way, I shall explain this further. One cannot claim that women are *inferior* to men in terms of intellectual talents; but one can claim that the minds of men and women are, by nature, very different. Man reduces everything that is in him and for him to clear concepts, and makes his discoveries through reasoning alone (i.e. if he is said to be truly convinced, and if his knowledge is not merely historical knowledge). Woman has a natural feeling for determining what is true, proper, and good. The point is not that this knowledge is given to her by mere feeling, for that is impossible, but rather that, when something is given to her from an external source, it is easy for her to judge whether or not it is true or good, based on mere feeling, without clear insight into the reasons for her judgment. It can be said that man must first make himself rational, while woman is already [352] rational by nature. This is easily derivable from the principles, given above, that distinguish woman from man. A woman's fundamental drive immediately and originally merges with reason, for without this union her drive would nullify reason; it becomes a rational drive, and this is why her entire system of feelings is rational and geared towards reason, so to speak. In contrast, a man must first, through effort and activity, subordinate all of his drives to reason.

Thus by virtue of her womanhood, woman is already supremely practical, but by no means speculative. She cannot, and ought not, go beyond the limit of her feelings and into the interior of things. (And this explains a very well-known phenomenon. For we have had women who distinguished themselves as geniuses in matters of memory – e.g. in languages and even mathematics, insofar as such things can be learned by memory; there are women who became famous in matters of fiction, in the milder forms of poetry, in novel-writing, and even in the writing of history. But we have not had female philosophers or mathematical innovators.)

Let me add a few more words about women's desire to pursue writing, which is becoming increasingly widespread among them.

There are only two conceivable goals of writing: either to submit new scientific discoveries to the scrutiny of the learned community or further to disseminate, through popularization, what is already known and settled. Women cannot make new discoveries, for the reasons given above. But popular writings for women, writings about women's upbringing, moral teachings for the female sex in particular, can all be best written by women; first, because they know the female sex better than any man ever will, since they themselves are members of it (assuming, of course, that they are also capable of raising themselves above it to some extent); and secondly, because – as a *rule* – it is easier for them to find acceptance from a female audience. Such writings can teach even an educated man [353] a great deal about the nature of woman. This assumes, of course, that these female authors also write as women, and want to appear in their writings as women and not poorly disguised men. As one can see, I have presupposed that women write only for their own sex, in order to be helpful and fulfill a need detected in their sex; but by no means for our sex, out of vanity or a thirst for glory. In the latter case, not only will their writings have little literary value, but also the moral character of the authors would be severely harmed. This writing will then be nothing to their authors other than an instrument of their coquetry. If a female writer is married, her authorial glory will give her a status that makes her independent of her husband, which will necessarily weaken the marital union and threaten to dissolve it. Or else, she will be criticized, and will perceive the criticism as an affront to her sex, which will cause bitterness in the life that she and her innocent spouse share.

FOURTH SECTION
ON THE RECIPROCAL RELATION OF RIGHT BETWEEN
PARENTS AND CHILDREN

§39

The original relationship between parents and children is determined not only by the mere concept of right, but by nature and morality, as is the relationship between spouses. Thus in the present investigation, as in the previous one, we must begin with principles that are higher than the concept of right, in order [354] first to have an object to which the concept of right can be applied. For in this relationship, which is grounded in nature and morality, there may well be further determinations that have to be ordered through the concept of right.

Those who want to regard the entire relationship as merely juridical have been forced by their presupposition into making fantastic claims, e.g. that in consequence of the act of procreation, as a form of production (*per formationem*), children are their father's *property*, and so forth.

§40

The fetus is generated in the mother's body as a part belonging to her. The health and preservation of the mother during pregnancy are tied to the preservation of the fetus; and – what is most important here – not as they are in irrational animals (namely, that *this is simply the case*), but rather in such a way that the mother *knows* about this necessary connection between her own preservation and the preservation of the fetus. It is not just a matter of mechanical necessity that she generates the fetus out of herself and forms it in her body; rather, her prudent and considered care for the preservation of the fetus is impressed even upon her consciousness.

In accordance with a completely certain, universal law of nature, the child's birth does not occur without pain. The moment the child is born is the moment the mother is relieved of pain, and thus it is necessarily a joyful moment for her. She is linked through joy to the child's existence.

Even after the child is born, the organic bond between mother and child is not yet dissolved. The child's nourishment continues to be prepared inside the mother, and the mother feels a need to give it to the child, just as the child feels a need to take it.

(An organic body contains parts such that one of the parts has a drive to remedy a need existing in another part and this other part is unable to remedy the need on its own; and the other part has a drive [355] to relieve a need existing in the first part and the first part is equally unable to relieve this need on its own. I refer to this relationship as the organic bond among parts. Since there is no place – except in the mother's body – where nature prepares nourishment that is most beneficial to the newborn child, and no channel – other than the child's mouth – that nature has established for relieving the mother of her milk, it follows that there is an organic bond between mother and child, even though they now exist in two independent bodies. It seems to me worthwhile to investigate whether and to what extent this law of nature applies to the plant kingdom as well, insofar as a plant that already stands on its own as offspring still does not immediately (*per saltem*) separate itself from the body of its mother plant.)

§41

The law of nature just mentioned – considered either in plants or animals – will immediately drive plants and animals to act so as to assist in the further development of a body outside them. In plants and animals, this drive commands with necessity; the activity the drive aims at will follow immediately from and upon the drive itself. But in intelligent beings, a third thing comes between this natural drive and the activity it aims at: consciousness. Intelligence becomes conscious of the natural drive as a feeling. Such feeling is the necessary product of the natural drive and follows immediately from it; or to be more precise, the feeling is itself the natural drive as it exists in intelligence. But the activity the drive aims at does not necessarily and immediately follow from the drive, but depends instead on the use of freedom.

The natural drive was a drive to take care of an external body as one's own. How will this natural drive be expressed in the human mother? Obviously *as a feeling of the needs of an other, just as she feels her own*. But such a feeling is called *sympathy*. Thus sympathy is the form under which the human mother's natural instinct towards her child appears.

This sympathy aims at the same object that the natural instinct was aimed at: the child's physical preservation.

[356] The mother – if she gives herself over to nature – is driven by the sympathy intrinsic to her nature to care for the child's preservation.

Here there is a mechanism of both nature and reason, together in unity, which necessarily leads to the child's preservation – of course, since reason is also at work here, this drive can be resisted if the human being sinks to doing what is unnatural. But in the natural course of things, it is not resisted.

What we are discussing here is certainly not yet a matter of right. One can just as little say that the child has a right to demand this physical preservation from his mother, as that a branch has a right to grow on the tree; conversely, one can just as little say that the mother has a duty to preserve her child which she can be coerced to fulfill, as that the tree has a duty to support the branch which it can be coerced to fulfill. What is at issue here is a law of nature, although in relation to reason. In animals it is a mere law of nature.

(For the sake of clarification, let me add this: there is originally just as little a moral duty, i.e. a *special* duty, to preserve precisely *this child*. But later, once the mother has felt this drive, it certainly does become her moral duty to preserve and support this child. Below, we shall say more about what the state might be allowed and able to do, through positive laws, so as to make the preservation of the child into a duty that the mother can be coerced to fulfil.)

§42

There is in human nature in general, and therefore also in the man, a drive to take care of (and even show affection for) the weak and helpless. Now in the *father*, this universal drive will doubtlessly speak out on behalf of his own child as well; but precisely because it is a universal drive aroused by the sight of helplessness as such, it will speak out on behalf of every child. And so the father has no reason to show any particular preference for *his* child. But we must establish that there is such a preference. Since the relationship between father and child is only physical, the father's preferential love could [357] have no basis other than a physical one. But such a basis is not to be found, for there is absolutely no physical bond between a father and his child; so one must conclude that the father does not immediately have any special love for his child. Nor can one draw any conclusions based on the only natural link that does exist between father and child, namely, the act of procreation; for procreation as such (simply as the procreation of this particular individual) takes place independently of consciousness.

The father's special love for his child arises *originally* – we are not considering how it might also arise out of *opinion* as shaped by our social institutions – it arises originally out of his tenderness for the mother. Through this tenderness, the father makes every wish and end of the mother his own; and so this also includes that of caring for the child's preservation. Since this naturally is the mother's necessary concern, it now also becomes, by transference, that of the father; for the two are one subject, and their will is only one will.

Even here one certainly cannot talk about a mother's natural right to coerce the father to support the child. The grounds one might think capable of establishing such a right of coercion are insufficient. One might think that the mother can say to the father: "You caused me to have a child; therefore, take from me the burden of supporting him." In response, the father can say, and rightfully so: "Neither I nor you intended this. Nature has given the child to you, not to me. Bear what has happened to you, just as I also would have had to do, if something happened to me."

It would be different if the two had perhaps made a contract regarding support for the child. But even then, the state would have to have guaranteed the contract. If it did not, the contract would still not establish a right of coercion valid for an external tribunal, but only an internal, moral duty; and in our theory, such a moral duty need not be established through any special contract, since [358] it is already grounded in the parents' marriage. But we shall see later what the state still can and should do about this situation.

§43

The parents live together, and the child – entrusted to their care by nature – must also live together with them; otherwise they could not take care to support him.

Human beings have a natural drive to suspect that reason exists in external objects (except where it is completely implausible to do so), and to treat such objects, e.g. animals, as if they had reason. The parents will also treat their child in this way, and will summon him to engage in free activity: and so reason and freedom will gradually manifest themselves in the child. According to the necessary concepts of human existence, freedom is part of well-being: the parents desire the well-being of their child, and so they will grant him his freedom. But some uses of freedom would be detrimental to the child's preservation, which the parents also desire. Thus the parents will unite these two ends and restrict the child's freedom so that the child's exercise of his freedom does not endanger his preservation. But this is the first concept of the child's upbringing [*Erziehung*].⁴ The parents will *bring* their child *up*; this follows from their love for him, and from their care for his preservation.

One cannot say that the child has a right of coercion to demand this upbringing, or that the parents have a duty and can be coerced to provide it. We shall see what the state might be able to do about this.

§44

It is the universal moral duty of every morally good human being to spread morality beyond himself and to promote it everywhere. But every free being, and thus also the child, is capable of morality. Now the child necessarily lives with his parents, for reasons unrelated to morality. But if the parents themselves [**359**] are moral, they will make use of every possible means to cultivate morality in their child; this is the concept of the child's *higher upbringing*.

(We are not teaching morality here. Thus we are not saying that the parents *ought* to do this, but only that they *will* do it. Here we are describing natural and moral dispositions only as facts, in order first to obtain content for applying the concept of right.)

This upbringing includes the following two ends: first, that the child's capacities are developed and cultivated so as to be made useful for all sorts of ends; and second, that the child's mind is directed towards morality. In order to achieve the first end mentioned here, the child's freedom, once again, must be restricted. Every use of the child's freedom that contradicts the end mentioned above (the child's preservation and health) or this end (the development of his capacities) must be prevented; and every use of the child's freedom that is in accordance with the parents' intentions must be promoted. The former forbidden, the latter bidden. It is only in connection with the second end mentioned here that the child's freedom may not be restricted; for an action is moral only if it arises out of free choice. Morality develops out of the human being himself and cannot be produced by coercion or artificial means.

One cannot say that the child has a right of coercion to demand this upbringing, or that the parents have a duty and can be coerced to

---

⁴ See n. 11, p. 132

provide it. Just as little can one say that the parents, in relation *to the child* – we shall see in due time how things might stand in relation to others – have a *right* to bring him up, or that the child has a duty to let himself be brought up by them; for the child, insofar as he is being brought up, is not at all free. Thus the child is not at all a possible subject of rights or duties, but rather – insofar as he is being brought up – only an object of the parents' activities; the child is and becomes what the parents make of him.

§45

Only parents can see the goal of their child's upbringing; [360] children do not, precisely because they first have to be brought up. Thus only the parents, and not the child, can determine which means are necessary for achieving this goal. In their relation to their child, parents are judges in their own case; they are sovereign, and the child is unconditionally subject to them insofar as they are bringing him up. Whether the parents make use of their child's subjection to them solely in order to give the child what, to the best of their knowledge, is the best possible upbringing, is a matter for their consciences alone, and is to be judged only by their own, internal [moral] tribunal.

§46

A condition of the possibility of the state is that the size of the population remain more or less constant; for the state calculates how much protection, taxation, and power are needed, all in relation to the size of the population. Now if the death rate should cause the population continuously to decrease in size, then the state's calculations would be inaccurate; the result would be disorder in the state, and finally – once there were only a few citizens left – the state would cease to exist altogether. But the population's remaining more or less constant in size requires that new citizens replace the deceased ones.

In the civil contract each citizen promises to help actualize, as far as he is able, all the conditions that make the state possible, and this includes the condition just mentioned. One can best help to actualize this condition by bringing children up to have the aptitude and skills for various rational ends. The state has the right to make this into a condition of the civil contract; and so the upbringing of children becomes an *external* duty that one can be coerced to fulfill; it is not a duty owed directly to the child, but to the state. It is the state that, as part of the civil contract, acquires the right to impose this duty.

I spoke of the upbringing of *children in general*; for through it, the state attains its end. But now it cannot be left up to each citizen's arbitrary choice to determine which particular child he wants to bring up, since the ensuing collision of arbitrary choices would lead to irresolvable conflicts of right; rather, there must be some arrangement for determining [361] which particular children each citizen is to bring up. The most prudent solution would be for the state to follow the tendency of nature and reason (contrary to which the state has no right to prescribe anything anyway) and to require that parents bring up *their own* children.

§47

If the children are the offspring of a rightful and rational marriage recognized by the state, there is no difficulty. But they can also be the offspring of unmarried parents: either as the result of a union that – apart from not being recognized by the state – resembled a marriage in every respect and so (in accordance with the principles given above) had to be formalized by the state, but that immediately thereafter ended in divorce; or as a result of a concubinage. In either case the care of the child belongs to the one to whom nature has immediately entrusted it: the mother. For parents who are separated cannot both bring the child up together. But in consequence of his duties as a citizen, the father is also obligated to contribute to the child's upbringing; thus he is to be required to make his contribution in the form of money and its equivalents. The father pays money for the child's upbringing, and the mother looks after his personal care.

§48

Infanticide committed by the mother is undoubtedly an atrocious, monstrous crime, for a mother who commits it must have silenced every natural feeling within herself; but it is not a crime against the child's external rights. A child has no external rights in relation to his mother.

Rather, it is a crime against the state's law requiring that children be brought up, and to that extent it is punishable. Infanticide exhibits monstrous coarseness and savagery, and so it is the kind of crime whereby the state should seek to reform the criminal. Infanticide is to be punished by imprisonment in a correctional penitentiary, until the criminal has reformed.

(Some ancient republics, [362] fearing that the population – especially of the privileged class, the real citizenry – might become too large, permitted the exposure of children, especially weak ones, to the elements; and so they indirectly permitted infanticide. No state has the right to *command* infanticide, for a state cannot command what is immoral or a sin against nature. Even just permitting infanticide through an *explicit* law is always immoral, and any state that does so dishonors both itself and its citizens. But there can be no rightful objection to a state's permission of infanticide through the silence of its laws, for the state has no positive concern for the morality of its citizens. But newborn children have external rights only insofar as the state has guaranteed their lives, and the state is responsible for guaranteeing their lives only to the extent that the possibility of its own preservation depends on it.)

§49

The state has the right to see that children in general are kept alive, nourished, clothed, and that they live among humans (since this is a necessary condition of their being brought up to be adult human beings and citizens); and it has this right in consequence of the above-mentioned condition of the civil contract. We shall soon see that this right does not extend to the means one might choose for the upbringing of children.

§50

The state makes it the duty of parents to give their children an upbringing. Thus it necessarily guarantees to provide them with the conditions of the possibility of such upbringing. This entails, first of all, that no other citizen may take custody of their children for the purpose of bringing them up. Therefore – *the state necessarily guarantees to parents, over against all other citizens, the exclusive right to keep their own children.* If a conflict of right should arise concerning this, the laws would have to decide in favor of the true parents.

In bringing up children, one must follow a consistent plan and uniform set of maxims. [363] But these would be interrupted if a stranger wanted to get involved in the children's upbringing and have an influence on them. The stranger's involvement would give rise to a legal complaint, and the state would always have to decide in favor of the true parents.

§51

If the parents are moral, their children's upbringing will be a matter of conscience for them. They will want to bring their children up in the morally best way they can. But everyone necessarily regards his own maxims as the best and most correct; otherwise, it would be unconscionable for him to subscribe to those maxims. But the state cannot encroach upon matters of conscience. Thus the state itself cannot interfere with the parents' upbringing of their children.

The state has the right to establish public institutions for the upbringing of children, but the parents must be allowed to decide whether or not they want to make use of them. The state does not have a right of coercion regarding the use of such institutions.

§52

Regarding the maxims to be followed in the upbringing of children, neither the state, nor other citizens, nor the child himself (since he is the one being brought up) can be the judge; therefore, the parents are their own judges in the matter. There can never be a conflict of right between parents and the children they are bringing up. In regard to their children's upbringing, parents are the highest court of appeal and sovereign. The state cannot pass laws regarding this relationship, any more than it may pass laws regarding the relationship between husband and wife.

§53

Thus the parents' dominion over their children is grounded solely on their duty to give the children an upbringing. This duty is established by nature and guaranteed by the state. The belief that children are their parents' property and that the parents' rights over them [**364**] are property rights is groundless.

§54

According to what has been said above, the state has the right to see that, in general, the child is given an upbringing. Therefore, it has the right to prevent any treatment of the child that would clearly nullify its being given an upbringing; thus the state cannot allow a child to be treated as if it were a piece of property, e.g. if a son were to be sold.

§55

Only one who is free can be made accountable before the courts. Children are not free, for they stand under the dominion of their parents. Thus the father – since he is at the same time also the legal representative of the mother – is their legal guardian. They have no rights that he needs to defend, for they are not yet actual citizens. But he is responsible for any injury they may cause.

The injured party will look to the father for compensation, and rightfully so, for the children stand under his authority, and he should have prevented them from causing the injury. Since he did not prevent it, he must pay for it. Children cannot be subjected to public punishment; for they are not at all subject to the state's external laws of coercion. They stand entirely under their parents' laws of coercion. Parents punish their children as they see fit; but the state does not punish them, for children are not yet its citizens.

§56

The sole ground of the parents' dominion over their children is that the children need an upbringing. If the ground of something ceases to exist, then what is grounded ceases to exist. As soon as the child's upbringing is complete, he is free.

But as a rule, only the parents can decide when the child's upbringing is complete, for it is they who [365] have posited, and they alone who know, the final end of this upbringing. Now either they themselves will judge that the child has been fully brought up and thus will voluntarily, at their own discretion, let him be free. As the child grows in understanding, they ought to give him increasingly more freedom, anyway – not in consequence of the child's rights, but in consequence of an important rule of upbringing. Now if the parents let go of the final tie by means of which they have until now restrained him, the child is completely free.

Or, in the second scenario: the very nature of the situation makes clear that the end of the child's upbringing has been attained. The general end of such upbringing is to make our capacities useful for the advancement of rational ends, and the external judge of this usefulness – a judge that the parents must respect – is the state. Now, to be sure, the state cannot directly liberate children from their parents, for then it would be interfering with the parents' upbringing of them: but it can do so indirectly, by giving the son a state office or some other civil right, e.g. the title of master in a trade as conferred by a guild (assuming that the guild has been authorized by the state to do so). The state can then render its judgment about the usefulness of the child's capacities. And a state office emancipates children from paternal authority.

Finally, in the third scenario: the children's upbringing – and along with it, their subjection to their parents – can be canceled if it is rendered impossible by the very nature of the situation. This happens when children marry. A married daughter becomes unrestrictedly subject to the will of her husband, and so cannot remain subject to any other will, including that of her parents. A married son must look after the happiness of his spouse with unrestricted tenderness; in doing so, he cannot let himself be interrupted by any external will, including that of his parents.

However: since the child's upbringing ends when the child is married, but since only parents are entitled to judge when their child's upbringing can end, parents have a right to withhold for a while their permission to marry, or a right to postpone the marriage.

[366] But parents do not have the right to prohibit their children from

marrying at all; just as little do they have the right to choose whom their children shall marry, for the reasons already presented above.

§57

Husband and wife hold property in common. Children have no share in this common ownership, and do not own any property at all. But then from where are they to get it? Parents are responsible for providing their children with nourishment and clothing as they judge appropriate; otherwise, the goal of giving their children an upbringing would not be attained. As already mentioned above, the parents can be coerced to fulfill this duty, which they owe to the state (not to the children); and the state has the right to see that they fulfill it.

But children labor, it is said, and thereby acquire property. One can make this claim only on the basis of the incorrect presupposition already refuted above, namely, that the right to property is grounded in one's formation of things. Children are made to labor so that they will exercise their capacities as part of their upbringing; and parents rightfully appropriate all the profits that incidentally result from their children's labor. The child cannot do anything at all apart from the will of his parents, and so he cannot acquire property apart from their will. Or is the child's right to property supposed to be based on a contract with his parents? Only one who is free can make a contract; but children have no self-standing freedom in relation to their parents. It is impossible for them to break away from their parents and have their own will and thus become an opposing party over against them.

§58

Every independent citizen must have his own property and must be able to tell the state how he makes his living. Thus the state can rightfully require of parents who release a child from their hands that they give the child a certain amount of property, or – to use a very descriptive word – that they *vest* [*ausstatten*] the child. But the state cannot prescribe how much they ought to give him; [367] that depends instead on the parents' own free discretion.

In the case of marriage, the bride's and groom's parents must reach an agreement as to whether both children or only one ought to receive something, and how much. The state has no right to inquire about where the property comes from. It may inquire only about whether the new family (which it knows only as a family) has enough to subsist on.

§59

It is entirely up to the parents' own arbitrary choice whether they want to vest one of their children more abundantly than another. It may well be unfair to show such preference to one child, but it is not contrary to external right. On what basis in right could the disadvantaged child complain? Everything he has, he has solely because of the voluntary kindness of his parents.

§60

When the parents die, their rights in the sensible world – and hence their rights to property – cease to exist altogether. Should children inherit equal shares of their parents' intestate estate? Should parents have the right to make wills? And how free should parents be to give their property to those who are not family members? How extensive should the legal formalities be? To what extent should parents have the right to disinherit their children? Answers to these questions depend solely on the state's positive laws, which decide such matters on political grounds. There are no *a priori* grounds for deciding them.

§61

Until now, we have refrained from answering the question: "If the parents divorce, how is the custody of their children to be divided between them?" For this question could not be answered apart from a well-founded insight into the relationship between parents and children.

First, since parents have unrestricted dominion [368] over their children, parents who divorce must be entirely free to arrive at a voluntary agreement between themselves. The state has no say in the matter, provided that the children's upbringing has been provided for. If the parents can reach a voluntary agreement (assuming that the agreement really is voluntary), then there is no dispute concerning right, and so there is nothing for the state to decide.

It is only when the parents cannot reach a voluntary agreement that the state enters its verdict.

There are only two conceivable reasons why this dispute might arise between parents: either because neither of them wants to take responsibility for the children's care and each wants to foist it on the other as much as possible; or because each of them wants to retain custody of the children and grant it to the other as little as possible.

The first scenario will be decided as follows: as stated above, the duty of caring for children is a direct duty only for the mother, but for the father it is merely an indirect duty, derived from his love for the mother. Since his love for her – and thus also the natural ground of his paternal tenderness – has ceased to exist in this case, the children are to be handed over to the personal care and attention of their mother. But the father must contribute (under the state's supervision and guarantee) to the costs of supporting the children; and it is necessary to establish determinate guidelines for this, depending on the parents' means.

The second scenario will be decided as follows: the state's rightfully grounded goal with respect to children is to see that they receive the best possible upbringing. Now as a rule – and general laws can be based only on what applies as a rule – the mother is best suited to bring up the daughter, and the father to bring up the son. Thus daughters are to be handed over to the mother, and sons to the father.

It is obvious that the true father – and not the husband – must pay the costs of supporting a child who is the offspring of an adulterous relationship.

[369] Outline of the right of nations [*Völkerrecht*] and cosmopolitan right [*Weltbürgerrecht*] (Second appendix to the doctrine of natural right)

(I) ON THE RIGHT OF NATIONS

§1

According to what was said above, every individual has the right to force any other individual he encounters either to enter into a state with him or to stay out of the sphere of his efficacy. If one of them already lives in a state and the other does not, then the first will coerce the other to join him in his state. If neither already lives in a state, then the two will unite to form at least the beginning of one. From this follows the proposition: someone who does not live in a state can rightfully be coerced by the first state that encounters him either to subject himself to it, or to stay away from it.

In consequence of this proposition, all human beings living on the earth's surface would gradually become united in a single state.

§2

But it is just as possible that geographically separate groups of human beings, knowing nothing of one another, would unite to form separate states. In one place on earth, the need for a state would be felt and remedied, and in another place on earth, the same need would be felt and remedied – even though the first group would know nothing of the second, and the second nothing of [370] the first. In this way, several states would come to exist on earth.

Proof that the state is not an arbitrary invention but commanded by nature and reason is provided by the fact that wherever human beings live alongside one another for a while and acquire a bit of cultivation, they establish a state, even though they are unaware that the same has happened or is happening with other human beings beyond their sphere.

The fact that oceans, rivers, and mountains carve up the earth's surface and divide the human beings who live on it, would be another reason why it was necessary for different states to come into existence.

§3

The human beings in these different states know nothing of one another, and thus they do not have a genuine relation of right with one another; for according to what was said above, the condition of the possibility of any relation of right is that there be an actual and conscious reciprocal influence.

§4

Two citizens from these two different, independently established states encounter one another. Each will demand of the other that his own security alongside the other be guaranteed – which, as we have shown, each has a perfect right to demand – through the other's subjecting himself, along with the first, to the sovereign under which the first lives. "Subject yourself to my sovereign" is what each demands of the other, and with equal right, for each lives under a rightful constitution. And so neither has this right; for their rights mutually cancel each other out.

But they must still give each other a mutual guarantee. Since this could not happen in the manner suggested above, how can it happen? The two ought to subject themselves to a judge common to them both; but each one already has his own separate judge. Their two judges must themselves reach an agreement and become the single, common judge [371] of both in matters affecting both; i.e. their two states must mutually promise one another to punish and make amends for any injustice done by one of its own citizens to a citizen of the other state, as if it were an injustice done to one of its own citizens.

Corollaries

(1) Any relation between states is grounded on the rightful relation between their citizens. The state, in itself, is nothing but an abstract concept; only citizens as such are actual persons. Moreover, this relation between states is grounded quite clearly on their citizens' previously mentioned duty of right to give each other a mutual guarantee of security upon encountering one another in the sensible world. At first, therefore, the only states that stand in relation to one another are those that *border* on one another. Later we shall see how states that do not border on one another can also enter into relation with each another.

(2) This relation between states consists in the fact that they mutually guarantee the security of the other's citizens, just as each guarantees the security of its own. The formulation of the contract between them is: "I make myself accountable for any injuries that my citizens might do to yours, on the condition that you are likewise accountable for any injuries that your citizens might do to mine."

(3) This contract must be expressly entered into; it is not already part of the civil contract. And there must be legislation announcing to the citizens that such a contract has been entered into. A citizen already satisfies the conditions of the civil contract if he simply refrains from violating the rights of his fellow citizens; the civil contract does not pertain to foreigners. Only in consequence of this contract does it become law that one also respect the rights of foreign states that are party to this contract; only in consequence of this contract does the violation of such rights become a punishable crime.

[372] §5

The contract between states as we have described it necessarily involves *reciprocal recognition*, which is presupposed as a condition of the contract's possibility. Each state, on behalf of its own citizens, accepts the other's assurance as a valid guarantee, and neither undertakes any further measures for its own security; thus each state presupposes that the other has a legal constitution and can speak on behalf of its citizens.

Thus each state has a right to pass judgment on the legality of any other state with whose citizens its own have a relation. But one should note well that this right to pass judgment extends only far enough to allow the state to determine whether an adjoining state is capable of entering into an external, legal relationship. It is none of its business to inquire about the other state's inner constitution, and it has no right to pass judgment on that.

This is what is meant by the reciprocal *independence* of states.

§6

Every nation [*Volk*], provided only that it does not exist in a condition of nature but has a government (no matter how that government is set up), has a right of coercion to demand recognition from the adjoining states. Proof of this follows from what was said earlier, and has just been given above. No state can force citizens of another state to subject themselves to its authority, for the adjoining state would then have the same right, which is self-contradictory. However, adjoining states must be willing to give and receive from each other guarantees regarding the security of their respective citizens; but this is possible only on the condition of recognition. One state's refusing to recognize another amounts to its regarding the citizens of the other state as not living under a rightful constitution at all; but that entails that the first state has a right to subjugate citizens of the second. Therefore, one state's refusing to recognize another gives the other state a valid right to wage war against the first.

[373] States are necessarily independent of one another and self-standing.

§7

If a nation has no government – and thus is not a state – then an adjoining state has the right either to subjugate it, or to force it to establish a constitution, or to drive it away from its vicinity. The reason for this is the following: whoever cannot guarantee the security of the other's rights has no rights of his own. Hence, such a nation would be an outlaw, devoid of all rights.

(Let no one fear that powers thirsting for conquest have anything to gain from this proposition. A nation of the kind described is unlikely to exist at all; this proposition has been introduced, not so much to be applied, but to make our argumentation complete. Any nation, provided only that it has someone to lead it in war, undoubtedly has a government. The Franconian republicans beat the coalition forces over and over again, while the coalition, doubting that the Franconians had a government of their own, asked, "With whom should we conclude the peace?" With the next onslaught they encountered, the coalition forces should have inquired of those who beat them, "Who is your commander in battle?" Perhaps those who had commanded them to beat the coalition forces could have also issued a command to leave them in peace. Finally, once they were sufficiently beaten, they, too, luckily hit upon this solution and discovered that the Franconians, after all, must have had a government.)

§8

Adjoining states reciprocally guarantee one another the property rights of their citizens. Hence, they must establish clear guidelines concerning the limits of these rights. These limits have already been *specified* in the contract that each state has made with its own [374] citizens, and so there is no need to specify them anew. A citizen of state A whose property borders on state B has declared to his own state that he wants to own property up to this point, and his state has granted it to him. The very same has transpired between state B and the citizen of state B whose property borders directly on the property of that citizen from state A. The adjoining states as such now also guarantee these contracts [to one another], on behalf of their citizens and in the interest of their citizens. What at first obligated only one's fellow citizens, henceforth also obligates the citizens of adjoining states. Any disputes that still might arise in this regard will be decided in the same way in which they are decided by individuals on the basis of natural right: through voluntary agreement, for there are no rightful, *a priori* grounds why one object should belong to this individual rather than another. Thus the first condition of a legal relation between states is the drawing of borders. The borders must be clearly and unambiguously established; otherwise, there would be future border disputes. This condition entails not only the drawing of borders with respect to land, but also with respect to certain rights, e.g. fishing, hunting, shipping, and so forth.

The borders between the citizens become the borders between the states themselves.

§9

In this contract, the two states are perfect equals. Whatever one does to protect the other's citizens from harm, the other must also do to protect the first one's from harm. Any laws that the first state passes in order to protect the other's citizens, must also be passed by the other state in order to protect the first one's citizens. But neither state is obligated to take more care to protect the other than the other takes to protect it. Thus it is quite possible for a state to give more protection to the rights of its own citizens than it does to the rights of foreigners – since the other state, for its part, may not have agreed to a higher standard of protection. It is even possible for a state to give better protection to the property of foreigners from *one* adjoining state than it does to the property of foreigners from *another* adjoining state [375] – since the first adjoining state, for its part, might give better protection to the property of foreigners within its own borders. The whole relation depends entirely on the agreement reached by the states in question.

§10

As a result of this contract, the states that are party to it acquire the reciprocal right to survey one another, in order to determine whether the other conducts its affairs in accordance with the contract and enforces the contract through the laws it has passed. The reason for this is easy to grasp. The contract is binding only to the extent that both parties live up to it; thus each party must know whether or not the other is living up to it, so that it can judge whether it, too, is obligated to do so.

This surveillance can take place only within the state being surveyed. Thus in order to conduct this surveillance, the two states must reciprocally send envoys to one another. Of course, envoys can be also sent from one state to another in order to sign either the contract just described or some particular contract; but an envoy's serving in that role is both temporary and incidental (envoys of this kind are called ambassadors). The true and original essence of a permanent, resident envoy (a resident agent, *chargé d'affaires*) is to survey the state into which he has been sent in order to determine whether it is fulfilling its obligations to the state from which he has been sent; and perhaps also to remind this first state of its duties and to demand that it not violate the contract. But he may not get involved in the internal, domestic affairs of the state into which he has been sent, for the state that sent him may not do so.

§11

Since the envoy's job is to survey certain aspects of the state into which he has been sent, he cannot become dependent on it; otherwise, he would have to become obedient to it, and the obedience demanded of him might defeat the purpose of his being sent. As long as he [376] stays within the limits of his role as an envoy, he stands entirely under the authority of his own government, which is his only judge. Therefore, he is sacred and inviolable in the eyes of the state into which he has been sent; he represents his own, independent state. (As a matter of right, the envoy is granted immunity from all taxation: taxes are a contribution to the state's protective power, but an envoy is not a citizen of this state. The idea that an envoy might make personal use of this immunity by trafficking in smuggled goods is so disgraceful and vile that the contracts states make with one another cannot reasonably be expected to contain provisions for dealing with it.)

If an envoy steps beyond the limits of his role as an envoy, either by trying to influence the domestic affairs of the state he is surveying, or by causing disturbances through his transgressions, then the state into which he has been sent acquires the right, not to become his judge – for he has never subjected himself to its laws – but to send him back and demand compensation from the state that sent him.

§12

As long as the contract between the two states is clearly and unambiguously formulated – and since it can never encompass a large number of provisions, precise formulation is very easy. Any lack of precision would already betray an evil intention to have a pretext for future wars – then it will be very difficult, if not impossible, for misunderstanding to be the cause of a violation. Thus if there is any violation, it was most probably caused by a bad will. But be that as it may: a state's violation of the contract – like a state's refusal to recognize another – gives the other state a right to wage war against it. In both cases, the state being warred upon has shown that it is incapable of entering into a legal relation and therefore has absolutely no rights.

[377] §13

The right to wage war, like every right of coercion, is infinite (§8 III). The state being warred upon has no rights, since it refuses to recognize the rights of the state waging the war. The state being warred upon may later plead for peace and offer to be just henceforth. But how can the state waging the war ever be convinced that the other is really serious and not just saying this in order to find an opening to crush the first state? What kind of guarantee could it possibly give to the first state? Therefore, the natural purpose of war is always *to annihilate the state being warred upon*, i.e. to subjugate its citizens. It may well be that from time to time a peace – actually, only a cease-fire – is declared, because either one state or both are presently exhausted; but the mutual distrust remains for both, as does the goal of subjugation.

§14

War is waged only by the armed forces of the warring states, not by unarmed citizens; nor is war waged against these citizens. Any part of a state's territory no longer protected by the troops of that state becomes the acquisition of the conquering state, for the purpose of war is to subjugate the state being warred upon; and a conquering state cannot plunder its new citizens or lay waste its own possessions without acting contrary to reason and its own purpose, and therefore without acting contrary to (military) right. As soon as the invading state drives away the armed defenders of a certain territory, the unarmed persons in that territory become its own subjects. But territory still under the protection of the defending troops is not subject to the invading state. In the first instance, the invading state cannot lay waste to the territory in question, since that would be contrary to its own purpose in waging war; in the second instance, it cannot do so, since the defending troops make it physically impossible. But of course, the usual method of waging war is barbaric and contrary to reason. The conquering state lays waste to the conquered territories in a hurried effort to strip them of as much as possible and to leave as little [378] as possible for the enemy. Thus the conquering state does not intend to keep the conquered territory. But if that is so, why did it wage the war?

Similarly, a disarmed soldier is no longer an enemy, but a subject. The fact that we regard him as a prisoner of war to be exchanged for other prisoners is an arbitrary contrivance of modern politics, which automatically expects to negotiate with the enemy and lacks any sound, self-sufficient purpose in warfare.

The purpose of a military campaign is not at all to kill, but only to disarm and drive away the armed forces protecting the citizens and land. In hand-to-hand combat, where one man goes up against another, one kills his opponent in order not to be killed by him, in consequence of *his own right to self-preservation*, but not in consequence of *a right to kill conferred upon him by his state*; for the state does not have that right, and so cannot confer it upon him. Even the modern method of waging war with cannons and other firearms can be viewed in this way. The purpose is not to kill with cannon balls and bullets, but only to keep the enemy away from areas where they are being aimed. If the enemy should nevertheless go into one of those areas, it is his own fault if he is hit by a projectile that is not directly aimed at him. (Reason would dictate that one first tell the enemy that one is going to fire on a post if the enemy does not depart from it voluntarily, just as one first demands that fortresses be surrendered before firing on them.) The only elements of our modern method of warfare that are absolutely contrary to right are the *snipers*, who lie in wait in the brush, safe from harm, and in cold blood take aim at human beings as if they were practice targets. Their purpose is to commit murder. (And their first use against policed states – by Austria against Prussia – actually provoked the indignation of all Europe. But now we have become accustomed to their use and imitate it, which does us little honor.)

[379] §15

As we have seen, the injured state has a perfect right to wage war against the unjust state until it has utterly destroyed it as an independent state

328

and combined the latter's subjects with its own. And so war would then be a sure and perfectly rightful means to secure legality in relations between states, if one could only find a means by which the state with the just cause would always be victorious. But since not every state has precisely as much power as it has right, war may well help to advance unjust causes as much as, if not more than, just ones.

But now war is the only means by which a state can be coerced: and so the only problem would be how to arrange things so that the just cause in a war is always the stronger and victorious one. Strength arises out of sheer multitude; thus several states would have to *confederate* for the purpose of maintaining rightful relations among themselves and using their unified strength to attack the unjust state. There can be little doubt that this would give rise to a power that is always victorious. But the more important question is: how can things be arranged so that this confederation of states always supports the just cause?

I shall first elaborate on the idea just mentioned.

§16

Several states unite and guarantee to one another – not only vis-à-vis one another, but also vis-à-vis any state that is not a member of this confederation – both independence and the inviolability of the contract just described. The formula of this confederation would be: "We all promise to use our united strength to destroy any state – be it a member of this confederation or not – that refuses to recognize the independence of, or breaks a contract with, one of our members."

[380] I call this the formula of a *confederation*: for it would be a *confederation made up of nations*, certainly not a *state made up of nations*. The basis for this distinction is as follows. The individual can be coerced to enter into the state, for otherwise a rightful relation with him would be absolutely impossible. But no state can be coerced to join this confederation, for a state can exist in a rightful relation even without this confederation. A state posits itself as existing in a rightful relation with adjoining states simply by recognizing them and entering with them into a contract of the kind described above. No state has a right of coercion *to the positive protection* of another state. Therefore, this is a voluntary association, one certainly not based on coercion; and this kind of association is called a confederation.

§17

It is possible to know right away whether one state has recognized another's independence, based on whether the first has entered with the latter into the kind of contract described above: if it has done so, then it has recognized the latter; if it refuses to do so, then it refuses to recognize the latter. And so in this matter, the confederation's verdict cannot be mistaken. But the confederation cannot knowingly and intentionally pronounce an unjust verdict without letting the entire world see that it is unjust; and one can, I hope, count on its having some shame. Determining whether a contract between states has been fulfilled or not will depend not only on the reliability of the facts as alleged, but also on the terms of the contract. First, regarding the facts as alleged: every state is already obligated – in consequence of the civil contract – to conduct its affairs publicly; therefore, one must be able to ascertain whether or not a particular event took place. The state charged with having defaulted on a contract must provide positive proof that what was required of it by the contract was actually done (e.g. that a criminal was punished, that an injury was compensated for, and the like); such things should not be too difficult to clear up. By refusing to appear before the confederation's tribunal, a state automatically forfeits its own case, and [**381**] judgment is to be entered against it. A state that is not a member of the confederation might say: "Why should this tribunal be of any concern to me? It is not my judge." The proper response would be: "You are, however, accountable to the party that is suing you, in consequence of the contract you made with it. Now if this party appoints the confederation's tribunal to stand in its place, it undoubtedly has a perfect right to do so."

As to understanding the terms of the contract: the confederation – precisely because its judgments should be based on the contract between the two states – acquires the right to see that such contracts are clear and precise. After all, every contract made by a confederation member is made under the confederation's guarantee. The confederation cannot tolerate imprecision in these contracts, since it should rely on them when adjudicating between the disputing parties. And by doing so, it affirms its own integrity as well. It cannot render an unjust verdict without everyone knowing about it. Consider, furthermore, that these different states, divided in their private interests, can have absolutely no common interest in acting unjustly. An unjust verdict by them is evidence against themselves. They shall be judged according to the principles they follow in judging others.

§18

The confederation must also be able to carry out its verdicts. It does so, as is clear from the above, by waging war to annihilate the state convicted by its tribunal. Thus the confederation must be armed. One might ask whether a special, standing confederation army should be established; or whether it is enough to have a militia comprising troops contributed by different confederated states and assembled only during an actual war. Since, as I hope, war will rarely – and, in the future, never – occur, I would favor the latter: for why have a standing confederation army which, based on our presupposition, would have to be idle most of the time?

[382] §19

But we have not yet established that it is absolutely impossible for this confederation of nations to render an unjust verdict. And this cannot be established any more than it could be established, in the context of political right, that it was absolutely impossible for the assembled people to render an unjust verdict. As long as pure reason does not make a personal appearance on earth and assume judicial power, there must always be a highest judge who – because he is finite – is capable of erring or having a bad will. The only real task is to find a judge who seems least capable of these things. Regarding civil matters, this judge is the nation; regarding relations between states, it is the confederation of nations as described.

§20

As this confederation expands and gradually encompasses the entire earth, the result will be *perpetual peace*, which is the only rightful relation among states. For war – if it is waged by states who are judges in their own cases – can just as easily cause injustice, as justice, to be victorious. Or – even if it is waged under the direction of a just confederation of nations – it is still only a means to the final end, the preservation of peace; but it is certainly not the final end itself.

(II) ON COSMOPOLITAN RIGHT

§21

Every citizen of a state has the right to pursue his activities throughout the state's entire territory. This right is part of the civil rights guaranteed to him by the state contract. The envoy of a foreign state, in consequence of the contract [383] between his state and another, has the right to enter the country of his destination, travel through it, and go wherever his mission calls him to go. He has a right to attain his end, which is to see that the other state is fulfilling the contract; and so he also has a right to the means. At the border, he shows his authorization papers; and it is now the duty of the state to which he has been sent to let him in. If the state unconditionally rejects him as an envoy – i.e. if it has no particular reason for finding him unacceptable as an individual and does not tell the other state that it would gladly accept another envoy – then the other state would have a right to wage war. Private persons from one state may visit another state, either for business or simply for pleasure, provided that the two states recognize one another and are on friendly terms. Anything that happens in connection with these visits is to be judged in accordance with the states' existing contract. If the two states have reciprocally guaranteed the security of one another's citizens – even when the other's citizens are in its own territory – then every citizen will be secure as a result of this contract between them. But the fact that one is a citizen of this particular state is established when he shows his identity card at the border.

But what is the right thing to do if a foreigner enters a state's territory, neither having been sent to do so by an allied state nor being entitled to do so because of a contract between the allied states? The task of answering this last, remaining question of right belongs to the doctrine of cosmopolitan right.

§22

All positive rights, i.e. rights to *something*, are grounded on some contract. Now this foreign newcomer does not have any contract at all with the state he is visiting; he has not personally made any contract with it, nor can he refer to any contract that his state has made on his behalf. For according to our presupposition, he does not come from any state at all, or else the state he is visiting does not recognize his state and has not made any contract with it. Is he therefore devoid of all rights, or does he indeed have any? Which rights, and on what [**384**] basis? He has that original human right which precedes all rightful contracts and which alone makes them possible: *the right to every other human being's expectation to be able to enter into a rightful relation with him through contracts.* This alone is the one true human right that belongs to the human being as such: the right to be able to acquire rights. This, and only this, right must be granted to everyone who has not expressly forfeited it through his actions. Perhaps this will become clearer by way of contrast. If a state cancels the civil contract it has made with a particular citizen, then that citizen loses all the positive rights he had acquired as a result of that contract. Moreover, he loses not only those rights, but also the right to acquire rights in this society, for he has already shown himself to be absolutely incapable of having a rightful relation with others. Now the newcomer in the foreign state has just as few positive rights as he does; but the newcomer does have the right to demand that others expect it to be possible to enter into a rightful relation with him.

This right entails his right to enter into the territory of the foreign state; for if one has a right to the end he seeks to attain, then one also has a right to the means. But he cannot attempt to enter into a rightful relation with this state if he does not encounter it on its own territory and offer to establish a connection with it.

It is this right to go about freely on the earth and offer to establish rightful connections with others that constitutes the right of a mere *citizen of the world*.

§23

The ground of the foreign newcomer's right to enter a state's territory was his right to offer and attempt transactions with the citizens of this state. First, therefore, the visited state has the right to ask the foreigner what he wants, and to force him to explain himself. If he refuses to explain himself, then the ground of his right ceases to exist, and he is to be sent away from the state's borders. By the same token, if he does indeed explain himself, but his offer is not accepted, then the [385] ground of his right is likewise nullified and he is rightfully expelled from the state's borders. But this must be done without harming him. For it is still possible for him to establish a connection with another state, after things have failed to work out with this one. This is his perfect right, and he may not be robbed of it.

§24

If his offer is accepted, then from now on he has a contract *directly* (i.e. personally, without the intervention of any state acting on his behalf) with this state, and this contract determines the reciprocal rights of the two parties. First, he has already recognized this state as a rightful subject, simply by virtue of having entered into a contract with it; and therefore he has at the same time recognized the property rights of the state's individual citizens. He need not make any express promise of such recognition; for his recognition follows immediately from his act of making the contract. He becomes subject to all the state's other laws, simply by having subjected himself to this one.

Moreover, this state necessarily becomes his judge. Since no other state intervenes on his behalf (as on behalf of an envoy), there is no other judge of his activities. As burdensome as this situation might be for him, he must subject himself to it, for it is unavoidable.

Index

Abbé de Saint-Pierre, 13, 13 n.h
agency, *see* efficacy
agriculturalists, 189–92, 193, 194, 198, 200, 202
animals, 74–7, 188–9, 242, 307
    property in, 194–201
aristocracy, xxiii, 143, 250
artists, 202–6, 207

Beccaria, 246
Beck, J. S., 8 n.5
body,
    articulated nature of, 57–8, 59–62, 64, 74, 112
    as agent of will, 56–60, 70, 103–4
    as condition of self-consciousness, xviii, 53,
        67–8, 70
    as criterion of rational being, xviii, 71–2, 75–6,
        78–9, 84, 112, 122
    influence by others upon, 58–67, 80–1
    rights associated with, viii, xx, 102, 103–4,
        107–8, 112, 113, 215–21
    see also efficacy; organ; organism

Catiline, 244
check (*Anstoß*), 32, 54 n.1, 175 n.1
children, rights concerning, 297, 305–19
    see also upbringing
Cicero, 244
coercion, right of (*Zwangsrecht*), xix, xx, 12, 14,
    88–92, 93, 102, 109, 113, 115–16, 119, 123,
    131, 144–5, 167, 186, 187, 299
community (of free, rational beings),
    as object of right, xviii, 10, 11, 15, 45
    conditions of, 68, 79–84, 86, 87, 94, 101, 226,
        233
    see also efficacy, reciprocal
confederation (of states), 329–32
constitution, 14, 16, 140, 148

defined, 162
    provisions of, xxiii, 150–1, 156–7, 159,
        249–54, 262
contract,
    civil (*Staatsbürgervertrag*), 135–6, 139, 162,
        173–4, 177 n.a, 179–80, 183
    provisions of, 146, 168–71, 206–7, 210,
        215–16, 234–5, 247, 256, 275–6, 311–12,
        322
    consequences of violating, 226–7, 241, 243
    expiation, xx n.7, 227–9, 236–7, 242
    general nature of, 165–8, 174, 169, 224
    property, xxi, 169–70, 171–3, 178, 183–7, 198,
        207, 214, 222, 224
    protection, xxi, 171–5, 178, 219–20
    subjection, xx n.7, 179
    transference, 14, 145–6, 155, 156, 251
    unification, xxi–xxii, 175–7

democracy, 14, 140, 141, 143, 250
despotism, 141, 149, 250 n.1
Dionysius II, 238
divorce, 281, 283, 286, 288–9, 291–7, 318–19

efficacy (*Wirksamkeit*)
    and body, 56, 104
    defined, xiv, 18, 20, 28
    requirements for, 24, 28, 29–33, 35, 36, 39–40,
        70, 105–6, 110, 115
    reciprocal, 33, 38, 65, 67, 79–80, 84, 183
    significance for right, xv
elections, 143, 145, 157, 161, 178, 251, 253–4
end (*Zweck*), xiv, 20, 35, 56, 67, 103, 105, 114,
    126–7
ephorate, xxvii, 16–17, 141, 142–3, 144, 151–61,
    164, 178, 251, 253–4
Erhard, J. B., 11 n.f, 12

335

Fichte, J. G.,
early political writings, x, xxiii–xxiv
System of the Doctrine of Morals, viii, ix
Wissenschaftslehre (1794), vii, viii, ix, 3 n.a, 5
n.b, 8 n.4, 22 n.a, 25 n.1, 32 n.3, 40 n.7, 54,
92, 175 n.1
Wissenschaftslehre nova methodo, viii n.2, 54 n. 1
finitude, subjective, xiv, xv, 18–19, 21
freedom, viii, 9, 40, 48, 126
formal, xxv, 41, 102
of reflection, 62, 63–4
of thought and conscience, 51, 102
personal, xi, xxv, xxviii, 9, 53, 56

Hegel, G. W. F., xvii n.5, xxii n.9, xxv, xxvi
human being, essential nature of, viii, xxii, 37, 48,
74, 76–8
Humboldt, W. von, xiii n.4
hunting, 200–2

I (*das Ich*), ix, xiii, 3–5, 18–19, 21–4, 25 n.1,
26–8, 32–3, 39, 49, 53–5, 126
identity card, xxiii, 257–61
imagination, 28, 55, 175
imperative, categorical, xxiii–xxiv, 75, 245, 246
individuality, xiii–xvii, xxiv, xxvi, 9, 40–9, 53,
58–9, 117
see also person
interdict, 151–6, 159
intersubjectivity, xvi, xxvi, 29, 37–8, 39, 48
see also recognition
intuition, 54–5

Jacob, L. H., 245 n.a
Jacobi, F. H., 28 n.b

Kant, I., vii, 3 n.a, 6, 7, 26, 54
Critique of Judgment, 35, 180 n.3
Critique of Pure Reason, 11 n.7, 28 n.2, 54 n.1,
55 n.2
Metaphysics of Morals, vii, xiv, xxv, 13 n.14, 245
nn.9,14
moral theory, xiv, xviii n.6, xxiii, 75
Perpetual Peace, 13–14, 17, 83 n.a, 141 n.14,
249–50
political theory, xxv, 12–14, 246–7, 249–50

labor, 185–7, 190, 204
land, property in, 190–2, 195, 223
law, civil, xxiii, 16, 135, 142, 163, 170, 183, 222,
256–7
constitutional, 139
moral, 11, 13–14, 47, 50, 83 n.a, 117, 221, 244,
269
of coercion, 126, 127–32, 133, 139, 146
penal (or criminal), 16, 126, 135, 136, 179, 211,
216, 227–48
permissive, 13–14, 83 n.a
police, 146, 256–7
positive, 95, 98–9, 132
see also right, law of
Locke, J., xxvii

marriage, 264, 271–5, 277–86, 287, 288–9,
290–1, 296–9, 312, 315–16
matter, 56–7, 64–8, 70, 76–7
subtler, 65–8, 70–1
men, nature of, 266, 268, 269, 271–3, 278, 284,
304, 308
see also sexuality
merchants, 204–6, 213
mining, 190, 192 n.1, 193–4
monarchy, xxiii, 143, 144, 250, 251
money, 207–9, 210–11, 213, 222, 258, 260–1
Montesquieu, 262, 280
motherhood, 306–9, 319
murder, 216–17, 218, 221, 241, 246, 257, 312–13

nature, 105
ends of, 86, 184–5, 264–6

organ, higher and lower, 60–2, 63, 65–8, 70–1,
77–8
organism (or organized product of nature), xxii,
72–4, 176–7, 180–2, 188, 262
oscillation (*Schweben*), 28, 72, 175–6

people (*Volk*), 154–5, 159–60
personhood, 94, 226
conditions of, xix, 56, 68–9, 79–81, 87–8, 101,
102–4, 105, 215
defined, xiv, xix, xxiv, 53–4
see also individuality
Pliny the Elder, 76
police, xxiii, 146, 148, 232, 243, 244, 254–63, 287,
290
populace (*Gemeine*), 139–41, 143, 144, 145–6,
148, 149–57, 159–61, 187, 193, 199
power,
executive, 14, 16, 135–6, 139, 141, 142, 144,
149, 160–1, 163–4, 186, 252
administrators of, 147–9, 151–4, 155–6,
158–61, 251–2
judicial, 88, 93–5, 96, 116, 135–7, 140–1,
142–3, 146, 147, 252–3
powers, separation of, xxiii, xxvii, 13 n.14, 14, 16,
17, 142
prerogative, royal (*Regale*), 192, 193–4

property,
  absolute, 158, 191, 207, 209, 210–14, 222–3,
    234, 248, 256, 258
  acquisition of, 222–6
  exchange of (via contracts), 165–7
  right to, xx, xxi, xxiv, 106, 113–22, 177 n.a, 179,
    183–6, 207, 218–19, 222–4
  see also animals; land; contract, property
prostitution, 268, 287, 289–90
punishment, capital, 242–6
  purpose of, 228, 230, 232, 233, 239–40, 245,
    247
  see also law, penal

rape, 276
reality, 5, 7, 25, 70
  ground of, 38–9
reason, nature of, xi, xiii, xiv, 3–5, 9, 18–20, 21,
    35–6, 39, 49–51, 55, 62, 63, 266
recognition, xvi–xvii, xxv–xxvi, 41–9, 79–80,
    111, 117–18, 119–20, 121, 123
representation (*Vorstellung*), 21–3, 27–8
representation, political, 141, 143–5, 251
republic, 143, 144, 150, 250, 251
right (*Recht*),
  as condition of self-consciousness, ix, xi,
    xii–xvii, xviii–xix, xxvi, xxvii, 9, 12
  as distinct from morality, xviii, xxiii–xxv,
    10–12, 13–14, 47, 50, 81, 102, 221, 230, 237
  concept of, vii, ix, xii–xxiii, 9–10, 12, 49–51,
    79, 84, 87–8
  cosmopolitan, 320, 332–4
  equilibrium of, 109, 123, 130, 136
  law (or principle or rule) of, viii, xiii, xix,
    10–11, 13–15, 49, 82, 83–96, 109–10, 114,
    115–16, 119, 123–4, 127, 135, 138, 144, 153,
    166–7, 221
  natural, vii–viii, xix, xx, 102 n.4, 132–3
  of nations (*Völker*), 320–32
  of necessity (*Notrecht*), 220–1
  political (*Staatsrecht*), xix, xx, 135, 183
  relation of (*Rechtsverhältniß*), xvi, 9, 39, 49, 51,
    109–11, 113, 114, 115, 116, 119, 120–1,
    123
  science of, ix, 3, 8, 11–12, 79–81, 92, 159–60,
    249
rights, vii–viii, xi, xvi–xvii
  of the dead, 224–6
  of the householder, 196, 211–13, 215–16, 219,
    258
  of humans as such, 333–4
  original (*Urrechte*), xix–xx, xxii, xxviii, 12,
    87–9, 101–3, 107–8, 109, 111, 117, 119, 183,
    184

see also coercion; property; self-defense,
    self-preservation, subsistence; wars
    (international)
Rousseau, J.-J., xxi–xxii, xxvi, xxvii, 13 n.b, 98
    n.a, 177 n.a, 246 n.16

Schleiermacher, Friedrich, xiii n.4
Schmid, C. C. E., 11 n.7
security, guarantee of, 90, 93, 95–7, 99–100, 115,
    118, 119, 123–5, 127–30, 133–4, 136–7,
    139, 146
self-consciousness, ix, xii–xvi, xxvi, xxvii, 4–5,
    19, 21
  conditions of, 9, 19–21, 24, 29–34, 39, 43, 49,
    56, 58–9, 67–8
  see also body; right
self-determination, xiii, xv, 18, 20, 31–2, 33, 48,
    135
self-positing, ix, xiii, 3–4, 18–19, 21, 22–3, 25
    n.1, 34, 40, 48, 54 n.1, 55, 58
  see also I
self-defense, right to, 218–21, 256
self-preservation, right to, xx, 102, 107–8
sexuality, 265–70, 284–5, 273, 275, 281
  see also men; women
Smidt, J., 66 n.3
Spinoza, B., 108
state, exclusion from, 227, 235–43, 245, 248
subsistence, right to, viii, 106–7. 184–7
summons (*Aufforderung*), xv–xvi, xix, 31–5, 37,
    39, 41

Tathandlung, 25, 100 n.3
taxation, 209, 252
testaments, 217, 223, 224–6
treason, 153, 156, 159, 234, 235, 238
trust, 123–5, 127, 130, 213–14, 240

upbringing (*Erziehung*), xxvi, 38, 132, 310–19

Voltaire, 214

war, state of (between individuals), 116, 118, 119,
    125, 166–7
wars (international), rights concerning, 326–9,
    332
will, xiv, xviii, 21–3
  arbitrary (*Willkür*), 14–15, 99
  general (or common), xxi, 16, 97–9, 117, 131,
    134–5, 136–7, 149, 152, 155, 160, 161, 167,
    176, 217, 2256
  private, 134, 136–7, 149, 166–7, 176
women,
  nature of, 266–75, 284–6, 295, 298, 300–7

women (*cont.*)
  social and legal status of, xxviii, 271, 275–83, 287–9, 294, 296, 297–303
  see also motherhood; sexuality
world, sensible,

deduction of, 24–7, 54
necessary features of, 68, 79,
right realized within, 42–3, 51, 104, 106–7, 111, 115, 118
  see also body

Cambridge texts in the history of philosophy

Titles published in the series thus far

Aristotle *Nicomachean Ethics* (edited by Roger Crisp)

Arnauld and Nicole *Logic or the Art of Thinking* (edited by Jill Vance Buroker)

Bacon *The New Organon* (edited by Lisa Jardine and Michael Silverthorne)

Boyle *A Free Enquiry into the Vulgarly Received Notion of Nature* (edited by Edward B. Davis and Michael Hunter)

Bruno *Cause, Principle and Unity* and *Essays on Magic* (edited by Richard Blackwell and Robert de Lucca with an introduction by Alfonso Ingegno)

Clarke *A Demonstration of the Being and Attributes of God and Other Writings* (edited by Ezio Vailati)

Conway *The Principles of the Most Ancient and Modern Philosophy* (edited by Allison P. Coudert and Taylor Corse)

Cudworth *A Treatise Concerning Eternal and Immutable Morality* with *A Treatise of Freewill* (edited by Sarah Hutton)

Descartes *Meditations on First Philosophy*, with selections from the *Objections and Replies* (edited by John Cottingham)

Descartes *The World and Other Writings* (edited by Stephen Gaukroger)

Fichte *Foundations of Natural Right* (edited by Frederick Neuhouser, translated by Michael Baur)

Hobbes and Bramhall on Liberty and Necessity (edited by Vere Chappell)

Humboldt *On Language* (edited by Michael Losonsky, translated by Peter Heath)

Kant *Critique of Practical Reason* (edited by Mary Gregor with an introduction by Andrews Reath)

Kant *Groundwork of the Metaphysics of Morals* (edited by Mary Gregor with an introduction by Christine M. Korsgaard)

Kant *The Metaphysics of Morals* (edited by Mary Gregor with an introduction by Roger Sullivan)

Kant *Religion within the Boundaries of Mere Reason and Other Writings* (edited by Allen Wood and George di Giovanni with an introduction by Robert Merrihew Adams)

La Mettrie *Machine Man and Other Writings* (edited by Ann Thomson)

Leibniz *New Essays on Human Understanding* (edited by Peter Remnant and Jonathan Bennett)

Malebranche *Dialogues on Metaphysics and on Religion* (edited by Nicholas Jolley and David Scott)

Malebranche *The Search after Truth* (edited by Thomas M. Lennon and Paul J. Olscamp)

Melanchthon *Orations on Philosophy and Education* (edited by Sachiko Kusukawa, translated by Christine Salazar)

Mendelssohn *Philosophical Writings* (edited by Daniel O. Dahlstrom)

Nietzsche *The Birth of Tragedy and Other Writings* (edited by Raymond Geuss and Ronald Speirs)

Nietzsche *Daybreak* (edited by Maudemarie Clark and Brian Leiter, translated by R. J. Hollingdale)

Nietzsche *Human, All Too Human* (translated by R. J. Hollingdale with an introduction by Richard Schacht)

Nietzsche *Untimely Meditations* (edited by Daniel Breazeale, translated by R. J. Hollingdale)

Schleiermacher *Hermeneutics and Criticism* (edited by Andrew Bowie)

Schleiermacher *On Religion: Speeches to its Cultured Despisers* (edited by Richard Crouter)

Schopenhauer *Prize Essay on the Freedom of the Will* (edited by Günter Zöller)

Sextus Empiricus *Outlines of Scepticism* (edited by Julia Annas and Jonathan Barnes)

Shaftesbury, *Characteristics of Men, Manners, Opinions, Times* (edited by Lawrence Klein)

Voltaire *Treatise on Tolerance and Other Writings* (edited by Simon Harvey)